Homeward Bound

SUSTAINED BY GRACE

ALBERT VELDMAN

To my wife for supporting and motivating me throughout this project.

To my children and grandchildren as a legacy of my active ministry.

Library and Archives Canada Cataloguing in Publication

Title: Homeward bound : sustained by grace / Albert Veldman.
Names: Veldman, Albert, author.
Identifiers: Canadiana 20220149038 | ISBN 9781777115593 (softcover)
Subjects: LCSH: Devotional calendars—Reformed Church. | LCSH: Canadian Reformed Churches—Devotional literature. | LCSH: Canadian Reformed Churches—Prayers and devotions.
Classification: LCC BV4811 .V45 2022 | DDC 242/.2—dc23

Copyright © 2022 Albert Veldman

All rights reserved. No part of this publication may be reproduced, transmitted, or stored in any form or by any means without the prior written permission of the publisher.

978-1-7771155-9-3

REFORMED PERSPECTIVE PRESS
Box 1039, Carman, MB R0G 0J0

Preface

During my years of active ministry, dealing with the Heidelberg Catechism in the preaching has always been a real joy. The reason for this joy is that as a confession the Heidelberg Catechism offers not only doctrine, but it also provides personal comfort throughout the 52 Lord's Days. It makes the doctrine come alive in a very practical way.

It has always been my desire to use my retirement to write a devotional on this beautiful confession. The challenge with a devotional is to provide a short meditation with a message for every day. In addition to the 52 Lord's Days of the Heidelberg Catechism, I have also included some devotions on the Fifth Chapter of the Canons of Dort. This chapter deals with the perseverance of the saints and offers real comfort for coping with the trials God puts on our path. Additionally, I have included some meditations from sermons on the alphabet of faith.

Homeward Bound – Sustained by Grace. This title brings together two passages of Scripture. In Hebrews 11:10 we read that Abraham was looking forward to the city that has foundations, whose designer and builder is God. Likewise, we are pilgrims on our way to the celestial city: homeward bound. The words 'sustained by grace' are a reference to 2 Corinthians 12:8 where we read that on our earthly pilgrimage, God's grace will always be sufficient each day anew, whatever lies ahead. I sincerely pray that these devotions may offer daily strength in pointing all who read them to the amazing grace of our faithful God and Father.

All Bible texts are quoted from the English Standard Version, while the quotations from The Three Forms of Unity and the occasional Psalm or Hymn come from the Book of Praise of the Canadian Reformed Churches, 2014 edition.

In conclusion, I thank God for giving me the health and strength to finish this project. It took longer than I expected, yet God was there to carry me by His grace along this road as well. I also thank my wife for supporting me and motivating me to finish it. Finally, I thank Sister Kelly Eikelboom for editing all of these devotions and for her support throughout this project.

31 July 2021

January 1

READING: PSALM 105:1-11

God's 'Yes' in Christ

"For all the promises of God find their Yes in Him (i.e., in Christ)…"

2 CORINTHIANS 1:20A

A new year – what will it bring for us personally, for God's churches in this world and also for God's churches in our own country, where hatred against Christianity is becoming increasingly fiercer? How is it possible to find peace and rest in a society where we hear about violence, terror, and other dreadful things on a daily basis? When thinking about all of these things, anxiety so quickly creeps in, especially also when thinking about the future of our children and grandchildren. What kind of a world will they grow up in?

Yet when we firmly believe in the truth of Scripture, there is no need for anxiety, since in faith we may cling to God's promises, which – as the apostle Paul writes – find their 'Yes' in Christ who came into this world to bring God's promises to fulfillment. Therefore, those who believe in Him have hope again - a future of everlasting peace; not as the world around us understands peace, but peace with God through the blood that our Lord and Saviour Jesus Christ shed for us on the cross.

In faith, it is no longer my strength or my money by which I must build a future. Instead, in faith, we may find our strength in God who will provide us with all that we need, also in times of sickness, sadness, and hardship. In Christ, God already said 'Yes' to us at our baptism, even though because of our sins we deserved God's 'No', and still we got a 'Yes'. The only thing God asks for is our 'Yes' in response, that is, a thankful 'Amen' to God's love for us in Christ, and this not just in words but also in deeds.

If we do so, we may have confidence that the coming year will be a blessed year whatever it may have in store for us, since God is there to carry us every day. We do not need more assurance than that.

January 2

READING: 2 CORINTHIANS 1:18-22

Our response to God's 'Yes'

"That is why it is through him that we utter our Amen to God for his glory."

2 CORINTHIANS 1:20B

Yesterday on the first day of the New Year, we focused on God's 'Yes', God's 'Amen' in Christ, in whom all God's promises came to fulfillment. The focus was on God's faithfulness, verse 18, on which we may also rely throughout the coming year. God is faithful. He will do what He has promised. This means we can be sure, as God promised at our baptism, that He will care for us as a Father, each day throughout this new year.

At the same time, as the apostle Paul says in 2 Corinthians 1:20b, God's 'Amen' **in** Christ must be responded to by our 'Amen' **through** Christ, who is our Mediator, in whom God speaks to us and through whom we speak to God. In heaven, Christ as our high priest brings our imperfect praising of God in perfect form before the Father, but also our supplications; yes, whatever we pray in His Name. That is how, through Christ, our prayers will bring glory to God.

Yet God wants to receive glory also on earth. That is why the Holy Spirit was poured out on Pentecost, who in the New Testament is called the Spirit of Christ. The life-giving Spirit dwells within us to renew us, so that also on earth God is receiving glory from us. This too is Christ's work, when we through the Holy Spirit, respond to God's 'Amen' with our 'Amen' towards God.

What is this 'Amen'? It is us saying that God's promises are trustworthy and that we firmly believe what Scripture tells us that God's love for us in Christ is true; that we never have to doubt this. Instead, in faith, we may thankfully embrace all of this and so glorify God each day.

 January 3

READING: GENESIS 4:17-26; 6:1-3

Walking with God (1)

"And Enoch walked with God…"
GENESIS 5:22A

What does it mean to live life to the glory of God each day? It means walking with God in every step we take, in every decision we make, just as Enoch once walked with God.

How should we picture this walking with God? Was Enoch perhaps a bit of a hermit, dreaming about God, an ascetic whose mind was occupied only with spiritual things? Was he a man entirely out of tune with the things going on in the world he lived in? This is not the picture Scripture presents us. Jude, in his letter, speaks about Enoch as a prophet who spoke publicly about God's coming judgment upon a godless society.

Enoch was the seventh from Adam in the line of Seth. This makes him a contemporary of Lamech, also the seventh of Adam yet in the lineage of Cain. The concluding part of Genesis 4, as well as the beginning verses of Genesis 6, gives us a glimpse of what life was like in those days. The dividing line between the church and the world was slowly fading away. World-conformity was creeping into the church. Especially the youngsters in the church had their questions about why they could not go out and have a look at the fascinating world of Jabal, Jubal, and Tubal-Cain. They also liked the girls they met there. In the tents of Cain, life seemed to be so much more fun than in the church.

Well, this was the time in which Enoch also lived – a time in which it became increasingly more challenging to keep the antithesis set by God in Paradise after the fall into sin. In Enoch's day, many a member of the church could no longer see why this antithesis was necessary. They were no longer happy with the isolation in which God had placed them.

Yet Enoch did not compromise on what God asked of His children. He kept walking with God, warning others to repent. This was a tough battle for Enoch every day. Yet, by the grace of God, he remained faithful. Likewise, God asks us to stay faithful, not compromising the truth, but to keep walking with God.

READING: JUDE 5-16

Walking with God (2)

"And Enoch walked with God…"

GENESIS 5:22A

When reading Scripture, one often has to conclude that there is nothing new under the sun. In today's climate, it is not any more challenging to live holy before the LORD than it was in Enoch's day, or for that matter in Jude's day. Both in Enoch's day and our days as well, society has become totally corrupt.

Thankfully, Scripture gives us guidance on how to remain faithful when living in such a society. In this respect, like many others also, Enoch serves as an example. From the letter of Jude, we learn that amid a dark world, Enoch caused the light of God's Word to shine. As a front line soldier in the army of God, Enoch did not desert but stuck to his post. He prophesied speaking of God's coming judgment not only upon the ungodly but also upon those who perverted the grace of God into licentiousness inside the church. Walking with God, Enoch surely did not live like a hermit, not being in tune with what was going on in the world. Instead, knowing full well what went on in the society he lived in, Enoch spoke the Word of God to all whom God placed on his path.

Enoch also had sons and daughters – children whom Enoch had to care for together with his wife, raising them in the fear of the LORD: as infants, but also throughout puberty and as growing teenagers, who were fascinated by all that was going in the world just as our children are today. Walking with God, Enoch must have spoken with his children about the vanity of all of this and how it grieved God. No doubt, he must also have told them how, in opposing all of this, they should remain faithful in serving God.

Well, God asks the same of us in raising our children. Just being faithful – walking with God, also together with our children, pointing them to the riches of God's promises, which are far more precious than all that this world has to offer, no matter how glamorous it may seem at times.

January 5

READING: ROMANS 8:1-11

Walking according to the Spirit

"For those who live according to the flesh set their minds on the things of the flesh, but those who live according to the Spirit set their minds on the things of the Spirit."
ROMANS 8:5

In Scripture, the verb 'to walk' often refers to the way we live our lives. Walking with God means living for God. The New Testament calls this living for God 'walking according to the Spirit', for example, in Romans 8:4 and Galatians 5:16.

When walking with someone, you talk with him or her on the way. If not, walking together can become very awkward. The same applies to our walk with God. When walking with God, we may open our hearts to God in prayer, whereas when reading the Bible, we listen carefully to what God has to say to us – how to live, how to serve Him from the heart and how to fear Him.

To fear God – this does not mean being afraid of God but instead living close to God in an intimate relationship, marveling each day at the fact that this is possible in and through Christ. This shows that the expression to 'fear God' and to 'walk with God' are almost identical.

Enoch walked with God. You could also turn the expression around: God walked with Enoch. Then you see God as a Father walking with His child, giving this child direction in life, protecting this child, keeping this child in His care. All of this is part of a life in which we walk with God.

Walking with God, walking according to the Spirit – this means, your heart desires to please God at all costs. Yes, walking with God also involves costs. You can no longer walk with evil people as companions (Psalm 1). We choose the narrow way over the broad way of destruction. We seek to eliminate everything from our lives that hinders our walking with God. Then whatever we do, we want to do it to the glory of God, obeying His will, desiring to be conformed to His image again. The more we grow in this through the powerful work of the Holy Spirit within us, the more walking with God will become a mere joy each day.

January 6

READING: HEBREWS 11:1-6

A living faith

"And without faith it is impossible to please Him, for whoever would draw near to God must believe that He exists…"

HEBREWS 11:6A

Walking with God also means that we must live by faith, like the Old Testament saints mentioned in Hebrews 11. Such living by faith has as a first requirement to believe that God exists. This involves more than just believing that God is there. Even the devil admits this. Believing in God includes much more, especially when considering that the word 'exist' in Hebrews 11:6 is a reference to the name of God – to the name 'I am who I am', the covenant name of God which refers to God's faithfulness, assuring us that God is there – undeniable. God is not somewhere far away, but He is near us by day and by night, surrounding us with His love and His power. In Hebrews 11:6, it reads: one must believe this. Otherwise, you will never go to God, never open your heart to God in prayer, trusting that He will provide.

Believing in God also means acknowledging God as the Lord of your life, being eager to open your Bible every day to learn more about God, and also how He wants us to live for Him, glorifying God in all that we do. This is all part of walking with God. It means having an intimate and open relationship with God where there is nothing to hide.

Who would not love to have such a relationship, and yet it is often lacking? Why is this? The main reason is that we look at ourselves. Yet, from ourselves, we will never come to such a close relationship with God. However, this inability should not cause us to despair since God Himself through the powerful work of His Spirit will work this sincere love for Him in us. So instead of looking at ourselves, we should look on high to Christ who at our baptism has promised not only that He will wash us in His blood, but also that He will renew us by His Spirit, that is, the life-giving Spirit who will help and guide us to walk with God every day; God holding our hand and us never letting go of this hand, through faith in Jesus Christ, our Saviour.

January 7

READING: GENESIS 5:21-32

A blessed walk (1)

"Enoch walked with God, and he was not, for God took him."
GENESIS 5:24

He fathered, had sons and daughters, and died – this is the continuous rhythm of Genesis 5. But then suddenly there is a breakthrough. Enoch did not die. While the world around him had given up on God, Enoch kept walking with God, remaining faithful in serving Him.

He too had sons and daughters. He also had to work for his livelihood. Yet while living his daily life, Enoch confided in God and trusted Him. That is why his life did not break off like the lives of all the others. Instead, God took him. Enoch walked with God. They were so close that they walked through everything, even through death. This is a crucial testimony also for us today.

I realise how God took Enoch was exceptional. Yet, it tells us something about the blessings of walking with God also for today, since ultimately death cannot take us either. Christ conquered death. Hence for all who believe in Christ, death is no more than a portal through which we may walk with God to a better life, a perfect life. This is the New Testament perspective of Genesis 5:24.

However, it is not just this future blessing, but there is equally a blessing for today when we walk with God. The prophet Isaiah speaks about this in Chapter 43 of his prophecies, albeit in different wording. He says there when you walk with God, He will always be near so that we have nothing to fear. In verse 2 of this chapter, the LORD assures His people of old – and the same promise also applies to us – "When you pass through the waters, I will be with you; and through the rivers, they shall not overflow you. When you walk through the fire, you shall not be burned, nor shall the flame scorch you." And, therefore, – verse 5 of this same chapter: "Fear not, for I am with you."

These are the abundant blessings which God will bestow upon us when we walk with Him. Then this walking with God will create such a strong bond that even death cannot destroy it. As the Lord Jesus Christ says in John 11:26: "He who believes in Me, though he may die, he shall live."

January 8

READING: REVELATION 21:1-5

A blessed walk (2)

"Enoch walked with God, and he was not, for God took him."
GENESIS 5:24

Due to sin, death entered God's perfect creation. It is because death did not belong that in Genesis 5, God breaks through that monotonous rhythm, "and he died". In taking Enoch, God showed that He was on His way to conquering death. After Enoch, we read about Methuselah who lived for 969 years. The longest a man ever lived on earth. Yet from him too we finally read, "and he died".

Nevertheless, Genesis 5 still bears testimony to the coming defeat of death, since in this same genealogy, we would read many ages later: "All the days of Jesus of Nazareth were 33 years and He died". Yet, we would also read: "He arose from the dead". Yes, Christ conquered death completely and this for us, so that one day we may live with Him forever.

Today, we still live in a world where death is the last enemy. This means, if Christ does not return earlier, it will also be said of us: he/she lived so many years and he/she died! However, because of Christ's victory over death, we also have the comfort of death only being a portal to a better perfect life. We have the comfort of one day receiving perfect glory in the New Jerusalem, of which we read in Revelation 21: "There shall be no more death, nor sorrow, nor crying. There shall be no more pain, for the former things have passed away".

One may wonder what comfort this gives us today. Well, for a moment, think of that empty seat in the living room, an empty bed, an empty cot, of which one day, God will wipe away the memory. The memory, for example, of that loved one suffering Alzheimer's, of a parent or spouse who has cancer, of children who died in infancy or before birth, and so much more that confronts us with the brokenness of this life.

Thinking about all of this suffering, we may cry. Yet in faith, we may also rejoice, because of the Lord Jesus Christ who in Enoch erected a stone amid a cemetery – a stone engraved with the following words: "Behold, I make all things new."

January 9

READING: PROVERBS 14:26-27

To fear the LORD

"The friendship of the LORD is with those who fear Him…"
PSALM 25:14A

Going for a walk with a close friend can be a real joy. Since you trust one another, you do not mind confiding in one another. This applies even more so to walking with God. It means we may open our hearts to God, and likewise, God in love towards us will open His heart to us. Psalm 25:14a speaks about 'friendship' – the friendship of the LORD is with those who fear Him (ESV translation). In the NIV translation, it reads: "The LORD confides in those who fear Him." Confide in – that is what you do with a true friend.

To fear God – in Scripture, this has nothing to do with being afraid of God. Psalm 25 makes this clear very beautifully. In verse 8a, we read God teaches sinners the way. This shows God is a forgiving God, who repeatedly calls us back to walk with Him, lest we might go on dangerous sidetracks away from Him. These sidetracks may seem attractive, but they will all end up in dead-end roads. That is how God teaches sinners the way.

When walking together this way, we will realise the love of God and in response, we will show our love to God in thankful respect. Well, this is what Scripture means when it speaks about 'fearing God'. It refers to a positive attitude in entrusting your life to God, rejoicing in walking with Him.

Such walking together will bring us closer to God, but it will also bring God closer to us. I mentioned the NIV translation "God confides in those who fear Him". Think of God confiding in Abraham when He told him what He was going to do to Sodom and Gomorrah (Genesis 18:17). I am also thinking of what we read in John 15:15, where the Lord Jesus calls His disciples 'friends' in whom He had confided, telling them all that He had heard from the Father. You could call this verse the New Testament equivalent of Psalm 25:14.

Walking with God in this way, what a joy it is each day.

January 10

READING: PSALM 25:1-10

Walking with God – who would not marvel?

"The friendship of the LORD is with those who fear Him…"

PSALM 25:14A

Walking with God – when thinking about it in the real sense of these words, one can hardly believe that this is possible: holy God walking with us sinners – nothing to fear, complete trust. It is a miracle that we may live in such an intimate relationship with God. Yet it is true, despite all of our sins. Psalm 25 beautifully shows this.

In this Psalm, we see David bowed down by enemies surrounding him, verse 2. Yet what worries David, even more, are the sins he has committed and testify against him. Outward circumstances can cloud our relationship with God to the extent that we may ask, "Has the LORD forgotten me?". Yet often, inward struggles do so when we feel unworthy of God's love because of our sins.

David thinks about his life, especially the sins of his youth. Yes, how often do the sins of our youth not haunt us later in life – the temptations we struggled with when we were still young, the times we could not be bothered to fight them? Sin can weigh heavily on our hearts.

In Psalm 25, sin also weighs heavily on David's heart: "LORD, remember me, not according to my sins, but according to Thy mercy" (verse 7). Yet, despite his sins, David keeps clinging to God. "Show me Thy ways, O LORD, teach me Thy paths," (verse 4). God's ways, God's paths – on them David wants to walk, since in verse 10: "All the paths of the LORD are mercy and truth."

Mercy and truth – these are the two keywords within the covenant that God has also made with us. God is merciful since He does not want the death of the sinner. Instead, God wants us to turn to Him and fear Him, trusting God as being reliable and truthful, always. With God, we are safe, even when we must travel through deep valleys and have to number challenging days, or when we struggle with sins committed in the past. When we confess these sins in true repentance and keep clinging to God, we may continue to walk with Him firmly confident and assured that by tightly holding God's hand, we are safe, always. What a miracle this is.

January 11

READING: PSALM 86:11-13

Walking with God – who would not listen?

"The friendship of the LORD is for those who fear Him, and He makes known to them his covenant."

PSALM 25:14

To fear God makes one marvel that God wants to walk with us in such an intimate way. LORD, how great are Thy mercies! We stand in awe! Yet when truly standing in awe of God, thanking Him for His mercies, a genuine desire will come not only to walk with God but also to walk in His ways, in every step we take.

To be able to do so, we must know His ways. That is why David asks God in verse 4 of Psalm 25: "Show me Thy ways, O LORD; teach me Thy path." In verse 9b, we read that the LORD teaches the humble His ways. This shows that God also asks humbleness of us in learning from Him, accepting that what the LORD teaches us in His Word is for our good.

Humble acceptance – this means we should not respond straightaway with comments like "What if…" or "This might be true, but…". Instead, we are to learn from God, accepting that the LORD knows much better what is right for us than what we often think is good for us.

The New King James Version of verse 14 translates the word 'friendship' with 'secret'. Reading this in connection with the second line of verse 14, it means that God wants to make known to us the secrets of His covenant, the secret of how our lives can flourish again – flourish as God intended it in the beginning before the fall into sin. God's ways lead us back to Paradise. That is the truth, even though we cannot always see it this way. So often we think we know better, but meanwhile, it is leading us away from the LORD. In actual terms, this means we no longer appreciate the love the LORD wants to show us. We are no longer appreciative of the intimate relationship the LORD wants to have with us.

So, in walking with God, the question is: are we appreciative of God's love and do we also want to respond to God's love in a way that is pleasing to Him? To do so, a meaningful beginning to every day would be to pray with David: "LORD, teach me and guide me!".

January 12

READING: PSALM 34:1-10

Walking with God – who would not open up?

"The friendship of the LORD is for those who fear Him, and He makes known to them his covenant."

PSALM 25:14

When walking with God, we may rejoice in His nearness, warming ourselves in God's love. Having this assurance, there should never be any fear of opening up to God. This is what you do when walking with a person you can trust and who loves you.

When we rejoice in the intimate relationship we have with God walking with Him, we will never begin a day without speaking to God first and equally never finish a day without speaking to Him. We will bring our joys, sorrows, and concerns before the Father in prayer, sharing with Him what weighs heavily on our hearts just as David does in Psalm 25. You can do this with a person who cares for you.

In walking with God, opening our hearts to Him, confiding in Him, we also may have the assurance that we will always find a listening ear – a listening ear even when speaking with God about what we may call the trivial things of life. Small, little things – and yet at times, they can really bother us. Well, should God – who has numbered all the hairs on our head so that no hair will fall to the ground without His will – should He not also be interested in even the smallest things in our lives, in every detail, despite how little it may seem to be in our eyes?

That is how we may walk with God each day, close to Him in every step we take, and this under an open heaven. Living with this reality, we should look on high towards heaven more, perhaps also in the literal sense of the word to make ourselves more aware of God's nearness, and never-failing love for us.

Where this awareness grows, prayer will become much more natural. Then, not only during our set times for prayer but also throughout the day, we will feel joy and will seek strength in opening up to God in prayer – for example, praising God in prayer during a nature walk, on the worksite or in the office when people mock us because of our faith. We will find strength in a silent prayer knowing God is near, also then.

January 13

READING: PSALM 119:1-16

Walking with God – making time for it

"The friendship of the LORD is for those who fear Him, and He makes known to them his covenant."

PSALM 25:14

Walking with God in a close intimate relationship – how wonderful this is. Yet this does not happen automatically. It takes time and effort.

In human relationships, it is already so that to keep up a close relationship, you must invest time in it. Think of marriage, for example. A husband and wife must work on their marriage each day – taking time for each other, appreciating each other.

Well, the same applies to our relationship with God. To keep this relationship close and intimate, it takes time, effort and energy in the most literal sense of the word. As a bare minimum, try to find half an hour a day of quiet time for and with the LORD, reading His Word and meditating on it, asking God: "Show me Thy ways, teach me Thy paths, help me to submit to Thy will and teach me to see that Thy paths are indeed good and upright always."

There is a children's song, "Read your Bible, pray every day... and you will grow". Grow in closeness to God by reading your Bible and praying, but then also in this order. Sometimes it seems that people find it easier to pray than to read the Bible. At times, speaking with God seems to be easier than listening to God's comforting voice as it comes to us in Scripture. However, to fear the LORD and walking with Him starts with being willing to listen to God, rejoicing in His nearness and learning from Him the paths He wants us to take.

In general, we are not such good listeners. We like to talk, reasoning why nothing is wrong with this or with that. We think we know it all. We are quick to speak, slow to listen. Before the other has finished, we have already butted in by saying, "I know, but....".

The same can also happen in our relationship with God by not allowing God to speak to us. Yet we should make time to read the Bible, listening quietly, asking ourselves the question: "What does the Lord teach me in these verses?" Pray like David: "LORD, show me Thy ways, teach me Thy paths." Then it would be as if we were practically walking with God, rejoicing in His nearness.

January 14

READING: PROVERBS 1:1-7

The ABC of all wisdom – to fear God

"The fear of the Lord is the beginning of knowledge…"

PROVERBS 1:7A

The Book of Proverbs is a book full of practical knowledge, teaching us how to live life in our daily walk with God. It gives advice and warnings often described in the vivid colours of the ancient East. Yet, at the same time, it is easy to recognise ourselves in the various proverbs of this book and how similar it is to our lives today.

The Book of Proverbs provides us with wisdom, yet not in the form of a textbook to gain a certain amount of knowledge. Instead, the wisdom offered in this book can only be made one's own when our life is rooted in the fear of the LORD. This is a pre-requisite to understanding the lessons provided in this particular book of the Bible. The author makes this clear right at the start of this book: "The fear of the LORD is the beginning of knowledge."

Throughout this book, it becomes clear that being wise is different from being knowledgeable or smart. After all, one can also be very wise without any higher education or specific qualifications. Think of a wise mother who has not had much schooling, but who lives close to the Scriptures in which she finds the source of her wisdom. What a privilege it is for children to have such a mother – a mother blessed by God with a living faith.

This example shows that true wisdom is received by living close to the LORD, having the desire to obey God's commandments, which God has given not to burden us, but instead to cause our life to flourish. In one of the last verses of the Book of Ecclesiastes, which is another book of the Bible full of practical wisdom, it reads: "Let us hear the conclusion of the whole matter: Fear God and keep His commandments, for this is man's all." Well, that is what Scripture understands as being wise. It is the wisdom we receive in Christ through the renewing work of the Holy Spirit within us. Wisdom by fearing God, which also will have an impact on how we live our lives. Then we will desire to walk with God daily.

January 15

READING: PROVERBS 4:10-27

To fear God – what does this mean?

"The fear of the Lord is the beginning of knowledge…"

PROVERBS 1:7A

The fear of the LORD – what does this expression mean? In the Form for Baptism, it reads as God's children, "we must not love the world, but put off our old nature and lead a God-fearing life." Yet what does such a life look like? At the baptism of our children, we promise to raise them in the fear of the LORD. What does this mean in practical terms to teach our children to fear the LORD? As it so often happens, well-known expressions run the risk of wearing thin. We use them without really knowing what they mean.

To fear the LORD means having respect for the LORD, entrusting yourself to the LORD in all circumstances of life. It also means listening respectfully to what God has revealed in his Word. In a nutshell, it means to love the LORD as the Redeemer of our life. This love, this fear, is the beginning of all wisdom.

Over against this wisdom stands the foolishness of this world – the folly of people who do not want to consider the LORD's will when it comes to the things of everyday life. Instead, they lean on their own understanding. Yet this is mere foolishness.

Scripture teaches the antithesis also concerning wisdom. Antithesis – again, a word often used but not always fully understood. Antithesis – this word points to the battle line that runs across this world between the seed of the woman and the seed of the serpent. These two are always at war with each other: the church and the world, the battle between belief and unbelief.

Well, this antithesis also has its impact when we speak about wisdom. With the help of all kinds of proverbs, the wisdom teacher teaches God-fearing wisdom, pointing out that there are also other teachers teaching the art of living, yet with the wrong objective in mind. They teach the youth: "Seek your own pleasures. Enjoy life and don't take everything so seriously". They often do so most convincingly and temptingly so that many fall for it. Yet, it leads to destruction. Therefore, be warned, just as we read in the Book of Proverbs. Do not fall for it.

January 16

READING: PROVERBS 6:20-23

Instruction in the ABC of true wisdom starts in the home

"Hear, my son, your father's instruction,
and forsake not your mother's teaching."

PROVERBS 1:8

To become truly wise, one should never forget what has been learnt at home – the place where, during our formative years, our lives are shaped. Parents should make the most of these years, realising how important these years are when the children are still young and also very receptive. Psalms learnt during our youth are often never forgotten. This equally applies to the Bible stories. Such simple things and yet of lasting value.

It is in these early years that parents should lay the foundation according to the vows made at the baptism of their children. These vows obligate us to raise our children in the fear of the LORD and to instruct them in the riches of God's Word – the ABC of all wisdom.

There are more people involved when it comes to the education of our children: Christian schools and the instruction given by the church. Yet, parents cannot leave it just to the teachers at school or the minister in the catechism class. It starts in the home when the Bible is opened and we speak with our children about how they should live according to God's Word. In Proverbs 22:6 it reads: "Train up a child in the way it should go, and when it is old it will not depart from it."

If young people really want to become wise, they would do well to listen to their parents. That is not a popular message in today's society. Today you hear more and more that parents should let their children make their own choices. We live in a different age. Times have changed. Yet also in this respect, there is nothing new under the sun. In Proverbs 30:11 and 12 we read: "There are those who curse their fathers and do not bless their mothers. There are those who are clean in their own eyes but not washed from their filth." Similar words could be used for today's generation. It is the way of folly as described in Proverbs 9. In contrast, blessed are those young people who do not despise the teaching of their parents, but instead rejoice in what they learn at home: the ABC of faith and true wisdom.

January 17

READING: PROVERBS 3:1-8

God's wisdom versus man's wisdom

"Trust in the Lord with all your heart,
and do not lean on your own understanding."
PROVERBS 3:5

Trusting in the LORD means placing your security in God alone and letting God's Word guide your life in all circumstances. Do not lean on your own understanding, the wisdom teacher says. Why not? It is because we are sinful, and this also affects our understanding of things. James, in his letter, writing about human wisdom in contrast to divine wisdom, says human wisdom is earthly, sensual, and demonic (Chapter 3:15). This is a devastating appraisal of the mind of man. The wisdom of man has nothing in common with the wisdom of God. The wisdom from below contrasts the wisdom from above. That is why the wisdom teacher says that we should not lean on human understanding – do not place your security in the wisdom of men. Instead, put full trust in the wisdom of God. Do not look for answers to your problems from within, but rather, from above. Trust in the LORD, and He will act according to the promises He has given us. On these promises, we can rely, always.

I realise the LORD has created us with a mind, giving us the ability to make plans, choices, and decisions. Yet we should also be willing to admit that the human mind is limited in its thinking as it also suffers from the consequences of sin, which often causes us to make the wrong choices and decisions. Hence, we should be willing to subject the thoughts of our mind to God's Word at all times.

In 2 Corinthians 10:5, the apostle Paul writes that we must take every thought captive to make it obedient to Christ. This means, though using our mind, God's Word should still rule all of our decisions and all the choices we make. It is no longer what I think but what God says, even if it goes against what we think might be better. Trust Me, says the LORD. Trust and obey. It will cause our lives to flourish.

January 18

READING: 1 CHRONICLES 28:9; PSALM 73:23-26

What place does God have in our life?

"In all your ways acknowledge Him…"

PROVERBS 3:6A

Not leaning on your own understanding and trusting God means you reckon with God each day, genuinely giving Him a place in your life. That is what David charged Solomon to do and what the author of Psalm 73 professes as mere joy.

The opposite of acknowledging the LORD is that you do not need Him for everyday life, do not need Him in the day-to-day decisions. This so quickly happens, by breaking life up into two departments: the religious department – our church activities, our daily Bible reading and so on, whereas during our regular activities – work and leisure – the LORD hardly gets a place.

Yet, acknowledging the LORD means more than just having a special department for Him. Instead, it means that we ask the LORD for guidance and help with all things, knowing that without the blessing of the LORD, everything we do is in vain. I think here of the explanation which the Heidelberg Catechism gives of the fourth petition: "Give us this day our daily bread." In praying this petition, we acknowledge God as the only fountain of all good. Indeed, <u>all</u> good: the income we earn, the food on the table. Yes, then we want to acknowledge the LORD in all of these everyday life things by thanking Him for what He in His grace gives us, often in abundance and this while we are totally undeserving of it.

In all your ways, acknowledge the LORD. In all your ways, for example, when it comes to choosing a boyfriend or girlfriend, in receiving children from the LORD as well as in raising these children. Acknowledge the LORD when spending our money and using our time – also our leisure time. Acknowledge the LORD in coping with sickness, in feeling lonely or having not found a partner in life. So many more things could be mentioned.

When walking with God, we will mention all of these things in prayer, asking Him for help, guidance and strength. If we do so and we are also willing to follow God's instructions, He will grant us travelling mercies on our journey towards the New Jerusalem. In verse 6b, it reads: "He will make straight your path."

January 19

READING: PSALM 121

Travelling mercies

"…and He will make straight your path."
PROVERBS 3:6B

The Book of Proverbs teaches practical wisdom for everyday life. Often, this book does so via short concisely formulated sayings of two or three thought-provoking lines. At times, they may even make us question whether a specific saying is true since they are mostly formulated somewhat one-sidedly, highlighting only one aspect of the truth. By way of example, at the beginning of Chapter 3, we read, when keeping God's commandments, length of days and years of life will be added to us. One may wonder whether you can indeed say this. Does this indeed always apply?

In Proverbs 10:3, it reads: "The LORD will not allow the righteous soul to famish." However, what about those seven thousand people at the time of Elijah? Were they never hungry? Moreover, in Psalm 34, it reads: "Many are the afflictions of the righteous."

However, whenever we read such a seemingly onesided proverb wondering whether it does not overlook other aspects of the matter, this does not deny the truth expressed in such a proverb. The point is, the wisdom teacher wants to emphasise the great blessing which serving the LORD fills our lives with in every respect.

The text above this meditation intends to make this clear as well. Trust in the LORD with all your heart, acknowledge Him in all your ways, then the road will be safe for you. This does not mean there will never be any difficulties on the road. Yet, these difficulties will never become insurmountable obstacles which will force us off the road so that we might get lost. With the LORD, we are safe, always. The journey through life might not always be an easy one. We might also have to number challenging days. Yet the LORD will help us through. The road of life is never a dead-end road. Though at times the way to travel might be very dangerous, even making us stumble, if we cling to the LORD, He will give us a safe arrival in the New Jerusalem.

READING: PROVERBS 15:13-17

Affliction

"All the days of the afflicted are evil…"

PROVERBS 15:15A

When confronted with the brokenness of life, how can joy prevail? Affliction can be hard to cope with. Scripture speaks quite openly about this. Yet it also mentions that suffering is a result of sin. In Romans 8, the apostle Paul says that because of sin creation groans and so do we, like a woman in the pain of childbirth. This woman cannot wait to see her child. Well, so do we groan, eagerly awaiting our complete redemption: life on the new earth where there will no longer be any pain, no longer any suffering and no affliction either.

At present, however, we are still pilgrims travelling towards this glorious future. On the road towards this future, many of us will face affliction. In this context, Scripture speaks about the poor and the needy – children of God hit hard by the misery of this present life.

Affliction – at times, this happens just occasionally, but there are also those who, so to speak, collect all the blows. By way of example, think of those who live at the lower end of society with little income. When there is an economic downturn, they are always the first to feel it.

Yet there are also other kinds of afflictions with which we often struggle the most. Affliction received from God's hand, yet we do not know why. Think of the Old Testament examples of Joseph and Job. They did not have any idea why all of this was happening to them. How often do we not struggle in a similar way, asking "Why, O LORD?".

Once, in a conversation with someone who blamed God for all the misery in this world, I said, "We cannot always explain everything, yet remember that to see a rainbow we also need dark clouds". I realise, when depressed, one does not always see it this way. Yet even though we struggle to see the positives, God is there. In Proverbs 14:31 we read that He has mercy on the needy. I also think of what it says in Psalm 10:14, namely that God sees our trouble and grief, therefore consider this and commit yourself to Him. That is how joy can still prevail: by looking on high and committing ourselves to God, assured that He will also provide amid affliction.

January 21

READING: PROVERBS 15:30-33

Cheerfulness amidst affliction

"All the days of the afflicted are evil, but the
cheerful of heart has a continual feast."
PROVERBS 15:15

All the days of the afflicted are evil. In most instances, tomorrow will not be any better than today. Each new day is filled with hardship and sorrow. Who would not get worn out by this?

However, even though not underestimating how hard all of this must be, the author of the Book of Proverbs teaches, we should not just stay focused on what we see and how we feel. Those who live by faith know there is more to life than the way we feel at times. The point is how we deal with these feelings. What is our attitude to all that we experience in life? Psalm 10 says: commit it to the LORD. Yes, give it to our Father in heaven, even if it is sometimes with no more than a sigh: "Father, I don't know anymore, but I lay it in Thy almighty hands."

In the text above this meditation, we read: the cheerful of heart has a continual feast. When suffering affliction, having a cheerful attitude can make a lot of difference. People with a cheerful character can often see light even in the darkness. They seem to be able to cope with life, even when there is affliction or hardship. Of course, this does not take the misery away – the days of the afflicted remain evil. Yet, when the heart is cheerful, life can still be a continual feast.

Evil and yet a continual feast – there seems to be a big gap between these two extremes. Yet the point now is a cheerful heart bridges this gap so that amidst all of the afflictions, joy still prevails, which is God's grace for the wounded!

Is this not beyond reality? No, it is not, since this cheerfulness also finds its roots in the fear of the LORD, which teaches us where to find strength amidst affliction and also how to cope in challenging times. How? By clinging to our Saviour, who went through the deepest darkness so that the light of God's grace will always keep shining even though we may sometimes find it difficult to see. Yes, when life is tough, keep remembering Christ is and remains the firm anchorage in our lives, also when we are bowed down by afflictions.

January 22

READING: PHILIPPIANS 4:4-13

Cheerfulness

" …but the cheerful of heart
has a continual feast."

PROVERBS 15:15B

Cheerful of heart – what does this mean? The New King James Version translates: but he who is of a merry heart is of a continual feast. Merry – the same word as when wishing someone a merry Christmas. Scripture, however, means a different kind of merriness. The merry heart mentioned in the text above differs entirely from the merriment today's society speaks so highly of – merriment to enjoy oneself, completely self-focused. When bowed down, these people will say to you: "Don't worry, be happy! Try to enjoy yourself". The superficial joy of the world!

Yet Scripture speaks differently about merriness and cheerfulness. When using these words, it is referring to the joy we experience in faith and which gives us the strength to cope, also in challenging times. It is the joy mentioned by the apostle Paul in Philippians 4 – a joy not depending on circumstances, but a feeling of deep contentment in the LORD, knowing that He will also provide in times of affliction. In the verses for today's reading, the apostle Paul is pointing to Christ as the secure anchorage in our lives. To say it with the words of our confession – Lord's Day 10 Heidelberg Catechism and Article 13 Belgic Confession – true wisdom rooted in the fear of the LORD makes us see that whatever befalls us comes from God's fatherly hand.

I realise that this does not suddenly make life easier to cope with, like an injection from a doctor to ease the pain. It is not like that. Yet, when we live close to the LORD in obedience to His Word, the LORD will give us the strength we need to also carry hardship and affliction, to carry it even with a cheerful heart, since God is near and His love goes out in particular to His afflicted children. In Him we may confide, in the LORD who is the Defender of the needy. That is how joy can prevail even when the days are evil. For God is at my side – in Him I may rejoice.

January 23

READING: LUKE 12:13-21

Contentment (1)

"Better is a little with the fear of the Lord
than great treasure and trouble with it."
PROVERBS 15:16

Today's text mentions two opposites: 'little' and 'great treasure'. Even though Scripture often speaks about riches as a covenantal blessing, this does not mean that being a covenant child will always bring riches. It can also be very different. There have been and always will be those who are needy among God's people.

Verse 16 speaks about 'better is a little with the fear of the LORD'. A little – that is a life with meagre wages where it is a struggle to make ends meet. In contrast, verse 16 also speaks about great treasure. The Hebrew word points to fullness of supply: never any worry about money, always having enough money in your account to buy what you want. It is the contrast between the rich and the poor, as we see in today's society and at times also in the church.

However, this is again just what is seen when looking at poverty and riches with the physical eye only. However, the physical eye never gives us the full picture. Also, concerning being rich and poor, the issue is how we deal with it. What is our attitude towards what the LORD in His good pleasure and wisdom has imparted to us? Proverbs teaches us that the fear of the LORD will help us with our attitude, also in how to deal with being rich or poor.

The second part of verse 16 speaks about having great treasure. However, a life of abundance often goes together with a lot of trouble. The Hebrew word used for trouble in this verse can also be translated with 'vexation' (being worried) or 'disturbance'. People holding their breath, for example, when the economy takes a downturn. What will happen, what will the future hold? Riches and great treasures, yet hearts are troubled. It is the anxiety of the Gentiles about which the Lord Jesus speaks in the Sermon on the Mount, people who are always worrying about what tomorrow will bring. Being rich often goes together with a lot of anxiety, a lot of tension, and unease. However, when we are rich toward God, all stress will be gone. Rich toward God – that is, having assurance in faith that Father will provide. Having this assurance, we can cope even when materially there are fewer supplies.

January 24

READING: LUKE 12:22-31

Contentment (2)

"Better is a little with the fear of the Lord
than great treasure and trouble with it."

PROVERBS 15:16

Yesterday we focused on a person having great treasure – having an abundance with never any worry about money – yet inwardly, they are often troubled about what the future may hold. Worried, since what he considers as his treasure can easily slip away and leave him empty-handed.

In contrast to this person, we read about someone who had but very little – struggling every day to get enough food on the table, living on a bare minimum. Yet he is better off than the rich person who is always worrying. He is better off because fearing the LORD causes this person to look at his poverty in a different way than the world around him, where things are looked at only with the physical eye.

Fearing the LORD – that is, living thankfully out of God's fatherly hand. It is living with the assurance that Father will provide, even though in our eyes, it might seem to be very little. It is living by faith, knowing that Father will always give us sufficient to serve Him. Yes, then we can be content even with a little.

Even though we know all of this, often we too do not look at things this way. Discontentment can easily take hold of us when looking at rich people while we ourselves are just struggling to make ends meet. Nevertheless, those who are poor are often more content than those who are rich. At times, wealthier people still want even more. On the other hand, those who receive every slice of bread out of God's fatherly hand are at peace and content, since Father provides what is needed – no more and no less. It gives peace, peace with God, established by the blood of the cross by the atoning work of our Lord and Saviour Jesus Christ. Yes, He is at the centre, also of the wisdom taught in the Book of Proverbs.

January 25

READING: MATTHEW 14:1-21

Mealtime

"Better is a dinner of herbs where love is
than a fattened ox and hatred with it."
PROVERBS 15:17

Proverbs 15:17 paints us two pictures. First, a family meal with little food – just vegetables and nothing else. Next, a family meal with food in abundance – a fattened calf. Verse 17 also speaks about the atmosphere around the table. In the family where they had nothing else but vegetables, they still had a lovely meal and encouraging conversation with interest in each other. Yet in the other family where they had plenty of food, there was no real happiness. Despite the abundance of food, hatred determined the atmosphere.

To give a bit more colour to each of these two pictures, I think of Matthew 14, where we also read about two meals. First the meal in the palace of King Herod, who on the occasion of his birthday had invited many guests. There was plenty of food and also a lot of wine. At the climax of the feast, the young girl Salome got all the men into a state of excitement with her dancing, which prompted King Herod to promise her whatever she asked for. After consulting her mother Herodias, she asked for the head of John the Baptist. A festive meal, but what hatred!

Next, we read about another meal in the open field. Five thousand people gathered around the Lord Jesus with no more food than just five loaves of bread and two fish. However, having blessed this simple meal, the Lord Jesus multiplied the bread and the fish and they all ate and were satisfied. A meal where God was given thanks for the food He supplied.

This teaches us it is not the amount of food that should determine the joy around a table. Better a meagre meal, eaten in peace and love for one another than a table with food in abundance, where the guests only cherish a deep-seated hatred towards each other. This does not mean that we are not allowed to enjoy a delicious meal with delicious food. The point is whether we enjoy our food in thankfulness towards God and when the need arises, we are also willing to share with our neighbour.

January 26

READING: PSALM 1

A joyful walk

"Blessed is the man… his delight is
in the law of the LORD…"

PSALM 1:1A + 2A

Walking with God means walking in His ways, finding joy in this. Well, who would not like this? Not the cheerfulness and merriment as the world around us finds joy in it, but as Scripture speaks about it: finding joy in being the Lord's. Yet, do we? Do we genuinely rejoice in walking with God each day?

It is easy to say 'Yes' to this question, but does this also show up in our lives? Is our life indeed a joyful walk with God every day, wanting nothing else? Psalm 1 says only this will cause true happiness: walking with God, having delight in His law, doing His will.

Agreeing with this is easy. Yet, there is also the daily temptation of enjoying life in this world, the temptation just for a moment to forget about all that God asks of us. One evening of fun. That cannot be too bad, can it?

Psalm 1:1 tells us about the danger of such an attitude. It pictures a downward trend: walking, standing, sitting. Just by way of example, you are young and having an evening of fun with your friends in the city. It is not your intention to go to a night club, but you walk by and just have a look – no more than that. You keep walking. Yet the next time you pass by you have a closer look – standing still, considering how nice it would be to have a look inside. Satan is busy with you and before you know it, you are inside sitting down. It is the slippery slope of sin. It may look like fun, but how empty this fun often is.

When looking through the window of the church at the outside world so quickly one can become discontent. Discontent because the outside world is attracting us. Would it not be nice to join in occasionally? That cannot be too bad, can it? Yet, while considering looking outside, we are standing with our back to the riches God is offering us inside the church. Do not do this, says the author of Psalm 1! Instead, keep joyfully walking with God.

January 27

READING: PHILIPPIANS 4:8-9

Meditating (1)

"Blessed is the man… who meditates on God's law day and night."

PSALM 1:1A + 2B

Meditating on God's law by day and by night – how can one keep this up in a hectic life where so many things are asking for our attention? You cannot spend the entire day reading your Bible, can you? Reactions like this make it clear that one has not really understood what Scripture wants to teach us in this verse.

Meditating – do we still know this skill? If we do not take time to do this, we will slowly drift away from the LORD. Moreover, we will fail to receive the happiness of which Psalm 1 speaks in such beautiful terms.

To meditate – this is more than just reading Scripture and pondering on it. The word used in verse 2 of this psalm means more literally 'reading in an undertone'. In those days, people never read softly but always used their voices just a little bit, in the same way as lonely people sometimes do today. When reading the Bible for themselves, they quietly use their voices to keep their attention, not only when reading the Bible, but also when praying.

From this explanation, we learn that the word 'meditate' used in Psalm 1 has nothing to do with musing in a somewhat dreaming way. Instead, it refers to a careful reading of Scripture, whereby one puts his mind to what he is reading, trying to understand the meaning of it, trying to make it his own to be able to work with it. After all, God's law is not just dry theory, but it will give us guidance, wholesome guidance for life, so that we may joyfully walk with God.

Through meditating on His Word, God will guide us so that we stay on track in walking with Him, also that we know what the LORD wants us to do in all the different circumstances of life that we face every day. We also need this guidance in learning to deny our own will. When meditating on God's Word in this way, it will no longer be a box we can tick off every day. Instead, we will start longing for that special time with and for the LORD each day, whatever time of the day or night this might be.

January 28

READING: PSALM 77:1-15

Meditating (2)

"Blessed is the man… who meditates on God's law day and night."

PSALM 1:1A + 2B

So far this month, we have focused on what it means to walk with God day by day. We learned that such a walk involves a close relationship with God. This close relationship will also create the desire to meditate on God's law, the desire to get to know the LORD better. By meditating on God's law and God's Word, we will see more and more who God is and what He did for His people throughout the time of the Old Testament, also realising this is my God and my Father! This made the author of Psalm 77 cry out: which god is as great as our God! Thou art the God who works wonders!

When studying God's Word this way and meditating upon it, it will indeed make us see more and more what great a God we have in the LORD, the faithful God of the covenant, who worked powerfully to save His people numerous times, even though God's children often rebelled against Him and yet, still there was redemption!

It is for this very reason that the author of Psalm 1 says: "Blessed is the man who meditates on God's law, day and night." Being busy with God's Word this way will cause our lives to flourish and also keep us close to God in a deep love for Him. This love will also grow in intensity when we take time to open God's Word and meditate on it daily. This same deep love towards God will also help us in the battle against sin.

Yet, none of us can do this of our own strength.. We need Christ, who never compromised but always delighted in God's will. It was His food to do His Father's will. On the difficult road He had to travel, He kept walking with God to the very end, obeying His Father's will, even when He was nailed to the cross. He did all this for us and in our place. Therefore, it is only by looking at Christ, our Saviour that we will find the strength to walk joyfully with God, also finding delight in obeying Father's will.

 January 29

READING: JEREMIAH 17:5-10

The fruit of meditation

"He is like a tree planted by streams of water that yields its fruit in its season, and its leaf does not wither. In all that he does, he prospers."
PSALM 1:3

Sincere meditation will also bear fruit. When meditating on God's Word with a genuine love for the LORD, it will create as fruit a holy desire to live accordingly, praising God not just in words but also in deeds. You could call this the purpose of all meditating. I think here of the charge the LORD gave to Joshua when he became leader of God's people, Joshua 1:8, "This Book of the Law shall not depart from your mouth, but you shall meditate on it day and night, so that you may be careful to do according to all that is written in it. For then, you will make your way prosperous, and then you will have good success." The same we also read in Psalm 1:3b, "… in all that he does he prospers".

Prosper – not first of all materially, but in finding peace even when facing difficulties and affliction. Prosper in finding strength in the LORD. Like a tree planted by a stream of water. Such a tree always has sufficient water and will never dry out. Likewise, when living close to the Word of God, we will always have enough; yes, even more than sufficient. Then God's Word will be our source, a fountain of living water from which we will drink daily with a holy desire. When drinking from that fountain, there will never be any dryness or withering of our life of faith. Instead, we will be like a tree that never disappoints, becoming a pleasure also for the community we live in, both the communion of saints as well as the wider community. Then whatever we do, we shall prosper. Prosper – perhaps not always materially, but we will be able to deal with matters in faith, also when facing difficulties or disappointments. Then even in the valley of life, the joy of faith will prevail; joy as the fruit of meditating on God's law and His wondrous deeds. Once we start to experience this, we will never give meditating on God's Word a miss, not even for one day.

January 30

READING: GENESIS 11:27-12:3

En route to the Promised Land – Isolated

"Now the Lord said to Abram, 'Go from your country and your kindred and your father's house to the land that I will show you.'"

GENESIS 12:1

Walking with God may also involve making sacrifices. I think of Abraham, who had to cut all ties when God called him away from his country, his family, yes even from his nearest and dearest family. Why was this necessary?

First, in Genesis 12, Scripture starts a new episode in the history of redemption. You could call it an interim when God starts channeling His salvation through the bed of Israel's history to bring the Messiah into the world. During this interim period, God leaves the nations in their evil ways. However, God did not cut them off altogether. At Pentecost, the call goes out once again also to the heathen nations.

Meanwhile, Abraham had to cut all ties. Why? Often the reason given is that God called Abraham away from the worship of idols. Yet also in Canaan, Abraham would be confronted with idol service. So, what else could be the reason?

For a moment, think of the story about the building of the Tower of Babel. The sin committed in this building project was that the people wanted to stay together as a support for each other. One may ask, what was wrong with that? Yet the underlying thought was, if we stay together, nothing will happen to us. The redemption motto of Babel was: stay within your country, close to your family, and your father's house, then you will be safe. Redemption was considered as something that lay within man's own reach. It is for this reason that Abraham had to cut all ties showing him that redemption is not within man's own reach! That is why God isolates Abraham from his country, his family, and even from his father's house.

Abraham also had to do this for our sake so that the coming of the Messiah could be safeguarded. Abraham had to, even for the generations to come: for believers from the Jews and Gentiles, who despite the ties they may keep, must still live by the same faith that safety is not guaranteed within the protection of a close-knit family, but in Christ alone. That is the parallel between Abraham and us today: seek your security in God alone!

January 31

READING: HEBREWS 11:8-16

En route to the Promised Land – With God's blessing

"And I will make of you a great nation, and I will bless you and make your name great, so that you will be a blessing. I will bless those who bless you, and him who dishonours you I will curse, and in you all the families of the earth shall be blessed."
GENESIS 12:2-3

In Genesis. 12:4, we read: "So Abram went, as the LORD had told him." Complete isolation, yet Abraham went accompanied by God's blessing. God promises him: "I will make of you a great nation" – a great nation, even though Sarah was barren. This shows that the blessing comes from above.

In Babel, people looked for security in making a name for themselves, yet God destroyed their work. Then in Genesis 12, we see how God makes Abraham's name great by blessing Him from above. For Abraham, this required full trust in God, breaking all ties, together with his wife entirely on their own. Yet it finishes with all the families of the earth being blessed in Abraham – a multitude too great to number.

For a while, God narrows the bed of the river of salvation, yet He still kept the nations in mind when He says to Abraham: "in you, all the families of the earth shall be blessed." In you – that is, ultimately in Jesus Christ, born from the lineage of Abraham. That is how the blessing given to Abraham also reached us. I think here of what the apostle Paul writes in his letter to the Galatians, Chapter 3:29, "If you are in Christ, then you are Abraham's seed, and heirs according to the promise." Being in Christ – this means together with Abraham and the whole cloud of witnesses in Hebrews 11: we too are heirs of that city that has foundations, whose designer and builder is God.

At times, this may also put us in isolation, when people mock us because of our faith or when, for the sake of the truth, family ties are no longer as strong anymore. This may hurt. Yet when hurting, let us never forget: we walk with God, who in Christ grants us His blessing day by day. Well, we do not need more, since God's blessing is sufficient, always.

February 1

READING: ROMANS 3:21-31

Upholding the Law

"You are not under law but under grace."
ROMANS 6:14B

Walking with God also means obeying His commandments. In the next set of meditations, we will turn to the Heidelberg Catechism and focus on what God asks of us in each of His Ten Commandments. Yet first, we will look at some texts from Scripture, which speak about how to obey God's commandments in love and not as a burden.

Today, many Christians believe that the Ten Commandments are no longer applicable in the same strict sense as they were given to the people of Israel during the time of the Old Testament. They defend this viewpoint by referring to some specific texts in the New Testament, for example, to what the apostle Paul writes in Romans 6, verse 14: "You are not under law but under grace." At first reading, this text seems to prove that the Ten Commandments are no longer in force for the New Testament church.

Those who make comments like these often overlook that, concerning the Old Testament laws, we must distinguish between ceremonial laws and moral laws. As to the ceremonial laws, the ceremonies and symbols of these laws functioned to teach the Old Testament Church about the coming of Christ, and therefore, when Christ came, they were no longer necessary. They ceased. At the same time, however, because they pointed to Christ, today, we still can learn from them.

Concerning the moral law, this is different, as it becomes clear from Christ's Sermon on the Mount. In this sermon, Christ says that He had not come to abolish the Law. He also shows this in the sermon, clearly explaining how we are to obey each of the Ten Commandments: not just superficially by adhering only to the letter of the law, but more importantly, we are to obey these commandments from the heart.

Living in the New Testament era, the Holy Spirit will enable us to do so. This is God's amazing grace in Christ, in whom we have been freed from the curse of the law. Yet, not from the law as such. The apostle Paul writes in Romans 3: living by faith in Christ, we still uphold the law.

February 2

READING: 1 JOHN 4:7-11

How can we ever give perfect love?
"Love is from God"
1 JOHN 4:7

The first commandment of God's Law reads: "You shall have no other gods before Me". Answer 94 of the Heidelberg Catechism summarises this as follows: God wants us to trust in Him alone, submit to Him, love fear and honour Him with all our heart, forsake all creatures rather than to do the least thing against His will. This means perfect love from an undivided heart and this always one hundred per cent, 24/7! One may wonder: who of us is ever able to give this perfect love? Who of us can live at this high level?

Yet there is no reason for despair, since God Himself will work this love in us. In 1 John 4:7 we read: "Love is from God". From ourselves, we would never be able to muster the unconditional love God requires. At times, we may think that if I try hard enough, things might change in my life. Yet, it is not our good intentions that will get us there in the end. It is beyond us. We will never attain it ourselves. It is only by abiding in God's wonderful love by which He loved us first that we too can express genuine love.

Yes, if we abide in that love, the love of God granted to us in Christ, the rest will follow. First, we have to turn to God's love for us, before we can extend any love ourselves. John writes in verse 9 of Chapter 4: "In this, the love of God was made manifest among us, that God sent his only Son into the world, so that we might live through him".

Love is from God! Hence, we need Christ who once said: "Apart from me, you can do nothing" (John 15:8). Nothing – therefore, to be able to love God and our neighbour as God requires from us, we need to abide in Christ. Thus warming ourselves in the love of Christ, also realising the great miracle of this love, we will know no other desire than also showing this same love to others. Love as God's gift for us to work with.

February 3

READING: JOHN 15:1-17

Abiding in Christ (1)

"Abide in Me…"

JOHN 15:4

Abiding in Christ – it is a well-known expression. Yet, how are we to do this? The image which the Lord Jesus Christ uses in John 15 makes clear what it means. Like a branch on a vine grows and produces grapes only when it remains firmly connected with the vine, so we can bear fruits of faith only when we live our lives close to the LORD.

From ourselves, we would never make an effort to live close to the LORD. We can do this only by the powerful work of the Holy Spirit within us; the life-giving Spirit by whom Christ wants to renew our lives. That is why Scripture warns us never to grieve the Holy Spirit. Instead, we should give the Holy Spirit ample opportunity to let the life sap of the vine flow into our lives. The Spirit does this by the Word. That is why we should never cut back on our daily Bible reading. At times this happens quite easily. For example, when we are in a hurry to get to work in the mornings or when we have slept in on a lazy day.

Abide in Me – says Christ – then I will abide in you. Abiding in Christ – that is, loving Him and loving God with all our heart, mind, and strength; to trust Him; to obey Him in all that we do! And this not as a burden, but instead, as Christ says it in John 15:11, that your joy may be full. This shows that true happiness will only be found when we live our lives daily close to the LORD every step of the way, holding Father's hand, clinging to the promises God has given us in Christ — abiding in Christ, by letting Christ abide in us, by the powerful work of the Holy Spirit in our hearts.

February 4

READING: JOHN 14:6-14

Abiding in Christ (2)

"As the Father has loved me, so have I loved you. Abide in my love."
JOHN 15:9

Small words can have significant meaning. Concerning John 15:9 I think of the word 'as'. It is quickly overlooked, yet it has great and deep meaning. Listen to what Christ says: "As the Father loved Me, I also have loved you." 'As' – with this little word, the Lord Jesus puts His love for us on the same level as God's love for Him, the Son of the Father.

Well, how did the Father love his Son? Our limited sinful human mind will never be able to fathom this love completely. We search for words to say something about it.

First, it is fatherly love. In many places, Scripture pictures this love as the most profound love there is: fatherly love! For us humans this often differs. Fathers can also leave scars behind because of how they have treated their children. At times, such children can have difficulty in understanding what fatherly love means.

God's fatherly love, however, stands above all of this. God's fatherly love means love in the deepest meaning of this word: real love as only God can give it. The love of God by which we may know our lives are surrounded, by day and by night. A fatherly love that can never be destroyed; it is there waiting for us, always. No matter how much we may sometimes have hurt God's fatherly love, it is there waiting. Think of the parable of the prodigal son.

"As the Father loved Me…". Of course, in the relationship between the Father and His Son, this was perfect, complete harmony. In John 14:10 Jesus says: "I am in the Father and the Father in Me." Completely one! With that love between the Father and the Son – with that very same love Christ now also loves us, with the same intensity and depth.

Christ showed this love in giving His life for us. That is how much He loved us and still loves us each day anew.

How are we to respond to Christ's love for us? The Lord Jesus says: "Abide in My love." Realise how much He loves you; do not walk away from it, but abide in it. Immerse yourself in this wonderful love. This will cause your life to flourish.

February 5

READING: 1 CORINTHIANS 13:1-7

True love

"If you keep my commandments, you will abide in My love."
JOHN 15:10

In John 15:9, the Lord Jesus Christ says: "Abide in my love." Unfortunately, today the word 'love' has devalued just to mean certain feelings you may have. Yet feelings often do not last. That is why we see the breakdown of so many marriages today. When the feelings for one another have gone, you simply quit. It is no longer 'for as long as we both shall live.'

So, what is true love? True love is a commitment; unconditional, self-denying, total! Unconditional – it does not depend on the other person's response. Self-denying – you always think of the other first. Total – you do not hold back. This is the love with which Christ loves us – now we have to abide in that love.

How are we to do this? By warming ourselves in the covenant relationship we have with God in and through Christ, our Redeemer. More practically, this means obeying God's commandments out of thankfulness for all that we have received in Christ. This is also what the Lord Jesus says in John 15:10, "If you keep My commandments, you will abide in My love." One may say, love should be spontaneous. How does this gel with the word 'commandment'? Yet, think of a little child who abides in the love of his parents and therefore has no difficulty in obeying them. Not because he has to, but by wanting to obey out of true love.

Abiding in God's love – then you rejoice in doing God's commandments, considering them as wholesome for life, causing life to flourish not only in our relationship with God but also in our relationship with one another.

When you find this difficult, keep remembering Christ's love, which we do not deserve. So often we hurt Christ by our sins and shortcomings and yet He keeps loving us. Well, if Christ so loves us, who am I then to be unwilling to show that love to my neighbour, even when I am disappointed. Just look at God's grace towards you, and you will become gracious as well in your attitude towards others. Then by abiding in God's love, love will also abide in our lives: unconditional, self-denying, total!

February 6

READING: ROMANS 13:8-14

Fulfilling the law through love

"Love is the fulfilling of the law."
ROMANS 13:10B

Love is the fulfillment of the law. What does this mean and how does this work? It means that love is to be demonstrated by our actions. It is a commitment. By way of example, think of the commitment given on the day of our profession of faith. On that day, we promised to commit our lives to the LORD. We vowed to love God with all our heart, soul and mind: a total commitment!

We fail to live up to this commitment every single day. Yet this should not cause us to despair, or cause us to make comments like "No one is perfect!", almost as an excuse. The truth is, God indeed asks one hundred percent love to fulfill the law.

One hundred percent – who can give this? No one! And still, there is no reason to despair, since in Chapter 10:4 of this same letter to the Romans, we read: "Christ is the end of the law for righteousness to everyone who believes." These words point us to the Gospel revealed by God in Jesus Christ, who brought the law to completion by obeying it perfectly and this for us and in our place.

The Lord Jesus fulfilled all the commandments. By doing so, He not only paid for all the times we fail to obey the law, but He also showed what a life of love looks like. If you want to know what true genuine love looks like, look at Christ. There was no moment in His life when love was merely a feeling or just a word to please. His love was always a pure action. In His love, there was no compromising, no excusing, no avoidance, no manipulation. He made no distinctions between people. He did not prefer one disciple over the other. His love was equal for all.

And, all of this completely unconditionally. Christ never demanded anything as a reward. His entire life, our Lord and Saviour had only one aim: to offer his life in service to God. In this way, Christ was the explanation of the law in one person. He was the end, the goal, the fulfillment of the law, which is love.

February 7

READING: EPHESIANS 4:17-5:1

A new life in love and holiness

"Therefore, be imitators of God as beloved children."

EPHESIANS 5:1

Love is the fulfillment of the law. We can give this love only in Christ. Therefore, we must become more and more like Him. The Lord Jesus left us an example to follow. Of course, we will not be saved simply by following the example of Christ . This is because only Christ can save us. Yet this does not take anything away from the fact that we are called to follow Christ's example – walking in love as He did and in doing so being imitators of God.

When reading these words in isolation, the call to be 'imitators of God' may come across as asking the impossible. Yet when looking at the previous verses, starting in Ephesians 4:17, we may learn what Paul means by this call. First, he gives us a picture of life in the world, and of the people who, in the blindness of their hearts, lived their lives without God. Then in verse 20, he continues saying: "But you have not so learned Christ …" In other words, in Christ, your life has changed, has taken on a different direction. Faith in Christ transformed you. In Him, you have become a new person. It is in this context that we must read the call: "Therefore be imitators of God."

Moreover, note how the apostle Paul addresses the Ephesians when he extends this call. He says: "Be imitators of God, as beloved children." With these words, Paul is saying: "Ephesians, never forget that you are children of a heavenly Father, who loves you in Christ." Well, this also has consequences concerning how to live now; how to live as children of this Father.

Often children have characteristics similar to their parents in their appearance, behaviour, attitude and abilities. "As is the father, so is the son", the saying goes. The same applies to us as children of God, being regenerated by the powerful work of the Holy Spirit. It is by this renewing power that we can reflect the image of God in our lives, as dear children of our heavenly Father.

February 8

READING: EPHESIANS 5:1-17

Walking in love

"And walk in love, as Christ loved us and gave himself up for us, a fragrant offering and sacrifice to God."

EPHESIANS 5:2

In the concluding part of Chapter 3 of his letter to the Ephesians, the apostle Paul prays that God may provide the congregation at Ephesus with inner strength, granting them to be strengthened with might through His Spirit in the inner man (Ephesians 3:16). This shows when Scripture calls us to love and obey God that we should never say "I cannot do this". The Holy Spirit who dwells within us will enable us to love and obey God. That is why in Chapter 4 verse 30 Paul warns: "Do not grieve the Holy Spirit of God". Instead, as God's children we should cling to that power by which we are able to produce fruits, the fruit of the Spirit, which also includes 'love'.

To love and obey God requires a conscious choice. It requires putting your trust in God alone, and submitting ourselves to God's perfect will for our lives, and this not because we have to but because we want to, out of thankfulness for all that God has given us in Christ.

That is why God's law is called the rule of thankfulness since the law has not been given to earn salvation, but as a guide to show thankfulness for God having saved us by grace alone. Thankfulness, that despite all our sins and shortcomings, God still allows us a place in His kingdom, in His church, and in His covenant.

In Ephesians 5:2 the apostle Paul writes: "And walk in love, as Christ loved us and gave Himself up for us, a fragrant offering and sacrifice to God." This is the norm for walking in love towards God and our neighbour. The norm is Christ's love for us: unconditional love, even to people we think might not be deserving of our love.

Be imitators of God as beloved children. Since we ourselves have been loved so much, we should show this same love towards others. Yes, walk in love each day.

February 9

READING: EZEKIEL 16:1-14

No other Gods (1)

"And God spoke all these words, saying, "I am the Lord your God, who brought you out of the land of Egypt, out of the house of slavery. You shall have no other gods before me.""

EXODUS 20:1-3

When God made a covenant with Abraham (Genesis 15) He also mentioned that Abraham's offspring would be strangers in a land that was not theirs and be afflicted for four hundred years. After that they would come back to Canaan. When God reveals Himself to Moses at the burning bush, He calls these promises to mind. God does this by revealing Himself to Moses with these words: "I am the God of your father – the God of Abraham, the God of Isaac, and the God of Jacob". Finally, four hundred years of affliction had come to an end. Having heard the groaning of the Israelites in Egypt, God was moved with pity out of love for His people.

Much later, during a time of deformation in the church, the prophet Ezekiel calls this wonderful love of God to mind. In a beautiful metaphor he speaks about God's compassion towards Israel – a people that had nothing to boast concerning its own background. "Your father was an Amorite and your mother a Hittite", says Ezekiel. Indeed, it was God's sovereign election that made Israel a people of His own possession. God's sovereign love – also in holding on to this love despite the many sins and shortcomings of God's people.

At Mount Sinai, before He proclaims His law, God reminds His people of this when He says: 'I am the LORD, your God, who redeemed you from your bondage, even though you did not deserve it. I loved you and I still do love you. However, My unconditional love also requires love in return from an undivided heart. That is why I command you, "You shall have no other gods before Me". No others gods – for they will only pull you away from Me'.

God says the same to us today. God also redeemed us from bondage out of sovereign love, namely from the bondage of sin and death. God did so in and through our Saviour Jesus Christ. Out of thankfulness for this redemption, we too should serve no other gods but give the love of our heart to God alone.

February 10

READING: DEUTERONOMY 6:1-9

No other Gods (2)

"Hear, O Israel: The Lord our God, the Lord is one."
DEUTERONOMY 6:4

Deuteronomy 6:4 emphatically stresses: there is only one God, "The LORD our God, He is LORD alone!" Therefore, we must serve Him alone and no other gods. God alone; that is, He who redeemed us. For the sake of our very salvation, the LORD calls us to obey His commandments. Living contrary to these commandments, we will become slaves again, slaves of sin, the very sin from which the LORD redeemed us. Living following God's commandments sets one free. This is why James in Chapter 2:12 of his letter, speaks about God's law as the law of liberty – freedom in obeying God's commandments. How does this work?

By way of example, think of a fish bound to water. Out of the water, a fish will die. That is why a fish is restricted to water, day and night. However, this is precisely how a fish can enjoy life, enjoying the freedom of an ocean of water. If this fish could reason in the same way as we sometimes do, saying that it wants to try what it is like to live on dry land, it would die. Well, likewise, we are bound to live following God's commandments. If we want to try enjoying life differently, it will only be to our detriment. In the end, we too would die; die spiritually, losing our redemption.

Bound by God's commandments, we are as free as a fish in the water, enjoying freedom in the ocean of God's love. In Deuteronomy 6:24, Moses says: "The LORD commanded us to do all these statutes, to fear the LORD our God, for our good always, that He might preserve us alive." This is the theme running throughout the book of Deuteronomy: "Keep God's commandments and it will be well with you." I once read that 'The law is the tune, in which our life before the LORD can rejoice.' One can even sing songs of praise about God's beautiful law, such as in Psalm 119 – a psalm that celebrates God's law as a wholesome guide for life.

February 11

READING: PSALM 115:1-11

No other Gods (3)

"You who fear the LORD, trust in the LORD!"

PSALM 115:11A

You shall have no other gods before Me – does this mean that there are other gods? The answer is a definite 'No'. Other so-called gods are images carved out of wood or stone – the work of man's hands that neither see, nor hear, nor eat, nor smell (Psalm 115:4 – 7). They are mere nullities, of no importance or worth. They do not really exist.

If they do not really exist, why does the LORD so strongly warn against them? It is because of the enormous power given to these gods by the people who worship them. Think of the worship of Baal, who was the personification of the fertility of the soil. The Canaanites worshiped Baal as the god of rain, thunder and fertility. When the sun scorched the land, it was said Baal dies. However, when the autumn rains caused everything to flourish again, the people said Baal arises.

Baal – just an idol invented by man; non-existent. Yet, the power of new life arising from dry soil does exist and is as real as the desire of man to get hold of this power. Having alienated himself from the Creator of rain, thunder and fertile soil, these powers within the realm of nature became threatening powers to man. Threatening forces – and therefore, they started worshipping them to keep these powers at peace, to make life more secure.

Sometimes we may have a bit of a chuckle about these primitive people serving idols such as Baal. Yet similarly today, people become so impressed by the power of money, sex and sport – to mention just a few – that they start worshipping them. This happens when we alienate ourselves from God and seek security and happiness elsewhere. Yet, in actual terms, it makes us slaves again – slaves to the lusts of our sinful hearts. Well, this is precisely the reason why the LORD warns us in the first commandment to have no other gods before Him. The LORD does not want us to live in bondage again. Instead, He wants us to enjoy the freedom we have received in Christ – freedom to find rest in a world full of unrest. Inward rest in Christ, which is the most beautiful rest one can get in this life.

February 12

READING: MATTHEW 6:19-24

No other Gods (4)

"No one can serve two masters…"
MATTHEW 6:24A

The Heidelberg Catechism explains idolatry as follows: "It is having or inventing something in which to put our trust instead of, or in addition to the only true God who has revealed Himself in His Word," Answer 95.

Instead of – this means God is no longer present in our lives. We have given up on God. However, it is also possible to invent something in which to put our trust in addition to God. We start compromising: the LORD dwells in His part of our heart, but there is also something else to which we give the love of our heart.

The LORD, however, requires love from an undivided heart. Serving the LORD involves a radical choice. One cannot serve the LORD and also give the love in his heart to something or someone else. "No one can serve two masters; for either he will hate the one and love the other, or else he will be loyal to the one and despise the other," Matthew 6:24. In the covenant relationship we have with the LORD, there is no room for a third party. Scripture often compares this covenant relationship to a marriage. Well, in marriage, there is no room for a third party either. Even thinking of someone else is already adultery. Similarly, it is adultery, when now and then we wish to be free of the commandments of the LORD – we still want to serve the LORD, but we also want more out of this world.

In marriage, a husband wants his wife for himself alone and would not be able to stand it if she would start flirting with other men. Similarly, God wants us for Himself alone. He cannot stand it when we start flirting with the world. He wants us to be faithful towards the covenant that He established with us. In Deuteronomy 6, we read that we must love the LORD our God with all our heart, with all our soul and with all our strength. We show this deep love by having only one desire: to keep God's commandments faithfully and this sincerely from the heart!

February 13

READING: 1 JOHN 2:15-27

For the sake of our very salvation

"Do not love the world or the things in the world."
1 JOHN 2:15A

In Answer 94 of the Heidelberg Catechism, it reads: "For the sake of my very salvation I must avoid and flee all idolatry." This means I must avoid and flee all idolatry as much as I love and yearn for the salvation of my soul. The Lord Jesus Christ set us free from the power of sin and death, making us His very own: body and soul. By serving idols, we may lose all of this; lose our salvation in Christ. Indeed, this may happen when we start living for the things of this world and start loving them as well. However, God calls us to love Him alone, and this from an undivided heart. When God commands us, "You shall have no other gods before me," we should never consider this as a burden, but instead look at God's love. Having redeemed us from the power of sin, God does not want us to become slaves of sin again.

In Christ, God redeemed us from the emptiness of life, giving our life meaning again. When looking around in this world, we see people grasping at happiness. In an attempt to find this happiness, they fill their lives with all kinds of pleasures. This may dope them or provide a quick fix for a moment, but then darkness sets in again. They live in bondage, being slaves of the lusts of their own sinful heart.

What a great privilege it is to know Christ as our Redeemer! He freed us from this bondage, and this while we were undeserving of it. When considering this, we can only marvel: who am I that I may belong to this Saviour? Therefore, out of thankfulness for this beautiful redemption, we should but have only one desire: namely, to serve this gracious God with our whole life, nothing excluded. Indeed, the LORD alone and no other gods, neither instead of Him nor in addition to Him. The fruit of living this way will give true joy, a joy far more precious than the empty pleasures of this world.

February 14

READING: ISAIAH 40:18-31

No images

"You shall not make for yourself a carved image."
EXODUS 20:4A

Why was it so tempting for the Israelites to make an image of God and to serve God through it? It was because the nations around Israel all worshiped their gods via images. Therefore, when the Israelites started to do this as well, they adapted their worship to what they saw around them. Today we would call this world-conformity.

So, why did the Gentiles make images of their gods? The reason was they did not have the security that the Israelites had. The gods they served often scared them. By creating an image of these gods and by worshipping them through this image, they thought these gods would no longer harm them.

By way of example, think of high voltage, which is very dangerous. If you are exposed to it, it can be fatal. Yet when using a transformer, you can decrease the voltage so that it becomes less dangerous. Similarly, the Gentiles tried to make the divine power of their gods less dangerous by the worshipping of images. This example makes clear that the worship of these images had to be conducted with great care. An elaborate system of all kinds of rites and ceremonies was necessary to receive the desired blessings.

In the second commandment, the LORD now says this is not how I want to be worshiped. I am the Almighty One, sovereign in all my acts. I am also the Holy One. Yet, this should not make you scared. Instead, remember: I made a covenant with you. You are my chosen ones. I have given you My Word and through that Word, I want to provide you with life, real life. That is how you may walk with Me daily, without ever having to be afraid.

In summary: in the first commandment, God teaches us that we must serve God alone. In the second commandment, the Lord says: You must also serve me in the right manner – loving me as I taught you to love Me. Not like the Gentiles, but by trusting me, trusting that I will be there for you always. You can count on that without any fear.

February 15

READING: DEUTERONOMY 30:11-20

God is near to us through His Word

"The word is very near you. It is in your mouth and in your heart."

DEUTERONOMY 30:14A

In Answer 98 of the Heidelberg Catechism, it reads: "God wants His people to be taught not by means of dumb images, but by the living preaching of His Word." This is the Word that is proclaimed to us every Sunday. Through His Word God, Himself is present among us. Submitting ourselves to this word brings us closer to God. Upon hearing the word, we rejoice in the covenant of love God has established with us.

In Deuteronomy 30, Moses says to the Israelites: "The word is very near you. It is in your mouth and in your heart, so that you can do it." The apostle Paul quotes these words in Romans 10:8, contrasting the righteousness based on faith and the righteousness that comes from the law. The righteousness based on faith clings to Christ, who dwelt among us. Yes, never did God come any nearer to man than in Christ. Today, God is near to us through the gospel that preaches Christ as our Saviour, who through the Holy Spirit dwells in our hearts.

In many churches, one can hear all kinds of pleas for alternatives to the preaching. The sermon, so people say today, stems from the time that conveying a message orally was the only means of communication. Therefore, a church that even today puts so much emphasis on preaching is considered old fashioned. This whole reasoning, however, fails to acknowledge that also in earlier centuries, alternatives to the preaching were used, for example, through the service of images, or by putting more emphasis on ceremonies. The point is that a sermon is more than just a means of passing on information. It is God who speaks to us through the preaching. God is the God of the Word. That is how the LORD already revealed Himself in Genesis. God spoke and this world came into being.

God started His relationship with Israel by speaking: calling Abraham and proclaiming His Law from Mount Sinai. This is how God speaks to us today through the preaching. Similarly, God is near to us, when at home we open His Word to listen to the voice of His love – that voice of love by which God wants to reach our heart.

February 16

READING: DEUTERONOMY 4:15-24

God's jealousy (1)

"For the Lord your God is a consuming fire, a jealous God."
DEUTERONOMY 4:24

Today, many people say that as long as you love God and serve Him, the exact manner in which you serve Him does not really matter. Everyone is allowed to decide for himself how to serve God. Worshipping God has become a matter of taste. If you are not happy in one church, you opt for another. People change churches like they change shops. That is why churches try to accommodate the tastes of man.

In the second commandment, however, God teaches His people that we are not to serve Him in any other way than He has commanded us in His Word. That is why Christ's church has to keep watch over the pulpit, so that no strange teachings creep in. The preaching should never give in to the wishes of man. A minister's task is not to satisfy the feelings of his audience, but to preach the whole counsel of God. Our worship of God has to be pure, i.e. in complete accordance with God's Word. Think of King Saul, when he brought sacrifices to God in a very pious way. Yet when Samuel comes to meet Saul, he says: "Behold, to obey is better than sacrifice and to heed than the fat of rams."

In the second commandment, we read that God is a jealous God. This means God takes sin against this commandment very seriously. The word 'jealous' has everything to do with the intimate relationship between God and His people. It points to the passion with which the LORD vindicates His rights and carefully watches over His people. More practically, this means two things. On the one hand, God's jealousy can take the side of His people in the battle against their enemies: "Do not touch the apple of My eye!". However, when God's people forsake His commandments and start serving the LORD in their own manner, God's jealousy can also turn against them.

In summary: God being a jealous God means He wants us for Himself alone because He loves us. That is why we should always treasure God's jealousy by serving Him in sincere love, walking joyfully in the ways the LORD has pointed out in His word.

February 17

READING: EZEKIEL 18:1-20

God's jealousy (2)

"You shall not bow down to them or serve them, for I the Lord your God am a jealous God, visiting the iniquity of the fathers on the children to the third and the fourth generation of those who hate me, but showing steadfast love to thousands of those who love me and keep my commandments."

EXODUS 20:5-6

In the second commandment, the LORD says that He will visit the iniquity of the fathers upon the children to the third and fourth generation of those who hate Him. For an example of this, I think of what happened to the Kingdom of the Ten Tribes, where almost every king walked in the sins of Jeroboam the son of Nebat. The result was that the LORD swept this kingdom out of existence. God is indeed a jealous God. Yet, the LORD also says: "I will show steadfast love to thousands of those who love Me and keep My commandments."

Of course, this does not mean that punishment and blessing will automatically be received in line with what our parents have done. The prophet Ezekiel makes this very clear. In Chapter 18 of his prophecies, he writes that we all have our personal responsibilities.

Nevertheless, when parents start serving the LORD in their own manner, they should not think lightly of what consequences this may have for their children. Children so easily walk in the footsteps of their parents, especially when parents start interpreting God's commandments less strictly. In the case where parents do not show much love and zeal in serving the LORD with all their heart, their children do not often exercise much zeal either. This is no excuse for the children, yet it shows what great responsibility parents have.

True, it also happens that parents do their utmost to raise their children in the fear of the LORD and yet the children still go their own way. It is not always the parents who are to blame. Parents cannot give their children their faith. However, when parents carry out their responsibility faithfully, the LORD may well bless this richly. Believing parents are a blessing for the coming generation. A faithful mother is a blessing for her children and her grandchildren.

February 18

READING: PSALM 8

God's Name (1)

"O Lord, our Lord, how majestic is your name in all the earth!"
PSALM 8:1A

Sometimes the third commandment is simplified as saying no more than "You shall not swear." True, this abuse of God's Name also has everything to do with the third commandment. Yet there is much more to this commandment. Even among men, there is more to a person's name than solely the name by which he is called. When saying that an accountant or a teacher has a good name, we do not refer to the actual name of that accountant or teacher, but to his reputation.

Well, the same applies to the name of the LORD. In many places, Scripture speaks about the name of the LORD as a name of great renown. God is the almighty One, the living God, to whom belongs the earth and its fullness. He rules all heaven's forces. That is why we are not allowed to use this name in vain, making it insignificant or unimportant, as a swearword or as a stopgap. The name of the LORD is too great for that.

Just consider in what beautiful way Scripture speaks about the greatness of the name of the LORD, for example, in Psalm 8. Impressed by God's creation and the place of man within creation, David exclaims: "O LORD, our Lord, how majestic is Thy Name in all the earth." When looking around the realm of nature – with eyes sharpened by the Word of God – one cannot but indeed come to no other conclusion than how great God is: the heavens, the work of His fingers; the moon and the stars, which He has ordained; the whole solar system, which God has in His mighty hands, so that it runs its circuit according to a well-ordered plan – considering all of this, who would not be overwhelmed by the greatness of God!

Even more so, when looking at man within creation: every birth is a miracle from God's hand – a baby growing in the mother's womb wonderfully made. I also think of the realm of nature: the flowers, the birds – all of these things! Therefore, who would not stand in awe of the greatness of this God, the greatness also of His great and wonderful Name! Yes, then we will make sure never to use God's Name in vain.

February 19

READING: ISAIAH 41:8-20

God's Name (2)

"For I, the Lord your God hold your right hand."

ISAIAH 41:13A

The name LORD written with capital letters is the name with which the LORD revealed Himself to Moses at the burning bush, the name JAWEH – I AM Who I AM.

I AM – this does not merely mean 'I exist', 'I live'. Instead, with this Name, God reveals Himself to His people as the One who will always be there for them. Therefore, you could also translate this name as "I will be there" or even more briefly as "I am there." Only three words, yet they contain tremendous riches.

To make this clear with an example: imagine you are hiking in the mountains, in very rough terrain with some steep cliffs. For a moment you lose concentration, you slip and fall from the cliff you were standing on. You fall very fast until you finally hit the ground in a ravine far away from everyone, almost unreachable. Yes, who will ever find you there with all the injuries you have? You are already considering that this might be the end of your life. For a while, you doze off but then all of a sudden someone whispers in your ear: "I am there!". How is this possible? Someone, risking his own life, still found you. I am there!

Well, this is how God is near to us in His Name, "I AM WHO I AM," and this not only in deep valleys, but always. This is how we may know God as the Redeemer of His people: "I am there." In Christ, God entered the depth of our existence where we were laying, lost in sin, totally undeserving of anything. Yet God had compassion. As the Triune God, He came to carry us, marking us as His own when we were baptised. At that moment, God promised us: "I will always be your Father. I will always be there for you, even though sometimes through weakness you may fall into sin. When in true repentance you cling to Me, I will still be there for you, while through My Spirit, I will also give you the strength to fight against sin." That is how God as the Triune God holds our hand and says: "Fear not, I am there to be your help and refuge always."

February 20

READING: PROVERBS 18:10-11

God's Name – a strong tower

"The name of the Lord is a strong tower;
the righteous man runs into it and is safe."
PROVERBS 18:10

God is near to us in His Name. God's Name is a strong tower in which the righteous man takes refuge. Think of a city under attack. The citizens of this city feel safe since the city was built as a strong fortress, which no enemy ever could take. Well, this is how the LORD with His glorious Name takes care of His people. God's Name is our refuge. Think of Psalm 124:8, where it reads, "Our help is in the Name of the LORD, who made heaven and earth." God's Name – a mighty fortress, a strong tower!

The tower mentioned in Proverbs 18 is in contrast to the tower about which we read in Genesis 11: the tower of Babel, in which sinful man tried to find his strength. Yet, it did not work. Moreover, there was no need for it either, since whoever calls upon the name of the LORD will find the strength he needs.

This same contrast between strength in the LORD and human strength one also finds in Proverbs 18. After verse 10, it reads in verse 11, "A rich man's wealth is his strong city and like a high wall in his imagination." Strength – but ultimately nothing more than pure imagination. It is a delusion to consider material wealth and all the pleasures that come with it as being a protective wall behind which one is safe. A delusion – since it does not offer real protection.

Think of the parable the Lord Jesus once told about a rich fool. This man thought he could enjoy life because of all the wealth he had accumulated and for which he had worked hard. However, the very night when this rich man was considering all of this God required his soul. A warning example, showing that earthly wealth does not offer any protection. Protection can only be found when we are rich toward God. To say it with the words of Proverbs 18: real security, we will find only when we take refuge in the Name of the LORD. The righteous run to it. Run – indeed! Amidst temptations, suffering afflictions, pain, sorrow – the righteous flee to God, taking refuge with Him, the only One, on whom we can rely in all circumstances.

February 21

READING: ISAIAH 1:10-20

Using God's Name in vain

"You shall not take the name of the Lord your God in vain, for the Lord will not hold him guiltless who takes his name in vain."

EXODUS 20:7

To take the name of the LORD in vain – what does this mean? The word 'vain' means worthless, futile. Hence it is a word that opposes the rich meaning of the name LORD. Using the name of the LORD in vain means you deny the glory of this name altogether. This happens not only by blaspheming and abusing God's name but also by cursing, perjury or unnecessary oaths. Of course, this is included as well. Yet there are many more ways in which one can become guilty of sinning against the Third Commandment using the name of the LORD in vain.

Let us say that you make plans which deep down you know quite well are not right in the eyes of the LORD, yet you still ask for His blessing – for example, by courting a girl or a boy who does not serve the LORD. You hope that the LORD will make you happy together. You may even pray, "Lord bring her to the church". Is this not a wonderful prayer? However, you made the wrong decision in the first place by going out with this girl even though you knew it was not right. Did you confess this to the LORD? Or did you pray just to get your way, still asking the LORD for a blessing? The same can also happen when doing business in a not completely honest way, yet still asking every morning in prayer that the LORD bless you in your work.

These are all practices similar to the ones listed in Isaiah 1. The prophet Isaiah also addresses people who faithfully brought their sacrifices and faithfully prayed to the LORD. Yet it was no more than just pious varnish. They used the name of the LORD to cover up their sins. Well, this is exactly what the LORD warns against in the Third Commandment.

That is why Isaiah says: "Wash yourselves, make yourself clean". Indeed, when there is something being covered up the LORD says: "Repent, no longer use my Name in vain! Instead serve Me in sincerity and truth. If you do so, I will forgive you. No matter how much you have messed up your life – sins red as scarlet, I will make them white as snow".

February 22

READING: LEVITICUS 24:10-16

No greater sin…

"Whoever blasphemes the name of the LORD shall surely be put to death."

LEVITICUS 24:16A

In Answer 100 of the Heidelberg Catechism it reads: "No sin is greater or provokes God's wrath more than the blaspheming of His Name". Why is this? The answer is: in blaspheming God's Name, we attack God's very person with all of its holiness, righteousness, goodness, justice and truth. Also, such an attitude in which God's Name and God's Person is treated without any respect for all that His Name represents is an attack on the salvation God offers us in Christ.

It is good to remember this when hearing the name of our Saviour being abused. It should be clear that whoever does so has no appreciation whatsoever for what the Lord Jesus came to do in this world: to save sinners! Abusing the name of the Lord Jesus, be it as a curse word or merely as a stopgap even in abbreviated forms, means one scorns the good news of the gospel. Moreover, we should not forget either that the name Jesus is the name of Him who today has all authority in heaven and on earth. Realising this, who would ever dare to use the name of this mighty King in vain? Yet it happens, not only in the world, but at times even by church members, believers who should know better since they have been taught about the rich meaning of the glorious name of their Saviour.

Indeed, no sin is greater or provokes God more than the blaspheming of His Name. God does not tolerate it that His Name is mocked or ridiculed. He does not tolerate this, today any less than in the days of the Old Testament during which time He commanded this sin to be punished with death. God will not hold him guiltless whoever takes His glorious Name in vain, be it in words or deeds. Therefore, let us never make light of this commandment. Instead, let us rather take refuge in this Name and honour it in all our words and works; that name of which we read in Proverbs 18: "It is a strong tower, the righteous run to it and are safe".

February 23

READING: MATTHEW 5:33-37

Oath taking

"Let what you say be simply 'Yes' or 'No';
anything more than this comes from evil."

MATTHEW 5:37

When reading Lord's Day 37 on the matter of oath-taking, one must consider the historical context, which goes beyond the issue of swearing an oath. At stake was whether the revelation of God's glorious name was of importance also for daily life. Rejecting the heresies of the Anabaptists, the authors of the Heidelberg Catechism wanted to make clear that as children of God, we cannot withdraw from this world. God has given us a place within this world, where we have a task to witness as shining stars. Therefore, we should not refuse to take an oath when the government asks it.

In a world full of lying and deceit, it is sometimes difficult to trust one another. People lie, at times, even in the church. 'Yes' stands over against 'No". How do we overcome this? We overcome this by taking refuge in the name of the LORD. Well, this is what we do when taking an oath.

Think of a court case. Someone is opposing you hard as nails. You realise that a great deal depends on the testimony you have to give, but you feel weak in a world full of lies. Would people believe you? You know I cannot solve this! However, you may call upon the Name of the LORD: "So help me God!". God will defend my cause. His name is a strong tower.

If the LORD is called upon, people ought to believe you, be it the judge, the police, or even in a conflict among church members. You call on the LORD and confess that you expect justice from Him.

This is swearing an oath in a godly manner. In a challenging situation, you call on the LORD for help. Of course, it is not always necessary to do this by taking an oath. We ought to live in this awareness always that our refuge is found in God's wonderful name alone. The Name LORD, in capital letters: I AM WHO I AM – our faithful covenant God who is always there ready to help us, even when we least expect it.

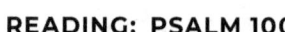

February 24

READING: PSALM 100

Sunday – a joyful celebration (1)

"Serve the LORD with gladness!
Come into His presence with singing."

PSALM 100:2

Thankful for all that God has given us in Christ – having freed us from the bondage of sin – obeying God's commandments should always be a real joy, including the fourth commandment. Joy in observing the sabbath day, not only when we go to church, but throughout the whole day. A day full of joy in every respect. How do we do this? How can we make the Sunday a day of thankfulness to God?

Of course, we should show this thankfulness to God every day. However, throughout the week, when we are busy, daily routine so quickly sets in. Yet on Sunday, we may rest. Rest – not just for ourselves, doing nothing. Instead, God gives us this day of rest to have time for Him. Time to worship Him, but also time for reflection, counting God's blessings – blessings in particular when we think of our redemption from sin and death! Sunday – a day of rest to pause, standing in awe of this redemption. I wonder how much time we spend on this when returning home after the church service. Do we rejoice on Sunday, receiving this rest? Rest not in the first place for ourselves, but rest to glorify God.

In our discussions about the observance of the Sunday, often the emphasis is on the things God has forbidden. Quite often also in a negative way. Negative – with questions about whether we are allowed or not allowed to do this or that on Sundays. Discussions like these can easily overshadow the joy of the Sunday.

However, should there not be joy? Joy that amid what is often a hectic life, the LORD gives us a day of rest, not in the first place as a day to charge up our batteries after a week of hard work. Instead, the LORD gave us this day as a feast day to rejoice in His works. To rejoice in the abundant blessing God has given us in Christ, the Saviour of our life. When observing the Sunday in this way, it will become a joyful celebration each week again.

February 25

READING: PSALM 84

Sunday – a joyful celebration (2)

"Blessed are those who dwell in your house,
ever singing your praise."

PSALM 84:4

In Deuteronomy, the motive for celebrating the Sabbath day differs from the motive given in Exodus 20. In Deuteronomy, it reads you shall keep the Sabbath day to "remember that you were a slave in the land of Egypt, and the LORD brought you out from there by a mighty hand and by an outstretched arm. Therefore, the LORD commanded you to keep the Sabbath day." This made the Sabbath day a real feast day – a special day, on which the Israelites rejoiced in their redemption from Egypt, in the rest God had given them.

In the wilderness, the Israelites could as yet not fully enjoy the redemption the LORD had promised them. Therefore, on the Sabbath they also looked forward to the rest that was still to come, i.e., the rest which God had in store for them in the Promised Land.

In the New Testament era, on the day of rest, we rejoice in the redemption God gave us, not from Egypt but from sin. We rejoice in the rest which Christ obtained for us. Yet, we too are looking forward to the perfect rest, which is also still to come for us.

We no longer celebrate this day on the seventh day of the week, but on the first day of the week. We do so since Christ, through His suffering and death, has fulfilled the Old Testament Sabbath. He fulfilled it. He did not abolish this day. 'To abolish' means: doing away with something. It means a law has lost its validity. Yet 'to fulfill' means: something reaches its final aim. Well, it is through the accomplished work of Christ that the Old Testament Sabbath achieved its ultimate aim: the eternal rest of which in this life we already may enjoy a foretaste.

On Easter morning in the garden of Joseph of Arimathea, when Christ rose from the dead, it came true, that which God had already promised in Paradise: namely that by Satan's defeat, we would again receive rest. By His resurrection, Christ defeated all the powers of unrest. That is why in the New Testament, not the seventh day, but the first day of the week has become a day of joyful celebration to thank God for what He has given us in Christ.

February 26

READING: HEBREWS 10:19-25

Sunday – a day of worship

"Not neglecting to meet together… encouraging one another…"
HEBREWS 10:25

Sunday is a day on which we come together to worship the LORD full of praise and thankfulness for the redemption received in Christ. When this thankfulness is sincere, we will be eager to come to church diligently each Sunday. Diligently – this means we make an effort to come since we do not want to miss out on this meeting with the LORD, the God of our redemption.

In Hebrews 10:25, the author warns the addressees of this letter not to neglect to meet together. For the sake of their faith, they had been exposed to abuse and affliction. Because of this, some had grown weary. They had become slack in faith, slack also in church attendance. Their spiritual buoyancy had gone. Yet the author urges them to remain steadfast in faith and to hold fast the confession of their hope without wavering. In this context, he also encourages them not to neglect the worship services, since it is primarily in the weekly worship services that God will strengthen our faith.

It is a tremendously precious privilege for us amidst the hardships, the sorrows, and difficulties we often face in this life, that on the first day of every week we may come together to be encouraged by the preaching of the gospel of hope and salvation in Jesus Christ, our Saviour. Who would want to miss out on this weekly comfort and encouragement? We need it each Sunday again to remain steadfast in faith.

In Hebrews 10:25, it also reads that we must exhort one another. How are we to do this? Not first of all, by visiting each other in our homes, but in church instead. In church, we may listen to the preaching, which gives us food for our discussions on Sunday, but also throughout the week. Strengthened by the preaching, we will speak about it, and where we see slackness, we will exhort one another. Even more so when we think that Christ can return at any moment. Let us pray that on that day He may find all of us active in His service.

February 27

READING: HEBREWS 4:1-13

A promise of the rest to come

"Let us, therefore, strive to enter that rest…"

HEBREWS 4:11

On Sundays, we rejoice in the communion we have with our risen Saviour. This joy should set the tone for the way we live our lives throughout the week. Having feasted on Christ's redemption, we also ought to live accordingly, resting from our evil works. These are the works Christ has redeemed us from. Thus, the blessing of the Sunday should have its effect also on all the other days of the week. Every day we should rejoice in the work God wants to do in our life by His Spirit, sanctifying us, so that already in this life we may begin the eternal Sabbath.

Indeed, the eternal Sabbath already starts in this life. This happens – as it says in Lord's Day 33 of the Heidelberg Catechism – when with heartfelt joy in God through Christ and with love and delight, we live according to the will of God in all good works. If this joy is not there today, something is lacking. Putting it even stronger with this question: "Would you feel at home in heaven, at home on the new earth, where everything will be focused on the LORD?". One can only answer this question in the affirmative if already today this focus is there.

Hebrews 4 speaks about the warning God gave to His people Israel during the time of their wanderings through the desert. In verse 2 of this chapter, it reads, "For good news came to us just as to them, but the message they heard did not benefit them." It did not benefit them due to unbelief on their part. The result was that God swore in His wrath, "They shall not enter My rest," verse 3. Only those who believed entered the rest of the Promised Land. A warning example for us! That is why the author writes in verse 11: "Let us, therefore, strive to enter that rest, so that no one may fall by the same sort of disobedience."

It is for this reason that we should make the most of the Sunday in joyful celebration and thankfulness to God. Next, in that same joy, we should also walk with God throughout the week.

February 28

READING: EPHESIANS 4:1-7

Unity

"…eager to maintain the unity of the Spirit in the bond of peace…"
EPHESIANS 4:3

The second part of the law focuses on the love we owe our neighbour. However, this love cannot be separated from our love towards God. Also in loving our neighbour, we are called to serve God. What does this mean concerning the Fifth Commandment?

In this commandment, the LORD teaches children to honour their parents. Yet in doing so, children are also called to honour God since it is God Himself who governs children by the hand of their parents. This shows even the Fifth Commandment still focusses on how to love God, namely how to practice this love in order to live together in harmony to God's glory, as a real covenant family within the communion of saints.

I add this aspect of the communion of saints since it is crucial that as families, we try to draw similar lines. So often, it happens that some families allow what other families do not allow. Why is this? The simple answer is, as families within the congregation, we are no longer on the same page in fighting world conformity. How are we to overcome this? Of course, it will always happen that as parents, we make different decisions. Yet especially in today's society, there is a need for more unity in building stronger families. Together we should fight today's world-conformity head-on without any compromise to make our homes safe havens for our children.

As parents, we should be more eager to become one in this, not only for the well-being of our children, but also for the well-being of God's church. Much is at stake here in a society where Satan is becoming increasingly active in making our homes less safe by way of such things as the internet, smartphones, and the use of social media. This requires effort on the part of the parents. Yet it equally requires effort on the part of the children, effort to obey. In this process, children also should have patience with the weaknesses of their parents. Likewise, parents should have patience with the weaknesses of their children, always teaching them in love.

March 1

READING: PROVERBS 4:1-9

Love and obedience

"Hear, O sons, a father's instruction."

PROVERBS 4:1A

The Fifth Commandment points first to the obedience children owe their parents, since God has placed these parents in authority over them. Today, these two words – obedience and authority – have simply become old-fashioned, because man does not like having any rule over him. Everyone should be free to make his or her own choices, even children. This is the climate in which our children grow up and it does not leave them unaffected. Think of some of the arguments you may have at times, for example about the way your teenage children dress or want to dress. You may even find it difficult to put your foot down. Of course, when asking obedience as parents we should make sure that we radiate love towards our children. We should never lay down the law with an iron fist, compelling them to obey, simply because we say it. Nevertheless, Scripture teaches very clearly that children have to obey their parents.

Children must obey their parents. From there on the Catechism also deals with other authoritative relationships. Yet the family relationship comes first. It is first of all in the circle of the family where children have to learn obedience. If they do not learn it at home, how will they ever be able to practise obedience in other areas of life? It is in the home where church members and citizens are raised for their future tasks. It is in the home where the future course and well-being of church and society is determined. It is in the home that the foundations are laid. Let us never think lightly of this. Parents who do not take this task seriously and children who do not heed the good counsel and discipline of their parents, do immense damage to the structures of life.

Today the vast majority of people no longer accept any authority. Today's society has become more and more what is called a permissive society, where each one is allowed to decide for himself what is good or bad. Yet, though society might have changed, God's commandments have not changed; commandments God has given to cause life to flourish. An harmonious family life – where parents show love and children obey – will not only cause church life to flourish, but will also be a blessing for the society we live in.

March 2

READING: PSALM 78:1-7

Tell the coming generation (1)

"We will not hide them from their children, but tell to the coming generation the glorious deeds of the Lord, and His might, and the wonders that He has done."

PSALM 78:4

Why is it so important for children to heed the teachings of their parents? As with all the commandments, also the Fifth Commandment must be read in close connection with the introductory words to the Ten Commandments, in which the LORD says, "I have redeemed you from Egypt, from the house of bondage, and now I will bring you into a land flowing with milk and honey". In the Fifth Commandment the LORD now adds, "When you honour your father and your mother, and all who are in authority over you, I promise you a long life in this wonderful land". In other words, if you want to continue to enjoy the freedom I gave you, you are to obey those whom I want to govern you. Otherwise, you will end up in slavery once again.

Israel knew first hand what slavery was like. Life in Egypt had become unbearable. In Egypt, they were forced to work seven days a week from early morning until late at night, continuously being supervised by ruthless taskmasters. It left them hardly any time to serve the LORD. To say it in today's language: no time to go to church or for any other special activity in God's kingdom throughout the week. The result was that they had grown weary in faith with little trust left in the promises God had once given to their ancestors. Yet despite all this, the LORD had not forgotten them. He had heard their groaning and had remembered His covenant. He came to redeem them out of bondage.

Yes, when Israel left Egypt, what a glorious event this must have been. Every year when Passover was celebrated, parents had to remind their children of this wonderful exodus; and of course, and of course, this was not the only thing they had to do. In Psalm 78 we read that this is what parents should do all the time: speaking with the children about the glorious deeds of the LORD. Telling them: this is your history, this is your God. Keep obeying His commandments for then it will be well with you and your children. This is how God wants to keep His people close to Him throughout the generations: close when as parents and children we walk together with Him.

March 3

READING: DEUTERONOMY 6:20-25

Tell the coming generation (2)

"When your son asks you in time to come…"

DEUTERONOMY 6:20A

In the concluding part of Deuteronomy 6 we find a beautiful example of how parents should tell the coming generation what a great God we have in the LORD. An example from which we can learn when our children come with questions like, "Why am I not allowed to do this?" or "What's wrong with that?" or "Why can I not go to that party?" How often are parents not confronted with questions like these?

Instead of getting upset when our children react this way, as parents we should make the most of occasions like these by taking the time to speak with our children in love. When they come with these questions, you can say to your child in a similar way as that Israelite father of Deuteronomy 6, but then in New Testament terms, "Listen my son, listen my daughter, we were dead in sin to the extent that there was no longer any hope for us. But then He came, Jesus Christ, God's only begotten Son. He took our hand and redeemed us from our misery. He freed our life from all those empty pleasures about which people outside the church often get all excited. This is what He has done for us, my son, my daughter; yes, for you as well. Therefore, to live in accordance with His commandments is not a burden, but this is how we may show our thankfulness. Through it God will keep us in this wonderful redemption. God does so by these wholesome commandments He has given us".

These are beautiful opportunities to speak with our children about what a joy it is to serve the LORD. However, such teachings will only bear fruit when parents show their children this joy also in their personal life. For how can we instil in our children love for the church if at home they hear nothing other than criticism of the church? How can we ask our children to love their fellow brother and sister in the church, when we as parents always speak negatively about certain church members? As parents we must live what we teach, making our homes true Christian homes where children not only hear all the good things, but see them practised as well. Practised when parents and children rejoice together in obeying God's commandments in their daily walk with God.

March 4

READING: PROVERBS 31:10-31

The blessing of a God-fearing mother

"Her children rise up and call her blessed."
PROVERBS 31:28A

Proverbs 31 speaks about an excellent wife, who at the same time is also a real mother for her family – a busy mother with surely not much time for herself. You sometimes wonder how she did it all, being busy from early morning until late at night. Busy for her family: for her husband and her children, who speak very highly of their mother, calling her blessed.

These words show they loved their mum. Even though she was busy, she was there for them at home.

Today oftentimes the task of a stay-at-home-mum is considered dull and boring. Wives too should have the opportunity to develop their God given talents. Why should the wife be the one who has to look after the family? To raise children is not specifically a female task, is it? Therefore, would it not be possible that a husband and wife each have a part time job so that they can look after the family in turns? Or when both parents are working full time, children are brought to a day-care centre? It sometimes seems as if children are a burden rather than a joy – hence not too many either. This way of thinking can so easily creep in also in the church.

When opening Scripture, however, nowhere does the Bible say that the task of a mother is something to be considered as inferior. Instead, Scripture always speaks very highly about mothers in Israel. A caring and faithful mother can have great influence on her children. This does not mean that husbands can leave the task of raising children to their wives. They too have their specific task in the upbringing of the seed of the covenant. Husband and wife should indeed do this together, each of them using his or her specific talents; talents, given by the LORD when He created man male and female. It would be foolish to ignore these differences with no appreciation for the way in which God created us: females differing from males, not just bodily but also emotionally with different talents. Because of these different talents, at times a mother may have better, more intimate contact with her children than the father. This does not matter, as long as there is a good marriage relationship, where husband and wife speak about these things with one another and together in prayer bring their children before the throne of God's grace.

March 5

READING: ROMANS 13:1-7

Other authorities

"Let every person be subject to the governing authorities. For there is no authority except from God, and those that exist have been instituted by God."

ROMANS 13:1

Because of sin we live in a broken world and therefore mankind is in need of authority. This is why our gracious God ordained kings, princes, and civil officers (Article 36 Belgic Confession). God did so in His grace and we can be thankful for this.

For if authority were just a human institution, most likely there would no longer be an existing government which people really would obey. After all, man does not like having people in authority over him. By nature we would all rather live our own life. But what kind of society would this create? That is why God in His grace gave us authorities to restrain not only the intemperance of children by the authority of their parents, but also the evil in society by the authority of the government.

What does it mean to have authority? It surely does not mean having the power to boss someone around. Instead, being in authority obliges a person to serve, to guide in order that life may flourish. This is the motive for this divine institution. By investing people with authority it was God's intention that everything among men be conducted in good order.

In the beginning, God created man in His image, giving man the mandate, "Let them have dominion over the fish of the sea and over the birds of the heavens and over the livestock and over all the earth and over every creeping thing that creeps on the earth" (Genesis 1:26). Man received the mandate to rule creation as a caring king, as a viceroy who in his ruling, in his authority over creation, had to reflect the image of God.

This still applies today to all authoritative relations ordained by God. This is how God has made the husband to be the head of his wife and how God has set parents in authority over their children. This does not mean that being the head a husband can boss his wife around. Instead, being the head a husband should use his authority to the glory of God and the well-being of his wife. This is also how parents are to treat their children when in authority over them. It is also in this way that the government should seek the well-being of its citizens for the good of the country as well as for the protection of the church.

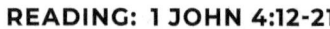 March 6

READING: 1 JOHN 4:12-21

You shall not murder

"And this commandment we have from him: whoever loves God must also love his brother."

1 JOHN 4:21

The Sixth Commandment of God's covenant law reads: "You shall not murder". God says this not in the first place to people living in the world outside the church, but to us His chosen ones within the church. Hence, when dealing with this commandment we should look not first of all at all that is going on around us in this world: the hatred, the envy, all the crime and violence we are confronted with almost on a daily basis, even though this too has everything to do with this commandment. However, when speaking about all the bad things in today's society, we so easily run the risk of no longer looking at ourselves, forgetting that the root of murder as described in Lord's Day 40 of the Heidelberg Catechism also lies at the bottom of our own hearts.

When testing our life to what God requires of us in the Sixth Commandment, we all have to admit that much is lacking. Think of the lack of patience we often have with one another. To love our neighbour as ourselves – how difficult this is also for us. Envy, hatred, anger and desire for revenge are also found in the church. At times, it also happens that church members live at odds with each other, refusing to resolve matters that keep them divided, trying to ignore it. So often we simply live on without really worrying about it, but meanwhile it grieves the Lord.

Therefore, when hearing the commandment: "You shall not murder", the LORD wants us to firstly look at ourselves. In a world full of envy, hatred, anger, and desire of revenge we, as redeemed children of God, should show a different lifestyle and this out of thankfulness for all that we have received in Christ. Love towards God must be reflected also in love towards our neighbour, this means first of all to our fellow brothers and sisters in the church. The apostle John writes in his first letter, "If anyone says, 'I love God,' and hates his brother, he is a liar; for he who does not love his brother whom he has seen, cannot love God whom he has not seen. And this is the commandment we have from Him: whoever loves God must also love his brother."

March 7

READING: GENESIS 1:26-31

Life – a precious gift of God

"Then the Lord God formed the man of dust from the ground and breathed into his nostrils the breath of life, and the man became a living creature."

GENESIS 2:7

Life is a gift of God. In the beginning God created man and made him into a living being, breathing the breath of life into man's nostrils. This is the main reason why in the Sixth Commandment God says, "You shall not murder". Life belongs to God. He gives it and He takes it in His time.

It is noteworthy that in the context of the Sixth Commandment the word 'life' has a much broader scope than the way we generally speak about life. Being alive – for us generally this means: we are breathing, our heart is beating, and blood is running through our veins. Yet from a scriptural point of view, there is much more to life than breathing and the beating of the heart. It also means living in a relationship with others. When God created man in His own image, He placed man in a relationship with his fellow creatures.

For a moment think of the opposite of life: death! Again, in this context we should think not only of physical death – being cut off from everything. It can have a wider meaning also.

Think of a family where there is always a lot of arguing and screaming going on. After visiting such a family, you may come home and say, "They have no life there." Death reigns, even though all family members are still physically alive and have not stopped breathing. Yet the air they breathe in is poisonous – fatal.

This shows the wider scope of the command "You shall not murder"; wider than the actual killing of a person. In today's Scripture reading it says that God created everything good and in harmony; perfect harmony also between Adam and Eve. Man blossomed in the relationship with his fellow creatures. God also had said that when you continue to walk in My ways this is how it will always be (and would have been, had sin not ruined it): a society where life flourishes without any arguments, no quarrels whatsoever; man always in tune with his fellow man. Life, as it will once again be on the new earth. No discord whatsoever, but perfect harmony in the communion we have with God and in the fellowship with one another: Paradise restored!

March 8

READING: GENESIS 4:17-24

The destructive power of sin

"For the wages of sin is death, but the free gift of God is eternal life in Christ Jesus our Lord."
ROMANS 6:23

In Genesis 3 we read that sin destroyed the beautiful life created by God. It destroyed not only the relationship between God and man, but also the relationship between man and his fellow creatures. Think of Adam and Eve. Before the fall into sin Adam thanked God for the wonderful gift of a wife – a helper next to him. Yet when God calls Adam to account in Genesis 3 nothing is left of this appreciation. Adam blames Eve. The harmony within their marriage is gone. In this we see the destructive power of sin, as is also seen later on.

Love gave way to hate, envy and jealousy. A satanic power took possession of man, which made Cain murder his brother. In this Cain showed himself to be a child of the devil, who was called by Christ "a murderer from the beginning" (John 8:44). First it was Abel, but from then on a large stream of blood ran throughout the ages. Genesis 4 tells of the family of Cain, among whom we find Lamech singing a song of revenge. In it he boasts to have killed a man for wounding him, also saying he would not mind doing it again. In the tents of Lamech people boasted about themselves and enjoyed life to the full – yet it was without God, which ultimately meant the destruction of life.

This happens when man starts living for himself and his own pleasures. When putting ourselves in the centre, hate, jealousy and envy quickly get the better of love. The Heidelberg Catechism describes these attitudes as the root of murder.

Looking around today, one sees this root having brought forth a complete plant, bearing poisonous fruit everywhere. Today there is little account for the life of fellow man, be it by way of violence or in favouring abortion and euthanasia. In this we see the truth of what the apostle Paul writes in Romans 6:23, "the wages of sin is death" – 'death' in its scriptural meaning as being opposite to 'life'. Life means being able to communicate, having relationships and enjoying fellowship, whereas death means these relationships are broken down and destroyed. Well, these are indeed the wages of sin. However, after having said this, the apostle Paul continues as follows: "but the free gift of God is eternal life in Christ Jesus our Lord".

March 9

READING: 1 JOHN 3:7-18

The root of all murder

"Everyone who hates his brother is a murderer, and you know that no murderer has eternal life abiding in him."

1 JOHN 3:15

The Sixth Commandment reads: "You shall not murder". One may say: I have never murdered a person. Yet the Heidelberg Catechism makes it clear that with this commandment God also looks at the root of murder.

As to the root of murder, the Catechism starts by mentioning envy: you begrudge your neighbour what he has. Such envy easily leads to jealousy. The grass on the other side of the fence seems greener to you and you cannot stand this. You are jealous. It makes you bitter, which in turn can lead to forthright hatred. We wish the other ill. Next, hate turns into anger. Scripture clearly teaches: all these attitudes must be considered as murder. Think of the text above this meditation, "Everyone who hates his brother is a murderer".

From a scriptural point of view there is much more to murder than actually killing someone. We may at times hurt our neighbour in a much more painful way with certain words or gestures than if he had been stabbed with a knife. A gesture – how quickly is it not made at times? You meet someone in the street, but you quickly look the other way because you do not want to greet him. If we are asked later, we could say "I did not see you." Yet in the meantime we have acted as if he were just not there. Sometimes we may greet our neighbour with a chilly look, a haughty laugh. When considering all of these things as a sin against the Sixth Commandment, who would be able to say: "I am blameless"?

You shall not murder – neither in thought, nor in word, nor in gesture. If we are honest, we all have to admit that we so often fall short in joyfully obeying this commandment – fall short in thankfulness for the renewal of life we have received in Christ by the powerful work of the Holy Spirit. Truly living a new life in Christ also means that in our relations with others we are willing to let go of all envy, hatred and anger. Instead – as it reads in the Form for the celebration of the Lord's Supper: "For the sake of Christ who so exceedingly loved us first, we shall now love one another, and shall show this to one another, not just in words but also in deeds".

 March 10

READING: COLOSSIANS 3:1-17

Showing love

"And above all these put on love, which binds everything together in perfect harmony."
COLOSSIANS 3:14

One of the rules for explaining the Ten Commandments is that the opposite of what is forbidden is commanded. Yesterday we dealt with what God forbids. He hates all envy, hatred, anger and desire of revenge, considering all of these as murder. The LORD calls us to break with all of these sins. Instead, we must show patience, peace and gentleness, loving our neighbour as ourselves.

Patience – this means you do not fly off the handle straight away when someone says something. You do not become angry with your fellow brother or sister.

It also means that when someone differs with you in opinion you will not condemn that person or start labelling him negatively straight away. Instead, when someone comes up with something new, we should open God's Word and on that basis be willing to listen to each other's arguments without entrenching ourselves in a certain position. This is the love Christ requires of us. Where this true genuine love is found, everyone will benefit from it.

Patience – this is what we should also show towards the wayward members of Christ's flock, not expecting great changes all of sudden overnight. Of course, this is what we pray for, but the reality is often different. This is why church discipline is often a long process before it comes to the final act of excommunication.

Patience is one of the main characteristics of true genuine love. Does this mean that we have to put up with everything, ignoring the wrongdoings in the life of a fellow brother or sister? Surely not! We are to call a spade a spade and so when there is sin in a person's life we should not try to cover this up or water it down. Sin is sin. I think of the apostle Paul who opposed his fellow apostle Peter when Peter refused to eat with the Gentiles at Antioch. At times, it might indeed be necessary to take a firm stand with a fellow brother or sister. Yet we should not do so simply to get our way, but out of love for the brother or sister, having his or her salvation at heart. This also means: never fight for personal opinions, but always seek the honour of God and the edification of His church.

March 11

READING: 1 CORINTHIANS 6:12-20

Flee sexual immorality

"For you were bought with a price.
So glorify God in your body."

1 CORINTHIANS 6:20

"You shall not commit adultery". From the explanation which the Heidelberg Catechism gives of this commandment, it is clear that it deals with more than just the actual sin of adultery. If this were the case, it would address only married couples. However, with this command, the LORD addresses also the unmarried, yes even the young people. As redeemed children of God we all, young and old alike, must put our life to the test of the Seventh Commandment to see whether we live holy before the LORD.

Holy – this word has as its first meaning 'being set apart', 'separated from'. When applying this to the Seventh Commandment, it means we must keep ourselves far away from all the filthiness we meet in today's society, where everything seems to be up for grabs. If it feels good, do it. Moral norms are no longer observed. Man has become a law unto himself. As God's children living amid this society, we have to make sure that we keep living holy lives without any compromise. This is a hard battle each day.

Today, the foundations of society are being destroyed. Former marriage and family patterns are considered old-fashioned. Everyone should be allowed to decide for himself how and with whom he wants to live. Hence, why be against same sex marriage? Moreover, when things no longer work out within a marriage why should a couple be compelled to stay together?

This is society today, but we should not be too quick to think that we are immune to all of this. I think of our young people: why wait with sexual intimacy when the world around us no longer makes any point of this? I think also of married couples, where there is friction between husband and wife. The thought can so easily arise: why carry on if things no longer seem to work? In today's society, couples like these surely do not have the incentive to put any effort into restoring their broken relationships.

We will only receive this incentive when we let ourselves be guided by God's Word. We have been bought with a price, the apostle Paul writes, which is a reference to the cross. We are Christ's – set apart. Only by rejoicing in this great redemption will we find the strength to flee all sexual immorality and to live holy before God, walking with Him also in all matters related to the Seventh Commandment.

March 12

READING: MALACHI 2:10-16

Covenant implications (1)

"Have we not all one Father? Has not one God created us?"
MALACHI 2:10A

Malachi fulfilled his prophetic ministry among God's people after they had returned from exile. You would have expected that after having spent 70 years in exile the Israelites would make sure that they showed true thankfulness to God, who in His sovereign grace had brought them back into the Promised Land. You would think that in true thankfulness for this undeserved redemption the Israelites would make sure the same sins were not committed again.

Yet after a while it seemed as if no lessons had been learnt. We read about all kinds of sins being committed again, amongst which also that of mixed marriage and divorce by which the Israelites profaned God's covenant. Pointing to these sins in particular, the prophet Malachi says, "Have we not all one Father? Has not one God created us?".

With these words Malachi wants to remind God's people of the wonderful relationship in which they were allowed to live. In sovereign grace, God had chosen them to be His people, a people of His own possession. With the words just quoted, Malachi is basically saying: do you still treasure these undeserved blessings? If so, why is it then so difficult to live accordingly and so difficult to live holy before the LORD?

At the time that Malachi fulfilled his prophetic ministry, you could hardly see that God's people took God's covenant seriously. It was a time of moral decline, which came to the fore in particular with respect to two sins: mixed marriage and divorce. With respect to these two sins, Malachi says that the bottom line is that you no longer honour God as your Father. For you cannot on the one hand put on a show as if you still honour God, whilst on the other hand you marry the daughter of a foreign god. In today's terminology, Malachi is saying that whoever starts a relationship with a boy or a girl, a man or a woman from outside the church is no longer seeing the unique position in which God has placed us.

God had said to Israel, "You are My people, My chosen ones!". Yet in Malachi's day, the Israelites failed to appreciate the riches of belonging to God. The result was that they could no longer see anything wrong with entering into a relationship with someone belonging to a foreign god. Yet through the prophet Malachi, the LORD now says: in this you put your relationship with Me at risk – you are profaning My covenant.

March 13

READING: 2 CORINTHIANS 6:14-7:1

Covenant implications (2)

"Do not be unequally yoked with unbelievers. For what partnership has righteousness with lawlessness? Or what fellowship has light with darkness?"

2 CORINTHIANS 6:14

Often the text above this meditation is quoted to warn young people against the dangers of mixed courtships, and this text can indeed be used for this purpose. Yet when looking at the context in which the apostle Paul writes these words, it is not just the issue of mixed courtship that is addressed here. With these words, the apostle warns against any unholy compromise which would hinder our life in the service of Christ. And then indeed, being a child of the Lord has consequences also when choosing which boy or girl we wish to marry.

In choosing a partner for life, the most critical consideration should be that we want to make our marriage instrumental towards the building of God's kingdom. Well, how can you ever do this with someone with whom you cannot share your mutual love towards the LORD? If a husband and wife are not one in the LORD, the foundation on which their marriage is based becomes very unstable. In the Geneva Study Bible there is this footnote, "Intimacy in its deepest dimension is impossible when husband and wife are not united in faith." Therefore, when looking for a marriage partner, the most crucial aspect is that we are spiritually one.

When we are young and start dating or courting, we should always keep this in mind. When you sincerely love the LORD, you do not look first of all for a good-looking girl, a nice-looking guy, or for someone with a good position who can bring in a lot of money. Of course, this does not mean that looks are not important. Yet, of greater importance is that you are one in the Lord, being heirs together of the grace of life. This is the only secure foundation for a good marriage relationship, which is also needed to deal appropriately with conflicts that may arise. Then as a couple, you can nip these conflicts in the bud by uniting in prayer and bringing them before the LORD. Therefore, most importantly is that the love between husband and wife is rooted in their mutual love for the Lord.

March 14

READING: MALACHI 2:13-16

Covenant implications (3)

"For the man who does not love his wife but divorces her, says the Lord, the God of Israel, covers his garment with violence, says the Lord of hosts. So guard yourselves in your spirit, and do not be faithless."

MALACHI 2:16

The LORD hates divorce. Why is this? Well, think of how much patience the LORD has with us repeatedly breaking His covenant. When looking at how often we have disappointed the LORD, the LORD would surely have every right to divorce us. Yet, all of our unfaithfulness towards God does not undo God's faithfulness towards us. He even gave His own beloved Son to restore the relationship with us. How great a miracle this is!

That is why the LORD hates it when amid ongoing conflicts His children end a relationship and are no longer willing to work towards restoration. When this happens, we may think that we can still serve the LORD. Yet the LORD is no longer pleased with being served in such a way, just as the LORD was no longer pleased with His people's offerings in Malachi's day. Why was this? The LORD says, "This is because I was witness between you and the wife of your youth, with whom you have dealt treacherously. Yet she is your companion and your wife by covenant".

"Your wife by covenant" – this is a reminder of the oath sworn at the beginning of marriage. God was witness to the oath we swore. Therefore, unfaithfulness towards our marriage partner also means unfaithfulness towards God.

Today, marriage vows are no longer regarded as a promise for life. If it does not work anymore, you just split up. We can quite easily be affected by this way of thinking. Do we still want to fight for our marriage when conflicts arise? Of course, things can go wrong even in a godly marriage. Even godfearing couples may wonder at times how to get things back on track again. How? When there is a willingness to seek help from above. Clinging to God in prayer, assured that He, who was witness to our oath we vowed on our wedding day, will help us when our married life goes through valleys, even deep valleys. As God promised, He will give His aid and protection, even when we least expect it.

March 15

READING: PSALM 127

Children – a heritage from the LORD

"And what was the one God seeking? Godly offspring."
MALACHI 2:15

In his day the prophet Malachi not only warned against all unholiness by which God's covenant was profaned, but he also positively called for holy service: the verses 15 and 16 of Chapter 2 of his prophecies. Even though the translation of these two verses is rather difficult, one thing is quite clear: God desires godly offspring. It is one of the purposes for which God instituted holy marriage. In marriage a husband and wife should not just live for their own pleasure. Marriage too is kingdom service first of all. This service includes a willingness to receive children from God's hand, if God pleases to do so.

God wants godly offspring. Concerning the Old Testament, God wanted to come to the birth of the holy seed: Jesus Christ. Well, if the Israelites married the daughter of a foreign god, how would this holy seed ever be born? Yet, even now the Messiah has come, God still seeks godly offspring to build His church throughout the generations.

I realise there is more to marriage than bearing children. Nevertheless, also with respect to receiving children, married couples in the church must be willing to make their marriage instrumental for the furtherance of God's kingdom. In this area too, worldly influences can easily creep in. I think here of the way in which people in the church also speak about this issue at times. For example, when a couple says: we do not want any children for the time being, or we are planning on having another child. All of this sounds more like what we want rather than what God wants.

Of course, there are more ways in which a husband and wife may make their marriage instrumental to the building of God's kingdom. Otherwise, what would be the meaning of marriage for couples to whom God in His wisdom does not give children? That is why the Form for the Solemnisation of Marriage mentions as its first purpose: "husband and wife shall live together in sincere love and holiness, helping each other faithfully in all things that belong to this life and to the life to come". Every marriage is temple service.

When summarising the meditations with respect to the Seventh Commandment, the bottom line is that in whatever state of life – married, unmarried, having children or having no children – the LORD wants all of us, young and old alike, to live holy before Him in temple service each day, never forgetting that our bodies are temples of the Holy Spirit.

March 16

READING: PSALM 89:5-18

The fullness of the earth is the LORD's

"The heavens are yours; the earth also is yours;
the world and all that is in it, you have founded them."
PSALM 89:11

When in the eighth commandment the LORD says: "You shall not steal", the first thing He wants to teach us is that we are only stewards of all the things He has entrusted us with. Only stewards, since God Himself is the absolute Owner of all that we have received: money, possessions and other things, yes even the time we have on our hands.

On the first page of the Bible we find the so-called cultural mandate. This mandate was given to man so that he would always serve God with all that he had received at creation. Via the same mandate God also teaches us today: I am the Giver of all that you possess. It is all Mine: everything you have and receive! Everything – including the money our employer puts in our bank account or the profit we make in our business, money for which, according to our own feeling, we have worked hard. It is all the LORD's. In fact, it was already the LORD's even before it showed up on our bank balance. It is all the LORD's, the earth and all that is in it, including the shares on the stock market. If we were to think a bit more about this, perhaps it would make us more humble. So easily, we forget and then boasting of ourselves, we look at how well we have done money wise or business wise.

It's all the LORD's, who according to His sovereign good pleasure provides to each one of us the allotted portion in such a way that even among God's own people there remains a difference between rich and poor. One of the reasons for this is to activate us to look after each other. God wants His people to be a living community that also has the interests of their fellow members at heart. In fact, not only the interests of its members, but also the needs of this suffering world. Since we have received so much, we should be willing to give readily and not use it all for our own pleasure. Remember we are stewards, who one day have to render account. By the grace of God, may we all be able to give a joyful account, whenever that day comes.

March 17

READING: 1 TIMOTHY 6:1-10

Contentment

"But godliness with contentment is great gain."

1 TIMOTHY 6:6

God distributes His gifts according to His sovereign good pleasure. He does so according to what He thinks is best for each one of us. We should be content with this wise distribution of God and not look over the fence thinking that the grass is much greener there. In 1 Timothy 6:6 the apostle Paul writes that there is great gain in godliness with contentment.

Godliness – this is when one fears the LORD. This fear of the LORD enriches life. In Chapter 4 verse 8 of this same letter the apostle Paul writes: "Godliness is of value in every way, as it holds a promise for the present life and also for the life to come". Hence there is indeed great gain in godliness. However, this godliness must be joined with contentment. This means that at all times we must be thankful and content with what we receive from the hand of the LORD.

At all times – so also when disaster strikes or when the economy goes in to recession and many families within the church may find it difficult to make ends meet. Should we worry when there are signs like these on the horizon? There is no reason for this, because God will also provide then and so we can be content. His fatherly hand never fails. He will never stop providing us with the food that is necessary for us. God will never stop providing us with the things we need to serve Him. With this we should be content, always, in riches and poverty, in good days and bad.

This is what true Christian contentment is all about. This is an attitude totally opposite to the climate we live in today; a climate in which people are often craving for more and better, never being content. A craving for earthly goods, which often brings with it lots of other sins: for example, corruption and dishonest practices in business. In this day and age, when you are in business it is surely not easy to stand up for Christian principles. We too can so easily be caught up in the desire for money. These are not things which will leave God's children unaffected. Therefore, let us take to heart the lesson of the apostle Paul that there is great gain in godliness with contentment.

March 18

READING: MATTHEW 6:25-34

Anxious for nothing

"Therefore, I tell you, 'do not be anxious'."
MATTHEW 6:25A

"Do not be anxious…", the Lord Jesus says, "Look at the birds …" Commenting on these words, John MacArthur in his book 'Anxious for Nothing' writes: "Birds do not get together and say, 'We have got to come up with a strategy to keep ourselves alive.' They have no self-consciousness or ability to reason. But God has planted within them the instinct or divine capacity to find what is necessary to live. God does not just create life; He also sustains it."

This is how birds work within the framework of God's design. Next the same author writes: "Birds do not worry about where they are going to find food; they just go about their business until they find it, and they always do because God is looking out for them. Birds have no reason to worry and if they do not, what are you worrying for? … Are you not much better than a bird? No bird was ever created in the image of God; no bird was ever designed to be a joint heir with Jesus Christ … If God sustains the life of a bird, don't you think He will take care of you?".

The author also writes: "Keep in mind, of course, that like a bird, we have to work. Just as God provides for the birds through their instinct, so God provides for people through their efforts".

God will provide and so for us there is no reason to worry. At the same time, God does so through our efforts. Hence, in business for example, there is nothing wrong in planning, even when it comes to expanding a business. This not only applies to the world of business, but equally to saving money to buy a house for example. We are allowed to plan. Yet when planning, do we do this prayerfully, making God part of our plans up front and not as an afterthought, having planned it all ourselves without God and after all of this asking God to bless our plans? This is wrong. At the very start of our planning, we should realise whatever we have been given, including the opportunity to save for our own home, has also been given to us out of Father's hand.

When walking with God in this way every day, it will give fewer worries. In actual terms, then we do not have to worry at all, because Father is there. He will provide!

March 19

READING: EPHESIANS 4:17-32

Being good stewards

"So then, as we have opportunity, let us do good to everyone, and especially to those who are of the household of faith."

GALATIANS 6:10

The eighth commandment not only negatively forbids all greed and squandering of God's gifts, but also with respect to this commandment the opposite of what is forbidden is required. This means, as it reads in Answer 111 of the Heidelberg Catechism: "I must promote my neighbour's good wherever I can and may, deal with him as I would like others to deal with me, and work faithfully, so that I may be able to give to those in need".

In Ephesians 4 the apostle Paul says: this also is part of the new life in Christ. In Christ we no longer live for ourselves. Instead with all that God has given us, as good stewards we will look out also how we can help our neighbour.

The way in which people spend their money is often a good yardstick to know how they live their life with the Lord. Spending money is not something that stands on its own. It shows a certain attitude to life. From the way one spends his money we can learn how a person thinks about love and faithfulness, learn whether people are Christians also in deeds.

When considering that everything we have received is the Lord's anyway, it should always be a joy and never a chore to give; a joy – out of thankfulness that the LORD has given us so much. Scripture often speaks about the first fruits. This also means when considering spending our money, God's kingdom should always come first.

When testing our hearts and lives against the eighth commandment in this way, there surely is room for improvement for all of us. Too often with respect to spending money we do not always seek God's kingdom first, with personal wants having greater priority than the needs of God's kingdom and the wellbeing of our neighbour. However, as stewards in God's service, we should make a daily effort to have our priorities right, not only money wise, but also time wise. Yes, also with respect to the abundance of time God has given us we should not think either that it is all for ourselves, but equally look out for what we can do for our neighbour: kingdom focused in self-denying love, realising that God is honoured in this. And is this not the purpose of all of our life: to honour God?

 March 20

READING: 2 CORINTHIANS 8:1-15

Rich in Christ

"For you know the grace of our Lord Jesus Christ, that though He was rich, yet for your sake He became poor, so that you by his poverty might become rich."
2 CORINTHIANS 8:9

Scripture teaches that we must do well to everyone. Hence our task is not finished when the needy within the church are sufficiently cared for. As God's children we should have an eye also for the needs in the world. Yet when doing so, it can overwhelm one: millions of people around the globe without food, without drink, often also without shelter, their lives in danger. And all of this while we live in wealth. We should not forget this, when it comes to donating money. This does not mean that we have to spend all of our spare money on these needs, as if going out for dinner is wrong while there are still people on the other side of the globe who are dying of hunger. When the LORD has blessed us materially, we may also enjoy this as a blessing from God, as long as we also give God thanks for this. After all, we deserve nothing. All that we have, even if it is in abundance, is received by grace alone.

Grace – this word points to Christ, who in heaven was as rich as one could be. Yet He became poor for our sake. He did not hold on to all this glory as something just for Himself but laid Himself in a manger as a son of impoverished parents. With His incarnation Christ laid down the glory He had with the Father to become a simple man on earth, poor indeed. A poverty not inflicted on Him, but voluntarily chosen by Him, so that He could make us rich, not materially, but spiritually.

Christ – He is the source of all our wealth. Out of thankfulness for all that we have received in Him, we should see it as a privilege whenever we are called upon to give to those in need. Most of us earn more than we need for our basic living. This is something to be thankful for. It is something we may also enjoy too, as long as we do not forget that God is the Giver of all of this. With all the wealth we have, we should never forget that we are but stewards in God's service. Hence God's kingdom should always have priority as we walk with Him.

March 21

READING: DEUTERONOMY 19:15-21

No false witness

"You shall not bear false witness against your neighbour."
EXODUS 20:16

In the time of the Old Testament, justice was administered in the open square at the gate of every town and city, where the elders were seated. Everyone who went out or into the city learned what was going on. One could also be called upon as a witness, whereby the elders functioned as some kind of jury making their judgment on the basis of the testimony provided by the witnesses. These testimonies played an important role, the more so since in those days there were no solicitors or lawyers who could defend the cause of the accused. One could be declared guilty even on the basis of the testimony of two or three witnesses – witnesses who at times could also come with false testimony. Think of the court case against Naboth and also of the lawsuit against the Lord Jesus before the Sanhedrin.

It is against this background that we must learn to understand the meaning of the ninth commandment. In a society that had become insecure because of sin, God wanted to give His redeemed children protection, saying: "Do not obstruct justice by false witness. There is no need for this. Just be honest. Do not try to help yourselves by all kinds of evil devices. It will only ruin life. Trust Me, I will provide. Therefore, do not speak false witness. Instead, live from the riches of your redemption."

Living from this redemption, even in the case of testifying against a person, we should still speak the truth in love, trying as much as possible to uphold the good name of our neighbour. We should do this not only in a court case, but always. When things go wrong in a person's life, we should not talk about him, but instead try to speak with him or her. Moreover, when speaking with the person concerned, we must always do so in love, even if a wrongdoing has to be exposed. In Proverbs 10, verse 11 it reads, "The mouth of the righteous is a fountain of life". May the LORD help us to always use our mouth like such a fountain. This means that instead of talking about others in a negative way through all kinds of gossip, slander, and condemning rashly and unheard, we should heed God's call to promote the good name and reputation of our neighbour under all circumstances.

March 22

READING: PROVERBS 12:13-23

The power of the tongue (1)

"There is one whose rash words are like sword thrusts, but the tongue of the wise brings healing."
PROVERBS 12:18

Words rashly spoken can do enormous damage. They can be like sword thrusts hurting a person more than physical stab wounds do. In most cases, physical wounds will heal over time. Yet emotional scars can last for life. Emotional scars – like being bullied at school, always being talked down to with little self-esteem left, and many other things. Often we have no clue as to what damage we do by the words we speak.

Lord's Day 43 of the Heidelberg Catechism speaks about twisting someone's words, gossiping, slander, condemning a person rashly and unheard. How often does this not happen even within the congregation of Christ? We do not always weigh our words as carefully as we should. It is so quickly done: sitting in a comfortable chair, chatting away with a friend over a cup of coffee. "Have you heard recently that such and such…". And there it begins – not realising that in passing on this latest news, we might well be busy ruining the good name of our neighbour. Our tongue is indeed a dangerous weapon. A word thoughtlessly spoken can be like the butt of a cigarette thrown away without thinking, yet when it falls in the wrong place, it can cause a massive bushfire destroying everything. This is what words can do, says James in Chapter 3 of his letter – destroying people's lives. We should think about this before we speak.

In Proverbs 18, verse 21, it reads, "Death and life are in the power of the tongue." Yes, also life! A word spoken in wisdom can have healing powers. How good is a timely word? It can lift a person up when he is down in the dumps. It may cause us to see things from a different perspective. It brings healing. With our words, we can comfort people, encourage them, yes, even make them laugh. This too belongs to the power of the tongue.

READING: 1 JOHN 3:7-10

The devil's own work

"He (the devil) was a murderer from the beginning, and does not stand in the truth, because there is no truth in him. When he lies, he speaks out of his own character, for he is a liar and the father of lies."

JOHN 8:44

Lying is a characteristic of the devil. This already started in Paradise. First, he caused Eve to wonder why it was somewhat strange that they could eat from any tree in the garden apart from the tree of knowledge of good and evil. Eve indeed starts wondering: "Why would God have given this command?". Trust in God slowly faded away, and doubts arose, with the devil making the most of this by saying: "You will not die, as God has said. Instead, He said this knowing that when you eat from this tree, your eyes will be opened, and you will be like God, knowing good and evil". This was a lie, and the devil knew this. Yet he wanted man to believe this lie to ruin their life. This is how it all started: with a simple lie. It meant the end to everything God had created so beautifully, and this is precisely what Satan wanted: total ruin!

Yet all of this did not leave man without hope. Straight away after the fall into sin, God came with that wonderful promise which spoke of the coming Christ who would crush the head of the serpent and so defeat the devil.

This means that in Christ there is redemption, also from all lying and deceit. He came into this world to bear witness to the truth. In doing so, Christ put His own life at risk, in particular when He stood up against the destructive power of the lie, against sin, darkness, and death. While hanging on the cross, it seemed that He would sink under this power. Life ended for Him in a terrible death. However, because of Christ's faithful testimony – for which He suffered a tremendous amount of injustice, lying, and deceit – He redeemed us from all of these destructive powers. Hence, in Him there is hope, a future again, even today!

 March 24

READING: REVELATION 13:11-18

The power of the tongue (2)

"It (the beast out of the earth) deceives those who dwell on earth, telling them to make an image for the beast that was wounded by the sword and yet lived."
REVELATION 13:14B

As to the power of the tongue, we should also consider the power of all kinds of false prophecies, by which Satan tries to lure God's children away from the truth of God's Word. False prophets, telling God's people that it is not necessary to be so strict about everything. That is how Satan was active during the time of the Old Testament, and he is equally busy today.

In Revelation 13, verse 11, we read about the beast out of the earth: "It had two horns like a lamb, and it spoke like a dragon." Outwardly this beast resembles the Lamb, yet inwardly it is in alliance with the dragon. You could say: the lie of Satan dressed up as the truth. Next, we read how people fall for what at best is nothing other than a pseudo-gospel. It appeals, since it is easier to listen to, easier for the sinful flesh. All of this is a picture of what will happen during the last days – the period between Pentecost and Christ's return on the clouds of heaven – when more and more people will believe the lie and no longer heed the truth, falling victim to the lying propaganda of the false prophet.

The lie, even today, makes people believe that they can enjoy life without being worried about morals. Eat, drink, and be merry, for before you know it, you will die. Therefore, make the most of life now! Many people fall for it. Yet it is a lie, by which the devil tries to ruin man's life. Yet, it does not bring real happiness. Often, it leaves man with an empty feeling and no security.

These are dangerous times for the church, challenging us to remain steadfast in our faith. Yet we are not without hope, because we may live from the assurance that the victory is Christ's, in whom we have been set free from the destructive power of the lie. In John 8, where Christ speaks about the devil being the father of all lies, He also says, "If you abide in My word, you are truly My disciples, and you will know the truth, and the truth will set you free" (verses 31 and 32).

READING: PROVERBS 23:19-26

A spiritual heart X-Ray

"My son, give me your heart."

PROVERBS 23:26A

Concerning the tenth commandment, we read in Lord's Day 44 of the Heidelberg Catechism what the LORD requires of us: "not even the slightest thought or desire contrary to any of God's commandments should ever arise in our heart." One may wonder: who of us will ever be able to live up to this rule? Is this not formulated too strictly?

It is not, when first we look at what the LORD has done for us: redeeming us from the bondage of sin that kept us captive in the clutches of Satan. This is not what sin may look like in our eyes. Yet, this is what sin is: something by which we are captivated. Yet it never satisfies. It often leaves us with an empty feeling instead. Well, by His death on the cross, the Lord Jesus Christ redeemed us from this captivity. Hence, should we not be thankful, enjoying this freedom, making sure never to fall into slavery again?

Living in the joy of holiness, in the joy of being set apart to live for God: the tenth commandment teaches that this involves more than just keeping some rules such as you shall not murder, you shall not commit adultery, you shall not steal. Many an unbeliever would not have much difficulty with these rules either. Yet, in the tenth commandment, the LORD says: there is much more at stake. In obeying these rules, your heart must be in it as well. Hence, not just some outward obedience, but obedience from a heart that loves the LORD sincerely. Thus with the tenth commandment, the LORD wants to find out what lives in the innermost recesses of our hearts. You could call it a spiritual heart X-ray. We all know what an X-ray is. It shows things we could not otherwise see. Well, that is how the LORD looks into our hearts with the tenth commandment, to see if it is indeed fully committed to Him.

This is nothing to be scared of, when we love the LORD sincerely out of thankfulness for the redemption He gave us. In the tenth commandment, the LORD says to us: "My son, My daughter give Me your heart!". Being genuinely thankful – who would not gladly do so?

March 26

READING: DEUTERONOMY 10:12-22

Love from an undivided heart

"And now, Israel, what does the Lord your God require of you, but to fear the Lord your God, to walk in all his ways, to love him, to serve the Lord your God with all your heart and with all your soul."

DEUTERONOMY 10:12

The LORD loves us from the heart. For this very reason, He also wants us to love Him from the heart undividedly! What does this mean in practical terms? Think of the following example. When a girl gives her heart to a boy, she gives herself with all that she has, unreservedly. In a good relationship, her boyfriend will respond in the same way. The same applies to marriage. Otherwise, it will never work. If a husband and wife give their bodies to each other but not their hearts, there will never be a healthy marriage relationship. Likewise, the LORD wants His children to give Him their heart so that the covenant relationship between God and us may flourish.

Having redeemed us and in this having shown us His love, the LORD is grieved when we give the love of our heart to something or someone else. The LORD wants to have us entirely for Himself alone. Well, this is what is at the heart of the tenth commandment: the LORD calls us to love Him with an undivided heart. In doing so, the LORD claims our entire life: all of our feelings, desires, and longings. Why is this? The answer is: the LORD does not want us to become slaves again – slaves of sin.

Satan too tries to take possession of our heart. Yet, he has no other aim than to ruin our life. Once Satan has taken possession of our heart, he will take us with him on the road to eternal death. Nonetheless – thanks be to God – Christ is there as well, and He is stronger than Satan. This is the comfort to which we may cling in our daily battle against sin.

Christ is stronger! However, this should not cause us to become complacent. Instead, we remain accountable for the response we make, when the LORD says: I want you to love Me from the heart unreservedly, as I love you unreservedly!

March 27

READING: PROVERBS 4:20-27

Watch the doors of your heart

"Keep your heart with all vigilance,
for from it flow the springs of life."

PROVERBS 4:23

The LORD wants our heart fully committed to Him, because if our heart is not fully dedicated to the LORD, we remain an easy prey to the attacks of Satan. In Proverbs 4, verse 23, it reads: from the heart flow the springs of life, including all sin! In Matthew 15, verse 19, the Lord Jesus says the same: "For out of the heart come evil thoughts, murder, adultery, sexual immorality, theft, false witness, slander." It is noteworthy that this lengthy list starts with evil thoughts incited by wrong desires that come from the heart with which all sin begins. James, in his letter, Chapter 1, verses 14 and 15, says the same: "But each person is tempted when he is lured and enticed by his desire. Then desire when it has conceived gives birth to sin, and sin when it is fully grown brings forth death".

Sinful desires always precede the sinful deed. Think of what happened in Paradise, when Eve ate from the tree. After being deceived by the devil, she has another look at the tree of knowledge of good and evil and considers in her heart that the tree was good for food, a delight to the eyes, and to be desired to make one wise. You see the distance between Eve and the forbidden tree become smaller and smaller. Her heart had already yielded to the sin, and then there is no longer any halt. She stretches out her hand, takes the fruit, and eats.

This is how it often goes. We stretch out our hand to sin. First hesitantly. However, slowly the distance becomes smaller, and finally it comes to the sinful deed. That is why the LORD says in the tenth commandment: "Watch the doors of your heart. Do not toy with sin. Do not dream about evil things. For in the end, it will lead to death". We would do well to take this severe warning to heart by keeping watch over the doors of our hearts so that not even the slightest thought or desire contrary to any of God's commandments should ever arise in our hearts. Instead, we should always hate all sin and delight in all righteousness with all our heart (Answer 113 of the Heidelberg Catechism).

March 28

READING: ROMANS 7:7-25

Only a small beginning (1)

"For I do not do the good I want, but the evil
I do not want is what I keep on doing."

ROMANS 7:19

We must keep watch over the doors of our hearts. We all have to admit that this is a hard battle each day again: having the desire to do good, and yet evil thoughts and desires still so quickly get the better of us. In this broken life, this will remain a constant battle. Why is that? Has Christ not set us free from all the power of the devil? This is true! Christ has set us free from the dominion and slavery of sin. Yet this does not mean that the battle is over. Although having been set free from Satan's dominion, there is still the flesh and the body of sin, from which daily sins of weakness spring up. In Article 15 of the Belgic Confession, we confess: "Sin continually streams forth like water welling up from this woeful source."

One may wonder, if this is true how it is possible to keep watch over the doors of our hearts. If our sinful nature is so much inclined to sin, does God not ask the impossible? The answer is: God does not! By asking for one hundred percent love, God wants us to become more and more aware of our sinful nature. We should not be too quick in saying: I am okay! Instead, we must learn to detest ourselves and humble ourselves before God, seeking our life outside of ourselves in Jesus Christ. After all, I am only acceptable to God on account of the satisfaction, righteousness, and holiness of Christ.

Answer 115 of the Heidelberg Catechism refers to this. The question asked is: "If in this life no one can keep the Ten Commandments perfectly, why does God have them preached so strictly?" The answer reads: "First, so that throughout our life we may become more and more aware of our sinful nature, and therefore seek more eagerly the forgiveness of sins and righteousness in Christ." The tenth commandment will drive us to Christ. In Him, there is hope in overcoming this daily battle, even though in this life, it will only be a small beginning.

March 29

READING: HEBREWS 11:39-12:4

Only a small beginning (2)

"Let us run with endurance the race that is set before us."

HEBREWS 12:1B

In answer 115 of the Heidelberg Catechism it says: empowered by the Holy Spirit, we must never stop striving to be renewed more and more after God's image, until after this life we reach the goal of perfection. Striving – running the race that is set before us, looking at Jesus, the founder and perfecter of our faith. This requires perseverance. Yet God promises that He will give us all that is needed to persevere. We may rely on this. The LORD will always be there.

We may rely on God's promises, yet at times it still can be very tiring to continue that daily battle. The battle of having a real desire to serve the LORD, yet also having to admit every day anew: it went wrong again! Article 1 of Chapter V of the Canons of Dort refers to this battle, saying, "By His Spirit God sets us free from the dominion and slavery of sin, but not entirely in this life from the flesh and the body of sin." Due to Christ's victory over sin and death, Satan's rule over us has been broken. Christ is our King. Yet within us, there is still some kind of magnet that is attracted to Satan's rule. A magnet that keeps pulling. You do not want to do certain things, and yet you do. At times, you even hate yourself for doing it again. You feel despondent and perhaps inclined to stop fighting against that sin, since it will never change anyway.

Yet the LORD says, do not give up. Instead, in prayer pour out your heart before Me and keep clinging to Christ. Stay focused on Him. Remember: whatever you have done and however hard the battle you have to fight in life might be, when you turn to God – even in a broken prayer – God's love still goes out to you. He is faithful and by His grace He will powerfully preserve us to the very end!

March 30

READING: 1 JOHN 1:8-2:6, CANONS OF DORT V, 1

Indwelling sin

"If we say we have no sin, we deceive ourselves, and the truth is not in us."

1 JOHN 1:8

Article 1 of Chapter V of the Canons of Dort gives a very realistic picture of the life of a believer. In doctrinal words, it says in this article: sin no longer rules our life, i.e. we no longer live in sin. He who abides in Christ does not sin. This means that that person no longer lives in rebellion against God, even though in this life we will never be entirely without sin. Note well: we should never use this as an excuse, as sometimes it is said: "No one is perfect; we all do sin."

In Chapter 1, verse 8 of his first letter, the apostle John writes, "If we say we have no sin, we deceive ourselves, and the truth is not in us." That is why we all need to pray each day again, "Lord, graciously forgive the things I did wrong again. Continue to help me in fighting against sin". These are the sins that still remain in us against our will. From a previous meditation, we learnt that even our best works in this life are still all imperfect and defiled with sin. And yet, after having written in Chapter 7 of his letter to the Romans about his own struggles, in Chapter 8, verse 1, the apostle Paul continues saying: "There is no condemnation for those who are in Christ Jesus."

In Christ, we have been set free not only from the guilt of sin (our justification), but we also have been set free from the dominion and slavery of sin (our sanctification). Our baptism is a sure pledge of this, assuring us that we have been washed not only in the blood of Christ, but also in the Spirit of Christ. In Christ, we have become a new creation. Meanwhile, this does not mean that the battle against sin has almost become a closed chapter in our life. If only this were true, yet it is not. Today we are still called to fight the battle, the battle also against our own old-self. However, because we are Christ's, we are not on our own in this battle. He is our King, and one day we will share in the complete victory together with Him.

March 31

READING: PHILIPPIANS 3:12-4:1, CANONS OF DORT V, 2

Daily sins of weakness

"Not that I have already obtained this or am already perfect, but I press on to make it my own, because Christ Jesus has made me his own."

PHILIPPIANS 3:12

In this life, we will not reach perfection. The battle against sin will remain. Nevertheless, in this battle we must press on to obtain the goal of perfection. These are the two sides of living a redeemed life in Christ. We should never settle for sin. Instead, we are called to put the sinful flesh to death by the power of the Holy Spirit, each new day again.

This is a tiring battle. So tiring, that at times we may even feel like giving up, especially – as it reads in Article 2 – when daily sins spring up, and defects cling even to our best work day after day, after day. Yes, who would dare to say that he or she never becomes tired or discouraged in fighting this battle? On the other hand, there is the danger that we become complacent, since we know that God is a forgiving God who loves us. Should we perhaps then not worry too much about the fact that in this life it will never be perfect?

Article 2 warns against such complacency, saying that whenever we make a mess of our lives, it should cause us to humble ourselves before God. When looking into the mirror of God's law, upon seeing my sin, I should not say this is life, we all struggle with the same problems, and so I am not worse than any other member of the church. Instead, we should say: I am as bad as that fellow member who I am inclined to sometimes look down upon somewhat when thinking about how he lives his life. I am as bad as he is. I am not one percent better, sinning each day again. "Lord, help me. I hate myself for being like this." I think here of the Form for Baptism, which says, "we should detest ourselves, humble ourselves before God, and seek our cleansing and salvation outside of ourselves." Outside of ourselves, to find it in Jesus Christ. That is the gospel to which we may cling in fighting the battle against sin. In Christ, there is a future. In Him, there is hope.

April 1

READING: PSALM 19:7-11, CANONS OF DORT V, 2

Holy exercises of godliness

"The law of the LORD is perfect, reviving the soul."
PSALM 19:11

In Article 29 of the Belgic Confession, it reads concerning the marks of Christians: "Although great weakness remains in them, they fight against it by the Spirit all the days of their life. They constantly appeal to the blood, suffering, death, and obedience of Jesus Christ, in whom they have forgiveness of their sins through faith in Him". Fighting against sin and praying – as we also often say: ora et labora – pray and work! In Article 2 of Chapter V of the Canons of Dort, we read because of this ongoing battle, we should humble ourselves before God, flee to the crucified Christ, put to death our sinful flesh more and more and by holy exercises of godliness.

To be well equipped for this battle, we should take time to read our Bible and meditate on it daily. These are the holy exercises of godliness mentioned in Article 2. As a bare minimum, just half an hour a day of reading our Bible, perhaps in conjunction with a meditation book, is a good start. We should also take time to reflect upon it, whereafter we may bring before Father's throne all of the things our hearts are often so full of. This will change the course of our day. It will give us a different outlook on life. It helps us to cope.

Thus these first two articles of the fifth chapter of the Canons of Dort highlight the wonderful comfort we will receive amid the brokenness of this life when living in this way. Comforting, since they are not phrased just doctrinally far and remote from daily life. Instead, they speak to us right in the middle of the lives we live, lives in which the battle is raging. When reading these articles, we receive encouragement not to give up, for Christ is near to us with His Spirit. Let us hold on to this, especially during days when everything may seem dark and gloomy. Christ is near, and in Him we are heading for the victory, of which the final sentence of Article 2 speaks: delivered from this body of death, we will reign with the Lamb in heaven!

April 2

READING: 1 CORINTHIANS 10:1-13, CANONS OF DORT V, 3

God preserves His own

"God is faithful, and he will not let you be tempted beyond your ability, but with the temptation he will also provide the way of escape, that you may be able to endure it."

1 CORINTHIANS 10:13B

In Article 3, it reads: God will make sure that we will not miss out on the victory promised to us in Christ. He will give the strength needed to persevere in the battle we still have to fight, confirming us in the grace once conferred on us and also powerfully preserving us in that grace to the very end.

This is a glorious promise. Yet it should not cause us to become complacent, thinking we will be okay in fighting the battle of faith. Those who think this often overestimate their own strength, at the same time underestimating the power of the adversary. True, God is near, yet this does not make the battle less severe. It is not for nothing that Christ also taught us to pray, "Lord, lead us not into temptation." If the battle were not so severe, there would be no need for this prayer. However, the power of the sinful magnet within us (our old self), and the craftiness of the adversary can so easily make us stumble and go down in defeat. That is the reality, and let us never make light of this. It would be better to own up to our weakness, acknowledging: "Lord, I cannot do this. I am weak, prone to sin. Lord, help me in keeping my eyes directed to Jesus, the Author and Finisher of our faith".

Yet, Article 3 also assures us: in the battle we still have to fight, God is there. By His grace, He will give us not only the strength we need today, but by relying on Him, we may also be assured that He will be with us to the very end, bringing us safely home! Again, this will not happen automatically. Yet it is the assurance we have, when living our lives with the LORD, each day anew, in every step we take, in every word we speak, in every thought that crosses our mind. Is this difficult? Not when we look away from ourselves and rely on God, seeking our strength in Him alone!

April 3

READING: PSALM 32, CANONS OF DORT V, 4-5

Guarded by God's power

"…who by God's power are being guarded through faith for salvation ready to be revealed in the last time."
1 PETER 1:5

Yesterday we focused on the promise that God will preserve His own. In our battle against sin, God is there with His grace to preserve us to the very end. However, if God is always there to uphold us in the battle we have to fight, why is it that at times even upright children of God can fall so deeply into sin?

According to the Arminians, this proves that God does not really preserve them, at least not infallibly. It is in response to this teaching that our forefathers confessed in Article 4: God's promises stand! The power of God, whereby He confirms and preserves true believers in the grace once conferred on them, cannot be conquered by the flesh. In other words, God's grace is greater than our sins.

This statement, however, does not undo the fact that because of the sinfulness of man's nature, even upright children of God still do walk away from God's grace, living a sinful lifestyle. Of course, God does not want this. Instead, it grieves Him. It kindles His wrath. Because of this, the life of these children of God can become very dark. They walk the Broadway of life and think it is great. Yet, God's fatherly face no longer shines upon them, and deep down they feel it, even though they do not want to admit it.

King David speaks about these struggles after he committed adultery with Bathsheba. It took quite some time before David owned up to this sin. During this time of covering up, David acted as if nothing was wrong. Yet, deep down he knew, and it was eating away at him (Psalm 32:3,4).

It is not difficult to recognise ourselves in this. We sin willfully, walk away from God, and act as if there is nothing wrong. Meanwhile, though, it is eating away at us. This pain shows that in His steadfast love towards us, God still holds on to us, guarding us by His power, so that we will not miss out on the inheritances He has in store for us. That is also why David's sin with Bathsheba did not thwart God's purpose for David's life. God remained in control.

April 4

READING: 1 PETER 5:6-11, CANONS OF DORT V, 4

Watch and pray

Be sober-minded; be watchful. Your adversary the devil prowls around like a roaring lion, seeking someone to devour."

1 PETER 5:8

Why does God allow His elect to fall into sin, while, at the same time, God is not the author of sin? These are matters we will never fully understand with our limited human mind. Yet Scripture does teach that God being in control uses it for the greater good. Think of Jacob's sons, who out of jealousy sold their brother Joseph as a slave. God permitted this, even though what the brothers did was a sin. However, God used the brothers' sin for the greater good, as we know from the concluding chapters of Genesis.

The difficulty is, that because we are so familiar with the Bible, we read stories like the one about Joseph being sold to Egypt knowing the outcome already. Because of the outcome, we know it was part of God's plan. However, when we are right in the middle of such a situation, we often struggle with the question 'why'. Jacob's sons just hated Joseph and wanted to get rid of him. At the same time, Jacob struggled with the question 'Why is this happening to me?'

From this example, it is clear that sin remains sin, even though God is in control. Sin remains sin, for which we must be continuously on guard. Scripture teaches us to watch and pray so that Satan does not lure us away from God. Without watching and praying, we become an easy target for the devil – like David, when on an evening while walking on the flat roof of the palace in Jerusalem, he saw a woman bathing. Instead of straightaway turning his eyes away, he looked on and saw that she was beautiful. David started toying with sin. How could this happen to David, a man after God's own heart?

Once I read a story of a teacher, who asked her Grade Two students the same question: how could this happen to David, since he loved the LORD? One of the students raised her hand and softly said: "I think that the king had forgotten to pray that morning."

Watch and pray, therefore! How often do we forget this when we start toying with sin? Watch, the LORD says. Guard the doors of your heart and hold on to Me. Only then will you be safe.

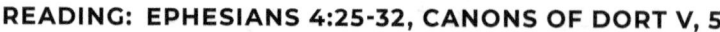

April 5

READING: EPHESIANS 4:25-32, CANONS OF DORT V, 5

Grieving the Holy Spirit

"Do not grieve the Holy Spirit of God, by whom you were sealed for the day of redemption."

EPHESIANS 4:30

Article 5 of the Canons of Dort shows the devastating effects of sin: it grieves the Holy Spirit. It may even cause us to lose the sense of Gods' favour. The Holy Spirit dwells in our hearts to guide us in the truth, giving us insight into how to live as a child of God. If we wilfully turn the other way, it grieves Him. The Spirit wants to put our sinful nature to death with its evil desires. Therefore, how much must it grieve Him, when instead we take delight in those sinful desires?

Sin ruins our relationship with God, and often we feel this as well. Bible reading becomes less frequent. Prayer is no longer as persistent as it should be. Because of this, faith no longer flourishes either. We may still go through the motions as no doubt David also did during that time he covered up his sin. He went to the tabernacle fulfilling his religious duties, but faith was no longer living, and this was inwardly eating away at him. This happens when we start toying with sin and no longer live life as the LORD wants us to live it. God becomes more and more remote. Instead of being God-centred, we live self-centredly. The warmth of the relationship is gone.

Sin deprives us of the joy of faith. Article 5 says: it will wound our conscience. For a while, we may even lose the sense of God's favour. I am sure we can all think of moments in our life when we simply went through the motions, or even worse did things which we knew full well were displeasing to God. But then there was that voice: "What are you doing?" You came home, opened your Bible, and started praying. Not just a routine prayer but pouring out your heart before God, and all of a sudden you felt God's face shining upon you again. You felt the warmth of the relationship. God did not let go of us. From ourselves, we are weak, prone to walk away from God, each day again. Yet God keeps watching over us, making sure that we do not fall away from His grace altogether. What a great comfort this is.

April 6

READING: 1 PETER 1:13-25, CANONS OF DORT V, 6-7

Preserving in them the imperishable seed of regeneration

"…since you have been born again, not of perishable seed but of imperishable through the living and abiding Word of God."

1 PETER 1:23

Article 6 states that God will not permit his elect to be lost. From Article 7, we learn that God does so by preserving in them the imperishable seed of regeneration. These words are a quotation from Peter's first letter, Chapter 1, verse 23. The apostle Peter is speaking about the power of God's Word, by which the LORD renews the lives of His children. Through it, we have become new creatures. We are born again through the Spirit, who worked this in us through the Word.

In the elect, the seed of this new life is rooted so deeply that it will never die altogether. That is why the voice of God's Word, no matter how soft it might have become, is still heard. Living in sin, we may try to push it away. However, as long as we live in today's grace, God is still calling out.

Whoever has been brought back to God in this way will grieve over his sins, grieve from the heart with godly sorrow for the sins committed, seeking forgiveness in the blood of Jesus Christ. When this happens, we are not just sorry because of the consequences of our sins. At times, this happens as well, but this is not the grief Article 7 is referring to.

God will preserve His elect, for as the apostle Paul writes in Romans 8: those whom God predestined, He calls effectually, and those He will also justify, and finally also glorify. In practical terms, this means God calls us each day anew to live from the riches of our baptism. If we genuinely do this, be it with many weaknesses and faults, we will never have to despair of God's mercy. When we live close to God in this way, no one will be able to snatch us out of Father's hand.

This is how God will powerfully preserve us in the grace bestowed upon us to the very end, making sure that none of His children sink so deeply that they will fall away from the grace of adoption and the state of justification. When we keep clinging to God, no power will be able to separate us from His love.

April 7

READING: JOHN 10:22-30, CANONS OF DORT V, 8

No one can snatch them out of the Father's hand

"My Father, who has given them to me, is greater than all, and no one is able to snatch them out of the Father's hand.."
JOHN 10:29

Many parents who have children who went astray, turning their back upon God, struggle with the text above this meditation. Did God not preserve them? Was Satan still able to snatch these lambs out of Christ's hands?

These are tough questions. Hence there is no easy answer either. However, questions like these do not negate the riches of Chapter V of the Canons of Dort. Firstly, these youngsters and others who have walked away, still wear the mark and emblem of Christ on their forehead. They are children of God, who received the same promises as we received, and therefore there is always a way back. To them too applies: God's grace is greater than our sins. Hence, there is forgiveness also for them, whenever they return to God in true repentance.

The Lord Jesus as the Good Shepherd laid down His life for the flock. He died so that His sheep might live. When we at times feel helpless and no longer know how to reach these wayward members, those prodigals, He still can. When we sometimes feel, if only we could give them faith – He can through His Spirit! His love also goes out to those lost sheep. He let His body be nailed to the cross even for them. He gave His life for us and our children. These are the promises parents may plead with.

Parents might be very faithful in the upbringing of their children, yet this is no guarantee that our children will always walk in the ways of the Lord. When they grow up, they themselves are also responsible for making the right choices, which they do not always do. However, as long as there is life, as long as we live in today's grace, there is hope. Hence, we may fold our hands to lay the names of our children in the hands of this Shepherd. As long as we live in today's grace, there remains hope, and as long as there is hope, we may pray that Christ will bring home safely also those prodigals together with all the saints.

READING: 1 JOHN 3:19-24, CANONS OF DORT V, 9-10

God's assurance of our preservation (1)

"For whenever our heart condemns us, God is greater than our heart."

1 JOHN 3:20A

The first articles of Chapter 5 of the Canons of Dort teach: God guarantees us a safe homecoming. He will finish perfectly what He for us has undertaken. When we continue looking at Christ as the Author and Finisher of our faith, God will give us what is needed each new day again. The question we often struggle with is: how can I personally be sure of this? Even more importantly: how do I receive this assurance?

Let us start with the second question. Concerning our election, likewise concerning our perseverance, we do not receive this assurance by a specific private revelation beside or outside the Word. Thus in a very clear way, the Canons of Dort refute the teachings of the Arminians, who claimed that without a special revelation, we can have no certainty of future perseverance in this life. Refuting this teaching, the Canons teach: in a similar way as our conversion is fruit of the powerful work of the Spirit, who uses the preaching of the Holy Gospel as a means, so the Spirit also assures us of our perseverance pointing us to God's sure promises.

Think of baptism, when God promised under oath that He would always be there for us. Even to the extent, when sometimes through weakness we may fall into sin, we never have to despair of God's mercy. Never, for in Christ, we have received the forgiveness of sin. Moreover, the Holy Spirit is there each new day again, helping us to make a clean start in the battle against sin.

Therefore, whenever we try to find assurance, we should think of the promises given to us at baptism. Promises we will find when we open God's Word. For example, the promise found in the passage of Scripture for today: "For whenever our heart condemns us, God is greater than our heart." Whenever there is doubt in your heart about God's promises, think of the greatness of God's love in Jesus Christ. Think of the assurance of which the apostle Paul writes in Romans 8 that there is no condemnation for those who are in Christ Jesus, and therefore – as it reads in the last verse of this same chapter: "Nothing will be able to separate us from the love of God in Christ Jesus our Lord."

April 9

READING: ROMANS 4:13-5:2, CANONS OF DORT V, 9+10

God's assurance of our preservation (2)

"No unbelief made him waver concerning the promise of God but he grew strong in his faith as he gave glory to God, fully convinced that God was able to do what he had promised."
ROMANS 4:20-21

Arminian teaching leaves man doubting when they look for an inward testimony to be sure of their salvation. This is why in many churches affected by Arminian teaching, conversion stories are so important. Their message is: The Lord Jesus called me to let the Spirit work in my heart, and the same can also happen to you, when you give yourself to Christ. In all of this, man's commitment stands in the centre, instead of God's sure promise. It is the voice I heard, followed by committing my life to Christ. It all sounds great, but what if I never hear this inward voice?

Yet, does Article 9 of the Canons of Dort not also say that faith gives assurance, and is this not something you must also feel in your heart? It even says that this feeling can be either strong or weak, depending on the measure of our faith. So, what is the difference, or is it just a matter of saying things differently? It is the assurance that God will indeed bring us safely home that is at stake here. Thankfully, concerning this assurance, we are not left to ask whether we feel it, or to listen for some kind of inward voice, but we may cling to God's sure promise instead.

The passage of Scripture above this meditation makes this quite clear. If Abraham had gone by what he felt and saw, he would soon have given up hope that God would fulfil the promise given to him. Yet Abraham lived by faith, which is the evidence of things not seen.

According to Answer 21 of the Heidelberg Catechism, living by faith is not only having a sure knowledge that God's promises are true, but also having the confidence that these promises are ours. Trust and assurance, which the Holy Spirit works in our hearts. This is how Abraham believed against all hope that God would fulfil His promises. We may live by this same assurance that God will also fulfil His promises to us, including the promise of a safe homecoming!

April 10

READING: 1 CORINTHIANS 1:4-9, CANONS OF DORT V, 9

God's assurance of our preservation (3)

"God is faithful ..."

1 CORINTHIANS 1:9A

In Lord's Day 7 of the Heidelberg Catechism, the question is asked, "What is a true faith?" The answer mentions two aspects: a sure knowledge and a firm confidence. These two aspects are inseparable, since the confidence that is mentioned here is not based on what I feel, but on what God has spoken. Satan may at times try to attack our confidence. Often these attacks are the strongest when we no longer live close to God's Word. That is why Article 9 also mentions the church – the place where God strengthens our assurance by the weekly preaching of the gospel.

Of course, this does not mean that merely by being a church member you can be assured that God will bring you home safely. Article 9 speaks about true and living members who do not go to church just out of routine, but with a burning zeal to be there to hear the gospel of our Saviour. To be there every Sunday to be strengthened in faith, to be reassured of God's wonderful promises, including the promise that God will preserve us to the very end.

A living member longs to be together with all the other members of Christ's body, knowing that not one member can be missed. After all, we are travelling together, and so we need each other. Individualism is the deathblow to a vibrant church life. This is why Article 9 also mentions the church, that is the place where the gospel is preached, strengthening us together in the assurance that God is faithful in preserving us to the very end.

The weekly preaching of the gospel should also help us to open God's Word throughout the week. And this also to receive assurance. Assurance, when at times we might feel or think that God is so far away or even doubt if God still wants to look upon us in mercy. Yet, thanks be to God, it is not our personal feelings that have the last say. Just take your Bible and believe what is written there in black and white. God's Word written in blood, the blood of Christ's love for us. Again, that blood is greater than our sins. Think also of the text above this meditation: God is faithful! Hence there is never any need to doubt the assurance God gives us.

April 11

READING: ROMANS 8:1-17, CANONS OF DORT V, 10

The testimony of the Holy Spirit

"The Spirit himself bears witness with our
spirit that we are children of God."
ROMANS 8:16

The assurance of our preservation does not come from an inward voice of the Holy Spirit in our hearts. Instead we receive this assurance by faith in the sure promises of God, which He has most abundantly revealed in His Word for our comfort. Yet Article 10 still speaks about a testimony of the Holy Spirit witnessing with our spirit that we are children of God. So what kind of testimony is this?

Scripture speaks about this testimony in Romans 8. In verse 15 of this chapter, we read: "For you did not receive the spirit of slavery to fall back into fear, but you have received the spirit of adoption as sons, by whom we cry 'Abba! Father!'". By God's sovereign grace, we are taken into the family of God, and inwardly we are persuaded by the Spirit that we truly belong. In the Form for Baptism, it reads: The Holy Spirit imparts to us all what we have in Christ. How does the Spirit do this? By working confidence in our hearts, pointing us to God's sure promises.

Often when it comes to security in faith, we look at our own life. Seeing our many weaknesses and shortcomings, we may so quickly start doubting, saying: "I am not good enough." This is the spirit of bondage, which causes us to fear. Yet when this fear arises, we start praying, "Our Father, who art in heaven…" We still say 'Father', even though we fear. Why is that? Because the Holy Spirit is at work in us, pointing us to Father's love, and hence we still dare to say 'Father'. There is no need for fear, for we are children of God, and if children, says Paul in verse 17, "then also heirs of God and joint heirs with Christ." This assures us: God will preserve us so that we will not miss out on the inheritance promised to us.

Whenever you struggle with sin and feelings of guilt, wondering: "Will God still look upon me in mercy?", always hold on to these riches. God is a waiting Father, waiting for us to come back to Him. When doing this in true repentance, clinging to God's promises, there is no reason to fear. We may be sure of this beyond any doubt.

April 12

READING: 2 PETER 1:1-11, CANONS OF DORT V, 10

The serious and holy pursuit of a clear conscience, and of good works

"Therefore, brothers, be all the more diligent to confirm your calling and election, for if you practice these qualities you will never fall."

2 PETER 1:10

When dealing with the source of our assurance, Article 10 also mentions: "the serious and holy pursuit of a clear conscience and of good works." What is meant by this? By way of example, think of today's society which lives by the slogan: "If it feels good, do it. I am my own boss. No one can tell me that this or that is wrong". However, when living by faith, the most important thing for us will be how God wants us to live our lives.

The fruit of this is, when doing something that displeases God, deep down we know that it grieves our Father in heaven. Where does this realisation come from? It is the echo of God's Word in our minds. The aerial tuned in to God, our conscience enlightened by the Holy Spirit. Because of this, we no longer worry about what people say about us. Instead, we want to have a clear conscience before God.

How do we get to that stage in life? Say you did something wrong. It weighs heavily on your heart. Where does this feeling come from? From God! A guilty conscience is often a result of having messed things up in our relationship with God. Yet when we go down on our knees and pour out our hearts before God, we feel relieved knowing that for Christ's sake God will forgive us whatever we did wrong. The fruit of this exercise is that our conscience is clear again. Also, it will bear as fruit that we want to live for the Lord with new zeal in all good works through the renewing power of the Holy Spirit within us. Throughout this process, we will also be reassured of being children of God, who have nothing to fear.

Doubt concerning the assurance of being preserved by God to the very end is often a result of not living close to the LORD. Hence, the call of the apostle Peter to be all the more diligent in confirming our calling and election. An election which is sure from God's side. Yet to receive this assurance inwardly in our hearts, it should also be our joy to do God's will.

April 13

READING: PSALM 88, CANONS OF DORT V, 11

God's assurance not always felt

"But I, O Lord, cry to you; in the morning my prayer comes before you O Lord, why do you cast my soul away? Why do you hide your face from me?."

PSALM 88:13-14

As children of God, we do not always live on the high mountains of faith. There might also be times when we struggle with doubts or temptations. Sometimes this can even take away the assurance of faith. Everything seems dark and gloomy. At moments like these, Satan might attack us with questions about whether what the Bible says is all true. What if it is all a hoax? Do not think this is bad if one were ever to think this. It leads one to wonder whether or not this is a testimony that our faith is totally gone. It is not. Instead, these are attacks of Satan. Attacks because we feel tired, even lost at times.

These are doubts from within. Yet, there are also the temptations from outside by which Satan tries to lure us away from God. All these things make life a real battle. Hence, the question can attack us – how will I ever be able to persevere to the very end? We struggle for assurance.

Yet this should never cause us to doubt. Instead, open Scripture and see how many of the saints before us struggled with similar questions. This is also the beauty of Scripture: it pictures people just like us – no heroes in faith, but people weak in themselves. You find this especially in the psalms: struggling children of God!

The author of Psalm 73, for example, became envious of the boastful, seeing the prosperity of the wicked. It made him question: have I cleansed my heart in vain? He found this too painful to consider, until he went into the sanctuary and started once again to look at life from God's perspective. I also think of Psalm 88 – one of the darkest psalms in the Book of Psalms. It is one long complaint to God from beginning to end. There is not even a turnaround to confidence in God. The only glimmer of hope in this psalm is that the author still pours out his heart before God.

In faith, we may have the assurance that when we do the same amidst our struggles and doubts, such a prayer will never go unheard, no matter how much we feel surrounded by darkness. God is still there!

April 14

READING: TITUS 2:11-14, CANONS OF DORT V, 12

God's assurance is an incentive to godliness (1)

"For the grace of God has appeared, bringing salvation for all people, training us to renounce ungodliness and worldly passions, and to live self-controlled, upright, and godly lives in the present age."

TITUS 2:11-12

The subject matter dealt with in Article 12 of Chapter V of the Canons of Dort is similar to what we read in Lord's Day 24 of the Heidelberg Catechism. Refuting the heresies of the church of Rome that the doctrine of being saved by grace alone makes people careless and wicked, the Heidelberg Catechism says: "It is impossible that those grafted into Christ by true faith should not bring forth fruits of thankfulness." This is what we also read in Article 12. Having full assurance of being saved in Christ will never lead to any form of pride or complacency, especially when considering the precious price that has been paid for this salvation.

Let me try to make this clear with a simple story, which I once read studying the Canons of Dort:

In a small village somewhere in India, two boys had been caught in a gambling game and had received severe punishment. The mother of one of the boys did everything to get her son free. She toiled long days, carrying stones, which caused her hands to bleed. However, she did not mind as long as she could earn sufficient money to buy her son free. She succeeded in her efforts. When the boy was just a few days back home, some old friends came along and asked him to join them once again in their gambling game. The boy responded: "How could I ever be so unthankful towards my mother. You go ahead with it, but I will never be able to do so again, when thinking of those hands of my mother full of blood".[1]

I think this story says it all – even though it is only a weak example. Also, when thinking of the fact of how weak we are from ourselves, prone to sin, who would ever walk away from the secure hand that is there each day again to lead us safely onward? Instead, considering all this, an upright child of God will make sure that nothing will ever put his restored relationship with Father at risk again.

---

1 See H. Drost, "Altijd Veilig", Woord en Wereld no. 75

April 15

READING: AMOS 6:1-8, CANONS OF DORT V, 12

God's assurance is an incentive to godliness (2)

"Woe to those who are at ease in Zion, and those who feel secure on the mountain of Samaria."

AMOS 6:1A

Article 12 of the Canons of Dort refutes the teachings of the Arminians who teach: if you know God will hold on to you from the start, then you have no reason to worry that anything can put this relationship at risk. This leaves a lot of room for complacency. However, this teaching makes a caricature of what Scripture teaches. A child of God, living a life in which there is no evidence of taking God's commandments seriously might think: just by going to church and ticking a few other boxes to keep the elders off my back, I will be okay. Yet Scripture teaches differently. Amos in his prophecies had to address the same issue in his day when the inhabitants of Jerusalem and Samaria thought they had nothing to fear from the world power Assyria. They were filled with pride and self-confidence. Yet the LORD abhorred the pride of Jacob. Pride and confidence are never fitting for God's cherished people; neither is complacency, thinking you will be okay.

A living faith that clings to God's sure promises never leaves room for any form of complacency. Instead, in humble gratitude it will cling to Christ, who said during His ministry on earth, "I am the vine, you are the branches. He who abides in Me, and I in him, bears much fruit…" (John 15:5). Abiding in Christ – this includes keeping His commandments as the Lord Jesus says in verse 10 of this same chapter: "If you keep my commandments, you will abide in My love." Keeping God's commandments, not because we have to, but because we want to out of thankfulness for our salvation in Christ.

We read the same in Article 12. It reads, "The certainty of perseverance, however, so far from making true believers proud and complacent, is rather the root of humility, childlike reverence, genuine godliness, endurance in every struggle, fervent prayers, constancy in suffering, and in the confession of the truth, and lasting joy in God." He, who truly loves God, has indeed no other desire than also showing this in fruits of thankfulness.

April 16

READING: PSALM 116, CANONS OF DORT V, 12

Thankfulness in deeds

"What shall I render to the LORD for all His benefits to me?"

PSALM 116:12

Psalm 116 is a clear example that being redeemed by the LORD, being set free from death, does not make an upright child of God inactive or careless. Instead, it will make the believer thankful also in deeds, showing the fruits of faith.

Article 12, dealing with this same issue, mentions the following fruits:

Humility: This is the attitude of knowing yourself unworthy of God's love, marvelling each new day again: "LORD, who am I that I may share in all these riches?"

Childlike reverence: This means rejoicing daily in Father's loving and almighty care, never wanting to let go of Father's hand. Thinking great of God and small of ourselves.

Genuine godliness: You desire to live close to God, walking with God in every step we take, but also in the thoughts that cross our minds, the words we speak, the decisions we make. It means avoiding all world-conformity, no flirting with the world, but in true love to God live close to Him.

Endurance in every struggle: This means in the battle against sin, we keep clinging to God, fighting the battle in the awareness God will provide the strength we need each day, no matter how hard the battle will be.

Fervent prayers: In the fight against sin, we also need to be active in prayer each day, asking the LORD: "Uphold me in this battle so that I do not go down to defeat". A living faith finds its strength in persistent prayer.

Constancy in suffering and in the confession of the truth: This means when being ridiculed for the name of Christ that we keep clinging to God even though the circumstances you are in might be hard to cope with.

Lasting joy in God: This is the joy of finding strength in God; joy in knowing that God's grace will be sufficient to carry us, always!

When considering all of this, it is clear that the certainty of perseverance will never cause an upright child of God to become proud or complacent. Instead, it will give us an even greater incentive to live a life of thankfulness, praising God for all that He has given us in Christ.

April 17

READING: PSALM 4, CANONS OF DORT V, 13

The contemplation of God's face is sweeter than life

"The Lord bless you and keep you; the Lord make his face to shine upon you and be gracious to you; the Lord lift up his countenance upon you and give you peace."
NUMBERS 6:24-26

God will preserve His own, even when through weakness they may fall into serious sin. He will not withdraw His Holy Spirit from them altogether. Preserving in them the seed of regeneration through His Word and Spirit, He certainly and effectually will renew them to repentance, bringing them back into His camp.

The question addressed in Article 13 is: what will be the response of such a person after having gone through all of this and being back in God's camp? Would that person really react with an attitude saying: the safety net is there, so a bit of carelessness does not matter? This is what the Arminians taught, trying to make a mockery of the doctrine of God's preservation. Yet Article 13 says: rather the opposite will be the case, namely a greater concern to observe the ways of the LORD carefully. For persons like these have come to realise how much they have grieved Father in heaven by their sins. They have experienced what it means to lose the sense of God's favour. Therefore, their prayer will be even more strongly: "Lord, let this not happen to me again."

In the last sentence of Article 13, it reads: "To those who fear God, the contemplation of His face is sweeter than life." In Psalm 4, David speaks about this as well. In verse 6a of this psalm, he says: "There are many who say, 'Who will show us some good?'" Many of the people who do not believe in God look for welfare elsewhere. David, however, does not want to fall into this trap. Instead, he prays in verse 6b, "Lift up the light of your face upon us, O LORD!" This expression is a reference to the priestly blessing recorded in Numbers 6.

The contemplation of God's face is sweeter than life. Therefore, those who have gone through a period of sin in their life, at times having lost the sense of God's favour – they will be careful that God will not hide His face from them again. To them, this is more bitter than death. For this reason, in many a psalm we read the prayer: "LORD, do not hide Thy face from me."

April 18

READING: ROMANS 10:14-17, CANONS OF DORT V, 14

The use of means in perseverance

"So faith comes from hearing, and hearing through the word of Christ."

ROMANS 10:17

Romans 10, verses 14 and 15 stresses that people need the gospel to come to faith. God works faith through the preaching of the gospel. Lord's Day 7 of the Heidelberg Catechism, speaking about true faith, says: "This faith the Holy Spirit works in my heart by the gospel." The same is also mentioned in Lord's Day 25 of the Heidelberg Catechism.

However, this is not the only way God works faith in us. He also maintains, continues, and perfects it as we read in Article 14, by the hearing and reading of His Word. This is why it is so important to be in church on Sunday. Our faith needs strengthening each Sunday again; strengthening to hold fast the confession of our faith without wavering (Hebrews 10:23).

Article 14 also mentions the sacraments, which function as a sign and seal to confirm God's promises to us even more strongly. Yes, we should also thank God for the wonderful gift of the sacraments to nourish and sustain our faith. They are added to the Word of the gospel to represent better to our external senses both what He declares to us in His Word and what He does inwardly in our hearts (Article 33, Belgic Confession).

Article 14 mentions not only the preaching of God's Word on Sunday, but also the daily reading of God's Word throughout the week, and the meditation on it. Meditation: this means we should not just quickly read a passage of Scripture, almost out of routine. Instead, we should make time for this, and having read it try to apply it as well through asking questions. Questions like: "What does the LORD want to tell me in this passage?" Perhaps the passage speaks of a beautiful promise to which we may cling. Article 14 speaks not only about promises, but also about threats and exhortations. There is surely a need to hear God's promises, but equally we should also listen to warnings in Scripture. In other words, we should read not just nice and comforting passages, but also passages that at times may cut deeply into our sinful flesh, exposing a sinful life, calling us to repentance. In summary: God causes the saints to persevere in faith and faithfulness through all of Scripture.

April 19

READING: PSALM 63, CANONS OF DORT V, 14

The blessing of meditating on God's Word

"My soul will be satisfied as with fat and rich food, and my mouth will praise you with joyful lips, when I remember you upon my bed, and meditate on you in the watches of the night."
PSALM 63:5-6

God will strengthen our faith by the hearing and reading of His Word and by meditating on it. It will help us in persevering in our faith and through it also become a blessing to others, radiating God's love to them. I think here of what it says in Psalm 1: He who takes his delight in the law of God – which is a reference to Scripture as a whole – meditating on it day and night, shall be like a tree planted by the river, bringing forth its fruits in its season, whose leaves shall not whither. How pleasant it is to sit under such a tree. How pleasant it is to be in the presence of such a person.

Many psalms speak about the blessing of meditating upon God's Word. I think of the verses from Psalm 63, quoted above this meditation. Meditating on God's Word, even in the watches of the night, David rejoices in the fellowship with God. At times when we cannot fall asleep, it can be helpful to focus on God's never-failing care for us. The author of Psalm 77 refers to this as well, verses 4 and 5: "You hold my eyelids open; I am so troubled that I cannot speak. I consider the days of old, the years of long ago".

This is how God wants to bless us when we take the time to meditate on His Word. Article 14 stresses that when doing so, we should not just stick to specific passages of Scripture but also listen to the warnings and admonitions by which God in His love wants to guide and keep us on the road of salvation.

Therefore, let us make time for this important exercise in godliness daily. Minimising it will only be to our spiritual detriment. To persevere in faith to the very end we must faithfully use the means God has provided, also exhorting one another all the more, as it reads in Hebrews 10:25, as we see the Day drawing near – the Day of Christ's return on the clouds of heaven. Who knows how close this will be?

April 20

READING: PSALM 138, CANONS OF DORT V, 15

For the glory of God's Name and for the consolation of the godly

"For you have exalted above all things your name and your word. On the day I called, you answered me; my strength of soul you increased."

PSALM 138:2B-3

Article 15 not only concludes the fifth chapter of the Canons of Dort, but it is also the final article of the Canons as a whole. This last article is a song of praise bringing glory to the Triune God: Father, Son, and Spirit.

This article mentions that the doctrine of the perseverance of the saints and the assurance of it has always been under attack, despite the fact that God has most abundantly revealed all of this in His Word for the glory of His Name and the consolation of the godly.

It is vital to hold on to this comfort, especially because of Satan's fierce attacks on the Word of God, also today. Attacks, not only from the outside world, but also from within the church through all kinds of modern interpretations of Scripture. We can be thankful for having a confession like the Canons of Dort, especially also because of the current rapid increase in Arminianism in many churches. A teaching, which not only robs God of His honour, but it also robs the church of the comfort that salvation is secure in Christ alone.

Article 15 gives a long list of all kinds of attacks, as our fathers saw in their day. Throughout history, these attacks have only become more severe, which Scripture also warns will happen as the end draws near. Behind all of this, we must see Satan attacking the church, the Bride of Christ. Let us keep our eyes open for these attacks and treasure what we have received, also in a confession like the Canons of Dort.

In Answer 54 of the Heidelberg Catechism, we confess that Christ gathers His church, also defending and preserving her by His Spirit and Word to everlasting life. Thus, the church as the Bride of Christ may know herself safe in the arms of the heavenly Bridegroom – safe because of God's preservation. Safe, because of the work of the Triune God to whom alone be all honour and glory forever. Amen.

April 21

READING: EPHESIANS 6:10-20

Persistence in prayer (1)

"Praying at all times..."
EPHESIANS 6:18A

Dealing with the perseverance of the saints, the Canons of Dort stress the importance of prayer. In Article 4 of Chapter V we read the warning that we should constantly watch and pray in order not to be led into temptation. We find the same warning in many of the apostolic letters in the New Testament. Prayer – one could call it the lifeline of faith, since a living faith cannot survive without also living close to God in prayer. This is the reason why, for the next set of meditations, we will focus on how to persevere also in prayer.

In Ephesians 6 which speaks about spiritual warfare, the apostle Paul also emphasises the importance of prayer. He urges his readers: persist in prayer so that you may remain steadfast in faith! This is a warning we too should take to heart, especially considering how difficult it can be at times to truly live our faith in a society that is becoming increasingly antichristian. Spiritually we live in a war zone where we feel the heat of battle daily, even though at times we might think it could still be a lot worse. This all depends on how one looks at things.

In Ephesians 6:12, the apostle speaks about the spiritual forces of evil in the heavenly places. You may have heard the expression, 'something is in the air'. It means you meet it everywhere. You breathe it in wherever you go. Well, this is what Paul is referring to when he speaks about the spiritual forces of evil in the heavenly places. It is in the air, the spiritually polluted air, which one simply cannot escape breathing in. Just to mention one aspect: think of the advertising in the media, which tells us that when it feels good, it is okay. Man is free to choose what he wants. It is the slogan of the society we live in today and one cannot deny that this has its influence also on the church.

How are we supposed to remain standing in this battle? The apostle says: Pray at all times. Cling to God in prayer daily, never doubting that He will provide whatever we are in need of no matter how severe the battle might be.

READING: 1THESSALONIANS 5:12-28

Persistence in prayer (2)

"Praying at all times…"
EPHESIANS 6:18A

Praying at all times! Literally translated, it reads: praying at every right moment. In other words: make sure that the opportunities to pray do not slip through your fingers due to a casual lifestyle, which at times so quickly can happen. Prayer should be a natural and consistent part of our lives. It should not be limited just to fixed timeslots during the day or special occasions only. Instead, we are to be people of prayer. Praying should be fundamental to living our lives for and with the LORD. Praying during the day at work, when you struggle or feel depressed, yet equally thanking God in prayer when enjoying a walk in creation, or out with the boat on the water. LORD, how great is Thy majesty! This does not always need to be a formal prayer. Instead, when spontaneously living with God it will rise from the heart. Prayer, as part of a life in which we walk with God always and everywhere.

The opposite can so easily happen. For example, on a lazy day off or on holidays when breakfast is skipped. Because of this, we did not start the day with prayer asking for God's blessing also when enjoying leisure time or having fun. I think it is not difficult to identify with this. Yet what blessings can we expect when we do not start the day with prayer? Prayer should be foremost in our mind at the beginning of every new day and equally throughout the day.

Praying at all times! This expression is very similar to how Moses taught the Israelite fathers to teach their children the riches of the covenant. In Deuteronomy 6, Moses says: You should do this "when you sit in your house, and when you walk by the way, when you lie down, and when you rise." Well, likewise we should make the most of the opportunities to draw near to God in prayer at the beginning of each day and throughout the day, praising and glorifying God; but also asking Him for His blessings over all that we do, in our work and leisure, and thanking Him for it!

April 23

READING: EPHESIANS 3:14-21

With all prayer and supplication

"Praying at all times in the Spirit, with all prayer and supplication."
EPHESIANS 6:18A

"With all prayer and supplication" – this expression refers to all kinds of prayers, with Paul's letter to the Ephesians itself giving some beautiful examples. Examples that show us something about Paul's own prayer life.

I think of the reading passage for today. In this specific prayer, the apostle asks God to strengthen the Ephesians in their inner being so that Christ would dwell in their hearts through faith. He also prays that God may give them a greater understanding of His incomprehensible love toward them. This prayer shows how the apostle Paul as a real pastor, bore the needs of the sheep entrusted to him in his heart, bringing them daily before God with all prayer and supplication.

With all prayer and supplication – how do we do this? Think of the acrostic word ACTS – which stands for Adoration, Confession, Thanksgiving, and Supplication.

Adoration – this is what prayer should start with, praising God, being aware also to whom we pray, and what a great God we have. This aspect is often forgotten. Adoration: LORD, how glorious is Thy Name in all creation but also in Thy care over our life! Care of which we are totally undeserving. Hence there is also a need for **confession**. Confession – not just generally, but by mentioning sins by name: "Lord, the sinful thought that all of a sudden crossed my mind, that word with which I hurt my brother in Christ, that wrong deed which I knew full well I should not do and yet I did. Lord, when looking into the mirror of Thy Word, I detest myself, knowing how unworthy I am of Thy love. Yet I plead with the sacrifice of Christ, asking Thee for mercy towards me a sinner, cleanse my life and renew it. Do not cast me away from Thy presence but restore to me the joy of Thy salvation" (Psalm 51).

When confessing our sins in this way, also knowing that in Christ they have been forgiven, we will grow in **thankfulness** and also express this in prayer. This also clears the way for humble **supplication**, firstly for others and then for ourselves as well.

April 24

READING: ROMANS 8:26-27

Praying in the Spirit

"Praying at all times in the Spirit …"

EPHESIANS 6:18A

The apostle Paul also says that we must pray in the Spirit. From Romans 8, we learn that the Holy Spirit not only works prayer in us, but also supports us when we pray (verse 26). We need this help. After all, how often are there not moments in our life when we find it difficult to put into words what lives in our hearts? Moments perhaps when we sigh, "Lord, I do not know anymore, it is all so dark, I do not know even what to pray" – indeed no more than a sigh, not of relief, but of complete tiredness!

It is the Holy Spirit working this in us, when amid the darkness we still cry out to God. At times, indeed no more than a sigh. Yet the Spirit with His power supports even this sigh so that it is heard by God and answered. This may give us enormous comfort, even though we do not always feel it inwardly in our hearts.

Praying in the Spirit – this is different than just a wish list to God. Instead, we are to draw near in humbleness as children, who through the Spirit have learnt what a great miracle it is that we may call upon God as Father. We see this even more when we link our prayer to the opening of the Scriptures. By first opening Scripture and then praying we will enrich our prayer life.

Also, we should not just read the Bible but also take the time to meditate on it. This will give direction to our prayer. For example, a promise you read to which you may cling in prayer. At other times, you may read a warning, and while meditating on it a bit more, you realise that the LORD is warning you here. And so you pray: Lord, help me in fighting this sin. This is what praying in the Spirit means. It is living close to God's inspired Word – delving into it as into a goldmine, discovering its treasures, and praying that we may cling to it.

April 25

READING: ROMANS 12:9-13

Keep alert with all perseverance

"To that end, keep alert with all perseverance,
making supplication for all the saints."
EPHESIANS 6:18B

The call to keep alert with all perseverance shows that prayer will not come automatically in our lives. We truly must make time for it each day with determination, in the knowledge that without prayer, we will not be able to stand. We all live busy lives. Yet, do we still know how to withdraw to our inner room in order to bring our needs before the LORD, and this not just by way of a quick prayer but really making time for it?

At times, we go through difficult seasons in our lives during which we feel close to the LORD, close also in prayer. However, when the difficulties have gone, and the sun shines again, the daily routine so quickly takes over. Often the result is that also devotion to prayer slackens. There seems to be less need for it. Yet is this really true? Perhaps in times of prosperity the need for prayer might be more important than in times of adversity. When things go well, we quickly forget our dependence on God. Paul says, be watchful to this end and persist in prayer also then, for the devil is out there to lure you away from God. Strong armour in itself does not help you. Before every battle, we should go on our knees, asking God for help and guidance.

By way of example, think of a situation when you do not feel so steady on your feet – you are almost falling. At such a moment, you like to hold on to something sturdy like a rope to remain standing. Well, in prayer we cling to a rope from heaven, which is our safety belt, our refuge in God. We should put on this spiritual safety belt at the beginning of each day before we do anything else!

Prayer – our spiritual safety belt. Not like the safety belt in the car which is just a routine before you drive off. Instead, a genuine prayer that comes from the heart! Daily, before we do anything else. LORD, keep me safe and close to Thee throughout this day. Be near to me, to all my loved ones, keep them close to Thee and grant that they too may seek this safety with Thee alone: our loved ones, but also all the saints, God's children around the globe. LORD, keep them all safe in Thy almighty arms.

April 26

READING: MATTHEW 6:5-13,
HEIDELBERG CATECHISM, LORD'S DAY 45

Why is prayer necessary for Christians?

"The eyes of the LORD are toward the righteous and his ears toward their cry."

PSALM 34:15

After some meditations on the subject of prayer in general, next we will turn to the section of the Heidelberg Catechism that deals with the theme of prayer, the Lord's Days 45 to 52.

In Lord's Day 45, the first question asked is: "Why is prayer necessary for Christians?" One may think: why this question? After all, who would ever doubt the necessity of prayer? Would a more practical question not have been of more benefit? Yet let us not judge too quickly. The question is not phrased generally about why prayer is necessary, but instead why it is necessary for Christians. For Christians – that is for those who have been anointed with the Spirit of Christ. Because we are Christians, because we belong to Christ, prayer is necessary.

Again, one could say: this is self-evident. After all, which Christian would not pray? It is part of our Christian life. Yet is it? How often does it not happen that there is slackness in prayer, or that prayer has become just a matter of routine? We still pray, yet using words we almost know off by heart our heart is no longer really in it.

No doubt, there will be other times as well; times when we feel very close to God, genuinely praying from the heart. Yet only a few days later, God may seem far away, which in turn affects our prayers negatively. For example, you have asked the Lord already so often that He help you in your battle against a specific sin in your life or to fight a certain character trait, but it does not seem to help. The result can be that we become tired of praying.

The secularisation of today's society can affect our prayer life negatively as well. If due to unemployment we have less income, we visit the social security office. If due to an increasing crime rate, we feel less secure, we speak about what the government should do. Occasionally matters like these may feature in our prayers, but perhaps not regularly.

This clearly shows that the question put to us by the Heidelberg Catechism is valid to teach us the necessity of prayer not just for certain things but for all things, making us realise our total dependence on God in every area of life.

April 27

**READING: PSALM 50:7-15,
HEIDELBERG CATECHISM, LORD'S DAY 45**

Prayer is the most important part of thankfulness

"Offer to God a sacrifice of thanksgiving."
PSALM 50:14A

The most important part of thankfulness! But why then did the Heidelberg Catechism not start with the subject of prayer? The point is that to show thankfulness to God, we first need guidance how to do so. Well, this guidance is found in the Ten Commandments. Through these commandments, God is teaching us: If you want to show thankfulness to Me for all that I have given you – live this way! It will make life wholesome, and it will glorify My name.

However, since we cannot do this of our own strength, we are to ask God for help, wisdom, and strength.

By way of example: The first commandment asks us to give all honour and glory to God alone. Yet how would we ever be able to do this without praying, "Father, hallowed be Thy name"? How would we ever be able to give our whole life to the Lord – as the tenth commandment requires – without that daily prayer, "Father, lead us not into temptation, but deliver us from the evil one"?

When considering prayer as the most important part of our thankfulness, we should think of all the blessings God has bestowed upon us in Christ. One of these blessings is that we may call upon God as our Father. A Father, to whom we may open our hearts in prayer: when there is joy to express thankfulness, when we struggle to ask for help, and likewise when worries overtake us. We may lay it before Father's throne, assured in faith that in heaven we will always find a listening ear. All of this should overwhelm us with thankfulness. Well, this is precisely what the Heidelberg Catechism teaches us when it speaks about prayer as the most important part of our thankfulness.

In many places, Scripture teaches that this thankfulness should come from our hearts. Psalm 50 is an example of this, saying all of creation is from God, and therefore God is not dependent on what we offer Him. Hence, it is not our material contributions that count in the first place or particular tasks by which we serve God. Most importantly, we should thank God daily in genuine humbleness from the heart for all that we have received from Him by grace alone!

April 28

**READING: LUKE 11:5-13,
HEIDELBERG CATECHISM, LORD'S DAY 45**

God promises His grace and the Holy Spirit

"And I tell you, ask, and it will be given to you; seek, and you will find; knock, and it will be opened to you."

LUKE 11:9

In Answer 116 of the Heidelberg Catechism, it reads: "God will give His grace and the Holy Spirit only to those who constantly and with heartfelt longing ask Him for these gifts and thank Him for them." This is why prayer is necessary. God requires it, so that we will acknowledge Him as the only fountain of all good. Of all good – hence, we should involve God in all the things in our lives, leaving nothing undiscussed with our great Father in heaven. If we truly do so, we will never rush our prayers but take the time for them, considering prayer a life-line to hold on to firmly.

We must be careful never to neglect prayer, which so quickly can happen. Think of our first prayer in the morning, which usually is prayed at the breakfast table. Yet, what happens when breakfast is skipped: for example, when we have to leave early for work or when during a holiday we have time to sleep in. In cases like these, prayer is so easily skipped. This means we start the day without thanking God for His protection throughout the night, nor do we ask Him for a blessing and protection for a new day. However, this essential prayer should not depend on whether we have breakfast or not. To overcome this: why not start the day with God as the first thing when waking up, similarly to closing the day with God before we go to sleep. In a living relationship with God, we will long for these moments to pour out our hearts before our Father in heaven.

As our heavenly Father, God longs for this as well. As a true Father, He takes an interest in all that we do: in our joys, but also in our struggles. All of these things we may bring in prayer before Him, assured of a listening ear in heaven, since God as our Father is eager to answer all of our prayers for the sake of Christ His Son, our Lord and Saviour.

April 29

READING: LAMENTATIONS 3:22-33

Wait for the LORD (1)

"Truly, I say to you, whoever says to this mountain, 'Be taken up and thrown into the sea,' and does not doubt in his heart, but believes that what he says will come to pass, it will be done for him. Therefore I tell you, whatever you ask in prayer, believe that you have received it, and it will be yours."
MARK 11:23-24

Scripture teaches in more than one place that whenever we bring our needs before the LORD in true humbleness and sincerity, not only will we find a listening ear in heaven, but we may also have the assurance that God will answer our prayers. In the text above this meditation, it reads: It will be done, it will be yours. Yet, what if contrary to what the Lord Jesus says, we have the feeling that those mountains have not moved? Things weigh heavily on our hearts. In prayer, we have brought it before the LORD, yet there seems to be no change.

We know the LORD will answer our prayers in His time. Yet, to accept this can be a real struggle at times. The result can be that we start to despair or even worse rebel and give up on the LORD. We have prayed so fervently, and yet there seems to be no change. Why does God not act, for example, in cases where children have walked away from the LORD? We pray and pray, but there remains a hardening of the heart. Why LORD? Think of childless couples, who would dearly love to have children, others who have one child and would love to have more children, or single people who would like to get married, but do not see their heart's desire fulfilled. Do all of these prayers go unheard?

When struggling with questions like these, we should try to bring our restless hearts to rest by giving our struggles to the LORD. We may say that we do so, but often we keep carrying these burdens. However, this creates only further unrest in our hearts. We have to let go by trusting the LORD fully with His plan for our lives. This means, each day again, we have to learn to wait for the LORD.

April 30

READING: PSALM 27

Wait for the LORD (2)

"Wait for the Lord!"

PSALM 27:14A

Psalm 27 shows us a struggling child of God, who the one moment feels very close to God: "The LORD is my light and my salvation, whom shall I fear?" Next, however, he wonders where God is: "Cast me not off, forsake me not, O God of my salvation." This swaying between different thoughts, different feelings, like the pendulum of a clock can be found in other psalms as well, for example, in Psalm 42. Yet, we also see that amidst these struggles, the authors keep clinging to God, keep waiting for the LORD.

Waiting for the LORD, crying out our heart before the LORD, our anguished feelings: "LORD, it is all so hard!" There is no need to hide this from God. After all, God knows how we feel, even before we tell Him. Moreover, God is our Father, who loves us. With Him, we will always find a listening ear, even though at times we might have the feeling that our prayers go unanswered. However, this is no more than just a feeling from our side. The reality is, God is still there: my Father, the faithful God of the covenant, whose love never fails and who will cause His promises to come true. To these promises we may cling, no matter how low we might feel at times.

David too clings to these promises of God, when in verse 8, he speaks about seeking God's face. God's face – in New Testament terms, this is God's love revealed in Jesus Christ, through whom God's face shines upon us. Through Christ, God has become our Father again. To this we may cling. That is why in the depths of life, there is still hope, restoration. Therefore, so David says at the end of this psalm, verse 14: "Wait for the LORD!"

In the context of Psalm 27, it is not difficult to understand what this 'waiting for the LORD' means. It is a waiting full of expectation, also knowing that this waiting will never be in vain. It is a confession of faith, knowing God is in control. He will provide. It is not a waiting for someone who in the end cannot do anything. On the contrary, it is a waiting full of assurance, no matter how difficult the present circumstances might be.

May 1

READING: PSALM 40:1-5

Wait for the LORD (3)

"I waited patiently for the Lord; he inclined to me and heard my cry."

PSALM 40:1

Waiting for the LORD is a waiting full of assurance. It is surrendering yourself, your whole life with all its worries, to Him who is all powerful and then let go of it, even though in the end the outcome might be different from what we would like to see. Waiting for the LORD means, whatever the future holds, I can have peace, for God will always work for my good.

Such waiting for the LORD requires a lot of patience. In Psalm 40:1, David writes: "I waited patiently for the LORD…" Waiting – this is not something that runs in our veins. To wait, to let go, knowing we are not in control. Instead, the LORD is. This is hard for us. Hence, 'to wait for the LORD' is a learning curve for all of us. Likewise, it was so for many a child of God in the time of Scripture. I think of Moses, who had to wait for 40 years before the LORD deemed him fit to deliver His people from Egypt. From a human point of view, one may wonder, why did this have to take so long? Yet Moses needed this time according to God's plan. He had to wait for the LORD.

Waiting can be one of the most challenging exercises in faith, especially for those of us who by nature are very impatient. Just wait – however, not in an inactive way. Instead, we have to wait actively in faith. Much of our trouble is that often we cannot wait for the fruit to ripen. Instead, we insist on picking them while they are still green. We find it difficult to wait for answers to our prayers, not realising that it may take many years for the things we pray for to be prepared. We are encouraged to walk with God. However, at times God may walk very slowly with us.

This may cause us to start doubting, wondering whether God really hears us. We find this also in Psalm 42, when the author cries out: "Why do I go mourning? Why is there this breaking of my bones?" Yet the author ends with: 'Hope in God.' This means: leave it to God, the Creator of heaven and earth, for whom nothing is impossible. With Him, our lives are always safe.

May 2

READING: ISAIAH 40:27-31

Wait for the LORD (4)

"Be strong, and let your heart take courage;
wait for the LORD."

PSALM 27:14B

Waiting for the LORD also requires the right attitude. In Psalm 27, David writes we must be strong, strong in faith, while our hearts should take courage. These are two necessary attitudes in waiting for the LORD. Once I read: "The fruitfulness of our time in God's waiting room is very dependent upon our attitudes and mindset in the process. Fretting and pacing not only fail to speed things up; they also result in emotional turmoil. Yet the LORD has a better way."

So what kind of attitude does God require? Waiting for the LORD requires patience. Yet this patience will only become ours when first we have truly submitted our lives to the LORD, firmly believing that He always has our best interests at heart, trusting Him also with His divine method and timing. When we do this, there will be no maneuvering, no manipulating, nor any rushing ahead from our side.

Fully trusting God also means relying on His secure promises alone. While waiting, God's Word should be our only secure anchor. Because of this, one of the wisest things we can do is to read Scriptures every day. It will bring stability to our lives. It will give direction also for prayer. Reading God's wonderful promises, how He cared for His people throughout the ages, will help us to cling to these same promises which were also given to us.

An example of such a prayer can be found in Psalm 57:2, "I cry out to God Most High, to God who fulfills His purpose for me." His purpose – for my daily work, for concerns beyond my control; His plan for children we worry about; His purpose concerning my battle with cancer not knowing what the outcome will be. While waiting for the LORD, we may find rest knowing that God will accomplish His plans for our lives perfectly.

This is the kind of waiting the LORD requires, and such waiting will also bear fruit. Having submitted ourselves to God, holding on firmly to the promises the LORD has given us in His Word, we can confidently watch God's will unfold in full trust that God knows exactly what to do, and this also always at the right time. We should live in that trust as we patiently wait for the LORD. That will give inward rest and peace!

May 3

READING: ISAIAH 55:6-11

Wait for the LORD (5)

"For as the heavens are higher than the earth, so are my ways higher than your ways and my thoughts than your thoughts."
ISAIAH 55:9

Wait for the LORD. Trust and obey. Why is it often so hard for us to live this way in childlike faith, walking with God, holding His hand? One of the reasons is that all too often we live hurried lifestyles in an action-oriented society. Because of this, it seems to become harder to create a quiet time with the LORD, bringing our needs before Him, asking God for direction with his Word open in our hands: half an hour a day! Just half an hour! And yet we find it hard to create time for it. We hurry on to the next commitment we have booked in our diary. Our schedules are full. Because of this, spending uninterrupted, unhurried time, seeking the mind of Christ seems impossible. And yet this is the only way to hear God's voice as it is found in His Word to give us direction in our waiting.

Another hindrance is that we often have a short-term perspective. The society we live in does not help us in this respect. Fast food restaurants, express checkouts, and drive-through coffee shops are proof of the "have-it-now" mentality in our society. We want everything quickly. However, there is no fast track to spiritual maturity in learning to wait for the Lord, which is crucial in developing a godly character.

Waiting for the LORD, taking God at His Word – it is the only way to find rest and peace, even if the journey of our life goes through deep valleys. Also then, we must learn to accept this from Father's hand and continue to wait for God to finish His plan with our lives.

This may take time. By way of example: we sow the seed, till the ground, and then wait and trust that God will cause the growth. We understand this principle when it comes to planting a field. Yet, we need to learn the same lesson concerning our prayer life. It takes time for God to answer prayers. Moreover, as it reads in Isaiah 55: God's ways are higher than our ways, and His thoughts than our thoughts. Trusting in this truth, leave it to God, and wait for Him!

May 4

**READING: PSALM 145,
HEIDELBERG CATECHISM, LORD'S DAY 45**

A God-pleasing prayer (1)

"The Lord is near to all who call on him,
to all who call on him in truth."

PSALM 145:18

After several meditations on the subject of 'waiting for the LORD', especially in the context of prayer, we will now turn back to the section on prayer in the Heidelberg Catechism to see what belongs to a prayer that pleases God and is heard by Him (Question 117). This question shows that not every prayer is pleasing to God. So, how can we pray in a way that is pleasing to God? Answer 117 reads: "First we must from the heart call upon the one true God only, who has revealed himself in His Word, for all that He has commanded us to pray."

This answer makes it clear that we cannot pray without also opening our Bible. Before we draw near to God in prayer, first we should listen to what God has to say to us in His Word. Many families, therefore, have the custom after having finished a meal and before closing off in prayer, that they first open God's Word. This is a good custom, not only for closing off our meals, but also when closing off the day with the Lord personally, at night. Also then, it is helpful first to take the time to open God's Word in which the LORD speaks to us about His promises and commands. This will give direction to our prayer, helping us to also give God and His kingdom priority, thanking and praising God for His manifold blessings and holding on to God's promises and commands in opening our hearts to Him. This is what a sincere prayer should be like. This also means we should take the time to meditate on the passage we have chosen to read. All of this is essential for a genuine willingness to listen to what God has to say to us.

When praying in this way, one will also have less difficulty with so-called unanswered prayers. Struggling with these so-called unanswered prayers can have its root in praying too selfishly at times, and because of it having the feeling that God does not hear us. Yet when praying with an open Bible and clinging to what God has promised us, we may have the firm assurance that no prayer will go unheard nor unanswered.

May 5

READING: DANIEL 9:16-19,
HEIDELBERG CATECHISM, LORD'S DAY 45

A God-pleasing prayer (2)

"For we do not present our pleas before you because of our righteousness but because of your great mercy."
DANIEL 9:18B

Concerning prayers that are pleasing to God and are heard by Him, Answer 117 of the Heidelberg Catechism also mentions: "We must thoroughly know our need and misery so that we may humble ourselves before God." This touches on the attitude with which to draw near to God in prayer. Because of our sins, we are unworthy to receive anything from God. Therefore, humbleness is required, acknowledging what a great miracle it is each day anew that God still wants to care for us, providing us with all that we need. This humbleness should be right there at the beginning of our prayer in the way we address God.

In society, we meet people who stand up for all kinds of rights they claim to have. Yet prayer is different. We do not make any demands on God. But in humbleness, we fold our hands, knowing that we do not deserve anything. This humbleness is reflected in many of the prayers we read in the Psalms. It is also reflected in the prayer of Daniel, recorded in Chapter 9 of his prophecies, where Daniel concludes with these words, "We do not present our pleas before Thee because of our righteous deeds, but because of Thy great mercy." It is after this confession that Daniel continues, saying: "O Lord, hear! O Lord, forgive! O Lord, pay attention and act!" One can only pray this way when indeed thoroughly knowing our need and misery.

Our need and misery – this is not the need we often think of when praying to God. When it comes to need, often we only think of sickness, hardship, affliction, and difficulties. All too often, it is particularly because of these things that we cry out to God. Of course, when drawing near to God in prayer, we may lay these needs before God's throne as well. Yet the Catechism, addressing our needs, probes deeper. It points to the cause of all hunger and misery, which is sin! This is our real need, which is something we should never forget when addressing God in prayer. It makes one humble. And as it reads in Answer 117, only such a prayer is pleasing to God and is heard by Him.

May 6

**READING: 2 CORINTHIANS 12:1-10,
HEIDELBERG CATECHISM, LORD'S DAY 45**

A God-pleasing prayer (3)

"But he said to me, 'My grace is sufficient for you.'"

2 CORINTHIANS 12:9A

As to a prayer which pleases God and is heard by Him, Answer 117 of the Heidelberg Catechism also mentions, "We must rest on this firm foundation that, although we do not deserve it, God will certainly hear our prayer for the sake of Christ our Lord, as He has promised in His Word."

God will certainly hear our prayers and will certainly answer them, even though we may struggle with this. Why we struggle can be a result of our attitude towards prayer. For example, at times, there can be an element of self-centredness concerning our prayers. Yet God wants us to pray in true faith, trusting Him with His plan for our life.

The fact that God promises to answer our prayers does not mean that God will always give us what we have asked for. God may also answer our prayers in a way different from what we had hoped for. The apostle Paul prayed in all sincerity that God would take away the thorn in his flesh. This thorn made life difficult for Paul, whatever it might have been. It hindered Paul in the execution of his apostleship. His prayer was a sincere pleading with God. Yet God did not take this thorn away. Instead, He said to Paul, "My grace is sufficient for you." In other words, I will give you what you need to carry out your task as an apostle even though there is a thorn in your flesh that hinders you. Paul too had to trust God with His divine plan for his life.

My grace is sufficient for you! This is a promise to which we too may cling, when going through trying times. When in genuine faith, we keep clinging to God, we will never be put to shame. Sincere prayers prayed in true faith will never be a leap in the dark. Instead, we may pray with confidence that God will cause His promises to come true in our life, no matter what befalls us. In prayer, we may lay our weak lives in the hands of our great Father in heaven, who alone knows what is good for us. In Him, we may put our trust.

May 7

**READING: JAMES 1:5-12,
HEIDELBERG CATECHISM, LORD'S DAY 45**

What to pray

"Every good gift and every perfect gift is from above, coming down from the Father of lights, with whom there is no variation or shadow due to change."
JAMES 1:17

One of the last questions in Lord's Day 45 deals with the content of our prayer: what are the things we should pray for? Even more importantly, what are the things God wants us to pray for? The answer says that we should pray for all the things we need for body and soul. This means, concerning everything in life, we should look on high and bring it in prayer before God.

All the things we need for body and soul. Yet how do we determine these needs? They may vary from person to person. So how do we decide what to bring before the LORD? When walking with God in every step we take, the answer to this question will not be complicated. Just speak with God in prayer about the things that are on your mind. As Father, God wants to hear this – to hear from us not only when we are bowed down by pain, sorrow, or hardship, but also when there is joy. All of this will deepen our relationship with the LORD. It will also bear as fruit that our love towards the LORD will grow in such a way that our wishes no longer come first in prayer, but instead the honour of God's Name, God's kingdom, and God's will for our life, as the Lord Jesus taught His disciples.

The prayer which the Lord Jesus taught His disciples serves as a model of how to pray, also when using different words. It shows what should have priority when drawing near to God in prayer. It will take effort to get these priorities right. It needs the renewing work of the Holy Spirit. He is there to guide us also in prayer so that – as the apostle Paul writes to the Philippians – in everything by prayer and supplication, with thanksgiving, we let our requests be made known to God. When praying in this way, we will find peace even amidst difficulties, hardships, and sorrow. This is the peace of God, which surpasses all understanding, which will guard our hearts and our minds through Christ Jesus, our Lord.

May 8

**READING: HEBREWS 12:18-29,
HEIDELBERG CATECHISM, LORD'S DAY 46**

Worshipping God with reverence and awe

"Let us offer to God acceptable worship, with reverence and awe."

HEBREWS 12:28B

Do you ever give it thought what a great miracle it is that we may address God as 'our Father' in prayer? As with so many things regarding our faith, also this – I am afraid – we so easily take more or less for granted. When addressing God as 'Father' do we still realise whom we are addressing? God, the Almighty One, Creator of heaven and earth, who is the Holy One, who loathes all unholiness, all unholiness also in our lives! And yet this great God allows us, sinful creatures, to address Him as Father. A great miracle indeed!

Answer 120 of the Heidelberg Catechism highlights this, saying that Christ has commanded us to address God as 'Our Father': "to awaken in us at the very beginning of our prayer that childlike reverence and trust toward God which should be basic to our prayer." Reverence is a word our modern society no longer knows. Think of the lack of reverence towards people in authority, let alone that people would show reverence towards God. It is the opposite, instead. God's Name is abused by many daily. No respect for God whatsoever. Yet God asks us to stand in awe of His Name, always to use His holy Name with reverence and awe.

Today's Scripture reading refers to what took place at Mount Sinai, where the Israelites stood in fear when God appeared to them. We do not feel that same fear when attending a worship service. There is no need for this either, since the veil was taken away on Good Friday. We may draw near to God in prayer without any fear in full confidence. Yet this should not become so common to us that we no longer stand in awe.

For this very reason, the catechism mentions that 'reverence towards God', 'childlike reverence' is essential to prayer. Also in this area, we have society against us. It is no longer a matter of custom that children address their parents with reverence. Let us be careful that this does not start to affect our families, for the result can so easily be that there is no longer real awe towards God. We may address Holy God as our Father. Yet we should never take this for granted. Instead, we should make sure that we always offer our prayers to God with reverence and awe.

May 9

**READING: ISAIAH 63:15-64:12,
HEIDELBERG CATECHISM, LORD'S DAY 46**

God – our Father!

"You, O LORD, are our Father, our Redeemer from of old is your Name."
ISAIAH 63:16B

God's people living in the Old Testament era also addressed God as 'our Father'. An example of this we find in today's Scripture reading. A prayer sent up to God by the Israelites in exile. A prayer of confession of sins and a request for mercy.

The confession of sins we find in Chapter 64:5b, "Behold you were angry, and we sinned …" I also think of verse 6b: "All our righteous deeds are like a polluted garment." Yet at the same time, they also prayed for mercy, addressing God specifically as 'our Father': "You, O LORD, are our Father, our Redeemer from old is your Name." With these last words, they call to mind the former days, when in mercy God saved them from their bondage in Egypt. Calling this very beginning to mind, the Israelites in exile ask the LORD to deliver them again pleading: O LORD, Thou art the God of the covenant. LORD, where are Thy zeal and Thy might, the yearning of Thy heart and Thy compassion? Return for the sake of Thy servants, the tribes of Thy heritage, for Thou art the One who once called us by Thy glorious Name. LORD, we do not deserve Thy love. Yet, all this does not alter the fact that we are Thy people, does it?

As God's children living in the New Testament era, we too may take this Father-Name of God on our lips. We too may plead by recalling that very beginning, the day on which God adopted us for His children and heirs, the day of our baptism, when God declared to us: I establish an eternal covenant with you and because of that covenant I will take care of you, always. True, as it also happens today that children of God stray away – stray away from Father. However, when there is true repentance, we may always return to God, especially since He is our Father.

Think of the parable of the prodigal son. The father in this parable cannot forget his child. When this son returns full of repentance, the father gladly accepts him in love again, for he is still his son. Whatever had happened, it did not undo the relationship between father and son. This father still cherished his son in love. Well, we may find this same love with God whenever we call on Him as our Father in Christ in sincere faith.

May 10

READING: HEBREWS 10:19-25

God has become our Father through Christ

"Let us draw near with a true heart in full assurance of faith with our hearts sprinkled clean from an evil conscience and our bodies washed with pure water".

HEBREWS 10:22

God has become our Father through Christ. Through His atoning sacrifice, Christ re-opened the way to God's throne for us. Whenever we draw near to God as our Father in prayer we plead with this sacrifice. Therefore, we will never plead in vain. In the Form for Baptism it reads: "And if we sometimes through weakness fall into sin, we must not despair of God's mercy". Why not? Because we have an eternal covenant with God, which was sealed at our baptism.

It can happen that because of our sins we drift away from God, which often affects our prayers negatively. We still pray, but no longer from the heart. They are just words! Prayer no longer has any real meaning for us. We should never let it get this far in our lives. Instead, at the end of every day, we should lay our lives before God including all the sins and weaknesses we struggle with. Bring it before the LORD through Christ who reconciled us with God by sacrificing His own life in our place. Because of Christ's precious sacrifice, we may come to God each day anew, no matter what sins we have committed. When there is true repentance, there is never any need to despair of God's mercy.

Through Christ, God has become our Father again. Through Christ – this also means it is not the pleasant-sounding words of our prayer nor our faith which makes God willing to listen to us, but only the blood of Christ. In the letter to the Hebrews, Christ is called the great Priest over the house of God, who by His priestly intercession continues to open the way to God for us. Therefore – so the author of this letter writes in Chapter 10:22: "Let us draw near with a true heart in full assurance of faith, having our hearts sprinkled from an evil conscience and our bodies washed with pure water." This is how we are allowed to draw near to God without doubting whether our Father in heaven will lend His ear to our prayer. For no matter how much we have incurred God's displeasure because of our sins, when there is true repentance we may still draw near to Him, fully assured that He will open His fatherly heart to us.

May 11

**READING: ROMANS 8:12-17,
HEIDELBERG CATECHISM, LORD'S DAY 46**

Adopted children

"…you have received the Spirit of adoption as sons, by whom we cry, 'Abba! Father!'"
ROMANS 8:15B

We are very privileged in that we may address God as Father, knowing that He will care for us always. These are riches beyond our human comprehension. Yes, who of us can comprehend that despite the many sins there are in our lives, God still loves us and cares for us each day anew? Who of us can understand that though we transgress God's commandments daily, we still may call upon Him as 'Our Father'? This is a miracle, indeed!

Since this is beyond our human comprehension, at times doubt might arise in our heart whether God will hear us. Yet, there is no need for such doubts. God's promises are sure and trustworthy because of the blood of Christ. And still, at times doubt does crop up.

The LORD also wants to help us in overcoming this doubt. In Romans 8:15, the apostle Paul writes: "For you did not receive the spirit of slavery to fall back into fear again, but you have received the Spirit of adoption as sons, by whom we cry, 'Abba! Father!'" God Himself through His Spirit wants to persuade us to call upon Him, taking our fear away.

This is the Holy Spirit, about whom Paul writes in verse 16 of this same chapter: "He Himself bears witness with our spirit that we are children of God." The Holy Spirit dwells in us to make us living members of Christ. In doing so, He also bears witness with our spirit, or more precisely to our spirit that we are children of God, lest we despair because of the many sins there are in our life, every day anew.

The Spirit bears witness to our spirit. How does the Spirit do this? Through the Word of God! This shows again how important it is to read from our Bible daily, as a family but also personally. For it is through His Word that God testifies to us Who He is and what we as His children may expect from Him. It is true that God's Word also points us to our sins, yet with the aim that we may confess them before our great Father in heaven. It is in this way that by the reading of Scripture, the Spirit wants to strengthen and nourish our faith so that we may live from the riches of it.

May 12

**READING: 1 KINGS 8:22-30,
HEIDELBERG CATECHISM, LORD'S DAY 46**

A heavenly Father

"O LORD, God of Israel, there is no God like you, in heaven above or on earth beneath…"

1 KINGS 8:23A

In Answer 121 of the Heidelberg Catechism, it reads that when addressing God as our Father 'in heaven' it will teach us never to think of God's heavenly majesty in an earthly manner. King Solomon, praying at the dedication of the temple, was fully aware of this when he prayed the following words, I Kings 8:27: "But will God indeed dwell on the earth? Behold, heaven and the highest heaven cannot attain you; how much less this house that I have built". God wanted to dwell among His people in the temple. Yet Solomon also acknowledges that God is too great to dwell in a house made with hands. When reading this beautiful prayer, it teaches us to always be aware of the greatness of God, His majesty, and holiness, whenever we draw near to God in prayer.

God is our heavenly Father, and yet He is not far away. Solomon speaks about the eyes of God. In other places of Scripture, we read about the ears of God. Of course, this does not mean that God has eyes and ears like we have. However, it does highlight that God sees us and hears us wherever we are and in whatever circumstances we find ourselves. In this way, God is always near to us.

Children like it when their father or mother has an eye or an ear for them. It shows that as parents, they are interested in what their children do. Well, this is how King Solomon speaks about the eyes of God. As our heavenly Father, God has the interests of us His children at heart. We may be confident of this. God knows our needs, our difficulties, and the hardships we go through at times. This may give us tremendous peace: my Father in heaven knows, so I no longer have to worry about it. These are the riches of prayer, as it reads in Answer 121 of the Heidelberg Catechism: God almighty is our Father, who with His power will provide us with all that we need for body and soul. In this trust, we may live each day.

May 13

**READING: PSALM 99,
HEIDELBERG CATECHISM, LORD'S DAY 47**

The LORD our God is Holy (1)

"Exalt the LORD our God; Worship at his footstool! Holy is He!"

PSALM 99:5

God is our Father, yet at the same time, He is and remains holy God, who hates sin. We know this. Yet, are we also always conscious of this? Conscious, so that it hurts when God's holiness is mocked or when His holy Name is blasphemed? Are we really hurting when this happens? I am afraid that this hurt is not always there. For example, when watching a movie or when listening to music. Sometimes it seems that we have simply accepted it as normal that not everyone honours God's name. Some do, others do not. That is the way it is. We can do nothing about it, can we?

The result is that this matter does not receive attention in our prayers either, at least not very often. There are other priorities which weigh much heavier on our mind than the holiness of God's name: matters like food and drink, health and work, etc. Yet, the remarkable thing is that when Christ taught His disciples how to pray, He said: When you pray, first you should say – above anything else – "Father, hallowed be Thy Name."

What is the meaning of this petition? In many places, Scripture teaches that God is Holy. Great and awesome is His Name, Psalm 99:3. Nothing can be added to this: perfect holiness. The point, however, is: God also wants all men to acknowledge this holiness. Well, this is what we pray when taking the first petition on our lips, "Father, hallowed be Thy Name."

When praying this petition, as God's children, we pray for the vindication of Father's Name. We pray for the vindication of the holiness of God in an unholy world. For the vindication of God's holiness also in our personal life.

Yes, in our personal life, so that once again we may show the image of God in which He created man with the aim – as it reads in Answer 6 of the Heidelberg Catechism – that we might praise and glorify God. Lord's Day 47 uses these very same words where it says that when praying the first petition we ask the LORD to so direct our lives – all thoughts, words, and deeds – that His Name is always honoured and praised by us.

May 14

**READING: ISAIAH 6:1-5,
HEIDELBERG CATECHISM, LORD'S DAY 47**

The LORD our God is Holy (2)

*"Holy, holy, holy is the LORD of hosts; the
whole earth is full of his glory!"*

ISAIAH 6:3B

In prayer, we may address God with that intimate name 'Father', assuring us of God's love and care for us. God is our Father! Yet, even though we may address God as our Father, we should still do this in the awareness that God is holy. A question that could be raised is whether this holiness of God is not in conflict with the intimate relationship by which we may call upon God as our Father. Whoever says 'Father' feels close to God. Yet, when thinking of God's holiness, one may feel a certain distance.

The prophet Isaiah felt this very strongly when God commissioned him to his task. In a vision, Isaiah sees the LORD sitting upon a throne high and lifted up, while the train of His robe filled the temple. Surrounding the LORD, he sees seraphim, angels full of glory, who are calling to one another, "Holy, holy, holy is the LORD of hosts, the whole earth is full of His glory." Praising the LORD, these seraphim draw attention to one of God's most distinctive characteristics: His holiness. Yes, this whole vision in Isaiah 6 points to nothing other than God's holiness, majesty, and fullness of glory.

All of this overwhelms Isaiah to the extent that he can think of nothing else but his own unholiness. He cries out: "I am lost, for I am a man of unclean lips, and I dwell amid a people of unclean lips." Yes, when considering the holiness of God, who can dwell in His presence?

At times, this fear can also take hold of us. God is holy, while we are unholy. When thinking about this, is it not dangerous for sinful children of God to pray: "Father, hallowed be Thy Name!"? Thankfully, the answer to this question is a definite 'No'! For, even though God as holy God is exalted far above the unholiness of this present world, this does not mean that God wants to have nothing to do with us sinful creatures. On the contrary, though holy, God still wants to confide in those who love Him, even despite of all the unholiness there is in our lives. How is this possible? The answer is: Christ's holiness covers our unholiness. How amazing this is!

May 15

**READING: ISAIAH 6:1-7,
HEIDELBERG CATECHISM, LORD'S DAY 47**

God's mercy

"And he touched my mouth and said: 'Behold, this has touched your lips; your guilt is taken away, and your sin atoned for.'"
ISAIAH 6:7

God's holiness did not consume Isaiah. Instead, one of the seraphim flew to Isaiah, and with a burning coal taken from the altar, he touched Isaiah's mouth, cleansing him from his unholiness, thereby enabling Isaiah to take up his task as prophet in the service of holy God.

Isaiah 6, thus, points not only to God's holiness, but also to God's mercy, which sounds through in the commission which Isaiah receives in verse 9: "Go and say to this people: 'Keep on hearing, but do not understand; keep on seeing, but do not perceive.'"

What do these somewhat paradoxical words mean? By way of example, think of a father saying to a stubborn child, "If this is what you want, there is no place in this house for you any longer. If you do not want to obey, you have to leave!" Of course, when saying this, such a father still hopes that the child will not leave home. By way of a paradox, he makes a last appeal so that this child may listen.

Well, this is how Isaiah is commissioned by God to make a last appeal to Israel, this stubborn child of God. In His mercy, God did not write Israel off. His holiness had not as yet consumed Israel. Instead, in holy jealousy God still had the redemption of those in mind whom He in sovereign love had chosen to be His own. Thus, though holy, God still wants to be near to His people.

God's holiness can indeed be a consuming fire. It destroyed Pharaoh and his entire host in the Red Sea, but at the same time, God's own people, Israel, went through the midst of the sea on dry ground, of which our baptism is a sign. For us, therefore, there is no need either to be frightened by the holiness of God or to be afraid of taking the first petition on our lips. For we do so after having said, 'Father'. It is true: God is holy. Yet this does not take anything away from the intimacy of the Father-name of God. As our Father, God wants to hold on to us, keeping us in His love.

May 16

**READING: REVELATION 15,
HEIDELBERG CATECHISM, LORD'S DAY 47**

Hallowed be Thy Name (1)

"Who will not fear, O Lord, and glorify your name?
For you alone are holy. All nations will come and worship
you, for your righteous acts have been revealed."

REVELATION 15:4

"Hallowed be Thy Name." With this petition, we pray for the vindication of God's holiness in a world full of unholiness. God is holy. Yet sinful human beings can tarnish and violate the splendour of the holy Name of God. Godless powers set in motion by hell itself darken the glory of God's Name in this present world.

By taking the first petition on our lips, we pray for counter-forces from heaven to fight this darkening of God's glorious Name. Father, hallowed be Thy Name – that is Father, vindicate Thy holiness by destroying the powers of hell so that Thy glorious Name may receive all honour; may receive all honour also in my personal life. Yes, Father, teach us as Thy children to stand up for Thy Name; to stand up for Thy Name amidst a society in which Thy holy Name is blasphemed and mocked almost everywhere.

God does not tolerate His holy Name being profaned. In praying "Father, hallowed be Thy Name", we pray that God may indeed burn away all that profanes His holy Name. Now just think about what this means in a world full of sin: "Father, burn away everything that cannot exist before Thee, let Thy Name be hallowed." Yet at the same time, we also pray: "LORD burn away from my personal life all that casts dishonour on Thy Name." Indeed, it is as serious as this!

One may wonder that if it is as serious as this, is it then not dangerous to pray this petition? The answer to this question is a definite no. After all, God does not seek the destruction of our life as such, but the destruction of our sinful life so that more and more we may hate and flee from sin and with love and delight may live according to God's will.

Father, hallowed be Thy Name. This is indeed a very serious prayer. Yet within God's covenant, it is also a very comforting prayer. For, within the covenant relationship we have with God, we do not pray for our personal destruction, but we pray that God will burn away all remaining sin from our life, so that our life may become more dedicated to Him.

May 17

**READING: PSALM 8,
HEIDELBERG CATECHISM, LORD'S DAY 47**

Hallowed be Thy Name (2)

"O LORD, our Lord, how majestic is
your name in all the earth!"

PSALM 8:9

Yesterday we saw that the fire of God's holiness is not meant to destroy, but to purify. God wants to cleanse this world and also our lives, so that once again our lives may serve the aim for which God had created them, namely to praise and glorify Him.

Paradise restored! More precisely, on the new earth life will be even more full than it originally was in the Garden of Eden. After all, at that time there was still the possibility of falling into sin. Yet on the new earth, that possibility will no longer be there. The new earth will be a place where righteousness dwells forever. On that day what is said in Psalm 8 will come true in perfect form, "O LORD, our Lord, how majestic is Thy Name in all the earth". Once again, creation will praise God in perfect harmony.

We read this also in Hebrews 2. In quoting Psalm 8, the author refers to God putting everything in subjection under man's feet. At present we do not see this. Yet, so the author writes, we see Jesus crowned with glory and honour. Yes, our Saviour is already there where we too will come, sharing in that same honour and glory, reigning with Him over all creatures. Reigning with Christ over an earth where God's Name no longer is mocked or abused, but glorified and praised by each and every one of us!

From the sermon delivered by the apostle Peter at Pentecost we know that this will come true through blood, fire, and vapour of smoke. These words refer to God's judgment as also described in the Book of Revelation. Through these judgements God shows that He does not tolerate any abuse of His holy Name. As we see these judgments unfold, it may cause us at times to tremble with fear. Yet at the same time we have the comfort that through these judgements God will come to the day that His Name will be glorified by all mankind and the whole earth will be full of the holiness of God. In the prophecies of Zechariah it reads: On that day, it shall be engraved even on the bells of the horses, "Holiness to the LORD." This is the glorious perspective of the first petition.

May 18

**READING: PSALM 47,
HEIDELBERG CATECHISM, LORD'S DAY 48**

The coming of God's kingdom

"For the LORD, the Most High, is to be feared, a great king over all the earth."

PSALM 47:2

With the second petition, we pray for the coming of God's kingdom. However, what do we mean when we pray this? After all, God is king, and He also rules as king. Many psalms in the Old Testament highlight this as a great comfort for God's people. God rules over all of creation. He has the whole world in His hand – so completely, that without His will no human being, no animal, no power whatsoever can so much as move. Even the devil and his henchmen are only instruments in God's hand. They too have to submit themselves to God's sovereign rule. In most instances, this is done unknowingly; at times, even in rebellion against the Lord. Unbelievers do not want to acknowledge God's kingship over this world, let alone over their own life. In self-deceit, they think they can do what they want. Yet without knowing it, they still execute God's will.

However, this is not the kingship God wants: people, who without giving it a thought, without understanding what they are doing, at times even in rebellion, do what God wants them to do. This does not bring any honour to God. God's Name is not hallowed, and His kingship is not acknowledged.

Instead, God wants to be feared. He wants people to sing praises to Him as the King of all the earth. This is how, in the beginning, God created man. This is how in Paradise, before the fall into sin, man served God in love and obedience, glorifying God's Name. God is looking for this acknowledgement again.

This is why in Paradise, after the fall into sin, God promised that the Messiah would come, in and through whom God would restore His kingship like it was in Paradise. This is why, as a herald of the coming Christ, John the Baptist preached the message: "Repent, for the kingdom of heaven is at hand!" During His public ministry, the Lord Jesus made a beginning with the restoration of life, which was broken by sin. Lost children were brought home again, home to Father. Many an Israelite turned to the LORD in repentance. These conversions proved to be the breakthrough of the kingdom of God. Well, this is what we continue to pray for: "Lord, may Thy kingdom break through mightily so that soon it will shine in fullness to the glory of Thy holy Name."

May 19

**READING: MATTHEW 6:25-34,
HEIDELBERG CATECHISM, LORD'S DAY 48**

God's kingdom – always first

"But seek first the kingdom of God
and his righteousness…"

MATTHEW 6:33A

When praying for the coming of God's kingdom, we often think primarily of the work of mission and evangelism. Yet the Catechism starts with ourselves saying, when praying this petition, first we pray: "So rule us by Thy Spirit that more and more we may submit to Thee." This means the Lord wants us to have a close look at ourselves first.

When doing so, we must all acknowledge that God's kingdom does not always come first in our lives. So often we are completely preoccupied with our own little kingdoms: our careers, our studies, our hobbies, that evening of sport – all for ourselves, meanwhile forgetting about what should be most important to us: God's kingdom!

When considering this, our lives often do not differ much from the people who do not serve God, always being worried about the things of this life: a healthy body, good food, nice clothing, a good job with good money, etcetera. However, this is not how it should be. The Lord Jesus in His sermon on the mount says: Make God's kingdom and His righteousness always a priority and stop worrying about all of the other things, for your heavenly Father will provide you with whatever you need. Trust Him!

In the passage above this meditation, the Lord Jesus says: "O you of little faith." That is us, often worrying in a worldly manner. Therefore, for all of us, there is a need to pray daily: "Father, help me to acknowledge Thee as King, also over my personal life. Help me to no longer take things into my own hands so that I may acknowledge Thy sovereignty and goodness over my life. Lord, help me to listen and to submit to Thy Word." This is the Word which is proclaimed to us every Sunday and from which we may read daily.

In summary, when praying for the coming of God's kingdom, we pray first of all for obedience to the Word of God. As God's children praying for the progress of Father's work in this world, we must pray for the progress of Father's work in our own life first, praying that our faith may always be a living faith in obedience to God. That is, in actual terms, seeking God's kingdom and His righteousness.

May 20

**READING: PSALM 122,
HEIDELBERG CATECHISM, LORD'S DAY 48**

Preserve and increase Thy Church

"Pray for the peace of Jerusalem!"

PSALM 122:6A

Concerning the second part of Answer 123, it is essential to note that even though there is a close relationship between the church and God's kingdom, they are still two different entities. The church is the instrument through which God brings people into His kingdom. It has received the keys of the kingdom to open it to believers and to close it to unbelievers. Hence, the church plays a central role in the kingdom. Where Christ plants His church, Satan is forced to retreat. Yet the opposite is also true: when a church becomes unfaithful, when it assigns more authority to itself and its ordinances than to the Word of God, the kingdom of God loses ground. Therefore, when praying 'Thy Kingdom come", we also pray: Father, amidst a climate of apostasy, preserve and increase Thy church. Keep her on that one foundation of apostles and prophets, of which Jesus Christ Himself is the cornerstone. Help Thy church to remain faithful in the battle it has to fight.

Next, we also pray: Father, increase Thy church. Increase Thy church from outside. Let Christ's church gathering work be dynamic. Bless to this end all work of mission and evangelism and bring in this way the final harvest home. Increase Thy church from outside, but also from within. Grant, Father, that Thy congregation may see it as a privilege when Thou blesses marriage with children. Grant that in this respect, a worldly way of thinking does not get a chance to infiltrate the minds of Thy children, but let joy continue whenever Thou opens the womb. Joy, that we may bear children for Thee; children who one day will inherit the New Jerusalem.

Preserve and increase Thy church. In summary, this means we pray that the Lord will make us faithful in the place where He has set us, steadfast in a battle that will become more and more severe. Yet, this should not cause us to become disheartened. For, even though at times it may seem to be the opposite, the victory will be ours. In Article 27 of the Belgic Confession, it reads that the church may look very small and sometimes as extinct in the eyes of man. But this same article also says: Christ is an eternal King who cannot be without subjects. God shall preserve His church, preserve her even against the fury of the whole world. That is the comfort we have, no matter how fierce the battle might become.

May 21

**READING: DANIEL 2:31-45,
HEIDELBERG CATECHISM, LORD'S DAY 48**

The fullness of God's kingdom

"And in the days of those kings the God of heaven will set up a kingdom that shall never be destroyed, nor shall the kingdom be left to another people. It shall break in pieces all these kingdoms and bring them to an end, and it shall stand forever."
DANIEL 2:44

Scripture is very clear that despite all opposition of Satan and his allies, God's kingdom will come to full glory. One day every person on earth will have to confess that all of today's attempted revolutions and rebellions against God were ineffective in preventing God's kingdom from coming to full glory.

The vision described in Daniel 2 makes this beautifully clear. It tells of a stone that is cut from a mountain but not by human hand, which breaks all the kingdoms of this world into pieces while the stone itself becomes a great mountain, filling the whole earth. That is how God will cause His kingdom to come.

God allowed his servant Daniel to already see something of it, which has been written down in Scripture for our comfort, assuring us that God's kingdom will triumph. It will prevail, yet not because of our work. The kingdom of God, at times also called the kingdom of heaven, comes from above. God is its King. He is also the One who cut out that stone in the vision shown to Daniel. When God rolls this stone, no world power can oppose its force. That is the comforting message of this vision. God's kingdom will break through with a power so great that no earthly power is able to withstand it. True, they will repeatedly try. But ultimately, it will all be in vain.

It is this triumph that we pray for every time we take the second petition on our lips. "Father, let Thy kingdom come. Grant that it indeed may break through with mighty power." Thus, amidst the heat of today's battle, we may look forward with eager longing to the fullness of God's glorious kingdom, to that great day on which God will finally be all in all, and the final harvest will be brought in, freed from sorrow, freed from sin.

The second petition, therefore, is also a prayer for the return of Christ. When He returns, He will have completed His mediatorial task and hand it back to the Father, so that God shall be all in all. Therefore, when praying, "Father, Thy kingdom come," we pray at the same time also: "Come, Lord Jesus, Maranatha!"

**READING: COLOSSIANS 1:3-14,
HEIDELBERG CATECHISM, LORD'S DAY 49**

Thy will be done (1)

"...we have not ceased to pray for you, asking that you may be filled with the knowledge of his will in all spiritual wisdom and understanding."

COLOSSIANS 1:9

When speaking about God's will for our life, do we mean God's hidden will, which is God's eternal counsel by which the LORD has determined but also executes everything that happens – hidden from us when it will happen as well as why it happens? Hidden, though in faith we have the comfort that it comes from God's fatherly hand.

Next, there is also God's revealed will, which we find in Holy Scripture where God teaches us His will for our life: how to serve Him in obedience. So what do we pray when saying: "Thy will be done?" Does this refer to God's hidden will or God's revealed will? Actually, there is no need to make a choice.

By way of example: say in your personal life you go through a rough time – disappointment after disappointment, sickness, concerns about your children, or perhaps some other trials which make life hard to cope with. In times like these, the Lord does not just simply ask us to say in a submissive way: "Father, Thy will be done." He also wants us to show that we are Christians, showing what it means to live by faith, also when life goes through deep valleys.

To live by faith – willing not only to accept the good and rosy things from God's fatherly hand, but also the trials we might have to face in life. Confessing God's providence that indeed nothing comes by chance, but that both health and sickness, prosperity and adversity come from the hand of Him who for Christ's sake is my God and my Father. When life goes through a rough time, the Lord asks for more than just dull resignation from us. Instead, He wants us – also then – to positively accept His direction for our life.

Well, that is what we pray for with the third petition. Father, Thy will be done – that is, Father teach me to be an obedient child of Thine, also in the valley of life. Father, help me not to rebel against the direction Thou takes with my life. Instead, even when it may seem to be all dark at times, help me also then to live by faith.

May 23

**READING: 2 SAMUEL 12:15B-23,
HEIDELBERG CATECHISM, LORD'S DAY 49**

Thy will be done (2)

"David therefore sought God on behalf of the child. And David fasted and went in and lay all night on the ground."
2 SAMUEL 12:16

When praying the third petition, we ask the LORD for help in accepting His will for our lives not just passively with a spirit of resignation, but with a positive attitude instead. In the case of a severe illness, for example, there is nothing wrong with praying for a miracle, unless God shows us differently. We find examples of this in Scripture as well.

I think of King David who had committed adultery with Bathsheba. Out of this adulterous relationship a child was born. Yet Nathan, the prophet, informs David that this baby will die. When David hears this, what does he do? Does he simply say, "LORD, Thy will be done?" No, instead, David pleads with God. For six days, he did not eat any food and prayed to the LORD that the child might live. David prayed for a miracle, not rebelling against God's will. Instead, through prayer David came to a positive acceptance of God's will. When there was still life, he prayed that God might save the child. Yet after it had died, he arose accepting the child's death from God's fatherly hand.

This example teaches the power of prayer. Instead of simply resigning ourselves to what God places on our path, we may bring our cause before the LORD, who at times indeed works miracles. Think of Peter, who was arrested, but upon the prayers of the saints in Jerusalem was freed in such a wonderful way that those who had prayed for it could hardly believe that God had really answered their prayers.

Likewise, we should never think lightly of the power of prayer. Our great Father in heaven is not a God of stone, but instead a God of plenteous redemption. He graciously listens to the prayers of His children when amidst the troubles of life, they cry out to Him. Then indeed the LORD might work miracles. No, not always. David prayed for six days and six nights, yet his son still died. To the apostle Paul the Lord said, "My grace is sufficient for you." The thorn in the flesh was not taken away.

All of this teaches us that it is through prayer that God will help us and enlighten us in understanding His will for our life. Well, this is what we actually pray when saying: "Thy will be done!"

May 24

**READING: PHILIPPIANS 2:12-18,
HEIDELBERG CATECHISM, LORD'S DAY 49**

Obeying Father's will (1)

"For it is God who works in you, both to will
and to work for his good pleasure."

PHILIPPIANS 2:13

In the two previous meditations, it was said that concerning the third petition there is no need to make a distinct choice between a positive acceptance of God's hidden will and a faithful obedience of God's revealed will. Nevertheless, the Catechism in explaining the third petition puts the accent on God's revealed will, explaining that with this petition we pray that we may faithfully obey God's will in the daily duties of our office and calling. In this way, the Catechism closely links the explanation of the third petition with the explanation of the second and first petition.

Concerning the second petition, the Catechism mentions: "So rule us by Thy Word and Spirit that more and more we may submit to Thee." However, this is only possible when we are determined to obey God's will. And why are we determined to obey God's will? For no other reason than that we also desire to hallow God's Name by praising Him in all our thoughts, words, and deeds. In connection with this, the Catechism mentions the following concerning the third petition: "Grant that we and all men may deny our own will, and without any murmuring obey Thy will, for it alone is good."

"Help us, Father, to deny our own will." Saying this, we pray for the miracle of regeneration, whereby through the powerful working of the Holy Spirit within us, God makes our will spiritually alive. As a result, where formerly the rebellion and resistance of the flesh fully dominated, now a prompt and sincere obedience of the Spirit begins to prevail, in which the true, spiritual renewal and freedom of our will consists (Canons of Dort, Chapter III/IV. Article 16).

This is what we pray for with the third petition. The word 'grant' makes this clear as well. Grant – this means God has to do it! God, who according to Philippians 2:13, works in us both to will and to do for His good pleasure. It is God Himself who brings this change about in our life so that more and more we learn to deny our own will and to obey God's will. This shows that even our obedience is God's work alone.

May 25

**READING: MATTHEW 16:21-28,
HEIDELBERG CATECHISM, LORD'S DAY 49**

Obeying Father's will (2)

"Then Jesus said to his disciples, 'If anyone would come after me, let him deny himself and take up his cross and follow me'."

MATTHEW 16:24

It is God who works in us to obey Him. Yet this does not make us altogether passive. In Matthew 16:24, the Lord Jesus says, "If anyone would come after Me, let him deny himself and take up his cross and follow Me." With these words, the Lord Jesus highlights that the call for discipleship demands self-denial, adding we are to take up His cross.

His cross! This means the Lord Jesus is not referring to any burden we may have to carry in life, even though these words are often interpreted this way, when we say, "Every house has its cross, its difficulties, to bear." This might be true, but that is not what the Lord Jesus is referring to. Instead, He is referring to the scorn one might have to suffer in following the Lord Jesus, in doing His will. People may laugh at us, ridicule us, when we simply want to do what Scripture teaches, convinced that God's will alone is good.

This is not always easy. On the contrary, every day anew it is a hard battle for every one of us not to take the easy way out, but to live by faith alone. It is hard to deny our own will and instead to obey God's will, always, under all circumstances. This is why we pray this petition, asking Father to help us in this daily battle. Yet also concerning this petition, may others also see that we enjoy doing God's will – that is, "pray and work".

In Romans 12:2, the apostle Paul writes: "Do not be conformed to this world, but be transformed by the renewal of your mind, that by testing you may discern what is the will of God, what is good and acceptable and perfect." Do not be conformed to this world, but instead show that the Holy Spirit has renewed your life. Reshaped by the knowledge of the gospel, our mind should be set on the things that are above. We should no longer be focused on the passing fashion of this age, but keen to do God's will, and in so doing prove that God's will is indeed good, acceptable, and perfect.

May 26

**READING: HEBREWS 5:1-10,
HEIDELBERG CATECHISM, LORD'S DAY 49**

As willingly and faithfully as the angels in heaven

"Are they not all ministering spirits sent out to serve for the sake of those who are to inherit salvation?"

HEBREWS 1:14

Explaining the second part of the third petition "on earth as it is in heaven," Lord's Day 49 refers to the faithful obedience of the angels in heaven, who today are standing before the throne of God, always willing and faithful to carry out God's command. After all, first of all, should we not as children have shown this faithfulness, especially when we consider God's love towards us? Yes, if we see how the angels, who are but servants of God, always hearken to God's voice, then we can only feel ashamed that we as His children so often disobey God's voice, acting contrary to God's command. A very humiliating example for us.

In Hebrews 1:14, it reads: the angels are "ministering spirits sent out to serve for the sake of those who are to inherit salvation." Sent out, obeying without murmuring, always active for our salvation. They keep watch over Christ's church. They protect God's children, whom they carry to Abraham's bosom upon their death. Being zealous for the holiness of God's Name and the coming of His kingdom, they fight against the devil and his whole dominion. This is how they serve as an example for us that we may carry out the duties of our office and calling with the same zeal and faithfulness as they do.

"Thy will be done on earth as it is in heaven." If only it were like this in our life, however, often the opposite is more accurate. For us, it is a constant battle to make the will of God the dominant force in our lives. A constant battle, which at times causes one almost to despair. What a great comfort it is, therefore, that also in this battle we may take our refuge in Christ.

In Hebrews 5:8, we read about our Saviour: "He learned obedience through what He suffered." This refers to Christ's struggle in Gethsemane, where He offered up prayers and supplications to Him who was able to save Him from death. Yet also praying: "Not as I will, but as Thou wilt." This is how Christ learnt obedience through what He suffered. Being true man, Christ struggled. Yet in this struggle, He remained obedient to the very end, so covering our disobedience in the sight of God. Through His Spirit He also gives us all that we need to obey Father's will today.

May 27

**READING: PSALM 111,
HEIDELBERG CATECHISM, LORD'S DAY 50**

A covenantal prayer

"He provides food for those who fear him;
he remembers his covenant forever."

PSALM 111:5

When considering the six petitions of the Lord's Prayer, often one can hear the following comment: first, we pray for God's cause, since in our prayer this cause should always have priority. Yet after that, we may also plead our cause with God. At face value, this seems to be a good way to show that God's cause should always have priority, also when we address God in prayer.

No matter how true this is, I wonder whether it is right to make such a sharp distinction between God's cause and our cause, especially when considering what praying means. In prayer, as God's children we draw near to God as our Father, who in His grace has established a covenant with us. Because of this, there is a close relationship between God and ourselves; a relationship in which Father and child not only live their own lives but are interested in each other's cause. God is interested in our lives. At the same time, when there is a living faith, we as God's children want nothing more than to live for the Lord, rejoicing in Father's cause. This should also be reflected in the way we pray. Concerning the Lord's prayer, this means God's cause and our cause are interwoven.

Concerning the three 'Thy petitions', our cause gets attention as well, since as God's children it should be our desire that Father's name is hallowed, Father's kingdom comes, and Father's will is done. Because of the covenant relationship, this is also for our benefit. God has given us a place on this earth to live for Him, to live for Him in everything. When this is the case in our life, God's cause and our cause are always intertwined.

This also means that concerning the three 'our petitions', Father's cause should still have priority. When praying for daily bread, we should not think of ourselves first. Instead, when praying this, we actually pray: "Father, give me daily bread, so that I may live to hallow Thy Name, to promote Thy Kingdom and to do Thy will." It is true with the fourth petition that we pray for our livelihood and all that is connected with it. Yet we pray for it so that we may receive all that we need to do our task in the service of the LORD.

May 28

**READING: PROVERBS 30:1-9,
HEIDELBERG CATECHISM, LORD'S DAY 50**

Provide us with all our bodily needs

*"Give me neither poverty nor riches; feed me
with the food that is needful for me."*

PROVERBS 30:8B

In Lord's Day 45, the question is raised: "What has God commanded us to ask of Him?" The answer reads: "All the things we need for body and soul." Yet how do we determine our needs? One person may think I need this or that for a decent living. Someone else in a comparable situation might be satisfied with less. From a human point of view, it is difficult to define what we need. So what determines our needs so that we may bring it properly before the LORD?

Concerning our needs, if God also comes first, our needs are decided first of all by the tasks we have to fulfil to serve the LORD. Because God has given each one of us different tasks, our needs differ too. However, one rule is the same for all of us: it is not my desires that determine what I need to serve God. Instead, God in His good pleasure determines what I need to serve Him. This rule has consequences when praying the fourth petition. It means that when praying this petition we do not ask the Lord to supply us with all that is needed so that our plans and ambitions may succeed. Instead, we pray in all humility, "Father, my aim in life is to serve Thee. Therefore, wilt Thou provide me with the things I need to serve Thee." No more, no less.

Agur's prayer gives us a beautiful example of this. Agur prayed: "Father, feed me with the food that is needful for me." Therefore, "LORD, do not give me too much. For if I were rich, the danger would be there that I forget about Thee, that I may think I can do without Thee. LORD, do not give me too much. Yet, do not give me too little either, for I may resort to things which are displeasing to Thee. My desire, LORD, is to live for Thee, for Thee alone. Therefore, simply give me what is needed to do my task in Thy service." We can all learn from this prayer in determining our needs when praying for daily bread.

May 29

READING: DEUTERONOMY 8,
HEIDELBERG CATECHISM, LORD'S DAY 50

Man does not live by bread alone (1)

"And he humbled you and let you hunger and fed you with manna, which you did not know, nor did your fathers know, that he might make you know that man does not live by bread alone, but man lives by every word that comes from the mouth of the Lord."

DEUTERONOMY 8:3

When praying for daily bread, we pray: LORD, give me what is needed to serve Thee! Yet when expanding on this need, what should we ask for? To answer this question, today we will turn to Deuteronomy 8, where Moses warns the Israelites not to forget to thank the LORD once they had entered the Promised Land; a land where they would lack nothing, but instead would have everything in abundance. Do not forget to thank the LORD – so Moses says – and this not only in words, but also by faithfully obeying God's commands. If you do not do this, the LORD who has given you all this wealth can also take it from you again.

Since we have been equally blessed with many material blessings, we too should not forget to thank the LORD daily for all these blessings, to thank Him as the Giver of it. In practical terms, this means when business-wise or job-wise we have done well, we should not start boasting of our capabilities and all that we have achieved. Instead, in humbleness we should bow our knees and thank God for it. God will bless such an attitude to life.

In Lord's Day 50 of the Heidelberg Catechism, it reads: our care and labour and also God's gifts cannot do us any good without the Lord's blessing. For what value does all of this have if God does not bless it for our salvation? From a material point of view, a person might be rich, but Scripture calls him poor. After all, as it says in Deuteronomy 8:3, "Man shall not live by bread alone."

Food is essential, but ultimately it cannot give life. Life is a gift from God. If the Lord does not bless our food, does not bless our physical well-being, we can eat the best of food trying to stay healthy, but all of this in itself does not help. Man does not live by bread alone, but – as Moses says – by every word that comes from the mouth of the LORD. Eating healthy food is essential, yet it is more important to obey God's commandments. This is the lesson of Deuteronomy 8, also for today.

May 30

**READING: MATTHEW 4:1-4,
HEIDELBERG CATECHISM, LORD'S DAY 50**

Man does not live by bread alone (2)

"But he answered, It is written,
Man shall not live by bread alone,
but by every word that comes
from the mouth of God."

MATTHEW 4:4

From yesterday's meditation, we learnt that obeying God's commandments is more important than food. The Lord Jesus made this clear as well, when in the wilderness the devil tempted Him. In this temptation, the devil was challenging God once again, as he also did in Paradise, tempting Adam. In Genesis 1, we read: God had created man good and in His image – perfect! Yet Satan challenged this, making Adam fall for a lie.

The Lord Jesus, being also true and perfect man, picks up this thread. Again, Satan tried to challenge God: man is not perfect. Yet the Lord Jesus – as the second Adam – withstands this challenge, even though He was tempted under much more difficult circumstances than the first Adam. The first Adam lived in a beautiful garden where he could eat from any tree except the one tree God had forbidden him to eat from.

Yet the Lord Jesus was led by the Spirit into the wilderness, where after 40 days of fasting, the devil comes to Him, saying "Why should you suffer hunger? One powerful word of your mouth can turn these stones into bread." Yet the Lord Jesus did not do this, knowing that this was against God's command. The Lord Jesus knew that if at that very moment He had turned those stones into bread, the bread would not have benefited him. After all, what value does food have if God does not bless it? And so in response to the devil, He quotes Deuteronomy 8:3, "Man shall not live by bread alone, but by every word that proceeds from the mouth of God."

This teaches us once again: obeying God's commandments is more important than the desire for food. Think of Adam in Paradise. He ate from the fruit of the forbidden tree, yet it caused his death. The same happened, when during their journey through the desert, the Israelites collected more manna than necessary: food in abundance, yet God punished them.

Man shall not live by bread alone, but by every word that proceeds from the mouth of God. It is good to remind ourselves of this every time we pray for daily bread.

May 31

READING: PSALM 37:1-11,
HEIDELBERG CATECHISM, LORD'S DAY 50

Acknowledging God as the only fountain of all good

"Delight yourself in the LORD, and he will give you the desires of your heart."
PSALM 37:4

When praying to God for our daily bread, we acknowledge God as the only fountain of all good. In doing so, we confess our complete dependency on God, including all our bodily needs. In that trust, we pray, knowing Father will provide.

This acknowledgement gives great comfort, assuring us that God is near, always present to give us what we need: no matter what difficulties we face, no matter what pain we suffer, or what kinds of sorrows oppress us, Father stands above it, and He is in control. Our need will never be greater than His power.

This is not just a matter of knowing it. God also wants us to acknowledge this in prayer, thanking Him for it. Thanking God for what He gives us day after day and this by grace alone. Thanking God not just in words but also in deeds. Concerning the fourth petition, the most important aspect of it is that we also live it, showing in our lives that we indeed fully trust God and are willing to live in complete dependence on Him. It cannot be that on the one hand we pray this petition acknowledging that our life is totally dependent on God, while on the other hand we try to work out everything ourselves: money-wise, business-wise, etcetera. Acknowledging our dependency on God, we must also live what we confess.

Often we pray the Lord's prayer before starting a meal, also praying for our daily bread, even though at times the food is already on the table. We do this, acknowledging that with this food, God as the Giver of it provides us with what we need to serve Him. He is the Giver and thus we want to thank Him for it.

When we live close to the LORD in this way, when necessary we are also able to wait until God provides us with the things we need, trusting that God will have His good reasons for letting us wait, even though we cannot understand it. Sometimes God may put our faith to the test. At times like these we should not become rebellious, but in childlike trust keep praying this fourth petition.

June 1

**READING: PSALM 62:1-8,
HEIDELBERG CATECHISM, LORD'S DAY 50**

Complete trust in God alone

*"Trust in him at all times, O people;
Pour out your heart before him,
God is a refuge for us."*

PSALM 62:8

The final sentence of Lord's Day 50 reads: "Grant, therefore, that we may withdraw our trust from all creatures and place it only in Thee." Father will take care in and under all circumstances. In that trust we must live, even when there is less food on the table, or when materially we have to live on a tight budget. Then in circumstances like these, we are not to look first to the government to see what it can provide us with, but in prayer we are to look on high. If the government makes provisions, we are allowed to use them, but we must do this in thankfulness to Father, acknowledging God as the fountain also of these blessings. This does not only apply to government money, but also to the wages we receive. It all comes from God. These are all ways and means by which God provides for our needs so that we can serve Him.

Sometimes God may let us wait, testing our faith. In times like these, we should realise God's timing and God's way of answering our prayers are wiser than we can think of. At times when struggling with this, we should remember that our lives are safe in Father's hands, and we could not wish them to be in any better hands. This is our comfort, also when life goes through valleys. Father is near, even in that valley.

With the fourth petition, we pray: Father, give me bread for this day, only for today, since our Saviour taught us that we do not have to worry about tomorrow. Therefore, putting our complete trust in God alone, we pray: "Father, give us this day what we need to do our task in Thy service. As for tomorrow, I trust Thou wilt take care of me then as well."

This sure knowledge gives rest and inward peace. Peace, of which the vast majority of the people around us do not know. They are always worrying about what the future may hold. Therefore, how blessed we are as children of God, who daily may look on high, assured Father is there. He will provide. Living in this full trust day by day will make life less worrisome. Instead of worrying about tomorrow, we will thank God for what He gives today.

June 2

**READING: 1 JOHN 1:5-10,
HEIDELBERG CATECHISM, LORD'S DAY 51**

Wretched sinners (1)

"Whoever conceals his transgressions will not prosper, but he who confesses and forsakes them will obtain mercy."
PROVERBS 28:13

Most of the prayers we send up to God also include a petition for forgiveness of sins. Quite often, it is used as a concluding sentence: "Lord, all this we ask of Thee in the forgiveness of our sins for Christ's sake. Amen." We are quite used to a formulation like this. Yet whenever we say this, do we also think about what we are saying?

By way of example, think of a meeting for Bible Study. The one who has to close off the meeting in prayer, also asks, "Lord, graciously forgive what was wrong this evening." Yet if at that moment we had to say what was wrong and sinful that evening, would we be able to do this? This shows how easily the prayer for forgiveness of sins can become just a matter of routine. However, at all times, we should make sure that we never take this petition on our lips in a superficial way, hardly thinking of what we are praying.

Often people find it hard to mention their sins by name. They do not find it hard to confess that they are imperfect. After all, everything we do is stained with sin. However, to mention sins by name, confessing to God at the end of the day: "Lord, this was wrong and I should not have done …" they find it challenging to give it real substance. Why is this? Do we still know the word 'wretched' as it is used in Lord's Day 51 of the Heidelberg Catechism? Wretched – this word means 'heartbroken' 'grief-stricken'. Do we feel this in our hearts, when we confess our sins? Broken-hearted, because we have grieved our heavenly Father?

The apostle Paul uses this word in Romans 7, when considering his actions: "What I will to do I do not practice, but what I hate, that I do." At times, we too do the very thing we hate. Well, let us not hide this from God. He knows it anyway.

The LORD longs for sincerity when it comes to our prayers, including the prayer for forgiveness of sins. As wretched sinners, we all need God's grace each day again. The more we live in the awareness of this, the more we will marvel at the miracle of being forgiven in Christ.

**READING: JAMES 4:1-10,
HEIDELBERG CATECHISM, LORD'S DAY 51**

Wretched sinners (2)

"Be wretched, mourn and weep."

JAMES 4:9A

In Lord's Day 2 of the Heidelberg Catechism, it reads that we know our sins and misery from the law of God. When looking into the mirror of God's law, we see the many sins that stain our lives. However, we will only see this when we are willing to admit our sins in all of its gravity. It is so easy to say that we are sinful. As such, this does not hurt. After all, we are all sinful. But if we sincerely mean it when saying that we are sinful, why on the other hand are we so quick to take offense and make all kind of excuses when certain wrongdoings are pointed out to us?

We are often good at mirroring our lives in the lives of others. When doing so, we mostly come out looking the best. Think of comments like, "How could that brother ever do this? I would never do that." We look at others. Yet, when mirroring our lives in the mirror of God's perfect law, we never come out as best. Instead, we will see how dirty we are, stained by sin each day anew.

Hence the question: How sincere are we when praying for forgiveness of sins? Are we genuinely brokenhearted for having grieved God again? If we could only see the hurt on Father's face, hurt even about those sins of which we might say at times, "It could be worse!" If we could only see the hurt on Father's face, perhaps we would ask more sincerely for forgiveness and marvel more at the miracle of it.

In becoming more aware of the things we do wrong, it can be of help to mention the sins by name. By way of example: that dishonest transaction, that dirty joke, that temper that once again got the better of me, things we should not have said, or our idling away of precious time, our wandering thoughts which we did not hold captive in obedience to Christ. Things, which happen at times without us even thinking about it. After all, it was not that bad. There are worse things one can do. However, it grieved our Father in heaven. Therefore, with a contrite heart we should bring them before the throne of God. When we do this, the more we will marvel at the greatness of God's love for us sinners and the miracle of His amazing grace.

June 4

**READING: PSALM 51:1-12,
HEIDELBERG CATECHISM, LORD'S DAY 51**

Wretched sinners (3)

"Create in me a clean heart, O God,
and renew a right spirit within me."
PSALM 51:10

The prayer for forgiveness of sins is necessary for all of us. For a moment, think of on whose lips the Lord Jesus laid this petition: His disciples, people active in church life, faithful in the service of the Lord. Yet even they could not do without this prayer. They too were not too good for it, nor are we. For as they are, so are we: wretched sinners!

Wretched – not because, unfortunately, we have fallen victim to sin. No, we are sinners because of our own guilt. The fifth petition speaks about 'debt'. This means we have failed to render God His due. Yes, we have even become incapable of doing this.

The Catechism also speaks about the evil which still clings to us. True, in Christ we have become new people. Regenerated by the powerful work of the Holy Spirit, we have been set free from the dominion and slavery of sin, but not entirely in this life from the flesh and body of sin. Therefore – as we confess in the Canons of Dort, Chapter V, 2 – "daily sins of weakness spring up and defects cling to even the best works of the saints." Spring up – from a woeful source, according to Article 15 of the Belgic Confession. A woeful source – that is our old nature still very much alive within us. Therefore, whenever we sin, it is not just an unfortunate mistake we are making. No, it goes much deeper.

David makes this clear in Psalm 51. In this Psalm, David confesses that his adultery with Bathsheba was not just an unfortunate incident, but this is 'how I am', says David – sinful from birth, yes even from conception. This is why David's prayer for forgiveness goes much further than just asking for forgiveness of this specific sin. He prays: 'what I need is a clean heart'.

Whoever sees his sins before God in this way, will humble himself before the LORD. When doing this sincerely, we will no longer find it difficult to mention our sins by name. Then we lay our hearts open before the Lord and say with the apostle Paul, "Wretched man that I am!" We will dislike ourselves because of the grief we are causing our heavenly Father. When we humble ourselves before God in this way, the more we will see what a miracle it is that God is still willing to forgive us our sins.

June 5

READING: MICAH 7:18-20

The joy of forgiveness

"He will again have compassion on us; he will tread our iniquities underfoot. You will cast all our sins into the depths of the sea."

MICAH 7:19

In Romans 7:24, the apostle Paul writes: "Wretched man that I am! Who will deliver me from this body of death?" Next, he writes: "Thanks be to God through Jesus Christ our Lord!" Yes, it is only because of Christ's sacrifice on the cross that God no longer looks upon us as we are but wants to adopt us for His children and heirs again. Christ is our righteousness before God. Therefore, though broken and contrite of heart, because of our sins, we still may rejoice. God will not cast us away from His presence. Instead, He will restore to us the joy of salvation through faith in Christ.

This does not mean that from now on, God turns a blind eye to our sins. It grieves Him every time we do wrong. Yet God will still forgive us. Why? On what basis? Is it because we have confessed our sins? Surely not! The only ground for God forgiving us our sins is the blood of Jesus Christ. This is the precious price which had to be paid to free us from our guilt before God. Whoever realises this will never make light of his sins: Christ had to die so that we could live – live eternally!

Live eternally! This means complete salvation in Jesus Christ, our Saviour. Complete – since God will never come back to any of our sins. In the Old Testament, this was symbolised by the ceremony of the scapegoat. This goat was sent away into the wilderness on the Day of Atonement. First, however, this goat was brought before the altar. The high priest would lay both his hands upon this goat as a symbol of all the sins of the people of Israel being put on the head of this goat. After this, the goat was sent into the wilderness.

Likewise, God also forgives our sins. God will never come back to any of them. In Micah 7:19, it reads that He casts them into the depths of the sea. They have really been forgiven – forgiven because of the blood that was shed on Calvary by which the Lord Jesus Christ secured for us an eternal redemption.

June 6

**READING: MATTHEW 18:21-35,
HEIDELBERG CATECHISM, LORD'S DAY 51**

The fruit of being forgiven

"So also my heavenly Father will do to every one of you, if you do not forgive your brother from your heart."
MATTHEW 18:35

In Matthew 18, Peter asks the Lord Jesus, "Lord, how often shall my brother sin against me, and I forgive him? Up to seven times?" Peter thought seven times was already quite something. Moreover, is seven not the perfect number? However, when answering Peter, the Lord Jesus teaches that forgiving is not a matter of mathematics, but that it must come from the heart. Not seven times, but seventy times seven – that is limitless. The parable that follows makes this clear as well.

The story told in this parable is easy to understand. After being released from such an enormous debt, why was this servant so harsh with his fellow servant? The answer to this question is straightforward. This servant had no real awareness of the greatness of his debt. This is the point the Lord Jesus wants to make in telling this parable. When asking for forgiveness, we must always do so fully aware of the greatness of our debt towards God. This awareness will help us in forgiving our neighbour whatever has happened. Trust might have been broken and perhaps will never be fully restored. Yet the bitterness has gone. We can look the other in the eye again. We extend the hand of forgiveness regardless of whether the other wants to accept it.

But what if the person acting against God's commandments does not show true repentance? This is something for God to deal with. What we can do is forgive the emotional hurt this person has caused us, so that it is no longer eating us away, almost cringing whenever we see this person. Christ wants to set you free of these feelings.

If you find it difficult to forgive, pray for strength from above. After all, none of us can do this in our own strength. Therefore, cry out before God. If you do so sincerely, God will provide. He is near to help us, so that we no longer harbour any grudges. Instead – as it reads in the Form for the celebration of the Lord's Supper – "For the sake of Christ, who so exceedingly loved us first, we shall now love one another, and shall show this to one another, not just in words but also in deeds." This should be the fruit of God forgiving us.

June 7

**READING: EPHESIANS 6:10-20,
HEIDELBERG CATECHISM, LORD'S DAY 52A**

Living in a war zone

"For we do not wrestle against flesh and blood, but against the rulers, against the authorities, against the cosmic powers over this present darkness, against the spiritual forces of evil in the heavenly places."

EPHESIANS 6:12

Although by God's grace we may live in a free and peaceful country, from a spiritual point of view we live in a war zone. A dangerous war is going on, and we are caught right in the middle of it. This war has already been raging since the beginning of history. After the fall into sin in Paradise, the LORD Himself declared this war. The war between the seed of the woman and the seed of the serpent. In Christ, we have been set free from the power of the devil. Yet the battle is still going. As God's children, we are fully involved in this battle, being called to live our lives for Him who redeemed us.

Because of our sinful nature, which so often is still very much alive within us, it is not always easy to take a firm stand when this is required. So quickly it happens that we do things which deep down we know quite well are not right. Decisions to break with certain wrongdoings are put off. We find it hard to do this. And it is hard! Hard, when looking at our own weakness.

However, the Lord does not leave us to our own resources. In prayer, we may call upon His Name, asking the Lord, "Lead us not into temptation, but deliver us from the evil one." Whoever prays this petition in sincere faith may have the firm assurance that the Lord will give the strength we need to persevere in fighting this battle. Weak soldiers receive a powerful weapon when praying the sixth petition. Weak from ourselves, we may look on high to receive the strength we need.

Weak from ourselves, indeed! In Lord's Day 52 of the Heidelberg Catechism, it reads that we are so weak we cannot stand even for one moment, while on the other hand our enemies do not cease to attack us. And what enemies they are! They are bloodthirsty. They have nothing other than our complete ruin in mind. This is why prayer is so important. It is the most effective weapon in fighting this battle.

June 8

**READING: JAMES 1:1-18,
HEIDELBERG CATECHISM, LORD'S DAY 52A**

Lead us not into temptation

"Let no one say when he is tempted, "I am being tempted by God," for God cannot be tempted with evil, and he himself tempts no one."
JAMES 1:13

What is the meaning of asking the Lord not to lead us into temptation? Are these temptations not there already? Living in a sinful world, one cannot escape being tempted. Moreover, it is God Himself who gives the church a place in this world. So, if we are already right in the middle of these temptations, how can we pray, "Lead us not into temptation"? Moreover, why ask this of God, since He will never lead us into temptation? Temptation is the work of the devil, as James makes it quite clear in Chapter 1 of his letter.

The subject at hand in this matter is the relationship between God and the work of the devil, as the Holy God loathes all evil. In his first letter, the apostle John writes: God is light and in Him is no darkness at all. Yet this does not mean that evil is an independent power on which God has no influence. If this were the case, God would not be almighty. In Article 13 of the Belgic Confession it reads: "God holds in check the devil and all our enemies so that they cannot hurt us without His permission and will." The devil does not have a free reign of power similar to God. Even Satan is no more than a creature, and not a free agent who can just do what he wants. Instead, you could say that God has Satan on a chain. Hence, Satan can only do things within the scope and reach of that chain. This is a tremendous comfort for the believers.

Yet this should not cause us to make light of the power of the devil. In Revelation 12, the apostle John sees Satan thrown out of heaven and cast to the earth. Next, it reads in this chapter: "Woe to the inhabitants of the earth and the sea! For the devil has come down to you, having great wrath, because he knows that he has a short time". Because of this short time, the attacks of the devil will be all the more severe. That is why we ask God in the sixth petition to help us in this fierce battle. We need this help. We cannot do without it.

**READING: REVELATION 12:7-14,
HEIDELBERG CATECHISM, LORD'S DAY 52A**

Nourished by God in the wilderness

"But the woman was given the two wings of the great eagle so that she might fly from the serpent into the wilderness, to the place where she is to be nourished for a time, and times, and half a time."

REVELATION 12:14

Satan cannot stand that Christ has defeated him. It enrages him in a fury against the offspring of the woman. To protect the church against this fury of the devil, God gives the woman a place in the wilderness. There she is nourished by God, hidden from the face of the serpent.

This picture of verse 14 functions as a reminder of what God did for the people of Israel when He freed them from Egypt and carried them on eagles' wings to Himself in the desert (Exodus 19:4). The wilderness symbolises a place of refuge where the church is safe against the attacks of its adversary. Safe, since in the wilderness God Himself will take care of His people and provide for them. In the same way as Israel received manna from heaven and could drink water from the rock in the wilderness, likewise the New Testament Church will receive its livelihood from God's fatherly hand.

For the people of Israel, the desert was also a place where they had to learn to put their complete trust in Him alone. Well, the same applies to the New Testament church which now finds itself in the desert. In this context, I think of what we read in Hosea 2. In Hosea's day, the Israelites no longer expected their wealth to come from the LORD, but from Baal instead. The church had become an unfaithful bride.

What does the LORD do with this unfaithful bride? In Hosea 2 we read that the LORD takes away all the wealth His bride received from her lovers. Next we read that the LORD will bring this unfaithful bride back to the wilderness to speak tenderly to her.

Why would God do this? We learn the reason from Hosea 2. The LORD wanted to renew the covenant with His people, for they would only be able to re-enter Canaan in this way. To say this in New Testament language: the church needs this period in the wilderness to learn her total dependence on the LORD again and not become conformed to the world. Only by putting our trust in God alone will we be able to withstand the attacks of the evil one.

June 10

**READING: REVELATION 12:13-17,
HEIDELBERG CATECHISM, LORD'S DAY 52A**

Attacks even in the wilderness

"The serpent poured water like a river out of his mouth after the woman, to sweep her away with a flood."
REVELATION 12:15

The church having received a place in the wilderness teaches us to put our complete trust in God alone, rejoicing in God's all-sufficient care. This is the only way to remain standing in spiritual warfare, seeking refuge with God. After all, Satan will continue to attack us even in the wilderness. Revelation 12 refers to the severity of these attacks, especially in verse 15. God had given the woman a place in the wilderness to protect her against the attacks of the dragon. Protection – as long as she was willing to put her trust in God.

Next, we read that the dragon tries to make the woman give up her trust in God, by pouring water like a river out of his mouth. What does this mean? The answer is that the dragon tries to do away with the wilderness, not as God did by giving water from the rock through a wonder from above. No, Satan tries, so to speak, to neutralise the wilderness, making God's people feel less dependent. There is water, even in the wilderness. Satan will make sure that it will be there. Satan is always eager to bring the world into the church: a bit of water in the wilderness. This is Satan's response to God's strategy. He tries to sweep the church away with his enticing flood. At times, posing as an angel of light, Satan tries to present sin in such a way that there is nothing wrong with it, making us fall for the lies of the devil.

We should be on guard daily for these dangerous attacks of the evil one, for sometimes the devil has caught us even before we know it. He knows our weak spots very well, often even better than we do ourselves. It is these weak spots which Satan tries to make the most of in causing us to sin. He laughs every time we give in. It is not for nothing that Answer 127 speaks about the devil as one of the sworn enemies who will not cease to attack us. Therefore, we should pray daily that God will uphold us in this severe battle, finding strength in clinging to God, holding Father's hand.

June 11

**READING: 1 JOHN 2:15-20,
HEIDELBERG CATECHISM, LORD'S DAY 52A**

Three sworn enemies

*"If anyone loves the world, the love
of the Father is not in him."*

1 JOHN 2:15B

The Catechism mentions three sworn enemies: the devil, the world, and our own flesh. In some of the previous meditations we focused on the first enemy: the devil. With respect to the world, we must remember that God has set us apart from the world, as a holy people. However, even though God has set us apart, the world still attracts us, tempting us with sweet tones. This is why, in more than one place, Scripture calls us to create distance by forsaking the world, making a clear choice where we stand: in the world, but not of the world!

We must forsake the world. In heeding this call, often the first thing that comes to mind is 'worldly places' and 'worldly things' we should avoid, and indeed we should! Yet there is much more to the call of forsaking the world. More positively, the point is this: the way in which we live our lives should show that we are a church living in the wilderness, rejoicing in living our lives for the LORD, living holy!

Living holy lives – not just outwardly, but also in our hearts, in our minds. Are we genuinely living witnesses of our Saviour: witnesses, in whose lives it shows that we have not set our hearts on the things of this world, but instead prove in our lives that the will of God is good, acceptable, and perfect?

The third sworn enemy mentioned by the Catechism is our own flesh. These are the sinful desires springing up from our hearts. One of the most severe battles we have to fight is to keep these sinful desires under control so that they do not cause us to sin. Indeed, most severe is the battle from within – much more severe than all the attacks that come from outside! This is because all that is in this world resonates with our sinful desires. It is the old nature that is often still so very much alive in us. This is why we pray: "Father wilt Thou uphold and strengthen us by the power of Thy Spirit, so that in this spiritual warfare we do not go down to defeat, but instead may persevere to the very end by clinging to Thee, seeking refuge in Christ as our Saviour."

June 12

**READING: LUKE 22:31-34,
HEIDELBERG CATECHISM, LORD'S DAY 52A**

Weak in ourselves

"I have prayed for you that your faith may not fail."
LUKE 22:32A

The Heidelberg Catechism mentions three sworn enemies who do not cease to attack us. A severe and tiring battle, especially when considering how weak we are in ourselves. Thankfully, every day our gracious God is ever there to provide us with strength to withstand the attacks of the evil one. God works this strength in us by the Holy Spirit, who in the New Testament is called the Spirit of Christ, by whom Christ wants to complete the work of redemption within us.

To the apostle Peter, Christ once said: "Satan has asked for you, that he may sift you as wheat. But I have prayed for you, that your faith should not fail." This same prayer is also prayed for us today. In heaven, as our Mediator, Christ intercedes for us before the Father so that amidst trials and temptations, we will not go down to defeat. To this comfort we may cling.

At present, God still gives Satan great power to attack us. In these attacks, Satan has an ally within us: our own sinful flesh. A hard battle, each day again. When confessing our sins at the end of the day, we often feel ashamed that it went wrong again. Yet, remember, as long as that shame is there, the Spirit is still at work. By this feeling of guilt, the Spirit wants to direct us to Christ, our Advocate before the Father. This again shows the power of prayer, by which we may also cling to that promise we read in Scripture that one day the God of peace will crush Satan under our feet. One day the battle will end. On that day, every child of God, who by grace from above remained faithful in the battle, will share in the victory which Christ obtained for us.

We read about this victory in the last book of the Bible. In Revelation 15, the apostle John sees the multitude of saints standing at the sea of glass singing the song of Moses and of the Lamb. These are – so we read there – "those who have the victory over the beast, over his image and over his mark and over the number of his name." In that hour, when the evil one is thrown into the lake of fire, Christ will triumph forever, and we with Him!

**READING: 1 CORINTHIANS 10:12-13,
HEIDELBERG CATECHISM, LORD'S DAY 52B**

The complete victory in Christ

"The God of peace will soon crush Satan under your feet."

ROMANS 16:20A

The concluding part of Answer 127 reads: "Until we finally obtain the complete victory." This shows the outcome of the battle is sure. One day, "The God of peace will crush Satan under our feet". Indeed, the God of peace! For through the battle, God is working towards His kingdom of perfect peace. The victory will come. In faith, we can be sure of this. For to God belongs the kingdom, and the power, and the glory, forever. He alone is King, and His dominion will be forever. He also has absolute control over all things, power even over Satan.

This almighty God, who has all things in His hands, is for the sake of Christ His Son, our Father. This is why there is no need to lose heart in the battle we have to fight. Our God is strong to save, even from mortal danger, from the grave, and every cruel oppression. He is our shield and tower. In His care, we are safe. We – who in ourselves are so weak that we cannot stand even for a moment. Yet if God is for us, who can be against us?

No, all of this does not mean that from now on, life will always be easy. We still have to fight the battle every day anew. But in faith we have the assurance that God will help us. In 1 Corinthians 10:13, it says: He will not let His chosen ones be tempted beyond their ability, but with the temptation He will also provide the way of escape, that we may be able to endure it.

For this reason, we may firmly conclude all of our prayers with that mighty word 'amen'. Amen – because in prayer we address our heavenly Father who always hears us and who will also answer us in a way that conforms to His holy will, which alone is good. God, as the faithful God of the covenant, will never put us to shame. We can trust Him always!

All of this shows the riches of prayer. In prayer, we cling to Christ, the Author, and Finisher of our faith. He will give us the strength to persevere to the very end, when we will share in the complete victory with Him.

June 14

READING: 1 THESSALONIANS 4:1-8

Living holy lives

"For God has not called us for impurity, but in holiness."
1 THESSALONIANS 4:7

From the meditations on the Ten Commandments, we learnt that God asks us to live our faith in thankful obedience for all that we have received in Christ. Such a living faith also needs sincerity in prayer, expecting all things from God alone, laying our weak lives in God's almighty hands.

Next, we will focus on whether we find genuine joy in living a life of thankful worship towards God and whether this is also seen in the way we live our life. Special attention will be given to the holiness God requires. Do we also find joy in living holy, and what does a holy life look like – holy in an unholy world?

In the text above this meditation, it reads: "For God has not called us for impurity, but in holiness." Although the emphasis in 1 Thessalonians 4 is on marriage, the command in verse 7 equally applies to those who are not married. We all must live holy in all our conduct each day.

To show what this involves, I would like to quote from some questions and answers from the Westminster Larger Confession. When dealing with the seventh commandment, this confession says: positively this requires chastity in body, mind, affections, words, and behaviour; watchfulness over the eyes and all the senses; temperance, keeping of chaste company, modesty in apparel, shunning all occasions of uncleanness, and resisting temptations thereof.

It also addresses the question of what the LORD forbids in this commandment. Some of the sins mentioned are: all unnatural lusts; all unclean imaginations, thoughts, idleness, gluttony, drunkenness, unchaste company, lewd songs, books, pictures, and all other provocations to, or acts of uncleanness, either in ourselves or others.

These words were written in 1646, but they surely have not lost their application today. In all of the things mentioned above, Satan is busy luring us away from the LORD. Therefore, the battle to stay holy is on for all of us. Let us never make light of this, but instead seek strength in the Lord to fight this battle faithfully each day, asking the Lord for strength not to give in to sinful desires. Instead we should find joy, that in Christ we have been set free from the slavery of all these sins. Set free – therefore, living holy before the LORD should always be a great joy for us each day.

June 15

READING: 1 PETER 1:13-21

Our hope in Christ is the foundation for living holy lives

"Set your hope fully on the grace that will be brought to you at the revelation of Jesus Christ."

1 PETER 1:13B

The call, in the text above this meditation, must be read in close connection with the verses four and five of this same chapter. In these verses, we read about an inheritance incorruptible and undefiled, ready to be revealed in the last time. We must set our hope on this inheritance as something that one day will be given to us. It makes the Christian life worth living for, since it is an inheritance which will not be affected by any economic downturn or by something else that may corrupt or erode it. It is safely stored away for us in heaven by God himself.

The question now is: do we appreciate this, or is this something we regard as "well that is for later!"? For later – if this is our reaction, it will also affect the way we live. Then the here and now of this life becomes more important to us than what God has in store for us. If we were to genuinely set our hopes on this great future, we would be like a little child that cannot wait until it is his birthday, for then he will get his presents. The mind of this child is continuously busy with this. It lives birthday focused. Comparably, we should live Christ focused!

Due to the fall into sin, our present life is broken in many ways. Yet in Christ, there is hope again. His victory over death has given our life perspective again. Perspective again, since – to quote from something I once read:
No despair so dark
No moral failure so grievous
No thundercloud so threatening
No disappointment so great
No future so bleak
No news so grim
No life in such peril
That our gracious God cannot remedy
through His power: to heal, comfort, restore, reconcile, and redeem!

In Christ, there is hope again, even beyond the grave. Because of Easter, we may look further than the horizon of this life. When we live our lives dedicated to Christ – we may struggle with problems, we may face illness, we may go through deep trials, yet we have a secure anchorage, a sure hope worth living for, which in this present life will help us to cope through ever-changing days and nights.

June 16

READING: 1 PETER 5:6-11

Be sober-minded

"Therefore, preparing your minds for action and being sober-minded...."

1 PETER 1:13A

Preparing your mind for action – literally it reads: girding up the loins of your mind. The reference is to the long clothes which people in eastern countries often wear down to their feet. These clothes make it hard to walk quickly. They make you stumble easily. Therefore, when travelling on foot, people would often gird or tighten up their clothes with a belt around their waist. Likewise, we should gird up the loins of our mind, bringing every thought into captivity to the obedience of Christ, so that our minds do not become too preoccupied with all kinds of things that cause serving the LORD to become secondary. Godly lives need godly minds. Similarly, holy lives need holy minds. Hence says Peter, be sober-minded.

Be sober-minded – first of all, this means: do not get drunk. Metaphorically it also means not to become intoxicated by the world. In other words, what are the things we are living for? Is it the here and now and the pleasures of this world, or do we as children of God show the people around us that we have something else to live for?

Be sober-minded – in Scripture, this call is often connected with the return of Christ. Hence, it also means not letting yourselves be taken up by everything this world has to offer: the lust of the flesh, the lust of the eyes, and the pride of life. When we do so, we so quickly lose sight of life's final destination. We are children of God, who have their commonwealth in heaven. This should also be clearly seen in the way we live our lives in this present world.

In Chapter 1 of Peter's first letter, we read that by the resurrection of Jesus Christ, we have been born again to a living hope. Is this hope alive in us? Is our life indeed full of it, so that we eagerly look forward to the return of our Saviour or is life at present too cosy for this? Yet how can children of the holy God ever be cosy or comfortable in a society full of unholiness and immorality? Hence in addition to the call to be sober-minded, we are also called to live holy; holy in all our conduct as obedient children who take delight in doing God's will.

June 17

READING: LEVITICUS 20:22-26

What is living a holy life?

"But as he who called you is holy, you also be holy in all your conduct since it is written, "You shall be holy, for I am holy.""

1 PETER 1:15-16

In the text above this meditation, the apostle Peter quotes from the Book of Leviticus. This book of the Old Testament especially emphasises that because of the covenantal relationship with God, the Israelites had to live holy lives. The same applies to the New Testament church. The apostle Peter makes it clear that in this respect nothing has changed.

We are called to live holy because we are children of the Holy God. Yet, do we truly rejoice in this? Do we see through the empty slogans by which Satan also tries to attract us? Or do we wonder whether one really has to live so strictly? Is everything in this world really so bad? We know how far we can go without compromising our faith. Do we? Or is it that we want the best of both worlds? Yet the LORD says that we must serve Him with an undivided heart otherwise we have no part in Him.

Living holy – this involves more than just living a decent life. Instead, it means: having a sincere desire to live for the LORD, not just every now and then, but always – not only on Sunday, but also throughout the week, both at work and during our leisure time. To see whether this really is our desire, it might be useful to examine ourselves with some of the following questions:

- Whom or what do I identify myself with – with the world or with God?
- Who or what rules my life, what do I get excited about?
- What are we busy with: everything the world around us is busy with as well, or does the reading and study of God's Word always have priority above all other things?

To live holy wherever we go and in whatever we do is possible only when we let ourselves be fed by the Word of God daily. Next, is there also a willingness to submit to God's Word; to submit also when it cuts deeply into our sinful flesh and may hurt? When we cling to God in prayer He will help us in this, giving as fruit that living holy will more and more become pure joy.

June 18

READING: HEBREWS 12:12-29

Strive for holiness

"Strive for peace with everyone, and for the holiness without which no one will see the Lord."
HEBREWS 12:14

The text above this meditation might cause feelings of uneasiness, especially concerning the words that without holiness no one will see the Lord. Feelings of uneasiness, since we all have a hard battle to live holy lives that are totally dedicated to serving the LORD in everything. If only this were true. Yet it is not. Daily we have to contend with the weakness of our faith and the evil desires of our sinful flesh. Living holy in everything is a hard battle each day again, for all of us. Does this mean we might miss out on seeing the Lord?

I think here also of what the Lord Jesus Himself said in the Sermon on the Mount: "Blessed are the pure in heart, for they will see God." Yet we are not pure, and so again does this mean we will miss out? Words of Scripture like these can cause us to worry. How will God look at my life, when with His holy eyes He sees the many sins there are, each day again?

In response, one can say there is no need to worry, since we are holy in Christ. He will cover all of our unholiness with his perfect holiness. This is indeed true. However, at the same time, we should be careful with a statement like this, lest we make light of the call to live holy lives. We are holy in Christ, yet this does not undo our responsibility to also strive for holiness. The word translated with strive refers to a determined effort on our part. It is a genuine and urgent call, lest – as it says in verse 15 of this chapter – we fail to obtain the grace of God.

We are saved by grace. From ourselves we cannot add even one inch to our salvation. Yet this does not mean that we can now simply sit back and rest on our laurels. Instead, God's grace in Christ will make us active – active also in striving for holiness. Slackness in this area might indeed cause us to miss out on seeing the Lord. Therefore, we should never make light of the call to live holy lives. The call to live holy – always.

June 19

READING: HEBREWS 13:20-21

Strive for peace and for holiness

"Strive for peace with everyone, and for the holiness without which no one will see the Lord."

HEBREWS 12:14

In Hebrews 12:14, it also says that we must strive for peace; not for peace with everyone – a call which we read more often in Scripture. Instead – as it can also be translated – strive for peace together with everyone and for holiness. It is the call to strive for holiness that is central in verse 14.

The addressees of this letter were in danger of slackening in faith. Living amid a hostile society, they found it more and more challenging to stand up for their faith. Hence, there was the inclination to compromise, to take God's commandments less strictly. They looked for peace within the society they lived in. Yet in doing so, they were in danger of losing their peace with God. This can also easily happen to us.

Today, many people live life to the full in immorality and all kinds of sinful lusts. Yet it does not make them happy. Instead, it often leaves them with an empty feeling and no inner peace. This is surely not the peace with which God will fill our hearts. Hence the call we read in verse 14! A call to make sure that no one lags behind in striving for peace and holiness.

Living holy – this is not popular today. It may cause you to lose friends, at times even within the church. Yet look at the gain. Living holy close to the Lord will give you peace with God, which is much more important.

Strive for peace together with everyone and for holiness. This means we should also encourage others to live this way, together pursuing this holiness to gain this peace. You may wonder who will be able to live at this high level. The answer is, no one of himself. That is why, in one of the concluding verses of this letter, the author says that God Himself will do this – Chapter 13 verse 21: He, the God of peace, will equip you with everything good that you may do His will, working within us that which is pleasing in His sight.

God will do it. Yet, this does not make the call to strive for holiness less urgent. The call is there! However, when we walk with God, holding Father's hand on every step of the road, He will give us what we need, also for living holy lives!

June 20

READING: HEBREWS 12:1-4

Living Christ focused

"Looking to Jesus, the founder and perfecter of our faith."
HEBREWS 12:2A

God will give us all that we need to live holy before Him. This does not mean that we can just sit back and let God do the work. The call to strive for holiness is a real call that sets us to work. At the beginning of Hebrews 12, we read about running a race. This involves effort. One must train for it very determinedly, which means one may need to skip some leisure activities. Yet what does that matter when the eye is set on winning the race?

This equally applies to running the race of faith. Chapter V, Article 2 of the Canons of Dort, speaks about holy exercises of godliness. Godly lives need godly minds. Hence, in training for the race of faith we should make the time and effort to read God's Word, to read a good book, or a good article. It means being involved with today's issues, trying to find Scriptural answers. To live holy, to live a godly life, we must train ourselves in godliness (1 Timothy 4:7).

All of this does not mean that by our efforts we can earn ourselves entrance into heaven. Christ cleared the way to the Father for us. No one can come to the Father than through Christ. Believe in Me, says Christ. Follow Me! Walk in my footsteps! Christ alone is the Author and Finisher of our faith. He alone can bring us safely home. To stay with the image of the race, He alone can make us reach the finishing line.

Hence the call to live Christ focused, always. As soon as we lose sight of Christ, it will also have its effect on the way we live, living more for ourselves than for God, with the result that we no longer see God in our life As it reads in Hebrews 12 verse 14: without this holiness, no one will see God. Seeing God – these words do not in the first place refer to the final day of history, but more directly to today. In the Sermon on the Mount, the Lord Jesus says, "Blessed are the pure in heart, for they will see God." When living close to the Lord in holiness towards God, we will see Him today, in the way He carries us by His love. What a great comfort it is seeing God in this way, every day as we walk with Him.

June 21

READING: ROMANS 8:5-11

Holy lives need the nourishment of holy minds

"Do not be conformed to this world, but be transformed by the renewal of your mind."

ROMANS 12:2A

Our redemption in Christ has consequences, also for the way in which we think. In Romans 8, the apostle Paul writes that we are not in the flesh but in the Spirit. Therefore, also our mind should be set on the things of the Spirit. Of course, we can only do this by the renewing power of the Spirit. Yet, this does not undo our own responsibility. It is true: the Spirit has to make us active in this, transforming us. However, the point is, are we willing to be transformed? Do we rejoice in this, or do we keep flirting with the world? Think of Lot's wife, who kept looking back. This means that in her heart and mind, she had not really cut ties with Sodom and Gomorra. A warning example!

Therefore, what are the things we fill our minds with? This is a very relevant question, especially when looking at today's society. Satan is busy, out there attracting our attention and in doing so, he is working foremost on our sinful desires – for example, when quickly flicking through the TV channels to see what is on, when browsing the internet, or via all kinds of pictures on our smartphones. I also think of all worldly advertising, making us believe that we can have it all.

Scripture calls us to live holy lives. Yet, we can only do so by filling our minds with holy things. How must we do this? The straightforward answer is to live close to Scripture – making time to read our Bible and meditate on it, time for and with the LORD, not only as a family at the dinner table, but also personally.

What are the things we fill our minds with? In 2 Corinthians 10:5, the apostle Paul says that we must bring all of our thoughts into captivity to the obedience of Christ. Only then will we be able to live truly holy lives. This shows that it all starts in the mind, a sinful mind that has to be renewed by the Holy Spirit. We must take our thoughts captive to the obedience of Christ, not just letting them stay in our mind only as thoughts, but also putting these thoughts into practice. In Philippians 4, the apostle Paul says: when you do this, the God of peace will be with you.

June 22

READING: PHILIPPIANS 4:4-13

Mind renewal

"...think about these things."
PHILIPPIANS 4:8B

Paul's letter to the Philippians is full of the theme of joy. Throughout this small letter, the word 'joy' is mentioned no less than sixteen times. This is remarkable considering that the apostle wrote this letter while in prison. One wonders how the apostle could write a letter so joyfully under such difficult circumstances. The answer to this question we find in the Scripture reading above this passage.

First, Paul says, there is no need to be anxious when you lay your life in God's hand and in prayer and supplication with thanksgiving give it all to God, assured in faith that He will provide. Trust that Father is in control, so why should I worry?

Next, Paul says that he has learnt to be content in whatever situation God places him. Content – this means living out of God's fatherly hand, whatever the circumstances are, fully trusting: God will provide!

Paul says that when you bring your life before God's throne in this way in prayer, you will find peace, real peace. Remember, the Lord is near. Christ is returning soon. Well, in that hour, the things we are so concerned about today, at times even grumble about – all this will disappear when Christ returns. Therefore, Paul says, stop doing this. Do not give yourselves over to doubt, to fear, nor to anger and bitterness, for this is sin. Instead, think of the purpose of your life. Live Christ focused!

Living Christ focused – this means focusing more on the cross where Christ gave His life for wretched sinners. Do we still marvel at this? Marvel daily, that Christ was willing to give His life for me, while there is still so much sin in my life? How often do we really think about this?

Think about these things. In order to do so, we all need some kind of mind renewal, whereby we get less busy with the things of this world, and as thankful children of God focus our mind more on how to live a life pleasing to God. Think about these things. Think about what is true: that is, about the things that God has said are true. This does not mean that we should only think about Christian subjects as opposed to secular matters. Instead, it means that whatever we are busy with in our mind, we should think about it in a Christian way. It means having a Christian mindset in everything.

June 23

READING: PHILIPPIANS 3:17-4:1

The battle of the mind

"...think about these things."

PHILIPPIANS 4:8B

Yesterday's meditation focused on thinking about all things in a Christian way. What does this mean more practically? For a moment, think of the society we live in today – a society full of crime and aggression. People are on edge, missing the safety of God's wholesome commandments for life. Think of marriage – a beautiful institution of God, which causes life to flourish. Yet those who oppose this institution, defending same-sex marriage and other freedoms, ruin the foundations of society. This clearly shows that when people set their mind solely on what they want, it goes wrong. Man's sinful heart fills the mind with sinful thoughts. Therefore, the apostle Paul says: make sure that you have the right mindset.

As God's children, we must live Christ-focused, also in our mind. Yet, this does not come just automatically. Even though God's Spirit has come to dwell within us, sin still often plays up. We are far from immune to all the temptations by which Satan also tries to lure us away from God.

In order to fight these temptations it is not good enough just to stop thinking bad thoughts that are dragging us down in our Christian life, but we must fill our mind also with good thoughts. The battle of the mind is to have a mind that is pure and honourable before the LORD. One has to learn this, says Paul, by busying the mind with other things like the virtues mentioned in verse 8.

When looking at these virtues one by one, they are formulated quite generally. Even an unbelieving person could agree that it is good to think of these virtues. This is not strange, when considering that these general virtues belong to man, having been created in the image of God. Yet, due to the fall into sin, these virtues have been stained. Even worse, these virtues are often turned into the opposite by people who do not honour God. Yet we are called to think about these virtues, not just in a general way as unbelievers perhaps would do as well. Instead, we must think of them in faith, out of love and thankfulness towards God. We are called to do this, since in Christ God wants to give these virtues back to us in their most beautiful form and this with the aim that we might practise them as well.

June 24

READING: PSALM 25:1-5

Thinking about the truth always

"Finally, brothers, whatever is true, whatever is honourable. whatever is just...think about these things."
PHILIPPIANS 4:8

In the next set of meditations, we will look in more detail at the virtues mentioned in verse 8 of Philippians 4. First, Paul says that we should meditate on whatever things are true, as opposed to things that are deceptive and dishonest. Meditating on what is true, showing the renewal of our mind by the power of the Holy Spirit. More practically, this means always thinking about things from God's perspective, be it at work, at home, or out for leisure. Do not just walk through life blindly, reacting thoughtlessly to whatever happens. Instead, remember daily that whatever God has revealed to us in Jesus Christ is true all the time, no matter where you are, no matter what is happening to you. When we start thinking in this way about the truth, the fruit will be that we also increasingly start living the truth.

Paul then mentions things that are honourable as opposed to shameful. More precisely, think about whatever brings honour to God, whatever brings glory to His great and wonderful name – meditate on this, says Paul.

Next, he says: whatever things are just – just in the eyes of God. Think about this when going to work in the morning. Think about how to live rightly before God. When we truly have this mindset at the beginning of each day, God will guide us and protects us. So quickly, we forget this. Hence, we should make our mind continually think about this, realising that the law of God is holy, righteous, and good, as the apostle Paul writes in Romans 7:12.

God's commandments are good and wholesome for life. Are we always convinced of this? If so, God's law will never become a burden to us. Instead, it will become a joy to do God's will. Again, this starts in the mind. Whatever is right, that is, whatever God approves of, whatever God has given us to live by. Constantly make your mind think about these things. Above all, do not just think about it but also live it to the glory of God's Name.

June 25

READING: COLOSSIANS 3:1-10

Setting our minds on the things that are above

"… whatever is pure, whatever is lovely, whatever is commendable, if there is any excellence, if there is anything worthy of praise, think about these things."

PHILIPPIANS 4:8

Whatever is pure, as opposed to impure. Again, the question is: what do we fill our minds with? For this will also reflect on the way we live. By way of example: at work, be it in the office or at the worksite, someone tells a joke displeasing God. What do you do? Do you show some dislike for the joke, yet meanwhile you still join in laughing? Yet, if our mind is set on whatever is pure, we would act differently with a correcting comment expressed in love.

It is sad to see in today's society that the idea of purity is rapidly disappearing. Fewer and fewer young people, when they approach their lifelong marriage partner, are pure virgins. This is not only happening in the outside world. It is also happening in the church.

Yet, again this starts with the mind and the desires of our hearts. Fleeing all immorality, including watching it on TV screens or videoclips on our smartphones, we should set our minds on what is pure and on how God wants us to live holy before Him. Think about these things, says Paul. Pure also in our mind, not only concerning sexual matters, but regarding every aspect of life.

Next, we read: "Whatever is lovely, whatever is commendable, if there is any excellence, if there is anything worthy of praise, meditate on these things." In all these virtues, the common denominator is that the LORD wants our life to be beautiful and so receive glory and praise through us. Again, this will only come about when our mind is also set on it. For, if our mind is full of what this world has to offer – earthly pleasures and earthly wealth – it will also have an impact on the way we live. Therefore, the LORD calls all of us to make a determined effort to busy our minds with things pleasing to Him, bringing every thought of our mind into captivity to the obedience of Christ. Only then will we also be able to live truly Christian lives.

June 26

READING: JOHN 14:15-27

The peace God will give

"...practice these things and the God of peace will be with you."
PHILIPPIANS 4:9B

From the previous meditations we learnt that in order to live holy lives to the honour of God, first we need a renewal of our mind, so that our heart's desires become pure. That is why the apostle mentioned several virtues to meditate on – things we should busy our mind with to have the right spiritual outlook on life. Yet it should not stop there. We must also practice this in living our faith in the daily routine of everyday life.

The apostle Paul says: practice what you have heard and seen in me. One may wonder whether this is not somewhat arrogant of the apostle Paul, putting himself as an example. After all, he too was but only a weak servant in the service of the Lord Jesus Christ. The apostle Paul too was far from perfect. How then can he say, do what you have heard and seen in me?

Yet the point is: what had the Philippians heard and seen from Paul? This: that Paul never boasted of himself. Instead, with all the weaknesses involved, his life reflected a total commitment to Christ. Paul not only taught but also showed by example what it meant to live by grace alone. The Philippians could see in Paul's life what it means when Christ becomes the Lord of your life: it produces life renewal in kindness and joy. In other words, when Paul says to do what you heard and saw in me, he actually says: commit your life to Christ, do so totally. If you do so, the God of peace will be with you.

However, if apart from our evening Bible reading, we hardly think of God throughout the day, it is unlikely that we will experience God carrying us throughout the day. We may feel unrest instead. Yet, when by the power from above we live our lives with the LORD, and we also cause our mind to dwell on the things of the LORD, God's peace surpassing all understanding will fill our lives. Even stronger, God Himself will be near to us each day, guiding and protecting us until we are home with Him forever. Then on our journey home, sustained by grace, the God of peace will be with us throughout the ever-changing day and night.

June 27

READING: PSALM 100

Living in the joy of faith (1)
"Serve the LORD with gladness..."
PSALM 100:2A

Many a Christian choir goes by the name of Jubilate Deo, which are words that come directly from Scripture. They are the opening words of the Latin translation, both of Psalm 66, as well as of Psalm 100. Literally translated, these words mean, "Make a joyful shout to God..." Psalm 66:1. In Psalm 100:1, it reads, "Make a joyful shout to the LORD..." Many a letter in the New Testament calls the congregation of Christ to express this same joy today, not only when there is something to celebrate, but always. In other words, we are to live this joy each day. In his letter to the Philippians, the apostle Paul writes in Chapter 4, verse 4: "Rejoice in the LORD always. Again I will say, rejoice!"

To rejoice, to jubilate – when hearing these words, we generally link them to a festive expression of joy, for example, in connection with someone celebrating an anniversary, a jubilee. Scripture, however, uses this verb much more widely, even in circumstances when perhaps we would never think of shouting for joy.

By way of example, 2 Chronicles 20 tells us that Judah and Jerusalem were under siege, and because of it fear spread throughout the country. Yet King Jehoshaphat did the right thing by calling a period of fasting throughout all Judah, during which time he brought the matter before the LORD who promises the victory. Next, we read that they went into battle. Yet before starting the battle, they sang a song of praise to the LORD, thanking God for His steadfast love. Thanking God even before they had won the battle.

As a New Testament example, I think of what we read about the Lord Jesus, singing the Hallel, just before He was about to bring His sacrifice on the cross. These are the Psalms 113 to 118 of the Book of Psalms, which were sung during the Passover. The last psalm of this section of psalms, Psalm 118, speaks about victory, yet the sacrifice was still to be brought. To sing, to shout for joy even before a challenging task is finished – this is possible only when we look on high and cling to God in faith. Singing our cares away, which is much more helpful than trying to reason them away. This is how we may live in the joy of faith as God's children, rejoicing in the Lord always, walking with God, holding Father's hand.

 June 28

READING: PSALM 106:1-5

Living in the joy of faith (2)

"…his steadfast love endures forever and
his faithfulness to all generations."

PSALM 100:5B

The last verse of Psalm 100 highlights God's covenant as an everlasting covenant. Hence, we never have to despair of God's mercy. When there is true repentance, we may always come back to God, no matter how much we have messed up our lives. God's mercy is everlasting. His steadfast love endures forever.

Psalm 100 also mentions that God's faithfulness endures throughout the generations. It does not stop when we die, since in that hour God will promote us to even greater glory: an everlasting covenant! Yet, because God's covenant is everlasting, it continues also through the generations. Generations come, and generations go – yet God remains the same in showing mercy to each new generation again. Every time a baby is baptised, we are reassured of this. God's promises stand from age to age unbroken, everlasting throughout the generations.

When considering all of this, who would not serve this God with gladness? It causes the mouth to speak from the fullness of the heart, bringing praises to God, shouting for joy.

Jubilate Deo – LORD, I stand in awe each time when I consider Thy love, of which I am totally undeserving; in awe when I consider Thy care even throughout the valleys of life, and above all when I consider Thy mercies, every morning anew. LORD, how great is Thy faithfulness. Hence, I shout for joy that I may belong. I shout for joy that this God is my God, my Father in Christ.

Psalm 100 calls us to worship the LORD with gladness, with great joy not only on Sunday but also throughout the week. It calls us to live our lives in the joy of faith, never being ashamed to also speak of this joy with others as true witnesses of Christ. It is nice to be a member of a choir that goes by the name of Jubilate Deo. Yet do we also jubilate the next morning back at work, radiating that same joy? If we indeed do so, who knows what fruit God will give. Jubilate Deo – these words are a call for all of us to live our lives each day in the joy of faith, rejoicing in God's steadfast love and never-ending faithfulness.

June 29

READING: 1 TIMOTHY 3:14-4:11

Upholding the truth

"…the church of the living God, a pillar and buttress of the truth."

1 TIMOTHY 3:15B

In 1 Timothy 3:15, the apostle Paul speaks about the church as a pillar and buttress of the truth. The truth – this is the good news of salvation in Jesus Christ as we find it in the Bible. In a world where this truth is continually under attack, the church has the calling to uphold or to bear the truth, as a pillar bears a bridge. The word 'pillar' serves as an image of firmness, and so does the word 'buttress'. These two words together show that the church must be a firm foundation on which the truth immovably rests. The church must be a place where the truth is safe.

Yet, how can a church consisting of weak and sinful members carry out this task? Only by strength from above. This is the only way in which a church, weak in itself, can uphold the truth amid a world where the vast majority of people no longer want to hear about the truth or accommodate the truth of God's Word to what they consider relevant. A church that still wants to uphold the Bible as the infallible Word of God will be increasingly under attack by the spirit of the time.

Today, many churches use the modern word contextualisation, which means the truth of Scripture must be applied to today's context. It is true that we must apply the Word of God to today's situation. However, today's situation is becoming increasingly more important than what God says. We see this concerning matters such as marriage, homosexuality and also concerning women in office. In all of these matters – so it is said – the Bible needs contextual interpretation in which the Holy Spirit guides us. Yet in most instances, it leads churches away from the truth of Scripture.

All of this makes the calling of the church to uphold and defend the truth an increasingly difficult task that needs our daily prayer. Our prayer that God will not only grant the office bearers, but all of us, faithfulness in defending the truth. A serious calling. Yet, in the heat of battle, we may also have the assurance that Satan will not succeed in his attempt to destroy the church. The victory is Christ's, our King, who will make sure that the church will not go down to defeat.

June 30

READING: EPHESIANS 3:14-21

Confessing the truth

"… the church of the living God, a pillar and buttress of the truth."

1 TIMOTHY 3:15B

As a pillar and buttress of the truth, the church not only has to uphold the truth, but it also must confess the truth. The word 'pillar' refers to this specific task of the church. In the days of the apostle Paul, pillars were also used to make things public. Announcements of the government, for example, were pasted to such a pillar, like our billboards today. Well, in a comparable way, the church of the living God is a pillar to make the truth public, defending it against all kinds of attacks which try to undermine the truth of the gospel. It is for this reason that we have confessions, which in a summary form say what the church accepts as the truth according to God's Word.

An example of such a confession is the Apostles' Creed. One could call this confession a first Form of Unity. Yet because of further attacks on this truth, it had to be elaborated on. Therefore, next to the Apostles' Creed, we also have the Nicene Creed, refuting the heresies of Arius who denied the deity of Christ. In the 16th and 17th Century, the Belgic Confession, the Heidelberg Catechism, and the Westminster Confessions were written to combat the heresies of the Church of Rome and the Anabaptists. Some time later, the Canons of Dort were written to defend the attacks from the heresies of Arminianism. By writing these confessions, the church understood its task of truly being a pillar of the truth.

Confessions should never be placed on the same level as Scripture. Confessions do not have divine authority. They are human documents, always subject to possible errors. Nevertheless, we accept them as a faithful interpretation of the truth according to the Word of God. In these confessions, the church confesses in summary form the catholic and undoubted Christian faith. It does so together with the church of all times and all places.

In the second half of the year we will go back to the Heidelberg Catechism, dealing with the Lord's Days 1 to 33 and this with the aim – as the apostle Paul writes in Chapter 3 of his letter to the Ephesians – of gaining a greater understanding of the love of God in Christ Jesus.

July 1

**READING: 2 CORINTHIANS 1:1-11,
HEIDELBERG CATECHISM, Q+A 1**

The comfort only God can give

"Blessed be the God and Father of our Lord Jesus Christ, the Father of mercies and God of all comfort, who comforts us in all our affliction…"

2 CORINTHIANS 1:3-4A

Comfort is a word we all know. Yet, what gives true genuine comfort? From a general perspective, comfort is something that provides relief, consolation. It is something we all need at times. Yet the point now is: where do we find this relief? Amidst the worries and anxieties of life, where do we look for an anchorage that can weather the storms?

Many things in life may offer a certain measure of security. An excellent job with a comfortable income gives at least some security. So does a healthy body and a good circle of supportive friends. These are all things which can make life less worrisome. However, what if all of these things fall away? What if you lose your job, or if all of a sudden you hear that you are terminally ill, or friends fail you – what then? Does life then just become one big worry, or do we still have a secure anchorage to weather all of these storms, which at times can indeed hit life very hard? This is what is at the heart of the first question of the Heidelberg Catechism: what is your anchorage in life, your only comfort when everything else falls away?

Today the vast majority of people are trying to find this comfort by indulging themselves in all kinds of worldly pleasures which for a while may help them to forget about the difficulties they struggle with. Yet does it really help? After a while, the reality only hits home harder. It does not ease the pain. How is that? The answer is: in seeking relief, people are driven by the wrong concept of comfort.

Finding true genuine comfort does not mean you no longer want to think of the difficulties, the hardship, and the pain you suffer from. Instead, one will find true comfort by facing all of these difficulties, trusting God will provide. This is the comfort about which the apostle Paul also speaks in 2 Corinthians 1: a unique comfort, the comfort only God can give. A comfort that never fails nor disappoints. It is a comfort we may cling to, even when facing death. Truly unique!

July 2

**READING: ROMANS 14:7-9,
HEIDELBERG CATECHISM, Q+A 1**

Belonging to Christ

"So then, whether we live or whether we die, we are the Lord's."
ROMANS 14:8B

Speaking about our unique comfort, the first thing the Catechism mentions is that we are not our own. One wonders what comfort this gives. In today's individualistic climate, many people would consider this to be a very strange comfort, not wanting any control over their lives. These days people want to make their own decisions, be it right or wrong. Moreover, who says what is right or wrong? People want to decide this for themselves. Postmodernism, we call this – a climate in which man claims total freedom. Yet it is a freedom which makes man a slave to his own sinful desires.

Already in the first pages of the Bible we can read what this delusive idea of freedom leads to. Adam and Eve also wanted to be their own boss, deciding for themselves whether it was good or bad to eat from the tree God had forbidden them to eat from. Yet they soon realised what an unwise decision they had made. In Article 17 of the Belgic Confession, it reads: man plunged himself into physical and spiritual death and made himself completely miserable. Trembling, he fled from God.

However, no one can flee from God. God will meet each person either with His grace or with His wrath. This is the reason why we read in more than one place in Scripture that there is no peace for the wicked. Those who speak so highly of their freedom and independence today, if they do no repent, will one day all perish.

Man wants freedom. Yet Satan uses this highly praised freedom to ruin man's life. It is a pipedream, appealing when you look at the glitz and glamour of all kinds of advertisements, telling us that we can have it all. However, it is nothing more than a delusion, which in the end only makes life miserable and leads to physical and spiritual death.

It is for this very reason that as God's children we confess: "Lord, I thank Thee that I am not my own, but may belong to Jesus Christ. I thank Thee that I may call Him the Lord of my life." Yes, thanks be to God, who in and through Christ has redeemed us from Satan's deadly grip. As a result, we are no longer on our way to death, but to life eternal instead.

July 3

READING: ISAIAH 43:1-5A,
HEIDELBERG CATECHISM, Q+A 1

Set free

"Fear not, for I have redeemed you; I have called you by name, you are Mine."

ISAIAH 43:1B

In the second part of his prophecies, Isaiah, enlightened by God's Spirit, addresses the church in exile, which he calls deaf and blind (Chapter 42:18). Deaf – because they did not listen. Blind – because they refused to see the hand of God in history, verse 20. Despite all that had happened (being robbed and plundered, having become prey with no one to deliver them (Chapter 42:22), they remained deaf and blind. Being stiff-necked, they still asked themselves the question, "Why did all of this happen to us?" Why? Because they had sinned against the LORD and they did not want to walk in His ways. Repeatedly, they disobeyed God's law. Therefore the LORD poured out the fury of His anger upon them and led them into exile. Humanly speaking, one would expect this must be the end.

However, turning to Chapter 43, we read something different. No judgment, but grace instead! Yes, the LORD still wants to redeem His people. Verse 3 speaks about a ransom. During the time of Israel's exile, God paid this ransom by bringing the people in the Middle East into motion, causing the Medes and the Persians to let Israel go back to their own country. Their armies moved more towards the South-West, capturing Egypt and Ethiopia instead. However, Israel was set free. This was sovereign love from God's side by which He still wanted to redeem His people – a miracle of God's grace.

Drawing the redemptive-historical line through to the New Testament, we know that in a comparable way as Israel's redemption from Egypt, this return from exile also foreshadowed the ultimate redemption God would give in Jesus Christ. Like so many of the Old Testament prophecies, Isaiah 43 also foreshadows the redemption from the power of Satan, to whom we, being blind and deaf as well, have yielded ourselves through sin. Because of it, we too deserved God's wrath and yet received grace in and through Jesus Christ. Yes, God so loved us that He did not spare His own Son but gave Him up for us. Christ came to ransom us from the clutches of Satan. The precious price paid for this was Christ's own blood. Set free by Christ, from now on, we may live in joy without fear, safe in life and death. A unique comfort, indeed!

July 4

**READING: MATTHEW 10:26-33,
HEIDELBERG CATECHISM, Q+A 1**

Have no fear

"Fear not, therefore…"
MATTHEW 10:31A

Not a hair can fall from my head without the will of my heavenly Father. Just one hair dropping on the ground when you comb your hair – would God really care about this; care about those most trivial things in our lives: that flu, which I only had for a couple of days, that mark for my test, that bruise I got when I fell? Yes, He does, and we do well to take note of this, lest we only speak about God's hand when something big happens: an earthquake, a flood or a tragic accident. Beyond that, those trivial things we can manage ourselves without God. Scripture, however, teaches differently.

In Matthew 10, the Lord Jesus says: not one sparrow falls to the ground apart from Father's will, and He adds, you are of more value than many sparrows. This teaches us: God concerns Himself with every little detail in our lives. The hairs on our head – they are indeed all numbered one by one, even when they fall out during chemotherapy. God also numbers these hairs. "Fear not, therefore," the Lord Jesus says. Fear not, because we may know ourselves safe always, safe in God's love in and through Christ, the Redeemer of our lives.

This does not mean that we will never meet with any harm. When Christ sent out His disciples, He also spoke about persecution. People will lay their hands on you. They will persecute you, He said. It might happen that you will be imprisoned. They may even put you to death for My name's sake. Yet not a hair on your head shall be lost.

How can the Lord Jesus say this? The answer is in John 10:29, where the Lord Jesus says: those whom the Father has given to Me, that is those for whom I shed My precious blood – they are Mine, My precious possession. Therefore, no one will be able to snatch them out of My hand. I have secured them with My blood, so that without My Father's will not a hair can fall from their head. Thus, God's protection is indeed all-embracing. Nothing – not even death – can separate us from God's love in Jesus Christ. This is the unique comfort confessed in Lord's Day 1.

July 5

**READING: ROMANS 8:31-39,
HEIDELBERG CATECHISM, Q+A 1**

We are Christ's in life and in death

"…(nothing) will be able to separate us from the love of God in Christ Jesus our Lord."

ROMANS 8:39B

Daily we may live from the rich comfort that there is no need for fear, since Christ is there for us always, with His all-embracing protection both in life and in death. A unique comfort, but also a sure comfort. Yet despite this assurance, there are also times when we do not always feel it that strongly – times when Satan is trying to deprive us of this sure comfort.

However, it is to be noted that it does not read in Lord's Day 1 that my only comfort in life and in death is that I feel that I belong to Jesus Christ, nor that I experience it. Thankfully not, since nothing is more fickle, more changeable than human feelings or experiences. Instead, the Catechism states the facts: I am Christ's with body and soul both in life and death. We can be one hundred percent sure of this. Why is this? The simple answer is: Christ paid my ransom! Because of that precious price paid for me – Christ's sacrifice on Calvary – there is never any need to doubt that He will always care for us, always preserve us as His precious possession.

In the concluding verses of Romans 8, the apostle Paul writes about tribulation, distress, persecution, famine, nakedness, peril, and the sword. Yet – says Paul – in all these things we are more than conquerors through Him who loved us. Therefore, nothing can separate us from the love of God in Christ Jesus, our Lord. Nothing – no matter how deep the valley we must travel through might be. Why can we be so sure of this? The answer is: all the waves and billows of God's anger and the fire of God's heavy wrath were poured out on the Lord Jesus Christ, who at the cross was forsaken by God so that we might nevermore be forsaken by Him.

Thus, our only comfort both in life and in death lies firmly anchored in Christ's sacrifice on the cross. Because of His perfect sacrifice, God will be near to us always, guiding and protecting us throughout this life, making all things work together for our salvation. There might be times when we do not understand God's way with our life, yet the LORD says to us: trust Me with My plan for your life. Then you indeed have nothing to fear.

 July 6

**READING: ROMANS 8:9-17,
HEIDELBERG CATECHISM, Q+A 1**

The renewing power of the Holy Spirit

"You, however, are not in the flesh, but in the Spirit…"
ROMANS 8:9A

Standing firm, even when the boat of our life hits gale force winds – one may ask how we can do this? Weak in ourselves, we would never be able to do this. However, in the concluding part of Answer 1 of the Heidelberg Catechism, we read that the LORD Himself will give us what is needed through His Holy Spirit who will make us heartily willing and ready to live our lives for and with the LORD, each day anew. In other words, to live for and with Christ is not something we have to achieve. Instead, it is the fruit of the Holy Spirit working within us.

In Romans 8, the apostle Paul writes: "You, however, are not in the flesh, but in the Spirit." The Holy Spirit dwells in us as a gift of the glorified Christ. From heaven, He poured out His Spirit not only to guide us in the truth, but also to help us live in the joy of faith.

In the Form for Baptism, it reads that the Holy Spirit imparts to us what we have in Christ. He does so by working faith in our hearts, which is the instrument by which we can embrace God's promises. He opens our eyes for the riches of these promises, so that we may live from them. By nature, we are inclined to turn our back on these promises. Yet the Holy Spirit powerfully renews our will so that the joy to be Christ's starts permeating our lives in everything. Our life receives a new direction. It gives us a different outlook on all that this world has to offer. We see through the emptiness of those worldly pleasures. Renewed by Christ's Spirit, our greatest desire will be to please Him who bought us with the price of His precious blood.

This is what a Christian life is all about. We no longer live for ourselves but for Christ, in thankfulness for the redemption He obtained for us. This too is part of our only comfort both in life and in death.

**READING: PSALM 130,
HEIDELBERG CATECHISM, Q+A 2**

The enriching knowledge of our unique comfort

"If you, O Lord, should mark iniquities, O Lord, who could stand? But with you there is forgiveness, that you may be feared."

PSALM 130:3-4

In the second part of Lord's Day 1, the question is asked: "What do you need to know in order to live and die in the joy of this comfort?" Three things are mentioned, only three. This does not seem to be too hard. Yet, who will ever be able to say that he has finished gaining sufficient knowledge concerning the three things mentioned in this answer?

First, it reads that we must know how great our sins and misery are. This is more than just a simple acknowledgment that we are sinful. This hardly hurts, since we are all sinners. The Catechism wants us to dig deeper, lest we gloss over our sins, saying it could be worse. Instead, the Catechism wants us to own up to our sins, admitting that all too often we make a big mess of our lives – a big mess in failing God and our neighbour. Yes, if the LORD should mark our iniquities, who could stand?

We all know that in Christ we have received forgiveness of sins and eternal life, but how often do we think about the precious price that had to be paid for this? Perhaps when praying for forgiveness, we should think more often of the cross, and of what Christ suffered there for us. This will also deepen our thankfulness. The more we see what Christ has done for us, the more we will marvel at all that we receive in Him.

Only in this way will we truly enjoy the comfort of Answer 1. Enjoy the knowledge that we are Christ's, who will take us with Him on His way to eternal glory. Meditating on the riches of this unique comfort will help us to live more in thankfulness to God, and this not just in words, but also in deeds. The more we realise what it means to be Christ's, the more it will increase our desire to render our life to Christ and live for Him alone.

July 8

READING: ROMANS 3:9-20,
HEIDELBERG CATECHISM, LORD'S DAY 2

Total Depravity

"None is righteous, no not one."
ROMANS 3:10

The first part of the Heidelberg Catechism is very brief. Yet this does not mean that it is less important. Without a good understanding of our sins and misery, we will never learn to appreciate what Christ has done for us. To see what a great Saviour we have, first we must learn what total depravity means.

Total depravity – in short, this means that because of the fall into sin we have become unable to serve God, unable even to accept the gift of salvation as it is offered to us. Those who are from a Reformed background will have no difficulty in embracing this as the true doctrine of faith. Yet to accept this doctrine as the reality of life seems to be more difficult at times, even hard to accept. Unbelievers – yes, they do not obey God's law, hating God and their neighbour. Nevertheless, even in the world, things are not always that bad either, are they? Outside the church, you can also meet people who still live a decent life.

Therefore, is the picture given by Lord's Day 2 not too dark? True, in the church everything is not rosy either. At times we are confronted with terrible sins, also inside the church. But to say that by nature we too hate God and our neighbour is hard to accept. Is our life indeed really so bad?

How is it that we struggle to admit the truth in Lord's Day 2? The reason is that too often we try to minimise the sins we commit. We shrug them off as not too bad, especially when comparing our lives with that of others. Yet in doing so we make light of the fact that with every single sin, no matter how small in our eyes, we grieve our great Father in heaven.

Think of an X-Ray, which is used as a diagnostic tool to help a doctor see what is wrong with our body. Without such an X-Ray, the doctor would never find this. The same applies to our spiritual life. When we let the Word of God shine into the deep corners of our life, it will show up dark spots which we would prefer to hide. However, see it as a spiritual X-Ray that shows where our life needs healing and repentance, so that once again, in total self-denial, God becomes the centre of our lives.

July 9

**READING: ROMANS 7:7-12,
HEIDELBERG CATECHISM, LORD'S DAY 2**

Sin exposed

"If it had not been for the law, I would not have known sin."

ROMANS 7:7

When asking the average person about what makes life miserable, in most cases the answer given would be: just listen to the daily news – what a misery in so many ways! War, crime, violence, famine, floods, etcetera. Misery, at times also in our personal lives: frustrations, worries, sickness, hardships, and trials.

Yet the Catechism, in answering this question, digs deeper by pointing to the cause of all misery. In doing so, it mentions not only the word misery, but also the word sin. This is a word that nowadays not many people want to hear. Yet it is the word 'sin' that points to the root of all misery. How so, one may ask?

Think of the following example. A patient in hospital who has a high fever may feel miserable and might even be critically ill. Yet this fever is only a symptom of the illness he is suffering from. Even stronger, it can be that a person does not feel sick at all, yet meanwhile a dangerous disease is eating his body away. Comparably, people can enjoy prosperity and life, utterly blind to the misery they suffer from: the sins they live in!

In other words, the root of our misery is something you cannot see. It is like your own face, which you cannot see either unless you look in a mirror. In doing so, we might not always like what we see. Likewise, the Catechism wants us to look into a mirror, a very special mirror, to show us what is wrong with our life. This mirror is the Law of God.

When looking in faith into the mirror of God's Law, we see that we are guilty before God and deserve His punishment. Not a nice picture. It can make one scared or depressed. Yet this is not God's purpose. If that were the case, how could we reconcile this with the mighty overture the Catechism starts with? We are redeemed. This is the wonderful comfort we may live from. So what is the aim of looking into the mirror of God's law? The aim is to convict us of sin, so that in total self-denial we learn to look away from ourselves to find salvation in Christ alone.

July 10

**READING: PSALM 19:7-11,
HEIDELBERG CATECHISM, LORD'S DAY 2**

God's perfect law

"The law of the LORD is perfect,
reviving the soul."

PSALM 19:7A

"From where do you know your sins and misery?" The answer reads, "From the law of God." When Lord's Day 2 mentions the law, it refers not just to the Ten Commandments but to the whole Bible. The Lord Jesus used these words in a similar way when He said to His disciples, "Is it not written in your Law?", meaning in the Scriptures of the Old Testament. Indeed, all of Scripture teaches us about our sins and misery. In His Word, His law, God teaches us about His perfect will for our lives, about who He is and what He expects from us. From all this teaching throughout God's Word, we learn how much we fall short in loving God and our neighbour.

The purpose of this teaching is not to depress us. Instead, God still seeks us in love even when He points us to our sins and misery. After the fall into sin, God could easily have left us to our fate and rightfully never looked at us again. Yet God did not do this. Despite all that had happened, God's heart still went out to sinful man. In Article 17 of the Belgic Confession it reads, "When He saw that man had thus plunged himself into physical and spiritual death and made himself completely miserable, our gracious God in His marvelous wisdom and goodness set out to seek man when he trembling fled from Him."

God's heart still went out to sinners lost in guilt. He still loved us. Yet, God's love for us did not cause Him to be silent about sin. On the contrary, by His law, God wanted to expose our sins. Yet not as a pitiless judge, but as our Father in Christ. After the fall into sin, God did not leave us to our fate. Instead, in love for us He called us to order. God did so quite soundly. It did not happen without any pain, yet it was still by His fatherly hand. By this hand, God wants to guide us in the right direction. This too is the purpose of God's law.

July 11

**READING: EPHESIANS 2:1-10,
HEIDELBERG CATECHISM LORD'S DAY 2**

The gospel of Lord's Day 2

"…by nature children of wrath, like the rest of mankind. But God being rich in mercy… made us alive together with Christ."

EPHESIANS 2:3B-5A

The Catechism makes it quite clear that by looking into the mirror of God's Law, the picture is a very horrible one, since the love God requires of us is lacking altogether. Even worse, by nature we are inclined to hate God and our neighbour. How can we reconcile this picture with the concluding sentence of Answer 1, where it reads that Christ through His Holy Spirit makes us heartily willing and ready from now on to live for Him?

We find the answer to this question in the passage of Scripture above this meditation where the apostle Paul writes that by nature we are not any better than those who do not love God. Yet in Christ this has changed, and this should also become visible in our life. This does not mean that our old nature will never play up anymore. It is rooted so deeply in us that we will never get rid of it altogether. The apostle John in his first letter writes that he who says that he has no sin deceives himself and makes God a liar. Therefore, also redeemed children of God must always be made aware of their sins and misery. Yet the aim of this is not to make us despair so that we start doubting our redemption. Instead, by pointing us to our sins and misery, God's Law wants to drive us to Christ in whom we have received the forgiveness of sins.

This clearly shows that Lord's Day 2 does not take away the comfort of Lord's Day 1. On the contrary, it deepens this comfort, making us more aware of the greatness of God's grace. When considering how great God's grace towards us is, it will also increasingly become our desire to live in obedience to God's law, out of thankfulness for the redemption we received in Christ. Thus, even in addressing the matter of our sins and misery, Lord's Day 2 still points us to the gospel of our salvation in Christ. Making us aware of how helpless we are of ourselves, we may flee to Christ, who through His Spirit will help us to live joyfully from the comfort of Lord's Day 1.

July 12

**READING: JOHN 3:1-8,
HEIDELBERG CATECHISM, LORD'S DAY 3**

The need for regeneration

"...unless one is born again he cannot
see the kingdom of God."
JOHN 3:3B

Lord's Day 3 of the Heidelberg Catechism deals with the bitter reality of sin and the consequences it also has for us. Not such an uplifting subject one may think, especially when this Lord's Day concludes that because of the fall into sin it even applies to us: no good left whatsoever. For many this is too hard a pill to swallow. In the last decade of the previous century, a little booklet was published which stated that the doctrine of man's total depravity as confessed in the Heidelberg Catechism could lead to severe depression. It had as title: Helpless and yet guilty. Would such a dilemma indeed not cause many people to despair; despair and this because of their faith?

Lord's Day 3 – a depressing Lord's Day, yet only when one reads this Lord's Day in isolation, not looking at the context in which this Lord's Day is placed. From Lord's Day 1 we learnt that to enjoy the comfort we have in Christ we must first learn how great our sins and misery are. Or to phrase this slightly differently: to know how great a Saviour we have, we must first know what He has saved us from.

We speak about amazing grace. Yet, this amazement will only be there when we first see the darkness of our own sins. Therefore, the dark colours pictured by Lord's Day 3 serve in showing the brightness of the light in Christ. By way of example, you will only see a bright colourful rainbow when there are also dark clouds.

Lord's Day 3 starts with the beautiful picture of man being created in God's image. Next, we read about the mess we made of it due to our willful disobedience. Yet, Lord's Day 3 does not end on this dark note. True, the last answer gives a bleak picture of man after the fall into sin. Man became so corrupt that he was unable to do any good and inclined to all evil. Totally corrupt unless a miracle were to happen. Well, this miracle did happen in and through the redemption Christ obtained for us. The miracle of a new life for people who deserved eternal death. Therefore, still good news! Yet, only when we first see very clearly what was needed to save us – **a miracle!**

July 13

**READING: GENESIS 1:26-31,
HEIDELBERG CATECHISM LORD'S DAY 3**

God created everything perfect

"And God saw everything He had made,
and behold, it was very good."

GENESIS 1:31A

Never can we blame God for all the misery we experience in this world. In the beginning, all of creation was perfect. Man lived in a good relationship with God and also with his wife. Never one bad word was spoken, never any argument, no troubles, everything perfect.

God created man good and in His image. The latter indeed means man looked like God. Not physically, like a mirror image, but being created in the image of God man was to reflect the characteristics of God: in faithfulness, gentleness, wisdom, righteousness, and holiness. With these characteristics, man was called to rule over creation, showing what God was like.

In exercising this rule, God had put everything into man's hands. All animals, the whole realm of nature, all raw materials, all the opportunities creation offered. God had put all things under his feet, we read in Psalm 8, yet not for man's own glory. Instead, man was to reflect the kingship of God, with God also creating man in such a way that he was able to do so.

Being created in true righteousness and holiness, man lived life to God's glory. There were no impure motives whatsoever. Man knew only one aim in life: to glorify God. We should never forget that this was the purpose right from the beginning for which God had created man, as it reads in Lord's Day 3: "So that man might rightly know God his Creator, heartily love Him, and live with Him in blessedness to praise and glorify Him." Considering this, one can only marvel at God's beautiful work of creation. Indeed, perfect in every respect.

Perfect also in the abilities and desires man had. After all, God did not create man to be like a robot, for a robot cannot show real love. Instead, God created man with a will and feelings, with talents to organise and to govern, so that in all this man could honour God His Creator, and in doing so respond to God's love. In the beginning, God indeed created everything beautifully, excellently, and gloriously. Perfect without any fault.

July 14

**READING: JOB 42:1-6,
HEIDELBERG CATECHISM, LORD'S DAY 3**

From where did man's depraved nature come? (1)

"Therefore I have uttered what I did not understand, things too wonderful for me, which I did not know."

JOB 42:3B

God created everything beautifully and perfectly. Therefore, in no way can God be blamed for all the misery we are confronted with today. But from where, then, did man's depraved nature come? If God meant it all so well, where did it go wrong?

For an answer to this question, once again the authors of the Heidelberg Catechism take us back to Paradise, to what happened there when our first parents, Adam and Eve, became disobedient and rebelled against God. This is where it went wrong with all the consequences involved, also for us.

Sometimes the question is asked, "But could God not have prevented this? Why did He not create man in such a way that he would never have fallen into sin?" Also, God knew beforehand that things would go wrong. Did He perhaps use sin to prove the greatness of His mercy, as some people have said?

These are questions that are on the borderline of being improper. Yes, are we allowed to ask questions like these? Is there not a danger that we are trying to call God to account, or even worse, somehow still trying to blame God?

This surely is not the intent of the Heidelberg Catechism. Even more to the point, questions like these are also found in Scripture. For example, I may refer to the Book of Job. When reading this book, we see Job struggling with the very same questions. However, in the concluding part of this book, God reveals His majesty to Job. God is God, whose ways are beyond our human understanding. This means there also comes a time when we must stop asking questions. Job did when he repented before God, saying: "I have uttered what I did not understand, things too wonderful for me, which I did not know… Therefore, I despise myself and repent in dust and ashes".

We may struggle to understand man's fall into sin: how could this happen? Yet we do not always need an answer to every question. There are also things which we may leave to God in childlike faith. Doing so will give inner peace, as Job found when he stopped questioning God.

READING: JAMES 1:12-17,
HEIDELBERG CATECHISM, LORD'S DAY 3

From where did man's depraved nature come? (2)

"Pride goes before destruction, and a haughty spirit before stumbling."

PROVERBS 16:18

At times there might be questions we struggle with which we should leave to God in childlike faith. Of course, this does not mean that we are not allowed to ask questions. We are allowed to do so, as long as we do it with reverence towards God. The Heidelberg Catechism does this by trying to answer the question of how evil entered into this world.

From Scripture, we know that it all started in heaven. One of the angels rebelled against God. One of the angels, and as such a creature, contended with God! This is where it started. Other angels joined this rebellion, no longer being content with the position God had given them.

When Satan, in his rebellion against God did not succeed in heaven, he turned to the earth, trying to ruin what God had created to be good and perfect. First, he sowed doubt into Eve's heart about the provisions God had made for man: why are you not allowed to eat from this one tree? Next, he defames God's motives and denies the truthfulness of what God had said, presenting God's words in such a way as if God had said all this solely for His own personal reasons, not wanting man to be like Him, knowing good and evil.

Eve falls for the lie of the devil, eats from the tree, and makes Adam eat as well. The result is that their eyes are opened. Yet it does not better their position as they had hoped for. Instead, their high position under God changes into a position without God.

In Proverbs 16:18, it reads, "Pride goes before destruction, and a haughty spirit before stumbling." It is this haughtiness that caused all the misery that followed. This is how it always goes when we sin. Man wants to be wiser than God. James writes in his letter that it starts with the wrong desire, then when desire has conceived, it gives birth to sin, and sin when it is full-grown, brings forth death. Sinful desires, which are nothing more than rebellion against God. They ignore God's love and goodness and bring forth only ruin and destruction, for which we can never blame God. God created everything beautifully, also giving man the ability to serve Him perfectly.

July 16

**READING: ROMANS 5:12-21,
HEIDELBERG CATECHISM, LORD'S DAY 3**

A sinful inheritance

"Therefore, as one trespass led to condemnation for all men, so one act of righteousness leads to justification and life for all men."
ROMANS 5:18

How can God keep us accountable for what Adam did? Can we be punished for the wrongdoings of our fathers? This is what the Israelites in exile thought. Yet then God says: the soul who sins shall die, Ezekiel 18:4. In other words, each one will be punished for his own sins. True, the second commandment teaches that the sins of the fathers do have consequences for the children, even in the third and fourth generations. Consequences – yet this differs from inheriting sin, that is, being held accountable for what Adam did.

In Romans 5:12, the apostle Paul says: "Therefore, just as sin came into the world through one man, and death through sin and so death spread to all men because all sinned …". There is a certain tension in this verse. On the one hand, it reads: through one man, sin entered this world. Yet, at the end of this verse, it reads "because all sinned". Both are true, and this because of our unique relationship with Adam. God looks at humanity in its totality.

For a practical example of this, I think of what David says in Psalm 51 after he had committed adultery with Bathsheba and had killed Uriah. How could this happen in the life of a man who lived so close to God? David says it is because he was brought forth in iniquity and was conceived in sin: "That is the source of my sins." In mentioning this, David is not trying to shift the blame, as we sometimes do by saying 'I cannot help that I am like this. I did not make myself.' No, in Psalm 51, David claims full responsibility for what he did. At the same time, he points to the source of it all, saying how deeply sin was rooted within him. 'It was not just an accident that this happened, but this is me', he says – 'I am sinful at the root of my existence.'

In concluding Lord's Day 3, instead of asking questions about God's fairness in holding us accountable for Adam's sin, we should instead thank God for the abundance of His grace, which is similarly given to us by being in Christ. When considering this, one can only stand in awe of God's wondrous works which still show so much love towards us sinners.

July 17

READING: ISAIAH 1:27-31,
HEIDELBERG CATECHISM, LORD'S DAY 4

God is just in all His ways (1)

"Zion shall be redeemed by justice and those in her who repent, by righteousness."

ISAIAH 1:27

Lord's Day 4 starts with the question, "But does not God do man an injustice by requiring in His law what man cannot do?" This question is not meant to blame God for any unfairness. Instead, the Catechism wants to highlight that God is just in all His ways. Yet not to condemn us, but to redeem us.

The LORD requires 100 % obedience, even though after the fall into sin we are no longer able to fulfill this requirement. The question could be asked whether this is fair? By way of example, consider the believers having become spiritually paralytic people because of the fall into sin. How can the LORD still ask us to walk before Him in perfect holiness? Why can the Lord not be content with less?

Even though the example sounds nice, it portrays a wrong picture. Our spiritual state is more like a man who received a purse full of money – enough money to live a wealthy life. Yet this man squanders his money. Next, he starts making irresponsible debts. If a creditor were to ask this man to pay his debts, no one would call this unjust or unfair. Comparably, we have robbed ourselves of the possibility of living in obedience and holiness before God. Therefore, it is totally out of place to accuse God of unfairness when He still asks us to do so.

Also, if the LORD had indeed lowered the requirements for obedience after the fall into sin, why did the LORD not lower these requirements before the fall? Perhaps we would not have fallen into sin after all. It is evident when we start asking questions like these that we get more and more entangled in it, getting nowhere. Therefore, we should begin with what Scripture teaches very clearly, namely that there is no injustice or any unfairness from God's side, when today He still asks us to render Him 100 % obedience. We can only be thankful for this, since this shows that God is faithful not only concerning His promises, but equally relating to His demands. If this were not the case, it would also make God's words of promise less reliable. Yet, now we never have to doubt this, since God is faithful always in all His ways. That is the comfort of Lord's Day 4. Comfort, even when it speaks about punishment.

July 18

READING: PSALM 5,
HEIDELBERG CATECHISM LORD'S DAY 4

God's justice shows God's faithfulness

"For you are not a God who delights in
wickedness; evil may not dwell with you."
PSALM 5:4

In Psalm 5:4, we read that God does not delight in wickedness. The LORD hates all evildoers. He will destroy them, verses 5 and 6. David, the author of this psalm, does not write these words because he wants revenge on his enemies. The purpose of this psalm is different. David knows: if the LORD did not abhor all evil, we would have to get used to sin with all the misery involved. Misery like war, crime, and violence, but also all lying and deceit – shameful things at times, even in the church. We would have to live with all of this brokenness without any hope. This would have happened if the LORD had lowered the requirement of 100% obedience.

The Remonstrants, whose teachings are refuted in the Canons of Dort, taught that God no longer requires perfect obedience from man, but instead considers our imperfect obedience as perfect. After all, man can still offer some obedience to God. Of course, it is grace from God's side in considering this obedience to be sufficient. This reasoning is appealing, but also very dangerous. It would mean that even though we fall short of the standard set by God, God would be content with it, especially when we have tried so hard.

Yet, if God would indeed be content with this, He would adapt Himself to the fact that we broke the covenant – adapt Himself to our unfaithfulness. This would also mean that God would go back on His demand of 100% obedience and no longer keep the words He had already spoken. However, this is impossible, and we can be thankful for this, since it reassures us that God is always faithful.

God is a just God. This means God does what we expect from Him. He sticks to what He has spoken, even after the fall into sin. God does not adapt Himself to the situation that man broke the covenant. But as the faithful God, He keeps reminding man of what is required of him: 100% obedience! Yet – and this is our comfort – God Himself opens up the ways in which this can be done. In wrath God also remembers mercy. Justice and mercy – for God, these are not two opposites, but in God's plan of redemption they work together for our salvation.

**READING: PSALM 5,
HEIDELBERG CATECHISM LORD'S DAY 4**

God's mercy

"But I, through the abundance of your steadfast love, will enter your house. I will bow down toward your holy temple in fear of you."

PSALM 5:7

In the concluding answer of Lord's Day 4, we read that God is also merciful, His justice nevertheless requiring punishment. In the proof text underneath this answer, we find a reference to Psalm 5, the psalm we also focused on yesterday to show that God hates all evil. God cannot let evil get its way by lowering His command for 100% obedience. Evil needs punishment. The boastful shall not stand in the sight of God. In verse 7, David confesses: "But I, through the abundance of your steadfast love, will enter your house."

How could David say this, knowing that he was not without evil either? Was he not afraid that God would punish him as well? Or did he perhaps think that he was better than all those others and therefore had nothing to fear? Surely not. David knew that if God did not have compassion on him, he too would perish under God's judgment. He knew that it was only because of God's grace that he could still enter the temple and appear in God's presence without any fear.

Grace, mercy – often, we are so used to these words that we no longer understand the real meaning of them. In Scripture, the term 'mercy' is a real covenant word. It includes concepts like loyalty and faithfulness. Like the word justice, the word mercy also points to God's faithfulness which the LORD surrounds His children with from their early youth. This is also how God showed His faithfulness to David. As a boy of eight days old he received the sign of circumcision by which God pledged: I will be your God – even though you too deserve eternal death, I will accept you in my love.

It is this love with which the LORD surrounded David while he was growing up, and also later when he was anointed as king over Israel. It is because of God's mercy that David could appear in His presence without any fear of God's just judgment. Without any fear, he could enter God's temple, where God's mercy was signified in the sacrifices which were brought; sacrifices also for David's sin to reconcile him with God. This sacrificial blood pointed both to God's justice as well as God's mercy.

July 20

**READING: ROMANS 3:21-26,
HEIDELBERG CATECHISM, LORD'S DAY 4**

Our redemption in Christ

"There is therefore no condemnation for those who are in Christ Jesus."
ROMANS 8:1

From yesterday's meditation, we learnt that for David to be reconciled with God, blood had to be shed. This sacrificial blood pointed both to God's justice as well as to God's mercy. Because the Old Testament sacrifices could not really take away man's guilt, they foreshadowed the coming of Christ, who became man for our sake so that in our human nature, He could bear the punishment of sin and so satisfy God's justice. Christ did so in particular when He suffered the most severe punishment of body and soul on the cross – eternal death!

God thus remained faithful to the justice that was required: full payment must be made. This is why in showing mercy to us, God made Him sin who knew no sin, so that in Him, that is in Jesus Christ, we might become the righteousness of God (2 Corinthians 5:21).

On the cross, Christ suffered for us and in our place. At Calvary, the wrath of God was poured out upon Him in all its severity. Being forsaken by God, Christ suffered the anguish and torment of hell. In doing so as a just judge, God maintained the ultimate seriousness of the covenant. The cross on which Christ was nailed shows how great the wrath of God against all sin and iniquity of man was. Yet by that same cross, God also revealed His love, His mercy, as we read in Article 20 of the Belgic Confession. In this article, it says: by laying our iniquity on Christ, God poured out His goodness and mercy on us, who were guilty and worthy of damnation.

At Calvary, it became evident very clearly that God's justice is not in conflict with His mercy. On the contrary, these two attributes of God are always in complete harmony with each other. God is a just judge. But God is not a judge who is unmoved when He must execute His righteous judgment. God does not rejoice in the punishment of the sinner. Instead, God wants the sinner to turn to Him that he might live. That is why in wrath, God also remembers mercy.

**READING: ROMANS 5:6-11,
HEIDELBERG CATECHISM, LORD'S DAY 5**

Amazing grace – are we still amazed?

"…but God shows his love for us in that while we were still sinners, Christ died for us."

ROMANS 5:8

The confession that we are saved by grace alone is fundamental to the Reformed doctrine. Those who have grown up with this doctrine are very strong in defending this confession.

However, we are called to live this confession as well, realising that we cannot contribute anything to our salvation. On the contrary, from ourselves we are inclined to all evil and unable to do any good.

From a doctrinal point of view, it is quite easy to confess this. However, to accept that these sinful inclinations also live within us might be much harder. Are things really that bad, even with us? We are not unbelievers, are we? With all the shortcomings involved, we try to live our lives according to God's commandments. Is this not of any merit at all? Of course, we are the first ones to admit that this is only because of the work of the Holy Spirit within us. Yet, at times the idea can creep in that we are not doing too badly, especially when comparing our lives with that of others. Of course, we do not say this in so many words. Yet when speaking about the sins of others, this can easily become an underlying current, whereby the miracle of God's grace towards us personally is no longer seen so sharply.

In the text above this meditation, the apostle Paul stresses this miracle, saying that Christ died for us while we were still sinners. Do we still marvel at this; marvel at the fact that Christ was willing to sacrifice His life for us, while we were utterly undeserving of this? Too often, we look at the sins of others, but we would do better taking a good look at ourselves first to see what great a miracle it is that Christ still wants to continue with us, despite the many sins there are in our lives each day again.

Amazing grace, yet are we still amazed? Does the gospel of salvation in Christ still excite us every new day when we wake up in the morning and as we warm ourselves in God's love – and all of this indeed by grace alone? Every heartbeat, every breath of life – it is all grace alone! Marvelling at this will surely help in living our lives in greater thankfulness.

July 22

**READING: PSALM 119:57-64,
HEIDELBERG CATECHISM, LORD'S DAY 5**

God's favour

"I entreat your favour with all my heart; be gracious to me according to your promises."
PSALM 119:58

From Lord's Day 4, we learnt that even though God is merciful, this does not mean that God will not punish us. The beginning of Lord's Day 5 also starts with this – Question 12:

"According to God's righteous judgment, we deserve temporal and eternal punishment." Yet, is there perhaps still a way in which we can once again be received into favour, which is even more important than escaping God's punishment?

It is a believer who speaks in Question 12 – a child of God, who in deep humbleness confesses his guilt and then asks whether even now God still wants to look upon him in favour. Favour – this word refers to undeserved love. In other words, the matter dealt with in this question is not, first of all, to receive forgiveness of sins and so to escape the punishment. But above all: Lord, please look upon us in favour again.

This aspect is of great significance when praying for forgiveness. Of course, we need forgiveness, yet of more importance is that God will look upon us in favour. To understand this better, consider how much we grieve our heavenly Father with every single sin we commit, ruining that precious relationship we may have with God. If only we could see Father's face, could see how deeply it hurts Him when we sin.

By way of example, think of a child that has hurt his mum. He sees in her face how much he has hurt her. At times, Mum's sad face haunts him when laying in bed at night, and therefore he wants the relationship restored so that mum looks upon him in favour again. This child is quite willing to accept the punishment for his wrongdoing, if only mum would still truly love him.

It is this love we should pray for when asking for forgiveness of sins. However, this will only happen when there is a real awareness of how much we grieve God with our sins. This awareness will bring us down to our knees, asking God: "LORD, I entreat Thy favour with all my heart. Please be gracious to me. I plead with Thy promises. LORD, without Thy favour I cannot live".

July 23

**READING: EPHESIANS 2:1-5,
HEIDELBERG CATECHISM LORD'S DAY 5**

God's grace

"… by grace you have been saved."

EPHESIANS 2:5B

God's justice required that full payment must be made. Yet how? In the continuation of Lord's Day 5 we read that man himself is unable to make this payment. It would take him an eternity, and even then, man would still never be able to say, "It is paid for." Man cannot redeem himself from the wrath of God. On the contrary, as it reads in Answer 13: "We daily increase our debt."

Doctrinally we all know this. However, we so quickly gloss over the profoundness of this confession. Do we live in the daily awareness that for every single sin we commit, Christ had to shed His blood, even for those sins which we regard perhaps as minor? Our Saviour was also crucified for those sins. Even for those sins – which we at times shrug off – our Saviour had to endure the anguish and torment of hell.

Thinking of this, do we still see the greatness of our debt? Too often, when considering our life, we think that in comparison to others we are not doing too badly. Yet we should not look at others but instead look at God's Word and what God requires of us. If we were genuinely to do this, we would all have to admit that we are making a mess of our lives on a daily basis.

Thankfully there are also good things, but these we can only credit to the regenerating power of God's Spirit being busy in our lives and turning things around. There is nothing from ourselves here. The Catechism confesses in Answer 13: in no way can man himself make any payment towards the debt he has with God. Even our best works are all imperfect and defiled with sin. Hence our refuge lies entirely in God's grace alone.

This grace is highlighted in Lord's Day 5, first by emphasising that full payment must be made and also by stating that man himself is unable to do this. However, where we from our side messed everything up with no hope left, in His unsearchable wisdom and love for us sinners, God cut a way right through the thick jungle of our sinfulness. God cut a way in which reconciliation could be achieved. Reconciliation, by grace from above. In sending His Son, God Himself provided a mediator who could pay our debt and bear the punishment for us wretched sinners. Amazing grace!

July 24

**READING: ROMANS 8:1-4,
HEIDELBERG CATECHISM, LORD'S DAY 5**

The extent of God's grace

"For our sake he made him to be sin, who knew no sin, so that in him we might become the righteousness of God."
2 CORINTHIANS 5:21

When the question is asked: "What did Christ do for you?", often the answer is given: "He died for us on the cross." Yet, Christ did more than die for us on the cross. By dying on the cross, He bore the punishment for us. Yet Christ also had to pay our outstanding debt. This debt was paid by the obedience He showed throughout His entire life on earth. In other words, Christ's whole life was a substitute for our life from the moment that He was conceived in the womb of the virgin Mary. As our surety, He assumed the legal responsibility for paying our debt, and in doing so He became liable for our failure to pay this debt. This is why He had to become man, one of us, one with us. Man had sinned. Therefore, man had to pay for sin. Yet God, as the heavenly Judge, assigned the responsibility of our sin to Christ, thus making it possible that He could pay our debt and bear the punishment for us.

Again, how great a miracle this is! Indeed, amazing grace! Amazing grace, not only where it concerns the love of the Father in being willing to send His Son to bear all this in our place. Yet, we should equally stand in awe of the love of the Son, in being willing to do this, not holding on to all the riches He had in heaven, but taking the form of a servant, born in the likeness of men. This is how, during His life on earth, Christ paid our debt and by His death on the cross bore the punishment, granting us complete justification.

In addition to justification, God also grants us sanctification. Having been received into favour again, through His Spirit, God will now also help us to live holy before Him. This shows that our redemption is a gift from the Triune God: Father, Son, and Holy Spirit working together. A precious gift, never to be taken for granted. Instead, it calls for a life of thankfulness, glorifying and praising God daily for such precious gifts, received by grace alone.

July 25

**READING: HEBREWS 2:14-18,
HEIDELBERG CATECHISM, LORD'S DAY 6**

Jesus Christ – Our Kinsman-Redeemer

*"Since therefore the children share in flesh and blood,
he himself likewise partook of the same things."*

HEBREWS 2:14A

To understand why the Lord Jesus had to be true man in order to redeem us, it is helpful to look at the Old Testament laws concerning redemption. When a life was taken, a kinsman had the right to avenge or redeem the blood of the victim. We meet the word 'kinsman' also in the book of Ruth. Due to a famine in the land of Judah, Elimelech and his family went to Moab. Yet in Moab they found the hand of the LORD against them. Elimelech died and so did both sons of the family who meanwhile had married Moabite wives. After all this, Naomi decided to return to her homeland, where she arrived poverty-stricken together with her daughter-in-law Ruth. It is in this sad situation that Naomi remembers God's law, which gave opportunity for redemption. God in His grace leads things in such a way that Ruth meets Boaz who was of the family of Elimelech, so a kinsman, and who became willing not only to redeem the land but also to marry Ruth.

In this whole story, the essential element is that Boaz was a family member. Well, the mediator of the covenant also needs to be a family member, one of us, a true man. According to God's law, our mediator could not redeem us unless he was of our flesh and blood. The justice of God required that the same human nature which had sinned should pay for sin. In Paradise, it was man who rebelled against God. That is why the mediator who would pay for us, also needed to be true man.

It is for this reason that the gospel narratives also put much emphasis on the fact that the Lord Jesus Christ was true man. As true man, He suffered hunger when in the wilderness and was tempted by Satan. As true man, He struggled in Gethsemane. As true man, He also gave His life for us when He died on the cross for our sins. He did so not like a remote Saviour, but as our Kinsman-Redeemer, like his brothers in every respect. Because of this, today in heaven, we have a merciful high priest who, from His own experiences, knows what it means to live life in a world full of suffering.

July 26

**READING: HEBREWS 7:26-28,
HEIDELBERG CATECHISM, LORD'S DAY 6**

A complete and perfect redemption

"For it was indeed fitting that we should have such a high priest, holy, innocent, unstained, separated from sinners…"
HEBREWS 7:26A

From Lord's Day 5, we learnt already that we needed a mediator who was not just one of us, true man, but that He also needed to be a righteous man, without sin, perfect in every respect. Yesterday we focused on the example of Boaz as kinsmen-redeemer. Just imagine that Boaz had been bankrupt or up to his eyes in debt himself. He could never have redeemed Naomi's land nor have married Ruth. Well, this is also how our Redeemer had to be debt-free, in this case free from sin. Only in this way could He obtain for us a perfect redemption and become our wisdom, righteousness, and sanctification, as it says in Answer 18.

First, it says that Christ became to us the wisdom of God, wisdom not understood by the world. The world does not understand how one can receive redemption from a king who died. They regard this as foolishness. Yet this was the only way in which God's wrath could be satisfied. It was the only way in which we could receive access to God again.

Christ also became our righteousness. He did so by obeying God's Law perfectly in our place and in bearing the punishment for our disobedience. This is how Christ gave Himself to us. Boaz, who not only said 'I know a solution; there is a kinsman who can do something for you', paid for the land and married Ruth instead of leaving it to an even nearer relative. Well, likewise, Christ not only told us about a solution how we could become righteous again, but he Himself paid for us.

Finally, Christ also became our sanctification. Again, this was not by trying to motivate us to live a holy life but by Christ Himself working this holiness in us by the power of His Spirit, by which we are renewed day by day.

This is how we received a perfect and complete redemption in Christ. Like Boaz made Ruth His bride and no doubt gave her a wedding dress and ornaments to wear on her wedding day, likewise Christ will clothe us in new clothes, in fine linen, the mantle of salvation; and this not because of us, but only because of God's sovereign love for us sinners.

July 27

**READING: 1 CORINTHIANS 2:6-16,
HEIDELBERG CATECHISM, LORD'S DAY 6**

The blessings of our redemption

"What no eye has seen, nor ear heard, nor the heart of man imagined, what God has prepared for those who love him."

1 CORINTHIANS 2:9

A final aspect mentioned in Lord's Day 6 is that our Mediator also needed to be true God. Every man, every creature, would have been utterly crushed if God's wrath had been poured out on them. Only a divine power could shoulder this burden and so survive the punishment. Also, only a divine person could do more than survive. After all, it was not enough for man to have God's wrath satisfied, enough to have his slate wiped clean. How quickly would we have fallen under God's wrath again? Christ, however, also covered this aspect of our redemption in granting us not only justification but also sanctification and with it complete redemption, as only a divine mediator could do.

When considering all of this, one cannot but stand in awe of God's goodness and wisdom. This same God, who had said that man had to pay so that His justice might be satisfied, in His mercy gave His Son to be sin for us, so that in Him we might become the righteousness of God. Such a love towards us sinners is indeed beyond our human understanding. We had become enemies of God, and yet God gave His Son, his only begotten Son as a ransom for our sins, that we might be accepted again as His children and heirs.

In Christ, God indeed gave us everything, not only when we think of what He did for us on earth, but also when we think of Christ's work in heaven today – where He is our high priest but also our kinsman who can sympathise with our weaknesses, one who in every respect was tempted as we have been, yet without sin. Yet being also true God, He not only sympathises but is able to help us, always. In Christ, we have a Mediator, who is there for us always. In Christ, we have received all things necessary for our salvation.

Every attempt for self-redemption goes to pieces in light of this wonderful gospel. This is the gospel teaching us that the only way in which we can be saved is by seeking our life outside of ourselves, finding it in Jesus Christ, our one and only Redeemer!

July 28

**READING: JOHN 5:30-47,
HEIDELBERG CATECHISM, LORD'S DAY 6**

The glorious gospel of God's redeeming grace in Jesus Christ

"You search the Scriptures because you think that in them you have eternal life; and it is they that bear witness about me."
JOHN 5:39

How do we know that the Lord Jesus Christ is the one and only Redeemer? Lord's Day 6 says that we know this from the holy gospel, that is from God's holy Word, which speaks about Christ on almost every page. As Christ Himself once said: "It is they that bear witness about me."

God had already proclaimed this holy gospel in Paradise, straightaway after the fall into sin. God did so in the promise about the seed of the woman crushing the head of the serpent. As time progressed, God unfolded this gospel more and more richly throughout a history of revelation. In Answer 19, we read, "He had it proclaimed by the patriarchs and prophets and foreshadowed by the sacrifices and other ceremonies of the law." A believing Jew could not put a foot in the tabernacle and later in the temple without seeing and hearing this glorious gospel. The daily sacrifices spoke of it. Yet, many other things as well, such as the bells of gold on the priest's robe and the stones in his breastplate. It all preached God's grace. More precisely, it foreshadowed the fulfillment of this grace in Christ Jesus.

The chief purpose of Scripture is to reveal all of this to us: God's redeeming work in Jesus Christ. This is something we should never forget when reading or studying the Scriptures. And this, not merely to grow in knowledge of the Bible or to receive guidance in how to live. Of course, this as well. Yet the primary purpose of studying God's Word is to drive us to Christ and an ever-increasing faithfulness in serving Him. This is also why every sermon should be Christ centred.

Studying God's Word in all its riches and depth will help in staying focused on Christ. We need this, lest we slacken in faith. Therefore, we should always keep studying God's Word daily, so that each day again we may stand in awe of God's redeeming grace in Jesus Christ.

July 29

**READING: EPHESIANS 2:1-10,
HEIDELBERG CATECHISM, Q+A 20**

Saved by grace, through faith (1)

"For by grace you have been saved through faith. And this is not your own doing; it is the gift of God."

EPHESIANS 2:8

From Lord's Day 6 we learnt that everything we receive in Christ is God's gift to sinful man. Yet does everyone also receive this gift from above? Answer 20 of the Heidelberg Catechism says "No' to this question, stating, "Only those are saved who by a true faith are grafted into Christ and accept all his benefits."

Remarkably, the Heidelberg Catechism does not mention God's decree of election. It simply says that one must believe in Christ. This is also the central message of Scripture. True, Scripture also speaks about God's election. Yet this does not undo man's responsibility. The gospel always comes to us with the call to repent and believe, that is, to believe in Jesus Christ and cling to Him.

It is good to stress this point since there are also people who reason as follows: once a person is elected, he will be saved, no matter what he does, while those who are reprobated by God are lost, even if they want to be saved. For already from eternity, everything has been determined by God. This, however, is a fatalistic approach, which does no justice to what Scripture teaches; instead, it is in sharp conflict with it. Whenever God in His Word addresses man, He always addresses him as a responsible creature.

No one will perish eternally, solely because God has reprobated him or her. Those who do not respond to the gospel do so because of their own fault. The cause of sin and unbelief lies in man himself. In this context, I think of a word the Lord Jesus once spoke concerning the citizens of Jerusalem, Matthew 23: 37, "O Jerusalem, Jerusalem, killing the prophets and stoning those who are sent to you! How often would I have gathered your children together as a hen gathers her brood under her wings, and you would not!"

Likewise, today, many people called by the proclamation of the gospel refuse to respond. They reject God's love in Christ Jesus, not because God causes them to do so, but by their own free will. Yet those who accept this love of God in true faith will be blessed – blessed eternally.

July 30

**READING: ROMANS 5:1-11,
HEIDELBERG CATECHISM, Q+A 20**

Saved by grace, through faith (2)

"But God shows his love for us in
that while we were still sinners,
Christ died for us."

ROMANS 5:8

Without faith, no one can be saved. Does this make faith a condition for salvation? Surely not! The LORD comes to us unconditionally. In Romans 5, the apostle Paul says that we were reconciled to God by the death of His Son while we were still enemies. Enemies – and yet God's love went out to us. When we in Adam turned our back upon God, God called out, "Adam, where are you? Although you walked away from me, I want you back, for I still love you." Yes, God's love for us was even so great that He gave His own Son to die for us, so that we could live – live eternally with Him. A miracle of grace!

Yet, it is only through faith that we can share in all of these riches. Article 22 of the Belgic Confession calls this faith the instrument by which we embrace Christ our righteousness; an instrument that keeps us in communion with Christ and all His benefits. Yet, even this instrument is given to us by God, who works this faith in our hearts. Thus, being saved by grace is indeed all God's work. Yet, all this does not undo our own responsibility.

God came to man in sovereign love. However, this divine love asks for a response from our side – an active involvement. The verb 'accept' in Answer 20 highlights this. God gives us the instrument to embrace Christ and all His benefits. We are called to use this instrument, otherwise we are still without salvation. In the Canons of Dort, Chapter III/IV, Article 16, it reads that God does not act upon men as stocks and blocks, but He treats them as responsible creatures, not taking man's will away but making it alive through faith in Jesus Christ. How does God do this? By the powerful work of the Holy Spirit within us. The Holy Spirit revitalises our will spiritually, powerfully bending and reshaping it.

In summary, redemption is a gift of God, which He sovereignly lays in our hands. Yet, we are called to open our hands. That is, we must accept this redemption with a believing heart.

July 31

READING: ACTS 16:11-15,
HEIDELBERG CATECHISM, Q+A 20

The call to be reconciled to God

"Therefore, we are ambassadors of Christ, God making His appeal through us. We implore you on behalf of Christ, be reconciled to God."

2 CORINTHIANS 5:20

To receive salvation, one must confess his faith in Jesus Christ as the only true Saviour. Without faith in Jesus Christ, the way to salvation is closed. God, through His Spirit, works this faith in our hearts, preparing our hearts so that we are willing to listen to the gospel preached to us. In Acts 16:14, it reads that God opened Lydia's heart to pay attention to what was said by Paul. That is how believers embrace the gospel, persuaded by God. Yet once persuaded, we are bound to make a move which is our response of faith to God's love shown to us in Jesus Christ. This should be a response not just in words but also in deeds.

Looking around in today's society, the vast majority of people despise the riches they could receive in Jesus Christ. Whenever they are confronted with it, they turn their back upon this beautiful gospel. 'It is not for me', so they say! They prefer darkness to light, being lovers of pleasure rather than lovers of God.

One may say that this might be true, but we cannot force people to believe, can we? Is faith not a personal choice, something we must leave up to the people themselves? That is how this matter is often spoken about. It is one's own choice, whether to believe. What you do is up to you, but do not interfere with my way of living.

However, concerning faith in Jesus Christ, this is a viewpoint that misrepresents the truth of the gospel. After all, the gospel of Christ is never preached in a non-committal way, something like 'take it or leave it'. Whenever a person is confronted with the gospel, it always comes with the command to repent and to believe. Through the gospel, people are called: be reconciled to God, as the apostle Paul says in 2 Corinthians 5, verse 20. Whoever does not positively respond to this call, will find himself standing there empty-handed in the end. Only true faith in Jesus Christ will save us and grant us the peace that only God can give us.

August 1

**READING: HOSEA 4:1-6,
HEIDELBERG CATECHISM, Q+A 21**

True Faith – a sure knowledge (1)

"And this is eternal life, that they know Thee the only true God and Jesus Christ whom Thou hast sent."
JOHN 17:3

Since only true faith can make us share in Christ and all His benefits, it stands to reason that the Catechism poses the next question, "What is true faith?" The answer mentions two essential components: a sure knowledge and a firm confidence. These two components are inseparably connected. One should never try to drive a wedge between these two components since this will lead to all sorts of distortions. Too much emphasis on the knowledge aspect can easily lead to an almost clinical faith. On the other hand, saying knowledge is not as important as confidence and trust can lead to placing too much emphasis on one's feelings. Therefore, we should always look at these two components as one unit. True faith means, with a firm confidence we render our life to God, trusting in the promises He has given us. Yet we can only do so when we also know these promises. Thus, knowledge is also a necessary element to believing.

Sometimes one can hear comments like, "Knowledge is not so important as long as one loves the Lord Jesus Christ." The thought behind this reasoning is that belief is something one feels in his heart. This is what you should go by to ascertain whether faith is real. If you feel close to the Lord, all that knowledge is not so important. Yet the Catechism does not speak about feelings, but about a firm confidence instead. Well, how can one have confidence without knowing what to put his confidence in? How would one be able to believe, if he does not know the content of his belief? Therefore, knowledge is a vital component of true faith. It is not for nothing that by the mouth of His prophet Hosea, the LORD utters the following complaint, "My people are destroyed for lack of knowledge," Hosea 4:6. I also think of what the Lord Jesus Christ Himself said in His high priestly prayer, John 17:3 "This is eternal life, that they know Thee the only true God and Jesus Christ whom Thou hast sent."

August 2

**READING: COLOSSIANS 1:1-14,
HEIDELBERG CATECHISM, Q+A 21**

True Faith – a sure knowledge (2)

"I am Thy servant; give me understanding
that I may know Thy testimonies."

PSALM 119:125

Whenever Scripture speaks about knowledge, it means much more than just intellectual knowledge. Instead, it refers to knowledge from the heart, knowledge based on a living relationship with the LORD. When this living relationship is not there, people may know a lot about God, yet such knowledge is not of any benefit.

That is why Paul in Colossians 1, writing to the members of this congregation, says that he does not cease to pray for them that they may be filled with the knowledge of God's will, that is, with the knowledge of how to live life according to God's will. True knowledge of God lights the lamp of the gospel, which gives a different outlook on life. It draws us from the darkness into the light. Without true knowledge of God and His will for our life, we continue to walk in darkness.

In the world, there is a saying "knowledge is power." In the church, knowledge gives the power to withstand the attacks of the evil one. In Proverbs 19:2 it reads, "Desire without knowledge is not good." It can easily lead to impulsive and unwise acts. It is for this very reason that the author of Psalm 119 prays, "LORD, I am Thy servant, give me understanding that I may know Thy testimonies." Thy testimonies – that is, knowledge of God's will for our life. This knowledge is also necessary for us, so that we may live a life worthy of the LORD, fully pleasing Him, being fruitful in every good work.

This knowledge is also necessary to be able to speak with the enemy in the gate, as Psalm 127 speaks about. Only when we are well conversant with Scripture, will we be able to refute false doctrine, evangelical influences, and you name it. Only then can we stand firm, firm to defend the truth out of love for God.

When there is a sincere love for God, there will also be a genuine desire to study God's Word in order to grow in the knowledge of God's will and to live accordingly. The fruit of this study will be that we keep marvelling at our wonderful God. Marvelling also at the covenant relationship in which we may live with God.

August 3

**READING: HEBREWS 4:14-16,
HEIDELBERG CATECHISM, Q+A 21**

True Faith – a firm confidence

"Let us then with confidence draw near
to the throne of grace..."
HEBREWS 4:16A

A firm confidence is also an essential component of true faith. It is not enough to know the content of the Bible. We must also firmly believe that what we read in the Bible is true, trustworthy. It is not sufficient to believe that God exists. For as it says in the letter of James, even demons believe this, and they shudder. True faith means that you also want to dedicate your life to the LORD, putting your trust in Him, building your life on the sure promises of God, believing that these promises are not only for others but also for us personally. That is what this firm confidence is all about, lest we may start doubting God's sure promises.

Doubt can easily creep in. We are not always as strong in faith as we should be. Yet, whenever doubt raises its head, think of the promises God gave us at our baptism. At that time, God promised always to be our Father. Therefore, we never have to despair of His mercy. This means we may have confidence that no matter how much we might mess up our life at times, in Christ there is always a new beginning. This is also the same confidence of which the author of the letter to the Hebrews speaks, saying to hold fast to this confession so that we may draw near to the throne of grace in confidence, knowing that with Christ, we will always receive mercy and grace in time of need.

True faith means putting your trust in God, knowing that His Word stands firm. He will never disown those who put their trust in Him alone. It is this living faith that enriches life and gives peace. A living faith – this means it must also show up in the way we live that we trust God with our lives and that the Lord Jesus Christ is the secure anchorage of our life. Then we make sure by the power from above that the cares of this present world do not choke our faith. Instead, we trust that Father will always provide.

**READING: 2 TIMOTHY 3:10-16,
HEIDELBERG CATECHISM, Q+A 22**

All of Scripture is Christ-centred

"...the sacred writings, which are able to make you wise for salvation through faith in Christ Jesus."

2 TIMOTHY:15B

Only those are saved, who by true faith are grafted into Christ and accept all His benefits. God Himself, through His Holy Spirit, works this faith in our hearts. Answer 21 says God does so by the Holy Gospel, which has as content Christ and His redeeming work. Therefore, Christ should always be at the centre of all preaching of the gospel. Answer 22 highlights this as well: we must believe all that is promised us in the gospel. To believe – that is, to accept it as true, without trying to twist it according to our own ideas about the truth. When we start doing so, we lose every secure anchorage.

By way of example, today, many people no longer believe that what is revealed to us in the first three chapters of the Bible is real history. Yet, by no longer accepting that this is real history, one also puts a question mark behind the trustworthiness of the mother promise (Genesis 3:15). In the end, one loses everything. Once one starts putting question marks behind certain passages of Scripture, one is on very shaky ground. Today many Christians are led astray by modern theologians who interpret the Bible according to their own ideas – theologians who blame us for fundamentalism and stiff orthodoxy. They laugh at us when we still want to read the Bible as it is presented to us.

Yet, this should not discourage us. Instead, let us live from the riches which have been entrusted to us. Let us continue to confess our faith according to the Word of God. Only then will we find real security, no matter what life might hold in store for us. True security – by holding on to the confession of our faith in Jesus Christ, the Redeemer of our life.

A miracle of grace! Sometimes it is good to pause and let this miracle sink in, so that overwhelmed by it, we indeed have only one desire – to live our life for God alone.

August 5

**READING: MATTHEW 28:16-20,
HEIDELBERG CATECHISM, LORD'S DAY 8**

The anchor of faith is found by believing in the Triune God (1)

"...baptising them in the name of the Father
and of the Son and of the Holy Spirit."
MATTHEW 28:19B

One of the last questions in Lord's Day 7 was, "What, then, must a Christian believe?" The answer reads, "All that is promised us in the gospel..." Next, we find these promises summarised in the twelve articles of the Apostles' Creed, one of the oldest confessions of the church, which in a nutshell gives a good summary of our catholic and undoubted Christian faith. Somewhere I read, "The Christian church has summarised the ocean of the gospel in the thimble of no more than twelve articles." These twelve articles bring together in summary form the whole doctrine of the Old and New Testaments. They summarise the content of our faith in God as the Triune God.

This doctrine about the Trinity has always been under attack. This started already in the early Christian church. A severe battle had to be fought from which we inherited the three Ecumenical Creeds: the Apostles' Creed, the Nicene Creed, and the Athanasian Creed. Three Creeds, which each in their own way defend the doctrine of the Trinity. They highlight that the Son and the Spirit are also true and eternal God together with the Father, and at the same time are two distinct persons next to the Father. If this were not true, we would still be lost in guilt. We learnt this from the previous Lord's Days, that our mediator needed to be not only true man, but also true God. Next, if the work of renewal in our life is God's work, then the Spirit also needs to be true God.

This shows how much was at stake in this battle fought by the early Christian church. The foundation of our faith was at stake, since our entire salvation stands or falls with what we believe concerning the Holy Trinity. It is true indeed what it says at the beginning and the end of the Athanasian Creed, "Unless a man keeps this doctrine in its entirety inviolate, he will assuredly perish eternally," Article 2, while in Article 42 the Creed closes off as follows: "This is the catholic faith. Unless a man believes it faithfully and steadfastly, he cannot be saved."

**READING: REVELATION 4,
HEIDELBERG CATECHISM, LORD'S DAY 8**

The anchor of faith is found by believing in the Triune God (2)

"Holy, holy, holy, is the Lord God Almighty,
who was and is, and is to come!"

REVELATION 4:8B

Answer 24 summarises the complete doctrine of the Old and New Testament in three short sentences, mentioning the work of God the Father and our creation, of God the Son and our redemption, and of God the Holy Spirit and our sanctification. This summary bears testimony to Scripture's profound insight in highlighting our riches, when in faith we cling to God as the Triune God.

However, how is this to be reconciled with the fact that we believe in but one God? If the Father is God, and the Son is God, and the Holy Spirit is God – rationally, does this not mean that there are three Gods? The answer in faith is 'No". With human arithmetic, no one can work this out. It is beyond that. Yet, this should not cause us to speak about the doctrine of the Trinity as a mystery, of which we basically cannot say anything. We should not say either: let theologians discuss this, it is not essential. Scripture never uses the actual words 'trinity' and 'triune'. Yet the doctrine of the Trinity is clearly found throughout all of Scripture, both in the Old and in the New Testament.

To find out whether something is truly scripturally, we should not just look at specific texts alone. We should always take into account what Scripture teaches as a whole. This is also what the Heidelberg Catechism does, highlighting how rich we are by believing in God as the Triune God. Reverend C. Bijl, in his commentary on the Heidelberg Catechism, writes that this doctrine gives us an answer to three vital questions.

The first question is: Who gives us food and drink, health, and strength? Who will take care of creation? The answer is: God the Father almighty, Creator of heaven and earth.

The second question is: Who will deliver us from all the evil powers in this world? The answer is: God the Son!

Thirdly: Who is the one who will radically change us for the better? Who will take care of our sanctification? The answer is: God the Holy Spirit.

 August 7

**READING: PSALM 147,
HEIDELBERG CATECHISM, LORD'S DAY 8**

Three in One always working together in harmony

"For from Him and through Him and to Him are all things."
ROMANS 11:36B

Concerning the doctrine of the Trinity, there is much that surpasses our human understanding. Yet this does not mean that we are totally unable to say anything about this part of our doctrine, especially since both in His works as well as in His Word God makes Himself known as the Triune God. Father, Son, and Holy Spirit – each having their specific task, but at the same time, always working together in complete harmony.

Starting with God's work of creation in Genesis 1, we read, "In the beginning God (single) created the heavens and the earth." Yet Scripture also teaches, Psalm 33:6, "By the word of the LORD the heavens were made." From John 1 we know the Word to be the Son of God, the second Person within the Holy Trinity. Finally, in Psalm 104:30, we read that God sent forth His Spirit at the time of creation to renew the face of the earth. Thus, when comparing Scripture with Scripture, even creation was clearly a work of the Triune God.

The same applies to God's work of redemption and sanctification. The Father so loved the world that He was willing to send His beloved Son to offer His life as a sacrifice for our sins: Christ, who died for our trespasses. After He died, the Father raised Him from the dead for our justification and gave Him a place on the throne at His right hand. That is how God in Christ reconciled the world to Himself. When speaking about this divine work of redemption, we mostly give thought first and foremost to what the Son did, yet it also shows us the sovereign love of God the Father.

The Father sent the Son. Yet, the Son Himself was also willing to be sent, willing to reconcile us with God through the blood of the cross. On the foundation of this precious blood, He gathers, defends, and preserves for Himself a church chosen to everlasting life – a church chosen by the Father, bought by the Son, and in the unity of the true faith sanctified by the Spirit.

The Holy Spirit brings God's work of redemption to completion. He does so by sanctifying the church and its members today already, while also finally presenting us without blemish among the assembly of God's elect in life eternal.

August 8

READING: PSALM 89:1-18,
HEIDELBERG CATECHISM, LORD'S DAY 8

The unique comfort received by believing in the Triune God

"Righteousness and justice are the foundation of your throne, steadfast love and faithfulness go before you."
ROMANS 11:36B

The comfort we may draw from the confession recorded in Lord's Day 8 is that our redemption is firmly anchored in the work of the Triune God. It is also the same comfort of which Lord's Day 1 spoke, namely that both in life and death, I am not my own, but belong to my faithful Saviour Jesus Christ. This confession in Lord's Day 1 is firmly anchored in the redeeming work of the Triune God, signified and sealed to us in our baptism. This also means that we never have to doubt the riches of these promises. They offer safety under all circumstances. They give us hope and a future.

Today, many people are living without hope. What does the future hold? It all looks gloomy and dark. The reason is that many of these people have lost God. They have exchanged God for the service of idols, whatever these idols might be (money, sport, sex). Yet these idols do not make man really happy. Is this not what we see everywhere around us? Those who have lost God ultimately reach the point that they no longer see any meaning in life. It is all vanity. It is the same vanity of which the Preacher speaks in the book of Ecclesiastes.

This vanity can only be overcome through faith in the Triune God, who, as the God of our redemption, surrounds our life with His love and faithfulness, every day anew. With this God, our life always has a secure anchorage even when we are unsure of what the future holds. We have this firm assurance: the LORD is with us, always, and that is sufficient.

In this God, we may put our trust. Let us then also do this, living from the riches that God is my Father, my Redeemer, and the Sanctifier of my life. Indeed, this is the catholic faith which unless a man believes it faithfully, he cannot be saved. Therefore, let us draw daily comfort and strength from the fact that we bear the mark of the Triune God on our foreheads. May we also always see this mark as a privilege and never as a burden.

August 9

**READING: GENESIS 1:1-9,
HEIDELBERG CATECHISM, LORD'S DAY 9**

I believe in God the Father almighty, Creator of heaven and earth

"In the beginning, God created the heavens and the earth."
GENESIS 1:1

When routine sets in, even the most beautiful expressions lose their meaning – think of the first verse of the Bible. We all know it, and we also believe it: God created everything. Yet, believing is more than just knowing things.

For a moment, imagine the following scenario. A minister visits a member of the congregation who is suffering from depression, and because of it does not cope so well. As usual, the minister reads from God's Word to offer some words of comfort and strength. This time he opens his Bible to Genesis 1. One may wonder about the choice of this passage in circumstances like these. Someone is down in the dumps and then the minister opens his bible and starts reading, "In the beginning, God created the heavens and the earth." What comfort does this give, as if this person did not know? Is this how we should use our Bible when visiting a sick or depressed person? Many would have opted to read Psalm 23, for example.

True, Genesis 1 is perhaps not the most appropriate passage to choose in the abovementioned scenario. Yet it is a passage that, in essence, gives the same comfort as offered in Psalm 23. Genesis 1 also proclaims the gospel – good news, glad tidings. This chapter tells us by whom we may feel secure, what a mighty God we have: the Creator of heaven and earth, who – according to what we confess in Lord's Day 9 – is, for the sake of Christ His Son, my God, and my Father.

Genesis 1 is not a chapter only informing us how it all began, how this world came into existence or a chapter with which we can refute the theory of evolution. Of course, these are also some of the purposes of this chapter. However, when reading Genesis 1, we should not forget that this first chapter of the Bible also teaches us what a mighty God we have. That is also how the Apostles' Creed refers to this chapter, when it says, "I believe in God the Father, almighty, Creator of heaven and earth." I believe in – that is, I entrust myself to this God. With Him, I may always feel secure.

August 10

**READING: PSALM 33:1-9,
HEIDELBERG CATECHISM, LORD'S DAY 9**

God's almighty power

"For He spoke and it came to be; He commanded, and it stood firm."

PSALM 33:9

When thinking about God's almighty power, mostly we straightaway think of what happened at the beginning of world history, when out of nothing God created heaven and earth. Speaking about God's almighty power, Lord's Day 9 also refers to this, and so does Psalm 33. The author of this psalm praises God for His mighty and wonderful deeds, directing our attention first of all to creation.

However, the author sings not only of God's almighty power, but he also rejoices in the fact that he knows this almighty God as the faithful God of the covenant. He feels blessed in being allowed to live in a close relationship with this powerful and awesome God. That is the primary message of Psalm 33!

It is the main message, also when in the first section of this psalm the author speaks about the LORD wielding His power through the word. He spoke, calling into existence the things that did not exist. "He spoke and it came to be," verse 9. In verse 6 we read, "By the Word of the LORD the heavens were made, and by the breath of His mouth all their host." Just by one single breath of His mouth, the LORD brought into being the whole celestial host. As to the word 'host' mentioned in verse 6, most likely it refers not only to the innumerable stars of heaven, but also to the angelic armies, by whom we may know ourselves surrounded by day and by night.

I believe in God, the Father almighty, Creator of heaven and earth. Well-known words. Yet, we so often forget how rich we are with our God and Father. At times we only look at what we see with our physical eyes: the struggles, the sorrows, the difficulties we face. We are snowed under. We can hardly see any light at the end of the tunnel. We do still pray, but it seems to have no effect. Down in the dumps, depressed, also faith-wise, we feel like we are in a valley.

Yet, when opening God's Word and not only reading it, but taking the time to also meditate upon it, we may again see what great a God we have, a mighty Father, who has power over all things. Let us never forget this.

August 11

**READING: PSALM 33:10-12,
HEIDELBERG CATECHISM, LORD'S DAY 9**

The almighty God also upholds and governs everything

"Blessed is the nation whose God is the LORD."
PSALM 33:12A

As the Almighty One, God not only created everything out of nothing but by that same power, He also upholds and governs everything – the entire universe. He has the whole world in His mighty hands, ruling this world for the sake of our salvation. He does so as the faithful God of the covenant. It is this particular aspect in which the author of Psalm 33 rejoices: God's power and majesty revealed not only in the realm of nature, but also in the history of humankind.

The rulers of this world make their plans. Yet God in His almighty power may all of a sudden cause these plans to fall through. Verse 10, "The LORD brings the counsel of the nations to nothing; He frustrates the plans of the people." We meet here the same thought as in Psalm 2, where we read about the rulers of this world taking counsel together against the LORD and His Anointed. Yet, He who sits in heaven laughs and holds them in derision. In the end, the counsel of the nations will come to nothing. However – Psalm 33:11 – the counsel of the LORD stands forever. Indeed nothing can threaten God's plans. He is in absolute control of everything, in control also of history. Hence, "Blessed is the nation whose God is the LORD, the people He has chosen as His own inheritance."

Knowing ourselves surrounded by the power of this God, the LORD almighty, the faithful God of the covenant, we are blessed indeed! In more common language, we are to be congratulated, since this God will always be there for us, caring for us, providing us with all that we need. In verse 13 of this psalm we read: He looks down from heaven and sees all the sons of men. He, who fashioned their hearts individually, knows them all. He understands all their works, all that comes from their heart. That is why God is able to frustrate the plans of the people, making these plans subject to the counsel of His perfect will. And, all of this for our sake, so that amid the trials of life we may feel safe always, rejoicing in God's power and wonderful care.

August 12

READING: PSALM 33:13-17,
HEIDELBERG CATECHISM, LORD'S DAY 9

God upholds and governs all things by His eternal counsel and providence

"The war horse is a false hope for salvation,
And by its great might it cannot rescue."

PSALM 33:17

Psalm 33 clearly shows that God is in control of world history. He brings the counsel of the nations to nothing. He frustrates the plans of the people. And all of this to bring His plan of salvation to fulfilment. How privileged we are to be part of this plan, to belong to that nation God has chosen to be His.

In the second half of this psalm, the author elaborates on the riches of belonging to God. In verse 16, we read that a king with a great army and a soldier with great strength are no match in comparison with the power of almighty God, who rules everything and carries out His plan. No one can withstand Him.

When looking at a world full of turmoil and international conflicts, what a great comfort this is for us as children of God. Often we pray for peace, and that is good. Yet, we should also remember that God is fulfilling His plan even through wars and rumours of wars. Therefore, when praying for peace, we should also pray, "Thy will be done!" That is how we may find comfort, comfort in knowing God rules, who is our Father in Christ.

At times, we so quickly forget how rich we are with this awesome God always caring for us. Too often, we tend to look at things only with our physical eyes, keeping the eyes of faith closed to God's almighty power and majesty. As a result, we start worrying about this and about that. Yet, there is no need for this. Instead, we should walk through this world always having the eyes of faith open – open to see Father at work, not only in the great and eventful things, like earthquakes, floods, a pandemic, and all kinds of international conflicts. Of course also in these things, God is at work, but equally we should see God at work in what we may call minor things, the little things of everyday life: the wages we receive, the food He provides us with. We should never forget that God's almighty hand is involved in all of this, even in the simplest things in our life. He rules it all, great and small.

August 13

**READING: ROMANS 8:18-27,
HEIDELBERG CATECHISM, LORD'S DAY 9**

A life of sorrow

"For we know that the whole creation has been groaning… and not only creation, but we ourselves… groan inwardly…"
ROMANS 8:22-23

As God's children, we may rejoice in God's fatherly care, since God is our Father in Christ. Yet, this does not mean that we will never meet with any difficulty, sorrow, or hardship. After all, Lord's Day 9 also speaks about this life as a life of sorrow. The Form for Baptism phrases it even more strongly, speaking about the life we live today as "no more than a constant death." This is not just some pessimistic outlook on life, but a reality which we experience even as children of God. It points to the brokenness of this life due to sin. Paul writes in his letter to the Romans that creation is groaning in travail, and we groan with it.

Yet amidst this groaning, as God's children, we also have the assurance Father is in control. We can trust Father, who will give us His aid and protection even when we least expect it. Through hardship and sorrow, Father is working for our salvation, even though we cannot always understand how. That is our comfort, also when at times our life may go through deep valleys. For even then, God is there to care for us, to lead us through; yes, perhaps even using that valley for our benefit. For us, this might be difficult to understand, but this should not cause us to doubt it. Otherwise, we will lose all our comfort – a comfort we in particular need when life goes through deep valleys.

We should never doubt the trustworthiness of God's sure promises. If ever this doubt arises in our hearts, think of your baptism, which will function as a guarantee to us that God will keep His promises. God's fatherly care for us is securely anchored in the promises of the covenant, which He established with us and our children, the seal of which we bear on our forehead.

We should never judge God's fatherly care through personal experiences. Instead, whoever wants to know how much God loves us should plunge himself into the gospel, which is the ocean of God's love. A love vast beyond all measure in that the Father would give His only Son to make us wretched sinners His treasure.

August 14

**READING: 2 CORINTHIANS 12:7-10,
HEIDELBERG CATECHISM, LORD'S DAY 9**

Trusting God without any doubt

"My grace is sufficient for you, for my power is made perfect in weakness."

2 CORINTHIANS 12:9

Our life is firmly anchored in God's love for us in Christ. This is the most secure foundation anyone could ever wish for. Sometimes in the difficulties we experience, with winds blowing at gale force, our life may be shaken even on this secure foundation. Yet it will still stand firm in Christ, our Rock and our Redeemer. It is because of Christ's redeeming work that we have the firm assurance that whatever adversity God may send us in this life of sorrow, He will turn it to our good. God will always be there as our Father, able and willing to help us. We may be sure of this since God promised this to us on the day of our baptism. He also reassures us of it every Sunday through the preaching of His Word. Therefore, there is no reason to doubt. Instead, we should always trust God with His perfect plan for our life.

At times, we still may struggle and wonder, "Why, O God?" Even the apostle Paul did so amid the trials he went through. In 2 Corinthians 12, he speaks about suffering from a thorn in the flesh about which he had prayed three times to the Lord, "Lord, please take it away." But then the Lord responds saying, "My grace is sufficient for you, for My power is made perfect in weakness." Weak – yet strong, namely in the Lord! He is there to help, and to carry us, also through difficult times. Strong, by entrusting our lives to God, the almighty One who for Christ's sake has taken us and counts us as His own. He will help. We never have to doubt this.

Lord's Day 9 points us to what a mighty Father we have. He loves us, and He will always care for us. Let us never forget this, especially not when our life goes through valleys. Never forget, as also then Father is there to help us. There is not one step in life that we have to take without Him. What a glorious gospel this is!

August 15

**READING: PSALM 147,
HEIDELBERG CATECHISM, Q+A 27**

God's Fatherly hand

"Sing to the LORD with thanksgiving; make melody to our God on the lyre!"

PSALM 147:7

From Lord's Day 9 we learnt that God upholds and governs heaven and earth and all that is in them "by His eternal counsel and providence." God's eternal counsel is His plan with this world, already made even before creation. As a skillful professional builder, God did not start creating before He had made a well-considered plan. Following this same plan, God also upholds and governs heaven and earth and all that is in them.

Sometimes we speak about the laws of nature, but in faith we know it is God, who with His mighty hand upholds the whole solar system. He causes everything to move in its circuit. The myriads of stars – God knows them all, each by its own name.

With this same almighty and ever-present power, God also governs everything. In Psalm 147 it reads: He covers the earth with clouds, prepares rain for the earth, makes grass to grow on the mountains, gives to the beasts its food, and to the young ravens that cry. God thus indeed rules everything.

We call this God's providence, which does not just point to the fact that God knows everything beforehand. Of course, this as well! Yet more specifically, it highlights that God is there to provide. He never loses control of any situation, since He is always present with His almighty power: in the realm of nature and to no lesser degree in the world of politics. God is never absent, never a silent bystander. God is always present also in the life of every person, even when what we would call evil strikes.

In Article 13 of the Belgic Confession, it reads that this does not make God the Author of the sins which are committed. Though God is in control, He is not the One who brings about evil. Yet He still uses it for His purpose. Think of Joseph and his brothers. What the brothers did in selling Joseph to Egypt was a sin, and it grieved God. Yet He still used it for His purpose. Despite the sins of the brothers, God did not lose control of the situation. This is how God with His almighty power is always present, watching over us with fatherly care. Such wonderful care makes one indeed sing to the LORD with thanksgiving.

**READING: PSALM 23,
HEIDELBERG CATECHISM, Q+A 27**

God's Fatherly care

"He makes me lie down in green pastures.
He leads me beside still waters."

PSALM 23:2

If God cares for us and loves us, why then at times does He lead the lives of His children through such deep and dark valleys? This is a question we will never be able to fully answer, but perhaps to some degree occasionally in hindsight. Yet more often, how God ordains and executes His work surpasses our limited understanding. What God asks from us is childlike faith and trust – the same childlike faith and trust as expressed by David in Psalm 23.

In Psalm 23, David uses the image of a shepherd. However, this image is not of a shepherd who, together with his flock, peacefully treks from place to place. The picture is much harsher. In those days, a shepherd often had to defend and protect his flock against prowling beasts of prey. To find the right pastures, a shepherd had to at times lead his sheep along cliffs and dark canyons. In caring for the flock, the shepherd's own life was often in danger as well. Yet, because he loved his flock, this shepherd did not mind. His sheep meant everything to him.

David uses this picture as an image of God's care for us, highlighting that with the LORD we may feel secure under all circumstances, no matter how critical these circumstances might be. The LORD, our Shepherd, will always be there for us, full of love, defending us. With Him we will be safe, never having any wants.

Lord's Day 10 opens our eyes of faith to these same riches, so that in childlike trust we may lay our lives, weak and frail, in the hands of our great Father in heaven. We should do so in the same way as those sheep in Psalm 23, which kept following the shepherd even along cliffs and through dark canyons. These sheep did not understand either why they had to go along such difficult paths. Yet they trusted the wisdom of the shepherd, knowing that even via these difficult paths he would make them lie down in green pastures and lead them beside still waters.

Likewise, we should trust in God's fatherly care over our lives. In stressful situations, we might weigh up the circumstances. However, Lord's Day 10 teaches us always to trust God's fatherly care, both in prosperity as well as in adversity.

August 17

**READING: ROMANS 8:28-39,
HEIDELBERG CATECHISM, Q+A 27**

All things come from God's Fatherly hand

"And we know that for those who love God all things work together for good."

ROMANS 8:28A

In Lord's Day 10 we confess that all things come to us not by chance but by God's fatherly hand. All things – good, but also what we may call evil! Many people find this hard to accept. If God is love, how then can God ever put calamity and disaster on our path? This does not fit in with the concept many modern Christians have of God nowadays.

However, assuming that what we call evil does not come from God, where would this leave us? These things would then come by chance, striking at any time without reason. There is not much comfort in that. It is rather scary. It is no wonder, therefore, that so many people feel insecure nowadays. Many live in fear. They try to be merry, seeking this in alcohol and drugs, but deep down fear is eating at them.

Turning to Scripture, we read something different. In the prophecies of Amos we read in Chapter 3:6, "If there is a calamity in the city, will not the LORD have done it?" And this, while Amos also says in Chapter 5:15 that God hates evil and loves good. How are we to gel these two together?

In Article 13 of the Belgic Confession, we read that God is not the author of evil. God is light, and in Him is no darkness at all as we read in 1 John 5:1. Yet Article 13 also says that God's power and goodness are so great, "that He ordains and executes His work in the most excellent manner, even when devils and wicked men act unjustly." In other words, God remains in control, always!

When reading Scripture, we see the truth of Lord's Day 10 clearly shining amid the shadows so often cast over our lives. Many a letter in the New Testament was written to suffering children of God. Suffering, coming from God's fatherly hand. And yet, even in suffering, God's fatherly hand did not fail. Instead, in ways beyond our human understanding, God is working out the beautiful plan for our salvation, even through difficulties and hardship. We may struggle at times and ask the question 'why?'. Yet amid these struggles, we may cling to God and find comfort. How otherwise would we ever be able to cope?

**READING: PSALM 23,
HEIDELBERG CATECHISM, Q+A 27**

Trusting God

"I fear no evil, for you are with me; your rod and your staff, they comfort me."

PSALM 23:4

When facing challenging circumstances, we may weigh up the situation, making our own calculations. Yet David did not do this. At the time, when he had to flee from Saul, he did not take matters into his own hands, but waited for the LORD to make him king. David waited for God's chosen time, even though those years of wandering through the desert must have been terrible years for David; years during which David often must have asked, "LORD, what is the reason for all this?" Yet he trusted the LORD.

We see the same during the latter days of David's kingship when he had to flee Jerusalem because of the rebellion of his son Absalom. Again, David laid the matter in the hands of the LORD. Imagine: your own son attacking you, willing to kill you if only it would bring him to the throne. How much hurt must this have caused David? Yet also in that deep and dark valley, David kept trusting God, who took care of him.

Through trusting God we may have that same assurance that the LORD will never let the difficulties in the lives of His children rise so high that they will lose all strength. He repeatedly gives us moments when we can drink from the brook beside the way to refresh ourselves, so that once again we can lift our head, as David speaks about in Psalm 110:7. The LORD will always be near to nourish and refresh us, giving power to the weak and increasing strength to those who have no might. The LORD will always be near, not only in times of prosperity but also when we find it hard to cope with life. Yes, even during times when we least expect it, the Lord is near with His aid and protection.

God promised this at our baptism, when He said: I will always be your Father, providing you with all good, averting all evil or turning it to your benefit. That is why we may trust that God's fatherly care will never fail us. Never, not even when He leads our life through the valley of the shadow of death. For even then, His rod and His staff are there to comfort us.

August 19

**READING: PSALM 42,
HEIDELBERG CATECHISM, Q+A 28**

Patient in adversity

"Why are you cast down, O my soul, and why are you in turmoil within me? Hope in God; for I shall again praise him, my salvation and my God."

PSALM 42:11

From Answer 27 we learnt that nothing comes by chance but all things by God's fatherly hand. This knowledge gives a secure anchorage to our life. The question now is, is this visible in our lives, also when adversity strikes? How do we react when this happens? Do we just resign ourselves to the trials God puts on our path, even though inwardly we struggle to find peace? Answer 28 speaks about patience in adversity. What kind of patience is this? To find an answer to this question, let us briefly look at Psalm 42.

In this psalm, we meet a child of God struggling with the trials put on his path. In prayer, he pours out his troubles before God, while at the same time mockers say to him, "Where is your God?" (verse 3). Why does God not help you? Is he not the living God, almighty in power? The author struggles. Yet amid these struggles, he remembers how God was there for him in former days. God, whose name is Jahweh, the faithful God of the covenant who will never forsake us. Hence, why are you cast down, O my soul? Keep hoping in God, who is also my God, my salvation. This is the refrain verse throughout this psalm, to which the author keeps clinging amid the struggles he still faces. This psalm goes like the pendulum of a clock.

Is this not how things often go with us as well? Down in the dumps, we read the Bible, and all of a sudden we feel lifted up. Hope in God. But then the next moment it seems gone again, especially when the afflictions of life press us down. One moment we feel close to God, yet the next moment it seems gone again. On Sunday, we go to church and feel strengthened by the gospel, but when Monday comes around, everything looks dark again. Yet in faith, we keep clinging to God. That is how we find peace, knowing that despite all the turmoil in our life, God is with us, and He will never forsake us.

August 20

**READING: EPHESIANS 5:15-21,
HEIDELBERG CATECHISM, Q+A 28**

Thankful in prosperity

"Giving thanks always..."

EPHESIANS 5:20A

Peace and joy in life will only be found when we entrust ourselves to God, without any ifs or buts. Peace and joy in Christ, under all circumstances of life. What wonderful news this is. The road we might have to travel may still be rocky. There might be days hard to number. Days we would rather skip. Yet God is there in every step of the road. Thus the joy of faith may still prevail.

This does not mean that I have to shout for joy when affliction strikes. Even in the lives of upright children of God, there are also times that we are far from shouting for joy. Days that are overcome by sorrow or grief, when we can only cry, pouring out our hearts before God. Is that wrong? Surely not! Even our Saviour wept at Lazarus' graveside. In Gethsemane, He struggled immensely to come to terms with what God asked of Him. He even prayed that if it were at all possible, 'please God let Me not drink this cup of Thy wrath. Yet not My will, but Thy will be done.'

Faith is not without emotions. When a long entertained heart's desire finally comes true, overwhelmed by joy and thankfulness, we sing our praises to God. However, when the next day, a severe accident happens affecting the family, not much of this joy is left. We can only cry, and there is nothing wrong with this. Even though living by faith, different circumstances create different reactions. Our reaction to prosperity differs from our response to adversity. The Heidelberg Catechism also points this out, saying that we should be patient in adversity and thankful in prosperity.

In 1 Thessalonians 5:18 the apostle Paul writes, "Give thanks **in** all circumstances." Note that he does not say **for** all circumstances. God does not ask us to thank Him for affliction, pain, or sorrow hurting us. God says to thank Him **in** these circumstances. This means even in the valley of life, we are called to thank God that He does not let go of us, but is still there to provide for us. How otherwise would we ever be able to cope? Yet thanks be to God He is still there, even then! As the apostle Paul writes in Romans 8, nothing can separate us from His love. Hence there is always a reason to thank God.

August 21

**READING: PSALM 37:1-6,
HEIDELBERG CATECHISM, Q+A 28**

Having confidence in God

"Commit your way to the LORD; trust in him, and he will act."
PSALM 37:5

Nothing can separate us from God's love in Jesus Christ, our Saviour. Hence there is never any need to live in fear whatever the future may hold. Answer 28 says, "We can have a firm confidence in our faithful God and Father." Our heavenly Father says to us, "Fear not! Trust in Me, and I will act." He is the Almighty One, who has all creatures so completely in His hands that without His will they cannot so much as move. In Article 13 of the Belgic Confession it reads: God even "holds in check the devil and all our enemies so that they cannot hurt us without His permission and will." Therefore, why should we be afraid or worry? Father is in control no matter what happens in this world. In Him, I may put my trust. He will provide me with whatever I need, even in the most challenging of life circumstances.

We might not always feel like this. However, it is not our feelings that count, but God's sure promises instead. Daily we may cling to what God promised us at the very beginning of our life, when we were baptised. Those promises will remain valid throughout our life, whatever may befall us. Let us keep remembering this, especially when we struggle in faith. When struggling, think of your baptism.

Father is always there to care for us. This does not mean that we can count on a comfortable life. We live amid a creation which is groaning in travail, a creation where we are confronted with the brokenness of life daily. Yet we have this comfort: God is near and working everything together for our salvation, which means whatever adversity He sends us in this life of sorrow, He will turn it to our benefit. We may not always understand how all this works for our salvation. Yet, this is not necessary either. God says: trust me, and I will work it out. The road of our life may lead through dark valleys and alongside steep cliffs, yet it will bring us to green pastures and still waters. Safe with Father. Greater comfort one will never find.

August 22

**READING: LUKE 1:26-38,
HEIDELBERG CATECHISM, LORD'S DAY 11**

The Triune God and our Redemption

"And the angel answered her, 'The Holy Spirit will come upon you, and the power of the Most High will overshadow you; therefore the child to be born will be called holy – the Son of God.'"

LUKE 1:35

With Lord's Day 11, the Catechism starts the second part of the explanation of the Apostles' Creed. It covers the Lord's Days 11 to 19 and deals with the person and work of Jesus Christ, yet not in isolation, since one can never speak appropriately about the redemptive work of Jesus Christ without also mentioning the work of the Father and the Holy Spirit. After all, it was God the Father who sent the Son into this world. Thus, Christ's work for us finds its roots in the love of the Father, while the Holy Spirit overshadowed Mary to bring the Son into this world. Also, in Hebrews 9:14, we read that the Holy Spirit was involved when Christ offered Himself to God as a sacrifice without blemish. This shows that Christ's redemptive work from beginning to end reveals to us the sovereign love of the Triune God; Father, Son, and Holy Spirit always working together in unity for our redemption.

It is vital to highlight this, especially since people often speak about Jesus in a very isolated way. By way of example, think of car bumper stickers that say "Jesus loves you" or "Jesus needs you". I also think of wristbands people wear with the inscription, "What would Jesus do?" Many of these slogans may sound good, yet they often ignore the purpose for which the Lord Jesus entered this world, namely to save us from our sins. Often people do not want to speak about sin. And yet, sin is the root of all the problems we face.

Why is it that people do not want to hear about sin? One of the main reasons is that the word 'sin' causes us to consider who we really are: people who deserve nothing; people who must seek their life outside themselves to find it in Jesus Christ alone. We are sinners lost in guilt, who can only be truly redeemed by a unique and perfect Redeemer. Well, God gave us this Redeemer in Jesus Christ, the Son of His love.

August 23

**READING: LUKE 2:1-9,
HEIDELBERG CATECHISM, LORD'S DAY 11**

A unique Saviour (1)

"In those days a decree went out from Caesar Augustus that all the world should be registered."

LUKE 2:1

The Lord Jesus is our Saviour who came into this world to redeem us. Yet when Christ was born, the Roman Emporer also let himself be called and worshipped as saviour, since he too desired to give peace to a chaotic world, the so-called Pax Romana. For this reason, when a new emperor ascended the throne, the gospel went out with the joyous news of having received a new emperor.

Just imagine what this meant for the apostles when they went out to proclaim a different gospel – a gospel of true peace given by Jesus Christ. The Redeemer who had come down from heaven to save people not first of all from political chaos, confusion and bewilderment as a result of all kinds of civil wars, but instead He came to save people from the cause of all this misery, that is from sin.

During Jesus' earthly ministry, many took offence at this gospel. It opposed their concept of the Messiah. They thought the Messiah would come to redeem them from the hated Roman yoke. Similarly, many people today interpret the words of the gospel in a horizontal way as a gospel that proclaims freedom from the evil social structures in society. They preach Jesus as the great Revolutionary, who came into this world to subvert the established powers. After all, did He not oppose the leadership of Pharisees and scribes, and turn over the tables of the money changers in the temple? Jesus thus becomes the great example we should follow to bring a better world into existence, by defending the rights of the poor and the oppressed.

A gospel pointing to sin as the cause of all misery is something people do not want to hear. This should not cause us to make light of the many problems we face today. God gives us a place in this world, where we too must fulfil our duty in a positive way, contributing to the needs in society. At the same time, however, we should never be ashamed to speak of the hope by which we may live, the prospect of a better world, when in true faith we embrace the Lord Jesus Christ as the true Saviour, who came to redeem us from sin.

August 24

READING: MATTHEW 1:18-25,
HEIDELBERG CATECHISM, LORD'S DAY 11

A unique Saviour (2)

"...you shall call his name Jesus, for he will save his people from their sins."

MATTHEW 1:21B

How is it that the gospel of true life in Jesus Christ often falls on deaf ears? The reason is that the message of Jesus redeeming our life from its root problem, from sin, is something people find difficult to work with. For many, there are problems of far greater importance than the problem of sin. What can one really do with a gospel that comes with the message of being freed from sin, when it comes to climate change, natural disasters, or a pandemic like COVID19? If Jesus is a genuine Redeemer and truly loves people, why then do all these things happen? If Christ indeed came to take away the cause of all hunger and misery, which is sin, why then do we not see any changes? Wars keep ravaging countries. Look at all the natural disasters and illnesses that are not cured. Also, in all this, Christians are as vulnerable as non-Christians. So, what does it mean – as it reads in Lord's Day 11 – that in the Lord Jesus, we find all that is necessary for salvation?

Jesus saves. This indeed is a joyous message. However, if we highlight only the saving from sin, as the Catechism seems to do, does it then not become a very minimal joy? Are there not other, perhaps even more pressing needs to which the gospel of salvation in Jesus Christ should give response to as well?

Looking at His three-year ministry, the Lord Jesus had a keen eye for the needs of the poor, the sick, and the needy. One of His first miracles was the changing of water into wine. Yet, one may wonder, what did this have to do with redeeming us from sin? He healed the blind, raised people from the dead, stilled the storm, and multiplied bread. Yet, all this did not make the gospel Christ proclaimed simply a social gospel.

During Jesus' earthly ministry, the people often looked in an isolated way at the healings, and all other miracles Jesus did, instead of seeing them as signs, festive signals of what was to come: a glorious kingdom. Yet to bring this glorious kingdom to reality, first, the main problem had to be tackled: breaking the power of sin. It is the breaking of this power that made the Lord Jesus a unique Saviour.

 August 25

**READING: LUKE 15:11-24,
HEIDELBERG CATECHISM, LORD'S DAY 11**

How to receive this wonderful salvation

"But when he came to himself ..."

LUKE 15:17A

Jesus came to redeem our life from its root problem, our sins. However, to receive the benefit of this redemption, first, we must acknowledge that this is our problem. Like an alcoholic – you can only help him, when first he has admitted that he has a problem with alcohol. Well, the same applies to our struggle with sin. First, we must acknowledge that this is indeed a severe problem in our life. It is this acknowledgment alone that will bring us to our knees to confess our sins, asking the Lord for forgiveness, and also for help to fight against sin. In other words, we are to humble ourselves, and that is often very hard, for it cuts deep.

In the parable of the prodigal son, we read that beautiful expression of the younger son: he came to himself, not just because he suffered hunger. Instead, he came to himself, meaning all of sudden he realised what was actually wrong with him, namely that he had grieved his father. I have to go back. This must have been a tough journey for this son. To go back and to confess his sins. This did cut very deep, also for this son. But only in this way could he become truly happy again. Truly happy, in feeling whole again.

This example makes clear that being saved by Christ entails much more than just having some feelings of happiness and peace. Today we live in a religious climate, in which many people limit salvation in Jesus Christ to personal feelings. Without saying that this is completely wrong, there is a danger that lurks here. The rich significance of our salvation in Christ contains much more than just emotions of happiness and peace.

To make this somewhat more transparent, I am thinking of a broader meaning of the word salvation: to be cured, to make sound or whole again. This is something we should also keep in mind when speaking about our salvation in Christ. In Christ, the original soundness which man had in Paradise before the fall into sin is given back to us. It means, we may live in a peaceful relationship with God again, which gives our life a new dimension – a dimension that also provides us with the ability to cope in the face of the problems and trials God may still place on our path.

August 26

**READING: ACTS 4:1-12,
HEIDELBERG CATECHISM, LORD'S DAY 11**

Complete salvation in Jesus alone

"And there is salvation in no one else, for there is no other name under heaven given among men by which we can be saved."

ACTS 4:12

In Lord's Day 11 the Catechism poses the question, "Do those who seek their salvation or well-being in saints, in themselves, or anywhere else, also believe in the only Saviour Jesus?" The answer reads, "No. Though they boast of Him in words, they in fact deny the only Saviour Jesus."

Seeking your salvation or well-being somewhere else – with these words, our fathers, living in the age of the Great Reformation, made a firm stand against the Church of Rome. Yet we should not only look in the direction of Rome here. Lord's Day 11 wants to stress that whoever confesses Jesus Christ as his only Saviour must learn to deny himself.

Self-denial – we all know how difficult this is. How often does it not happen that we still expect it through our own efforts? We promise ourselves to make sure to break with a lifestyle that is displeasing to the Lord. **We** will make sure – instead of, in total self-denial, acknowledging that it comes entirely from the grace of God and the renewing power of the Holy Spirit. Why is this? Because it is hard to seek our life outside of ourselves to find it in Jesus Christ alone. Yet that is what God requires of us: to deny ourselves! We cannot contribute even one inch to our salvation. After all, Christ did not enter this world to redeem holy people, but He gave His life for sinners lost in guilt, who can appeal but only to His blood, suffering, death, and perfect obedience.

We should not seek our salvation and well being anywhere else. This also means we should not put our trust in gold, silver, money, or luxury. This does not mean that we are not allowed to enjoy what God has given us. The point is that our well-being does not depend on gold, silver, money, or luxury, but only on Him who has given His life to redeem us from the cause of all hunger and misery, which is sin. Gold and silver can quickly fall away. Yet, our salvation in Christ will never fall away. We can be sure of this, especially when considering the precious price Christ paid to make us His own.

August 27

**READING: MATTHEW 3:13-17,
HEIDELBERG CATECHISM, Q+A 31**

Anointed with the Holy Spirit

"And the Holy Spirit descended on Him
in bodily form, like a dove…"
LUKE 3:22A

To be a Christian means to be a follower of Christ. Yet to be able to follow Christ, first one must know who Christ is. The first Question and Answer of Lord's Day 12 tells us in a very detailed way who Christ is and also what He has done and still does for us today. In doing so, it first explains the name Christ, which functions as a title. By way of example, when speaking about Queen Elisabeth, Elisabeth is her name and queen is her title. Similarly, when speaking about Christ Jesus, then Jesus is His name and Christ is His title.

Christ is the Greek word for the Anointed One. In Hebrew, this word is translated with Messiah. As such, this is a name that does not say much, especially since we are no longer familiar with the custom of 'anointing'. This was different in the time of the Old Testament. In those days, 'being anointed' meant being appointed by God for a particular task, whereby the oil functioned as a sign that God would also enable that person to fulfil this task by the power from above, that is, by the power of the Holy Spirit. That is why in the Old Testament era, prophets, priests and kings were anointed with special oil. This oil was a symbol of the Holy Spirit, who would enable the person to fulfill the task to which he was called. In I Samuel 16 we read about David being anointed by Samuel. After the anointing with oil, it reads, "and the Spirit of the LORD came upon David from that day forward."

Through the service of these anointed persons – prophets, priests, and kings – God cared for His people. Yet these prophets, priests, and kings, though endowed with the Holy Spirit, remained sinful and weak in the execution of their respective offices. None of them could bring about a perfect redemption for the people of God. That is why the Messiah had to come – the Anointed One, our Lord Jesus Christ.

Also, whereas in the Old Testament, these three offices were separated and executed by different persons, our Lord Jesus Christ took all of those three tasks upon Himself, fulfilling them in and through His perfect ministry.

August 28

**READING: LUKE 4:13-30,
HEIDELBERG CATECHISM, Q+A 31**

Our Chief Prophet and Teacher

"Today this Scripture has been
fulfilled in your hearing."

LUKE 4:21

Answer 31 first mentions that Christ has been ordained as our chief Prophet and Teacher, who fully revealed to us the secret counsel and will of God. During the time of the Old Testament, God also sent prophets to reveal His will. Yet until Christ came, full revelation regarding our redemption had never been given. Moreover, many of these prophets had fulfilled their task in weakness. At times some of these prophets even had been unfaithful. That is why, during the time of the Old Testament, God's people continuously looked forward to the Great Prophet and Teacher, promised by God. In Christ, this promise came true, as He mentioned when He preached the gospel in the synagogue of his hometown Nazareth. Reading a passage from the prophecies of Isaiah, He said, "Today this Scripture has been fulfilled in your hearing." Meaning, I am this anointed One of whom this passage speaks.

Although the people initially spoke well of the sermon delivered by Christ, this enthusiasm faded soon after when Jesus did not perform any miracles. After all, that is why they had come to listen. But then Jesus makes it clear that the Word that is preached is what counts. Yet this was asking too much. True, Jesus was a good Preacher, but to indeed accept Him as the anointed One from Isaiah 61, to accept Him as the Messiah sent by God, they did not want to believe that.

And yet, Christ was indeed that anointed One. He was and is! He is the chief Prophet and Teacher, who also speaks to us today through that very same Word, that is through the Holy Scriptures which fully contain the will of God, and all that man must believe to be saved, as we confess in Article 7 of the Belgic Confession. That is the Word ministered to us every Sunday. Perhaps not always as astounding and astonishing as we would like it, yet it is preached with authority. Through this weekly preaching, Christ will also make known to us the counsel and will of God concerning our redemption. Every Sunday, we may listen to His voice and even daily when we open our Bible. This is how we may experience Christ's loving care as our Chief Prophet and Teacher.

 August 29

**READING: JOHN 10:1-18,
HEIDELBERG CATECHISM, Q+A 31**

Our only High Priest

"I am the good shepherd. The good shepherd lays down his life for the sheep."
JOHN 10:11

Christ is our only High Priest, who as the Lamb of God takes away the sins of the world. Concerning the high priests of the Old Testament, they were not able to take away even one single sin, let alone the sins of the world. Yet Christ came to bring that perfect sacrifice by His very own blood. He came as the Good Shepherd to give His life for the sheep.

It is noteworthy that in John 10:11 it does not read, "the good shepherd died for the sheep." Of course, He did. But that is not what the Lord Jesus teaches here. The truth is far more wonderful. Christ is saying that as the Good Shepherd, He came to give a voluntary sacrifice of Himself, laying down His life for the sheep, and this of His own will, as becomes clear in verse 18. In this verse, Christ speaks about His priestly activity and fulfilling it according to the task the Father had given Him.

The difference between the death of Jesus and the death of every other man is that He was personally active in it. For every one of us, when death comes, we will be victims, but this was not so for the Lord Jesus. When death came to Him, He was not its victim, instead He was its conqueror. He took death to Himself when He said, "Father, into Thy hands I commit my Spirit." Death was not His fate, but a triumphal act instead.

Through His suffering and death, Christ reconciled us with God. He died so that we may live, and to live eternally. He died, yet He also rose, so that He could make us share in the righteousness which He had obtained by His death. How? By interceding for us before the Father.

Since the sacrifice which Christ brought was a perfect sacrifice, we may have the assurance that God will hear us always, whenever we pray to Him in Jesus' Name. He is our Advocate in heaven, praying for us; praying not only for the forgiveness of our sins, but also as a High Priest who sympathises with us, praying that we may persevere in faith to the very end.

**READING: JOHN 10:28-30,
HEIDELBERG CATECHISM, Q+A 31**

Our eternal King (1)

"I give them eternal life and they will never perish."

JOHN 10:28A

As Prophet and Teacher, Christ revealed the plan for our redemption. As High Priest, He caused this plan to take effect. As King, Christ will now also preserve us in the redemption He obtained for us. If this were not the case, how quickly would we lose this redemption again? We are often nothing but very stubborn sheep, more interested in turning to our own ways. Yet Christ is there, even then, to care for us. Despite all the sins we commit, every day again, His love still goes out to us. How is this possible?

Christ knows our sins. That is why He came into this world to bear our sins in His body on the cross. For this very reason, we should never be afraid to dig out our sins and show them to Him. Christ ransomed us to set us free. He did so by laying down His life for us. Having paid such a high price for our freedom from sin and death, you can be assured that Christ will also make sure that none of those precious sheep will get lost again. We are dear to Him. As the Good Shepherd, Christ has set the love of His heart upon us. That is why today, as our eternal King, Christ will defend and preserve us in the redemption He obtained for us.

During our journey, on the road we must travel through life, questions may at times arise about difficulties and hardships the Lord places on our path. Questions we do not always get answers to. Why all these difficulties? Who are we to query the Shepherd, as long as we know that his eye is on us? He watches us, and therefore we are safe, whatever happens. This is something we simply must believe.

The shepherd's eye is on the sheep all the time. He knows them one by one and will provide for them accordingly, also when danger surrounds them. He never slumbers. He never sleeps. He watches over us, even in our trials, and when we struggle or find it hard to cope. Also then, the eye of the shepherd is on us all the time!

August 31

**READING: JOHN 10:28-30,
HEIDELBERG CATECHISM, Q+A 31**

Our eternal King (2)

"No one will snatch them out of my hand."

JOHN 10:28B

No one can snatch them out of His hand. As our eternal King, Christ will defend and preserve us in the redemption He obtained for us. He will bring us safely home. When we cling to Him, no power will be able to separate us from His love. What a great comfort this is in a world where Satan prowls around like a roaring lion, seeking whom he can devour. Satan is out there to lure God's children away, attracting them with enticing slogans. And at times we indeed see some young people falling for it. Children of God – baptised in front of the church – young members, who full of enthusiasm confessed their faith, but who strayed away from the church, following the lusts of the sinful flesh.

Was Satan able to snatch these lambs out of Christ's hands? Many a parent who has a child that no longer goes to church struggles with this very question. It is a tough question with no clear-cut answer. Yet the promise of John 10 stands and to that promise parents may cling, as long as we live in today's grace. For these children are still God's children to whom God gave promises, and therefore there is always a way back.

Sometimes we can no longer reach our children. Our arms are too short to reach them. How often do we not have that feeling, when children stray away from the Lord? Yet, there is one whose arms are never too short to help. When we can no longer reach our children, Christ can, through His Spirit renewing their faith. The faith that we cannot give to our children, Christ can. His love also goes out to those lost sheep. He let His body be nailed to the cross even for them. He gave His life for us and our children. That is the promise parents may cling to. No, this promise does not mean that our children will always walk in the ways of the Lord. When they grow up, it is their own responsibility to make the right choices. Yet as long as we live in today's grace, there is hope. We may therefore fold our hands, day and night, to lay the names of our children in the hands of Christ, the heavenly King.

September 1

**READING: MATTHEW 10:26-33,
HEIDELBERG CATECHISM, Q+A 32**

As prophet confess His Name

"So everyone who acknowledges me before men, I also will acknowledge before my Father who is in heaven."

MATTHEW 10:32

How can I as a Christian confess Christ's Name? First, by listening to His voice and listening to it with a believing heart. In Answer 32 it reads, "I am a member of Christ by faith." It is this faith, worked in us by the Holy Spirit, that makes us listen and also listen obediently. Obediently, when choices at times have to be made, so that I do not make the wrong choice, going against the voice of my chief Teacher.

We should listen to the voice of the Good Shepherd, also where it concerns the promises God has given us. For example, when struggling with doubts, since by these promises God will strengthen and comfort us as well as guide us so that we do not follow the voice of our own sinful heart, but instead open our hearts to Christ.

When we do this, we will stand more and more in awe of what a great Saviour we have. Yes, when overwhelmed by it, from the fullness of the heart the mouth will speak. As true Christians, we cannot stand it when the name of our Saviour is spoken about badly or blasphemed. Then we will stand up for His name and not keep silent.

Also, when considering our riches – which we too received undeservedly – we will become keen to share these riches with others who are still wandering around in the dark, so that they may also come to this wonderful light that clears the darkness.

This is what it means to confess Christ's Name. This indeed starts with listening. After all, a prophet must first listen before he can speak. First listen, since a prophet does not speak his own words, but the words of Him who has sent him. It is good to stress this, in particular in today's postmodern climate where everyone is allowed to air his own view. However, confessing Christ's Name is not giving my personal opinion about Christ. Instead, it is speaking the truth about Christ as it has been revealed to us Scripture. It is only this truth that gives rest in a world full of unrest. This truth should always be dear to us, thereby confessing this and nothing else.

September 2

**READING: 1 PETER 1:13-25,
HEIDELBERG CATECHISM, Q+A 32**

As priest present myself as a living sacrifice of thankfulness to Him

"But as he who called you is holy, you also be holy in all your conduct."
1 PETER 1:15

In the Old Testament era, the life of a priest was devoted entirely to the Lord's service. Likewise, we must dedicate our lives to Christ as a living sacrifice. This means our whole life – every aspect of it.

Christ laid down His life for us, even though we did not deserve this at all. He set us free from the slavery of sin and death. As the Good Shepherd, He did and still does everything for us. When thinking about so great a love for sinners, who would not give his life to this Saviour? Would this be asking too much; asking too much to give up certain sinful habits in our lives?

In the Old Testament, a priest not only had to offer sacrifices, but also prayed and blessed. This also belongs to our priestly task when we carry the needs of others in prayer before the Lord. Next, we should also try to be a blessing to others. Instead of living solely for our own interests, as priests we should care for others wherever we can.

We should also remember that priests, in particular, had to live holy. Well, we too are called to live holy. The apostle Peter in his first letter writes, "As He who called you is holy, you also be holy in all your conduct." In Chapter 3 verse 3 of his first letter, the apostle John writes, "And everyone who thus hopes in Him purifies himself as He is pure." In a nutshell, true Christians live for Christ, for Christ alone. He bought us with the price of His precious blood, so our life belongs to Him. This should never be a burden to us, but pure joy instead. Look at the world, where people are enslaved to sin. Yet, does it really make them happy? Perhaps for a moment, but that is all. Let us show the people around us that we have something better to live for. Share it. Do not be ashamed to show that you live for Christ, your Saviour.

September 3

**READING: 1 PETER 3:13-22,
HEIDELBERG CATECHISM, Q+A 32**

As king fight with a free and good conscience against sin and the devil in this life

"Baptism, which corresponds to this, now saves you, not as a removal of dirt from the body, but as an appeal to God for a good conscience."

1 PETER 3:21

We may fight with a free and good conscience. For even though our conscience may accuse us at times, we are Christ's who fully paid for all our sins. The apostle Peter in Chapter 3 of his first letter, speaking about baptism, says that our baptism is an appeal to God for a good conscience. Some translations use the word 'pledge' instead of the word 'appeal'. A pledge, a guarantee – of what? Of this, concerning God's coming judgment, we may have a clear conscience, for we are cleansed from all our sins by the blood of our living Saviour, who today is seated at God's right hand and who one day will return as judge. Our baptism testifies and guarantees, not as a pillow to fall asleep on but by living from it, that we do not have to be afraid of this judge, no matter how terrible the coming judgment might be. We do not have to be afraid, since in faith we have this assurance: my Judge is my Redeemer.

In Lord's Day 1 we confess this as our only comfort. We have been set free. However, there should also then be a desire to remain free. Therefore, sustained by power from above, it should be our desire to fight against sin and those sinful desires Satan so often uses to try and lure us away from Christ. Let us be faithful soldiers in Christ's service. Do not desert your Saviour. Instead, be thankful to be His.

Sharing in Christ's anointing, we are indeed also kings. True, as yet there is no throne for us. That is for later. Today we still have to fight against sin and the devil. We are still involved in a severe battle, whereby at times we may wonder whether we are not at the losing end. After all, true Christians are becoming more and more of a dwindling minority in a society which is growing increasingly secular. Yet, the victory is ours, since already today we are more than conquerors in Christ.

September 4

**READING: MATTHEW 16:13-20,
HEIDELBERG CATECHISM, Q+A 33**

God's only begotten Son

"Simon Peter replied, You are the Christ,
the Son of the living God."

MATTHEW 16:16

Throughout Christ's public ministry on earth, people wondered who He was. In Matthew 16 the Lord Jesus puts this very same question to His disciples. "Who do men say that I, the Son of Man, am?" Various answers follow. But He continues asking, "But who do you say that I am?" In response, Simon Peter answers, "You are the Christ, the Son of the Living God." This confession of the apostle Peter is central to all preaching of the gospel: Jesus Christ is the Son of the living God.

I believe in Jesus Christ, God's only begotten Son. This is not just a dogmatic statement where one could say that we should not make too much of a fuss about whether one firmly believes this, as long as one loves Jesus. Comments like these undermine the foundation of our salvation, since the confession about the deity of Christ is essential. In one of the commentaries on this Lord's Day, I read the following:

"Was it really necessary for our salvation that Jesus is the Son of God? Or is this not essential, something that does not alter the quality of His work? For example, we can wholeheartedly agree on the good qualities of an architect, but at the same time disagree on the point whether he is the natural son of his father. As far as his work is concerned it is of no importance whether he is a son of his own flesh and blood.

Could something like that perhaps apply also to Jesus? Surely not! Not only His godly honour, but then also our redemption would be completed negated. We could only be saved by the natural Son of God, who at the same time is also God Himself. Otherwise we would still be lost."[1]

It is of crucial importance to uphold this confession, without compromising. After all, no one will find salvation unless he confesses that Jesus Christ is the Son of the living God. Those who only glory in Jesus as an excellent human being will be ashamed and cast out when this Jesus returns in glory on the clouds of heaven. Let us therefore hold fast to this confession without wavering.

---

1 Drs. C. Bijl, "Wat het geloof verwacht. Het apostolicum volgens de Heidelbergse Catechismus. Zondag 8-24." Barneveld, 1989. Page 51.

September 5

**READING: PHILIPPIANS 2:5-11,
HEIDELBERG CATECHISM, Q+A 33**

Children of God by adoption

"He humbled himself by becoming obedient to the point of death, even death on the cross."

PHILIPPIANS 2:6B

When Scripture speaks about Jesus as the only begotten Son of God, it never does so at the expense of us who are children of God by adoption. On the contrary, God loved us so much that He did not even spare His own Son but gave Him up for us all. God poured out His wrath upon the Son of His love so that we could become adopted children, who with Christ share in the same inheritance which He also obtained for us (Romans 8:17).

However, not only the Father, but also the Son loved us so much that He did not feel ashamed to call us His brethren. He too gave everything up for us, even the glory He enjoyed in heaven. We read about this in Philippians 2:6 where it says, "He who being in the form of God did not consider it something to be held onto to be equal with God." This means Christ did not cling to the privileges which were His. He did not cling to His divine power and majesty to glorify Himself, but He emptied Himself of these privileges. This does not mean that He removed from Himself His identity as God, but He humbled Himself, relinquishing His exalted status, however not His divine being. The rhymed version of Philippians 2 verses 5 to 11 phrases this very beautifully:

> "Though God's equal, though eternal King,
> He did not to His rightful glory cling.
> Himself He emptied that He us might save;
> Himself for us, God's chosen ones, He gave,
> And, born as man, our Lord became a slave".

By way of example, think of a prince living among the homeless. Such a prince can never undo the DNA of his royalty.

That is how, in His love for us, the Son of God desired to unite Himself with our human nature. Though He was without sin, He took our sins upon Himself to bring us back to the Father, so that once again we might obtain the right of being children of God. Yes, on account of Christ's perfect obedience, God adopted us as His children and heirs.

September 6

**READING: 1 PETER 1:13-25,
HEIDELBERG CATECHISM, Q+A 34**

Our Lord

"Knowing that you were ransomed… with the precious blood of Christ."
1 PETER 1:18-19

We are children of God. Yet, Christ is also our Lord. He has ransomed us body and soul. We are no longer ourselves, but we are His precious possession. Does this not conflict with our status as adopted children, who share with Christ in the inheritance? Not when we consider the following.

When Christ ransomed us to make us His possession, we were far from free. We were slaves of Satan. This surely was not a position to take delight in. This is not always how it may look in our eyes. At times, we may think that people outside the church can do what they like, they are free, and that God's commandments burden us. As a child of God, you are not allowed to do this, and you cannot do that. Sometimes it may seem that you are not really free. However, this is Satan deceiving us. Satan likes to leave his slaves under the impression that they are free. You can do what you want without worrying about God and His commandments. Often we fall for this lie, envying those people who seem to be able to make the most of life. However, the freedom of this world will end in the prison of hell.

In Christ, we have been freed from this. Christ ransomed us to make us His possession. He did so for a very precious price. The apostle Peter says in his first letter that Christ did not ransom us with silver or gold, but He gave His life for us. That is how precious we were in His eyes. That is how much God loved us.

When considering all of this in faith, who would still say they do not want to be a slave of this Lord? Instead, we then rejoice in being Christ's possession. After all, the yoke of this Lord is not hard to bear. He is not a slave driver, but gentle and lowly in heart. With Him, we will find rest for our souls. That is why, full of confidence, we can entrust ourselves to Him. This Lord will carefully watch over us so that nothing happens to us, especially because of the precious price He paid for us. He will protect us to the extent that no hair will fall from our head without the will of His Father.

**READING: GALATIANS 4:1-7,
HEIDELBERG CATECHISM, LORD'S DAY 14**

At the time appointed by God

"When the fullness of time had come."

GALATIANS 4:4A

At the time appointed by God, Christ was born. Throughout the entire time of the Old Testament, God had been working towards this specific time, ruling history. God did so according to His decree, made already before the foundation of the world. That is how our gracious God rules history, also today, to come to the final day when Christ will come for a second time.

In Galatians 3:24, the apostle Paul speaks about the function of the law during the time of the Old Testament, calling it a guardian until Christ came. Paul uses this image to make a distinction between the Old and New Testament. During the time of the Old Testament, the law aimed at leading God's people to Christ. Yet often, God's people forgot about this aspect of the law. They saw the law as a burden, and therefore they often rebelled against it. This kindled God's wrath. As bitter fruit, God's people were exiled to Babylon.

However, after exile, there was not much change of heart. The majority of the people lapsed into a doctrine of self-righteousness, whereby they considered the law no longer as an instrument to lead them to Christ, but instead as a set of rules they had to meet to be saved. That is why they took offense at the preaching of Christ, offense at the gospel of being saved by grace. They refused to accept Jesus of Nazareth as the Messiah sent by God. They could not see that finally the time had fully come, of which the prophets of the Old Testament had so often spoken.

When this time finally came, the vast majority of the Jews were not ready to meet their Saviour. There was only a small minority still awaiting the redemption of Jerusalem. Yet this did not make God change His plans. God remained faithful towards the promise He had already given in Paradise, that one day the seed of the woman would crush the head of the serpent.

Throughout a history stained by sin from the side of God's chosen people, God kept working towards this great date, to bring His Son into this world to redeem those who were under the law. Yet He would save not only them, but also all who in sincere faith would acknowledge Jesus as their Saviour, Jews and Gentiles alike without any distinction.

September 8

**READING: GALATIANS 4:1-7,
HEIDELBERG CATECHISM, LORD'S DAY 14**

Redemption from the curse of the law

"… born of woman, born under the law to
redeem those who were under the law …"

GALATIANS 4:4B

Born of woman – the apostle Paul does not speak in actual terms about Jesus being born of a virgin. Yet implicitly he does. He speaks about God sending His Son, and about a woman. There is no reference to an earthly father. Therefore, even though in concealed terms, we still may see a reference to the virgin birth of Christ in these words.

Christ was also born under the law. Born of a Jewish mother, into a Jewish family, He was subject to the Jewish law. The Lord Jesus always submitted to the requirements of this law. He perfectly fulfilled all the righteousness of God's law for us and in our place. We call this Christ's active obedience. Burdened with our sins, He also submitted Himself to the curse of the law by giving His life on the cross for our disobedience to God's law. We call this Christ's passive obedience. Thus He reconciled us with God. Through faith in this Saviour, we may consider ourselves righteous in the sight of God – righteous by faith and not by works of the law.

In the beginning, God gave His law as a way unto life. Yet to obtain this life, one had to obey God's law perfectly. Our misery, however, is that we are incapable of doing so. Thus we were lying under the curse of the law. But then God sent His Son, born of a woman, born under the law. This also applied to the Son of God, "Do this, and you will live!" Well, Christ indeed obeyed God's law perfectly, and this not with aversion, but with joy. It was His food and joy to do the will of His Father in heaven. He never failed to keep God's commandments. He thus took the burden under which we would have perished on His shoulders. As fruit of all this, we are no longer slaves who are burdened with a job we could never finish. Instead, we have been set free. Having freed us from the curse of the law, Christ then leads us to the Father, who once again adopts us as His children and heirs.

September 9

**READING: JOB 14:1-12,
HEIDELBERG CATECHISM, LORD'S DAY 14**

A new beginning

*"Who can bring a clean thing
out of an unclean?"*

JOB 14:4A

In Answer 36 of the Heidelberg Catechism it reads, "With His innocence and perfect holiness Christ covers in the sight of God my sin, in which I was conceived and born." This means, God no longer looks at our unholy beginnings, but instead at the holy beginning of Jesus Christ. Our life has been removed from its old foundation. In Christ's holy conception and birth, it received a new foundation. Since Christ became our Mediator from the very beginning of His life, we are counted righteous before God. Though conceived and born in sin, we are sanctified in Christ. We are no longer subject to the condemnation of Adam.

Thus there are prospects again. We were corrupt into the very root of our existence. But Christ has given our life a new foundation. He sanctifies us from our early youth, even from conception. Thus the very beginning of Christ's life is also of great significance for our redemption and gave our life new roots.

This is something we should keep reminding ourselves of. At times, we can become depressed because we would like to do away with certain sins in our lives, as it seems that we will never succeed. Every day again, we fall into the same pattern of sins. We start doubting whether there will ever be a possibility for a new beginning. We start doubting, since we are looking for a new beginning of ourselves. Yet, we should look at Christ in whom God has given us this new beginning already. What is impossible for us is possible with God. Yes, with God, everything is possible, as long as we believe. And even this is not because of any efforts we could make. Faith is also God's gift! This gift enables us to accept what God has given us in Christ, whereby we must give thought not only to what Christ did for us on Calvary, but that this had already started with what God gave us in Christ's holy conception and birth.

Lord's Day 14 tells us in doctrinal terms what Christmas is all about. It tells us how richly God has blessed us by the child in the manger. Christmas speaks of a new beginning for people lost in guilt. Having been conceived by the Holy Spirit, Christ brought about a clean beginning, and by faith in Him we may share in this new beginning. Amazing Grace, how sweet the sound!

September 10

**READING: ISAIAH 53:1-3,
HEIDELBERG CATECHISM, LORD'S DAY 15**

A life-long suffering

"He was despised and rejected by men;
A man of sorrows, and acquainted with grief."
ISAIAH 53:3A

When reading the Apostles' Creed, it seems as if the major part of Christ's ministry on earth receives hardly any attention. It speaks about Christ's birth, but then straightaway it goes to the end of His life, saying, "He suffered under Pontius Pilate, was crucified, dead and buried." One could ask, but what about the period in between, especially the three years of His earthly ministry, about which all four gospel-narratives speak so extensively? What about Christ's redeeming work for us? Was all of this of less importance and is not worth mentioning at all?

Lord's Day 15 answers this question, saying that the word 'suffered' in the Apostles' Creed refers not just to the end of Christ's life. Instead, Christ suffered all the time He lived on earth, from His birth to His death. Indeed, right from birth, right from conception, when the eternal Son of God assumed human flesh and blood from the virgin Mary.

As such, there was no suffering in Christ becoming man. Think of man in Paradise. However, Christ did not start His life in Paradise, but in a world broken by sin – the same world where we also started our life. In Romans 8:3 it reads that He came in the likeness of sinful flesh. This means, when Christ became man, He took upon Himself a human nature with all of its infirmities. Also, although He Himself was without sin, right from birth Christ carried the burden of our sins, also suffering the consequences of them, living life as we live it in a world broken by sin.

Christ experienced this brokenness right from the very beginning of His life. Instead of receiving the red-carpet treatment when coming as the Saviour of this world, there was no place for Him in the inn. A little while later, He had to flee from King Herod. This clearly shows that His suffering started straightaway. Concerning the three years of His public ministry on earth, preaching the glad tidings of salvation, the vast majority of the people despised and rejected Him, as Isaiah had already spoken about. At times, even His own disciples failed to understand Him. How much must the Lord Jesus have suffered during all of this!

September 11

**READING: ISAIAH 53:4-8,
HEIDELBERG CATECHISM, LORD'S DAY 15**

A life-long suffering, but especially at the end

"But he was pierced for our transgressions;
he was crushed for our iniquities."

ISAIAH 53:5A

Towards the end of Christ's life on earth, His suffering increased in intensity. The Jewish authorities hardened themselves in their opposition towards Christ, plotting to put Him to death, even finding help with one of Jesus' own disciples. Finally, at the end of His life in the Garden of Gethsemane, we see our Saviour crawling in the dust like a worm, sweating blood, with the soldiers coming to arrest Him as if He were a criminal. At His trial before the Sanhedrin, He was scorned and accused. Before Pontius Pilate, He was tortured and disrobed, and then He was put to death on the cross.

Yet, no matter how terrible this already was, it was not the anger and hatred of man in the first place which caused Christ to suffer so severely. Many Christian martyrs also suffered terrible pain and agony. In that respect, one could wonder whether there was much difference between Christ's suffering and the sufferings of so many martyrs throughout history.

Yet there was: a distinct difference! For concerning those martyrs, although their suffering was also a result of being faithful to the LORD, they did not seek death. Yet, Christ did. He had to suffer and to die, and this for the sins of others, including our sins. In all this, Christ bore the wrath of God for us.

It is this particular aspect that made Christ's suffering completely unique, different from whatever any other human being would suffer. Throughout His whole life, Christ felt burdened with this wrath, with it coming down on Him to its fullest extent at the end of His life, especially during those three hours of darkness on the cross.

Because Christ stilled the wrath of God for us and in our place, we may live in the assurance that God's face shines upon us, with the assurance that God is there to care for us. Because of what Christ did for us, we may once again live in the light of God's favour. We may take shelter under His wings. Because of Christ's suffering on the cross, nothing can separate us from this wonderful love. Thus, we can cope in this often so broken life. We can cope by living from the riches of the wonderful gospel of God's amazing grace for us wretched sinners.

September 12

**READING: JOHN 19:1-16,
HEIDELBERG CATECHISM, LORD'S DAY 15**

He suffered under Pontius Pilate

"So he delivered him over to be crucified."
JOHN 19:16

As to Christ's suffering on Good Friday, many people were involved, yet the Apostles' Creed only mentions the name of Pontius Pilate. Why is this? The answer is: because Pilate proclaimed the final sentence, and as Answer 38 mentions, it was as an earthly judge. As a judge, Pilate initially declared Christ innocent, yet in the end he still sentenced Him to death.

One may wonder what legal authority this death sentence had, especially when taking into account the fraudulence of this Roman judge. Yet, we must not look here first of all at the person Pontius Pilate, but at his office. As a judge, Pilate was the official representative of the Roman government, and in this capacity, he was a servant of God. The Lord Jesus also testifies to this, when He says to Pontius Pilate, "You would have no power at all against Me unless it had been given to you from above." Pontius Pilate thus condemned Jesus with the authority given to Him from above.

Yet Christ was innocent. Therefore, was He not condemned unjustly? It is true, Christ did not deserve to die. No charge of any personal wrongdoing was ever made against Him. As far as that is concerned, Pilate indeed abused the power he had as an official judge. Yet, we should not forget that throughout the unjust actions of Pilate, God was sentencing Jesus. Even though Pilate did not find any guilt in Him, God in heaven considered Jesus guilty, since He stood there as our representative, carrying our sins. That is how Christ must also have experienced this sentence, pronounced not in the first place by Pontius Pilate, but by God, His heavenly Father.

Thus, though innocent, Christ was sentenced to death. In this, He experienced what we deserved. It was our guilt which was judged in that hour. At the time Pontius Pilate condemned Jesus to temporal death, God condemned us to eternal death. He brought the chastisement down on Him, who had taken our place. Christ the innocent One stood in the place of the guilty. The verdict we deserved was directed at Him and was carried out on Him. Thus, He freed us from the severe judgment of God that would have fallen on us.

September 13

**READING: GALATIANS 3:10-14,
HEIDELBERG CATECHISM, LORD'S DAY 15**

He suffered under Pontius Pilate, was crucified

"Cursed is everyone who is hanged on a tree."

GALATIANS 3:13B

Christ died by way of crucifixion. Was this because crucifixion was more painful and terrible than death by execution? The answer to this question is 'No'. Instead, we have to look at the meaning of death by crucifixion. Crucifixion was indeed a terrible way to die. Just think of it: Christ's blood dripping out of His wounds, while the fierce sun burned on His body. Yet this was not the worst part. The worst was the knowledge that this crucifixion pointed to the curse of God. The one who was crucified was considered to be cut off from heaven and earth – His place was in hell. Well, that is what Christ experienced while hanging on the cross. That is why words fail to describe the terrifying reality of what Christ suffered. This cannot be captured by a movie either, like the Passion of Christ. Christ's most severe suffering – being forsaken by God – was even hidden from the eyes of men when darkness fell over Calvary.

And again, it was us who deserved all of this. The Catechism speaks about the curse, which lay on me – yes, on every person. The curse rested upon the life of mankind – a life subject to futility, if Christ had not redeemed it. No one can escape this curse without rendering his life to Christ. Only faith in Christ removes this curse and futility, causing us to flourish again.

In the book of the law, it reads: cursed is everyone who does not abide by all the things written in this book and does them. However, Christ took this curse upon Himself. He hung on the cross as a person cursed by God. However, when He was taken from the cross, this curse was taken away as well, and this permanently. Having suffered, Christ received the crown of glory, and we may share in this same glory through faith in Him, even today. Since the curse has been lifted, Christ now fills our life with His blessing. We are no longer under the law, but may live by grace. It is this grace alone that constitutes true life; a life that is no longer subjected to futility, but bearing fruit in and through Christ.

September 14

**READING: GENESIS 2:15-17,
HEIDELBERG CATECHISM, LORD'S DAY 16**

The necessity of Christ's death

"...in the day you will eat of it you shall surely die."
GENESIS 2:17B

One of Christ's last words, which He spoke from the cross, was: "It is finished." Christ spoke these words just after the light had returned over Calvary. During three hours of thick darkness, Christ had endured the full wrath of God against the sins of the whole human race. Three hours of darkness, during which Christ emptied the cup of God's wrath to its last bitter drop. In doing so, Christ paid the full penalty for our sins. When Christ said, "It is finished" all of this now lay behind Him. This begs the question: Having paid the full price for our sins – why, after all of this, did Christ still have to humble Himself unto death? Does this mean God's wrath still had not been satisfied, and thus more suffering was needed? However, what then did those words "It is finished" mean?

The point is that even though the hardest work had been done, Christ still had not yet reached the end of the road of His work in humiliation. Christ still had to die, also physically. The Catechism in its proof texts refers to Genesis 2:17, where we read about the punishment God had set in case man transgressed the commandment not to eat of the tree of knowledge of good and evil. God had said very clearly, "In the day that you eat of it you shall surely die." Well, God always does what He says. Scripture calls this God's justice. God is always true to what He has spoken.

Because man had sinned, he deserved punishment and the punishment set by God was death! This speaks in the first place of eternal death. This is what Christ suffered when God forsook Him. Yet when God spoke about death, it also included physical death. By also dying for us physically, Christ removed the sting from our death. That is why, for our sake, He also had to die physically.

Since the fall into sin in Paradise, the word 'death' is written above every cradle. We live to die. No human being can escape death, unless we cling to Christ in faith, who also bore this part of God's punishment for us. True, we still have to die, but now even in death there is hope again.

September 15

**READING: PHILIPPIANS 1:19-26,
HEIDELBERG CATECHISM, LORD'S DAY 16**

Why do we still have to die?

"For to me to live is Christ, and to die is gain."

PHILIPPIANS 1:21

If Christ's death is a substitute for the death of the believers, why do the believers then still have to go through the trauma of physical death? If someone has paid my debt, I do not have to pay it anymore, do I? Well, if Christ died in order for me to live, why do I then still have to die?

Upon dying, the believer enters into eternal life. To die is gain! What a great comfort this is! Yet is this indeed the only way in which we can enter eternal life, only through death? Are there no other options? Enoch and Elijah, for example, went to heaven without dying. Why is this not an option for us?

In Answer 42, it reads: "Our death is not a payment for our sins, but it puts an end to sin." These words highlight that there is only one way to get rid of all our sins, namely through death. Sin is so ineradicably interwoven with our earthly existence that the last string can only be cut when the last string of our earthly life is also cut. Until that time, we will never get rid of our sins completely, no matter how sincerely we are fighting the battle against sin.

Sin runs in our blood. We are totally infected by it. Yet it has to go, otherwise we cannot enter the full glory of the kingdom of God, since flesh and blood – and that is what we are now – cannot inherit the kingdom of God.

Death is the last enemy we meet on our way to God. True, it is still an enemy. Death will never become a friend. However, the truth also is that this enemy has lost its strength. It cuts all ties we have with this earth, which causes pain and grief in particular for those who are left behind. Yet for the believers, it means gain, since upon death, we enter eternal glory. When our earthly ties are cut, the gates to heaven open. Think of this: when death comes to take God's children away out of this life, it does so with gnashing teeth, knowing that yet again a battle has been lost. Lost, since for us to die is gain!

September 16

**READING: ROMANS 6:1-14,
HEIDELBERG CATECHISM, LORD'S DAY 16**

Freed from sin

"For one who has died has been set free from sin."
ROMANS 6:7

For us to die is gain! Christ's mediatorial work benefits us from the cradle to the grave, yes even from before the cradle until after the grave. So, what further benefit can we receive from Christ's death?

The answer is that Christ not only covers our sins by His blood, but by His Spirit He will also help us to fight sin, so that already in this life, we may grow in holiness towards God. This too is fruit of Christ's death.

When on the cross, Christ was not hanging there just by Himself. Our old nature was hanging there together with Him. Next, Christ also took our old nature with Him into the tomb. Our old nature – that is our sinful flesh with all of its evil desires – died with Christ and was buried with Him.

One may wonder whether this is true. After all, how often does our sinful nature not play up, still getting the best of us? If it died with Christ, how then can it still play up time and again? Can one really say, "My evil desires have been buried with Christ?" The answer is 'yes' and 'no'.

Romans 6 makes clear that our baptism serves as a sign and seal that we have died and been buried with Christ. That is the principle from which we should start. In Christ, we have been freed from sin. In practical terms, this means: in and through Christ, we have become new people. That is why we must consider ourselves to be dead to sin, but alive to God in Christ Jesus, our Lord. However, this does not mean that sin is altogether gone from our life. Paul says that we must consider ourselves dead to sin. This means sin should no longer rule our lives, and that Christ instead should. That is why we must fight sin with all of its evil passions to become more and more like what, through Christ, we already are: new creatures! Of course, we cannot do this through our own strength. We can only do this by the same power by which Christ conquered death. Christ will give us this power when we cling to Him in faith.

September 17

**READING: ROMANS 8:31-39,
HEIDELBERG CATECHISM, LORD'S DAY 16**

The comfort we receive from the bitterness of Christ's death

"(nothing)… will be able to separate us from the love of God in Christ Jesus our Lord."

ROMANS 8:39B

When reading the Apostles' Creed in chronological order, "He suffered under Pontius Pilate, was crucified, dead and buried; He descended into hell," it seems to say that after Christ died and was buried, He descended into hell. Yet Scripture does not give any proof of this. Therefore, the confession "He descended into hell" should be read as a summarising word, in which the bitterness of Christ's death is described: the anguish and torment of hell. Christ suffered the full extent of God's wrath, especially when He struggled in Gethsemane and then later on the cross, when He was forsaken by God Himself. During these three hours of darkness, He was left alone with the devil and all the powers of hell. Three hours, during which the devil was present and during which Christ's suffering reached its deepest level, in tasting eternal death in all of its bitterness.

Christ suffered all of this so that we might be delivered from the anguish and torments of hell. Breaking the power of darkness, He saved us from the clutches of the Prince of darkness. That is why the apostle Paul wrote in Romans 8: "We are more than conquerors through Him who loved us." More than conquerors – this seems to be a very bold statement. Yet there is no need to doubt this.

At times, when we fall for the temptations of the evil one or when reflecting upon life, guilt and doubt can start overwhelming us. We struggle with our faith. How can we overcome such a crisis in faith? By opening our Bible and by firmly believing that it is true what God says in His Word. Satan will sift us like wheat – and let us never make light of that! However, there is also the sure promise that Christ prays for us that our faith will not fail, as He did for the apostle Peter when he was tempted.

When we travel through valleys, these will never be as deep as the valley Christ had to travel through. We will never be deprived of God's favour. He was forsaken by God, so that we might be accepted by God and nevermore be forsaken by Him. Nevermore, not even in the deepest valley! For in that valley, we may look on high to Christ our Rock and our Redeemer.

September 18

**READING: ISAIAH 53:10-12,
HEIDELBERG CATECHISM, LORD'S DAY 17**

Christ's resurrection and our justification

"By his knowledge shall the righteous one, my servant, make many to be accounted righteous."
ISAIAH 53:11

On Easter morning, Christ rose from the dead. Yet we also confess that the Father raised Him. In so doing, the Father accepted the sacrifice which Christ had brought on Good Friday, proclaiming that His justice had been satisfied. On Easter morning, the Son received the wages which God in Paradise had already promised to Adam, namely that in the way of obedience he would receive eternal life. Christ received this life on Easter morning, and as our living Saviour He now wants to distribute this life also to us.

Death ... sin ... they have been conquered in the death and resurrection of our Lord and Saviour Jesus Christ. Easter signals a turning point in history. The downward line changed to an upward direction.

It is this upward line to which the Catechism also points in Lord's Day 17. Christ rose so that He could make us share in the righteousness which He obtained by His death. By His resurrection, Christ overcame death. In Hebrews 2:14 and 15, it reads: "Through death He destroyed him who had the power of death, that is, the devil, and this to release those who through fear of death were all their lifetime subject to bondage." Because of Christ's death, our sins have been paid for. Therefore the devil's power to kill has been destroyed. His accusations against us no longer have any grounds. In heaven, we now have a High Priest who, based on His accomplished work, pleads for our acquittal.

Just imagine that this grip of death had not been broken. There would be no hope. That is the picture of life without Christ, no matter how much people might be enjoying life at present. One day, we all must stand before God, and without Christ this would only lead to condemnation. Without Christ, there is no hope, no future. Yet whoever embraces Christ in faith as His Saviour no longer needs to fear the judgment of God. In Christ, God will declare us righteous, granting us eternal life. This changes the picture altogether. Faith in Christ as the risen Saviour makes all the difference. For through faith in Jesus Christ, I am righteous before God and an heir to life everlasting.

September 19

**READING: EPHESIANS 2:1-10,
HEIDELBERG CATECHISM, LORD'S DAY 17**

Christ's resurrection and our sanctification

*"God… made us alive together with Christ…
and raised us up with him."*

EPHESIANS 2:5-6

Christ not only justifies us, but He also sanctifies us. Having redeemed us from sin, having overcome death, Christ also gives us the strength to fight the powers of death and the powers of sin. In Ephesians 2, we read, "He made us alive!" We receive this new life from Christ. In Lord's Day 17 it reads: "by His power – that is the same power by which Christ rose from the dead – we too are raised up to a new life."

This is not just a once-only affair, but a continual process. Every day anew by the power from above, we are called to fight the powers of sin, so that more and more we may become what in Christ we already are: new creatures, born again by the powerful work of the Holy Spirit who dwells within us. Through His Spirit, Christ makes our lives holy lives. This too is an essential part of Christ's redemptive work: our sanctification, and not as something we have to achieve ourselves. Christ imparts this to us through the work of the Holy Spirit. As fruit rendering our life to Christ, we no longer want to live in sin, but it will instead become our heartfelt joy to live according to the will of God in all good works. These are the works which God prepared beforehand that we should walk in them.

How are we to understand this? By way of example, good works are like a beautifully laid out garden in which we as believers may walk and work to the glory of God. Likewise, our good works are prepared by God, like a garden. Looking at it from this perspective, being a Christian can never be a burden, as we rejoice in being allowed to walk in this garden of good works. Next, we will also make sure that this garden stays nice and does not get overrun by the weeds of our sins. Then we will be able to rejoice daily and thank God that by the power of Christ's resurrection, we have been raised up to a new life in which we may live for Christ, our risen Saviour.

September 20

**READING: 1 CORINTHIANS 15:35-58,
HEIDELBERG CATECHISM, LORD'S DAY 17**

Christ's resurrection and our glorification

"Death is swallowed up in victory."
1 CORINTHIANS 15:54B

In 1 Corinthians 15:20, the apostle Paul calls Christ the first fruits of those who have fallen asleep. From the Old Testament, we know that these first fruits represented the whole harvest. Likewise, Christ being called the first fruits represents the whole harvest, which gives us as believers the assurance that one day we too will receive a glorified body. Paul writes that this corruptible nature must put on the incorruptable, and this mortal nature must put on immortality. In that hour shall come to pass the saying that is written, "Death is swallowed up in victory."

Death did not belong to creation. It is an enemy to which man wilfully yielded himself. Having eaten from the tree of knowledge of good and evil, Adam knew what would happen. God had forewarned him, "You will surely die!" That is how death entered creation. Death became like an insect with a deadly sting. This was a result of our sins. That is why the apostle Paul writes in 1 Corinthians 15:56, "The sting of death is sin." Therefore, the only way in which to destroy the power of death was to remove our guilt.

That is what Christ did on the cross, especially during those three hours of darkness when God's wrath burned as an all consuming fire that burned the guilt of our sins away. That is how the power of death was broken on Calvary, when Christ took away the deadly sting of sin.

One may say that we still have to die and ask what the actual benefit of all of this now is. Dust we are, and if Christ does not return any earlier, to dust we will return. This is indeed true. Yet, those who believe in Christ as the risen Saviour have the assurance: what is sown in dishonour will be raised in glory. One day our mortal body will be made like Christ's glorified body. In Christ's resurrection, we have received a guarantee of all of this. He is the first fruit of an entire harvest that one day will be gathered in, freed from sorrow, freed from sin.

Thus though mortal, we may live joyfully, for:
"What is weak and mortal here,
Prey to illness and destruction,
Shall with glorious power appear
In the hour of resurrection.
What today is sown disgraced
In great honour will be raised."

September 21

**READING: ACTS 1:1-11,
HEIDELBERG CATECHISM, LORD'S DAY 18**

Christ's ascension into heaven

"...as they were looking on, he was lifted up."

ACTS 1:9

Concerning Good Friday and Easter, generally even people outside the church still have some notion of the meaning of these days. Yet when it comes to Christ's ascension, how are we to explain this event to those who are unfamiliar with the gospel? Within the planetary system, where is heaven located? During the early years of space travel, some astronauts came back saying, "We haven't discovered heaven, nor have we seen God!"

Modern Christians today, in a similar way as the doctrine of the virgin birth, also consider Christ's ascension as a myth from which we must deduce the message. According to them, the Bible contains the imperfect human witness to God's truth written down following the ideas and concepts of that time, which do not always run parallel with the views of the time we live in. Sometimes, people wove stories to place events on a divine level. We should not simply accept these stories as historical truth. It is a bit like receiving a present packed in beautiful wrapping paper. You may like the wrapping paper, but ultimately what counts is the present. Likewise, as with these stories, they are nice to listen to but what matters is the message they want to convey.

As to Christ's ascension, the message is that we should believe that Jesus is our living Lord. To accept this message, one does not necessarily need to believe that He actually ascended into heaven in the way the evangelist Luke speaks about it at the end of his gospel narrative and at the beginning of the Book of Acts.

How are we to respond to this? For a start, one who firmly believes the infallibility of Scripture will also accept the narrative about Christ's ascension as trustworthy without any doubt. Moreover, whereas no one was present at Christ's resurrection, as regards His ascension, we have the firm testimony of eleven eyewitnesses, who saw that He was taken up. Hence, this is not just a fairy tale, but a reliable message. The disciples saw it with their own eyes. True, they did not see Jesus arrive in heaven. A cloud took Him out of their sight. However, two angels came down from heaven, testifying that Jesus had been taken up into heaven, where today He is seated at the right hand of God for our benefit.

September 22

**READING: EPHESIANS 4:1-10,
HEIDELBERG CATECHISM, LORD'S DAY 18**

Unity between heaven and earth

"He who descended is also the one who ascended far above all the heavens that he might fill all things."
EPHESIANS 4:10

In our estimation, there is an enormous distance between heaven and earth. Yet originally, it was not like this. True, also in Paradise, there was distance between heaven and earth. However, there was also an intimate relationship between God and man. God walked with Adam and Eve in the garden in the cool of the day. All this came to an end after Adam and Eve fell into sin. Yet God wanted this communion back. That is why He sent His Son into this world, so that creation could still reach its glorious destiny: man living with God to glorify and praise Him forever.

Our Lord and Saviour came down to earth to reconcile man to God. He did so by fulfilling all the righteousness of God's law for us. By His death on the cross, He also paid for our sins. In this reconciled relationship, man could again live in perfect harmony with God: a restored unity between heaven and earth. Christ's ascension into heaven was the first stage on the road leading to this unity. Today in heaven, He is preparing a place for all whom the Father has given Him. Christ's ascension is a sure pledge for us that one day heaven and earth will indeed be completely one again. In Revelation 21, we read about the New Jerusalem, coming down out of heaven from God, prepared as a bride adorned for her husband.

In Answer 49 of the Heidelberg Catechism, it reads that Christ took our flesh into heaven as a sure pledge that He, our head, will also take us, His members, up to Himself: complete unity! This makes clear that with His ascension, Christ did not put a full stop behind His work on earth – not even temporarily. The Catechism says that He ascended into heaven for our benefit. From heaven, Christ continues to work for us. In his letter to the Ephesians, the apostle Paul writes that Christ went into heaven so that He might fill all things, that is, to obtain the full blessing for His people. If Christ had stayed on earth, He could not have sent His Spirit, nor would He have been able to intercede for us. That is why Christ's ascension was not a loss for the church, but a mere gain instead.

September 23

**READING: JOHN 14:1-4,
HEIDELBERG CATECHISM, LORD'S DAY 18**

Christ ascended into heaven for our benefit (1)

"...I go to prepare a place for you."

JOHN 14:3B

John 14 starts with Jesus saying to His disciples: "Let not your heart be troubled." Why these words? Well, humanly speaking, there was every reason to be troubled, especially because of the words Christ said just before that about Judas' betrayal and Peter's denial. And yet, "Let not your heart be troubled." With these words, Christ ministers to the fears of His disciples rather than to His own needs.

"Let not your heart be troubled: you believe in God, believe also in Me. In my Father's house are many mansions; if it were not so, I would have told you." Do not start doubting! There is indeed a house for you, and this house has many dwellings. There is room for many, for a great multitude that no one can number. Why is Christ speaking about the house of the Father? The answer is given in verse 3: "I go to prepare a place for you."

These words refer to one of the beautiful benefits of Christ's ascension. The house of the Father is a house with many dwellings. A house, where Christ has also prepared a place for us. A place with the sign 'reserved' on it. A reserved place for everyone who clings to Christ in faith as the Saviour of his life. Today Christ is busy making everything ready so that when the time comes, we may enter this dwelling. For as Christ says, when He has finished preparing this place: "I will come again and receive you to myself; that where I am you may be also."

Christ's presence in heaven serves as a guarantee that no power in this world will be able to take that place away from us. It is reserved! Hence, your hearts should not be troubled. In heaven, Christ as the heavenly Bridegroom is preparing a home for His Bride, the church, of which by God's grace we are members. One day we will sit with Christ at the wedding feast of the Lamb. What a great comfort this is, already today! Hence, let not your heart be troubled, no matter how severe it all may become. If we fix our hearts exclusively on Jesus, we will find rest, and an inner peace that only Christ can give us. Peace, since no one can touch those who rest securely in Jesus' care.

September 24

**READING: JOHN 17:20-26,
HEIDELBERG CATECHISM, LORD'S DAY 18**

Christ ascended into heaven for our benefit (2)

"Father, I desire that they also whom Thou gave Me may be with Me where I am…"
JOHN 17:24

The words above this meditation are part of the prayer that Christ prayed with His disciples the day before He died on the cross. It is known as Christ's high-priestly prayer. In this prayer, Christ expresses as His desire, "Father, I desire that they also whom Thou gave Me may be with Me where I am, that they may behold My glory which Thou hast given Me."

This desire is expressed by Him, who today is our Advocate in heaven. In Article 26 of the Belgic confession we confess about this heavenly Advocate: "No one loves us more than He does, no one has more authority than He has and finally, who will be heard more readily than God's own well-beloved Son." Therefore we can be assured, based on what Christ Himself has spoken, that our Saviour will bring us safely home. Our place has already been reserved.

How comforting this gospel is. Whether we grow old, or die in the prime of life, or perhaps even as a child, there is a home for us: an eternal home. Christ's physical presence in heaven functions as a sure guarantee for the fulfilment of this wonderful promise.

Christ is our Advocate in heaven. Answer 49 mentions this as one of the first benefits of Christ's ascension. To do this work as Advocate, Christ needs to be in heaven. For which guilty person would ever benefit from an advocate, a lawyer, who would do no more than just give his client the occasional encouragement at home? To be able to help his client, an advocate must be present in the court of justice to defend his client's cause. Well, that is what the Lord Jesus is doing in heaven: defending our cause before God's judgment seat.

What are the grounds for Christ's defence? The strength of Christ's defence lies in the fact that He is the Lamb that stands though it had been slain, as it is mentioned in Revelation 5, which describes in visionary language the heavenly throne panorama. This Lamb was slain, led to the slaughter, bearing our iniquities. He died, but He also rose and ascended into heaven, where He now pleads our cause as the one who conquered. We can never wish for any stronger defence.

September 25

READING: HEBREWS 4:14-16,
HEIDELBERG CATECHISM, LORD'S DAY 18

Christ ascended into heaven for our benefit (3)

"Let us then with confidence draw near to the throne of God…"

HEBREWS 4:16A

In this meditation, we will look at some of the practical benefits of Christ being in heaven, pleading our cause.

A first practical benefit is that when praying for forgiveness of sins in Christ's Name, we have the assurance that God will not hold on to His anger forever. Whenever we pray for forgiveness, in genuine faith with a true and contrite heart, Christ will bring this prayer before His Father and say: "Father, I have paid for these sins with My precious blood. Therefore, Thou can no longer keep this child of Thine accountable for it." This is the strength of our prayers, whenever we say, "Lord, I pray all this in Jesus' Name."

A second practical benefit is that when going through a rough time, it can happen that we almost feel forsaken by God. However, when down in the dumps in the valley of life, we may direct our prayer to God assured that God will never forsake us. For, Christ will also bring this prayer before His Father. Then at times, our prayer might be no more than just a sigh, "O Lord, help me!" Yet in heaven, it is taken up by Christ who will plead, "Father, stay with this child of Thine, do not forsake him. I was forsaken, so that Thy children may be accepted by Thee and nevermore be forsaken."

A third practical benefit is that when confronted with temptations, we may pray to God, assured that Christ will also bring this prayer before His Father, pleading our cause to keep us safe in Father's care, to help us so that we may withstand the evil one. Christ will pray, "Father, let not the devil have any chance of snatching this child of Thine out of Thy almighty hands."

This is how, in very practical terms, Christ will intercede for us before the Father. He is the best Advocate we could ever wish for, since the price for God's answer to all our prayers has been paid for on the cross at Calvary. Thus, our prayers have a firm foundation. That is why we may always draw near with confidence to the throne of God so that we may receive mercy and find grace to help us in times of need.

September 26

**READING: COLOSSIANS 3:1-4,
HEIDELBERG CATECHISM, LORD'S DAY 18**

Seeking the things that are above

"...seek the things that are above, where Christ is seated at the right hand of God."
COLOSSIANS 3:1B

Answer 49 speaks about the Spirit as a counter pledge by whose power we seek the things that are above. The word 'counter pledge' must be read in connection with the word 'pledge' in this same answer. Think of two wedding rings, exchanged by a husband and wife on their wedding day as a symbol and reminder of their constant faithfulness and abiding love. Looking at the wedding ring, the husband will not forget his wife, and the wife will not forget her husband.

Using this example, one could say that Christ's body is the ring He took from us, to remember us in heaven. In return, Christ also gave us a ring as a counter pledge to make sure that we would never forget Him. This counter pledge is the Holy Spirit, by whose power we seek the things that are above.

With these words, the Catechism does not teach us a world-avoiding attitude. As Christians, we have our place in this world: in the workforce, at school, at home, or wherever. In His high priestly prayer, Christ did not pray, Father take them out of this world, but protect them in this world, keep them from the evil one. It is for this very reason that Christ gave us His Spirit to guide and protect us. The Spirit provides this guidance and protection by working faith in our hearts. He also speaks to us through Scripture, so that our steps do not stray from the straight and narrow way.

Seeking the things that are above does not mean that this earthly life becomes less important, but they highlight that in this earthly life, God's Word should give us direction in all that we do. Then we can rejoice in doing God's will, not by world-avoidance, but by living holy and obedient lives in whatever station God has given us in life. We will then no longer feel ashamed of our faith, but stand up for our Saviour. We will not forget about Him, since Christ will not forget about us either. For what bride would ever forget to think about her bridegroom and his love for her, even when her bridegroom might be far away at times. Well, let us do the same with regards to our love for the heavenly Bridegroom, seeking the things that are above.

September 27

**READING: MATTHEW 26:57-64,
HEIDELBERG CATECHISM, LORD'S DAY 19**

Seated at the right hand of God (1)

"It is as you said. Nevertheless, I say to you, hereafter you will see the Son of Man seated at the right hand of Power, and coming on the clouds of heaven."

MATTHEW 26:64

Upon entering heaven, the glorified Christ took His seat at the right hand of God. This expression 'the right hand of God' points to a position of honour. In Hebrews 2:9, we read that in heaven Christ is crowned with glory and honour. As well as glory and honour, Christ also received authority to reign. This too has everything to do with being seated at God's right hand. This becomes clear when looking a bit closer at how the term 'God's right hand' is used in Scripture. I think of Psalm 118:15-16, where it reads: "The right hand of the LORD does valiantly." It is at this right hand that Christ took His seat upon His ascension into heaven.

Christ had spoken about this already, even before He died on the cross, namely during the night before His death, when He was cross-examined by the Jewish council. All kinds of charges were brought against Him. However, to no avail, since Jesus Himself kept completely silent throughout His whole trial, fulfilling the prophecy of Isaiah 53:7 where it reads: "He was oppressed and He was afflicted, yet He opened not His mouth; He was led as a lamb to the slaughter, and as a sheep before its shearers is silent, so He opened not His mouth." It is only at the end of the trial, when they could not find anything to accuse Him of, that Caiaphas, the high priest, stood up, asking Jesus to declare by oath: "Tell us if You are the Christ, the Son of God." At that moment, Christ finally spoke and declared: "It is as you said. Nevertheless, I say to you, hereafter you will see the Son of Man seated at the right hand of Power, and coming on the clouds of heaven."

"Seated at the right hand of Power" – with these words, Christ called to mind what had already been testified about Him in the Old Testament, namely in Psalm 110 where David prophesied about his great Son, saying: "The LORD said to my Lord, 'Sit at My right hand, till I make Your enemies Your footstool.'"

September 28

**READING: MATTHEW 22:41-46,
HEIDELBERG CATECHISM, LORD'S DAY 19**

Seated at the right hand of God (2)

"The Lord said to my Lord, 'Sit at my right hand,
until I put your enemies under your feet.'"
MATTHEW 22:44

Christ also quoted Psalm 110 in an earlier discussion with the Pharisees, namely, when they asked the question, "What do you think about the Christ? Whose Son is He?", The Pharisees, knowing the Scriptures quite well answered readily: "The Son of David." But then the Lord Jesus continues by asking them a next question, "If you say that the Christ will be the Son of David, how then does David in the Spirit call Him Lord?"

Due to their ideas about the Messiah, the Pharisees could not answer this question. They expected the Messiah to be David's great son who would deliver them from the Roman yoke, restoring the kingdom of David to its former glory. But then Christ points them to Psalm 110, where David acknowledges the Messiah to be superior to himself, calling Him his Lord.

Why did David do this? When reading Psalm 110 a bit more carefully, the answer is not so difficult. In Psalm 110, the Messiah is spoken about not only as king, but also as priest – priest after the order of Melchizedek. Like Melchizedek, the Lord Jesus united in Himself both the office of priest and king.

During the time of the Old Testament, these two offices were separated. However, Christ united them, being Priest and King at the same time. That is why He was superior to David. Christ too would obtain royal dominion, yet through priestly service. In doing so, Christ's rule would rise far above the rule of His father David. After all, Christ became King of the whole earth.

Through His death on the cross, Christ fulfilled His priestly office to obtain royal dominion.

The Sanhedrin did not understand this. It was their wish to get rid of this rabbi of Nazareth. That is why they sentenced Him to death. God, however, raised Christ from the dead, took Him up into glory, and gave Him a place at His right hand. In so doing, Christ received the crown upon His priestly office, which He had fulfilled in complete obedience on earth. Thus, as the Priest-King through suffering, He obtained eternal glory. That is how we may today know Him, crowned with honour and majesty.

September 29

**READING: REVELATIONS 5,
HEIDELBERG CATECHISM, LORD'S DAY 19**

Seated at the right hand of God (3)

"Worthy are you to take the scroll
and to open its seals."

REVELATION 5:12A

In Answer 50 of the Heidelberg Catechism, we read that the Father governs all things through Christ. What does this rule of Christ involve, and how do we benefit from it? Revelation 5 gives us some answers to this question. In a vision, the apostle John sees a scroll in the right hand of Him who was seated on the throne. This scroll contained not only God's plan for this world but also God's plan for the church. However, the scroll was sealed with seven seals, and no one in heaven or on earth or under the earth was able to open it. This meant that God's plan could not be revealed. Even worse, it could not even be executed.

In visionary language, we receive a picture here of the result of the fall into sin. Sin hindered God in unfolding His plan for this world. The scroll was sealed, and who would open it? Who would take this hindrance, that is, who would take sin away? One can well understand that the apostle John starts weeping when no one in this vision is found worthy to open the scroll. If the scroll remains sealed, there would be no hope and no future for the church and the believers. Yes, who would not weep here?

But then all of a sudden, he hears one of the elders saying, "Weep, no more; behold the Lion of the tribe of Judah, the Root of David has conquered, so that he can open the scroll and its seven seals." These words refer to the accomplished work of Christ. In conquering Satan and bearing the full burden of God's wrath, Christ indeed proved to be the Lion from the tribe of Judah, the very root to which David owed his origin (David's Lord!). As the Lion from the tribe of Judah, as the Root of David, Christ obtained the victory and thereby the right to open the scroll. That is how God's plan for this world could continue: only in and through Christ.

September 30

READING: ACTS 7:54-60,
HEIDELBERG CATECHISM, LORD'S DAY 19

Seated and Standing

"But he (Stephen), full of the Holy Spirit gazed into heaven and saw the glory of God, and Jesus standing at the right hand of God."

ACTS 7:55

With the words of the Apostles' Creed, we confess that Christ is seated at the right hand of God. Seated – usually, you do this when your task is finished. Yet Christ's task is not finished. In Acts 7, contrary to what we confess with the words of the Apostles' Creed, we read that Stephen, upon his death, saw the Son of Man standing at the right hand of God, standing to defend the cause of His chosen ones.

Seated and yet standing – these two expressions together show how Christ is active for the sake of His own. Active, even though He sits at God's right hand. From heaven, having all authority, Christ reigns over this world, having everything under His control. Everything – this means no one and nothing is excluded from Christ's reign.

At times, we so easily forget that Christ is King over everyone and everything – King over His people, but also over His enemies. Where it concerns the church, perhaps we do not find it so difficult to speak about Christ's kingship. The point, however, is that Christ's kingship goes further than the realm of the church. We are to acknowledge Christ as King not only within the realm of the church but also in the things of everyday life, in whatever we do and wherever we are. After all, a king requires his subjects to honour him always. Hence, we must proclaim Christ's kingship in every area of life. That is how, as Christians, we are to take our stand amidst this godless society; a stand also in social and political matters. No, the church is not a political party with its own political platform. Nevertheless, as God's children, we must show our fellow citizens that God's commandments are wholesome for life, in matters of marriage, in matters of family life and in so many more areas of life. God's commandments are also given for the well-being of society. That is why Christ as King seeks the best for all men. If only people would acknowledge this. That is why, having been blessed with the riches of the gospel, we should tell others about it, so that they too may acknowledge Christ as King.

October 1

READING: ACTS 2:22-36,
HEIDELBERG CATECHISM, LORD'S DAY 19

The blessings of the glorified Christ (1)

"Being therefore exalted at the right hand of God, and having received from the Father the promise of the Holy Spirit, he has poured out this that you yourselves are seeing and hearing."

ACTS 2:33

Lord's Day 19 speaks not only about Christ being King of this world, but it also speaks about Christ caring for us as Head of the church. Ascending into heaven, Christ did not forget about us. Instead, through His Spirit, He is still with us every day and every night. We so easily forget that Christ is still near to us in this way, always, in whatever we have to face in life. Christ is there to lead us through. What a great comfort this is.

In Answer 51 it reads, "By His Spirit Christ pours out heavenly gifts upon us, His members." Reading this, we should not forget that the Holy Spirit Himself is the first and most important gift which Christ gave to His church. As well as through His Spirit, Christ gives us other gifts as well.

First, there is the gift of God's Word through which the Spirit speaks to us and makes the riches we have in Christ known to us. Daily we may read from the Word of God, the Bible, learning who God is for us – our Father, who cares for us – learning also about Christ – our Redeemer – and the Holy Spirit – the Renewer of our life.

From the Bible we also learn that we are sinful of ourselves and cannot stand before God unless we appeal to the blood, suffering, death, and obedience of Jesus Christ. The Bible also teaches us how to live amidst a godless society. It is through the Bible that the Holy Spirit guides us and also encourages and comforts us. These two always go together: Word and Spirit.

For a moment, try to realise what it would mean if Christ had not entered our life through His Holy Spirit. There would be no anchorage, no comfort, no hope, and no future. We would be altogether lost. Yet, we may now rejoice in this glorious light: the light of God's Word by which the Holy Spirit guides us in the truth to bring us safely home, where Christ our Head already is.

October 2

**READING: EPHESIANS 4:11-16,
HEIDELBERG CATECHISM, LORD'S DAY 19**

The blessings of the glorified Christ (2)

"And he gave the apostles, the prophets, the evangelists, the shepherds and teachers, to equip the saints for the work of ministry, for building up the body of Christ."
EPHESIANS 4:11-12

In this meditation, we will focus on the gift of the offices within the church. They too are a gift of the ascended Christ, who gave office bearers to His church for the building up of His body in equipping the saints for the work of ministry. When the office bearers come to visit us, we may see them as gifts of the ascended Christ to support us, help us stay focused on Christ and live kingdom focused.

With the help of the office bearers and other gifts, Christ equips us for the battle we have to fight to remain standing in today's spiritual war. After all, Satan is out for nothing other than the destruction of the church. This should not cause us to despair, for stronger than Satan, who prowls around like a roaring lion seeking whom he can devour, is the Lion of the tribe of Judah. Christ: King of the whole earth and Head of His church. He will defend us. He will surround us with His almighty power by day and by night, preserving us against the attacks of the evil one.

This does not mean that because of this preservation, life will become less difficult. There may be many trials and hardships, also for upright children of God. Christ's care for us does not mean that we will never be affected by any temporal affliction. The Bible does not say this either. Instead, Scripture also speaks about the oppression and persecution which believers may face. Professing the name of Christ may even involve the loss of life. However, no matter how hard Satan may try, he will never be able to separate us from the love of Christ. Thus in faith, we are on solid ground, always!

In faith! After all, we are not automatically protected, but only through faith and obedience in Christ, acknowledging Him as King. Yes, then Christ will fill our life with His blessings, defending and preserving us against all enemies. That is a promise. Yet this promise comes with an obligation. This is inherent in God's covenant. We can never separate the one from the other.

October 3

**READING: PHILIPPIANS 3:17-4:1,
HEIDELBERG CATECHISM, LORD'S DAY 19**

Christ's return

"But our citizenship is in heaven,
and from it we await a Saviour,
the Lord Jesus Christ."

PHILIPPIANS 3:20

Concerning the authority Christ received by taking a seat at the right hand of God the Father, Lord's Day 19 also speaks about Christ as Judge, who one day will return on the clouds of heaven to judge the living and the dead. This return will be the final part of Christ's redemptive work for us, when He will cast all His and my enemies into everlasting condemnation, but will take all His chosen ones to Himself into heavenly joy and glory.

All His and my enemies! This begs the question: are the enemies of Christ indeed also our enemies? Because we belong to Christ, we cannot maintain a close relationship with those who live as enemies of Christ. How could one ever rejoice in such a relationship? Then at times, it might be challenging to take a stand or even to break off specific relationships, but you do it for Christ who is our Saviour! Would this indeed be asking too much? Surely not, when considering that choosing Christ today means that one day we will be with Him in eternal glory. On the other hand, whoever chooses to be against Christ today will not partake of that glory. It is indeed as serious as that.

In summary, this means that the outcome of Christ's judgment on the last day is closely connected with the way we live our life today. All who live for Christ and Him only do not have to fear this judgment. They may know Him as my Judge and my Redeemer. Yes, then one can indeed look forward to the return of Christ as Judge, even with a most ardent desire. For on that day, Bridegroom and bride will be reunited for the great wedding day – the marriage feast of the Lamb.

It should always be visible in our life that we are on our way to that great day. It should determine our life in every way. We have something to live for, but this should then also be able to be seen. We should never compromise our faith. Instead, we should always stand firm by the power from above. The Lord will surely bless such an attitude, not because of us, but because of His marvellous grace.

October 4

READING: JOHN 3:1-8,
HEIDELBERG CATECHISM, LORD'S DAY 20

The regenerating work of the Holy Spirit (1)

"The wind blows where it wishes, and you hear its sound, but you do not know where it comes from or where it goes. So it is with everyone who is born of the Spirit."
JOHN 3:8

The word that Scripture uses for 'spirit' can also be translated with 'breath' or 'wind'. Job, for example, speaks about the Spirit as the breath of the Almighty (Job 33:4). After His resurrection, the Lord Jesus breathed upon His disciples as a sign of them receiving the power of the Holy Spirit. One of the signs with which the Spirit came on Pentecost was as the sound of a mighty rushing wind. This sign revealed something about how the Spirit works. He works like the wind, as the Lord Jesus spoke about when He met with Nicodemus. In Psalm 104, we read that the Spirit changes the earth. In spring, He gives the soil a new appearance. What was dead comes to life again. Likewise, the Spirit works in people, bringing what was dead to life, causing it to be spring in hearts of stone. The Spirit did so already during the Old Testament. In his defense before the Sanhedrin, Stephen speaks about the fathers of the Old Testament as "stiff-necked and uncircumcised in heart and ears, always resisting the Holy Spirit."

Apart from what we would call this 'normal' work of the Spirit in the Old Testament, we also read about people who experienced the Holy Spirit working powerfully in a more specific way. The Holy Spirit enabled ordinary men like the judges Othniel, Gideon, and Samson to do things which they would never have been able to do of themselves. The Spirit gave the farmers' sons Saul and David everything they needed to be able to reign as kings. The Spirit also inspired prophets so that they could pass on God's Word to Israel infallibly.

Thus, the Holy Spirit has dwelt and worked among God's people right from the beginning of this world. In Lord's Day 21, it reads that Christ has gathered a church chosen to everlasting life from the beginning of the world by His Spirit and Word. Even in the Old Dispensation, no one could come to faith without the Spirit working this faith in their heart. Also then, it was the Spirit who gave the people a new heart, making that which was dead alive.

October 5

**READING: LUKE 4:16-30,
HEIDELBERG CATECHISM, LORD'S DAY 20**

The regenerating work of the Holy Spirit (2)

"Today, this Scripture has been fulfilled in your hearing."

LUKE 4:21B

Explaining the prophecy of Isaiah 61 in the synagogue of Nazareth, the Lord Jesus pointed to Himself as the One upon whom the Spirit of the LORD rested. Never before had the Spirit worked more mightily in a person than He did in Jesus as the Messiah, and yet it was entirely in line with the work the Spirit had done during the time of the Old Testament. In the same way as the Spirit gave Samson, David, and all of the prophets power to fulfil their task in the service of the LORD, likewise He filled the Lord Jesus with power, enabling Him to accomplish His messianic task.

Having accomplished His task here on earth, Christ ascended into heaven from where He poured out His Spirit upon us, so that we too, enabled by the Spirit, can do our task in the Lord's service. But so did God's people during the time of the Old Testament. So what changed after Pentecost? Was it only a matter of the Spirit's work becoming more intense? If this were all, there would only be but a slight difference between the Old and New Dispensation. Yet there is also a new element with Pentecost. God moved further in the history of redemption.

Being filled with the Spirit after the time of Pentecost means being united with Christ through the Spirit. In Lord's Day 20 it reads that the Spirit is given to me "to make me by true faith share in Christ and all His benefits." The Spirit imparts to us what we have in Christ, working faith in our hearts by which we may embrace the riches we have in Christ. If the Spirit were not there, all the riches which Christ obtained for us would remain inaccessible to us.

Think of the preaching of the gospel. By nature, we do not like the gospel. Spiritually we would rather starve to death than to feed ourselves with the Word of God. It is mere foolishness to our human mind to believe that the one who died on the cross laid the foundation for a perfect world. Without the Holy Spirit's regenerating work, none of us would ever accept this message. Mission, evangelism, education – in itself, these means are powerless to bring someone to the confession that Jesus is Lord. Only the Holy Spirit, by His divine power, can bring people to faith in Christ.

October 6

READING: JOHN 7:37-39,
HEIDELBERG CATECHISM, LORD'S DAY 20

The fullness of Christ

"Whoever believes in me, as the Scripture has said,
'Out of his heart will flow rivers of living water.'"
JOHN 7:38

Only the Holy Spirit, by His divine power, can bring people to faith in Christ. This is how the Spirit already worked during the time of the Old Testament. So, what changed at Pentecost? Salvation in Christ was also granted to God's children living at the time of the Old Testament. Yet, this was done in anticipation of what was still to come. This shows that we must not overstate the difference between the Old and New Dispensation. However, with Pentecost there is progress in God's redemptive work. From then on, the Spirit draws on the fullness which is in Christ. Because of this, all former limitations fall away. The sphere of work of the Holy Spirit broadens.

Since Pentecost, we are all prophets, priests, and kings. Also, salvation is no longer for the Jews only but for the Gentiles as well. From then on, when it comes to receiving salvation in Christ, there is no longer any difference between Jew and Greek, male and female, between black and white or poor and rich. All of this is because of the fullness received in Christ. Since Pentecost, we have entered the last stage of world history. With the outpouring of the Holy Spirit, God brought His final gift into this world, which no longer gives people any excuse not to believe.

If Pentecost had not come, people would still be rejecting the Christ in ignorance, as many of the Jews did when they cried out on Good Friday: "Crucify Him." Yet on the day of Pentecost, many of them came to repentance, cut to the heart by Peter's Pentecostal sermon. Yet, whoever still refuses to accept Christ as his Saviour after Pentecost no longer has any excuses. Whoever rejects Christ after Pentecost also rejects the Spirit who preaches Christ as the only Saviour, and as a result, that person cannot be saved.

That is why the apostle Paul says in Ephesians 4 to make sure, by your way of life, that you never grieve the Holy Spirit by whom you were sealed for the day of redemption. In the letter to the Hebrews we read to be diligent in attending the worship services, since by listening to the preaching we may drink from the fountain of salvation.

October 7

**READING: ACTS 2:37-41,
HEIDELBERG CATECHISM, LORD'S DAY 20**

The Holy Spirit has also been given to me (1)

"For the promise is for you and for your children and for all who are far off, everyone whom the Lord our God calls to himself."

ACTS 2:39

The Holy Spirit has also been given to me. How do I know this so certainly? When saying this, does this not mean that I am speaking somewhat boastfully? No, we are not, since the point here is not what I think of myself and whether I am good enough to receive the Holy Spirit, but what God says to me in His Word. In his Pentecostal sermon, Peter says: "For the promise is for you and for your children and for all who are far off, everyone whom the Lord our God calls to himself." The truth of this promise has been sealed to us in Holy Baptism.

According to Lord's Day 20, the Holy Spirit has been given to us to comfort us, reassuring us that we never have to doubt what we confess in Lord's Day 1, that we are Christ's in life and in death. How does the Holy Spirit do this? Firstly, by the weekly preaching of the gospel. Wherever the gospel is preached in all its truth, the Spirit is active as well. That is why, at times, the church is called 'the workshop of the Holy Spirit.' Through the preaching, offering comfort and extending warnings, the Spirit is active in strengthening our faith, so that daily we may remain standing in the spiritual battle we have to fight. Therefore, we are risking our life, our spiritual life, by neglecting the weekly church services. Instead, we should come faithfully each Sunday to receive that much-needed comfort and strengthening of faith that the Spirit wants to give us through the preaching.

Finally, Lord's Day 20 also says that the Spirit will remain with me forever. Of course, this promise is not given to us as an insurance policy which covers one against any losses. On the contrary, this promise must also be accepted in faith. God will powerfully preserve us in the grace once conferred upon us, but He does so by faith alone. When we cling to God in true faith, He will not permit His elect to be lost. Then, during the times when we slide away, God will never withdraw His Holy Spirit from His chosen ones completely.

October 8

**READING: PSALM 51:1-12,
HEIDELBERG CATECHISM, LORD'S DAY 20**

The Holy Spirit has also been given to me (2)

"...take not your Holy Spirit from me. Restore to me the joy of your salvation ..."
PSALM 51:11B-12A

God preserves His own, but this does not mean that upright children of God cannot fall into serious sin. The Canons of Dort refer to the lamentable fall of David, Peter, and other saints. It may even happen that children of God sin so severely that for a time they lose the sense of God's favour, and yet through the working of His Spirit, God prevents them from plunging themselves into eternal ruin.

Of course, this is not a license to sin as if we could never do ourselves any harm. Even upright children of God can commit grave sins. Yet, as long as they do not continue living in sin, but instead repent with a contrite heart – worked by the Holy Spirit – there is forgiveness of sins, no matter how much we mess up our lives at times. That is the comfort the Spirit gives, thus preserving us for the inheritance stored up for us in heaven.

This is the comfort we receive when we listen to the gospel preached to us every Sunday. However, this gospel always comes with the command to repent and believe. After all, God's promises never come true in life automatically. Scripture is full of warnings that we must love the Lord and live accordingly, living our faith by walking with God in every step we take and in every decision we make. This applies not only to the big decisions, but also to the small decisions of everyday life. This is how, in a very practical way, God will remain with us forever through His Spirit. He will remain with us also in the heat of the battle.

It is so that life may not always be easy. God may even lead us through deep valleys. Yet, even in these valleys we are still comforted, since through His Spirit, God is with us, also promising that His Spirit will remain with us forever. We do not need anything more. When we cling to this promise – even though the road we travel may be rough, full of potholes and a bumpy surface – with the nearness of the Spirit, God promises us a safe arrival. In the end, this is the only thing that truly counts: a safe arrival in the New Jerusalem.

October 9

**READING: JOHN 10:1-5,
HEIDELBERG CATECHISM, LORD'S DAY 21A**

I believe one holy catholic Christian church

"When he has brought out all his own, he goes before them, and the sheep follow him, for they know his voice."

JOHN 10:4

What do you believe concerning the holy catholic church of Christ? What do you believe? Believe – after all, the Catechism is not interested in what I think about the church or how I may feel about the church. Instead, what we confess is based on what the Bible teaches us about the church. This makes all the difference.

What we confess about the church has everything to do with our faith in Jesus Christ as our Saviour. At times, this is so quickly forgotten. For example, when people express all kinds of criticism concerning the church, saying that a thing is wrong or something else should be done differently. At such a moment, do we still realise that the church is not an organisation run by men? Instead, the church is the Lord's. It is the Son of God who gathers for Himself a church chosen to everlasting life.

The church is the Lord's, and it is only by God's grace that we may belong. Indeed, it is by grace alone that we may belong to the congregation chosen to everlasting life which Christ gathers, defends, and preserves for Himself. When speaking about the church, we should always keep this in mind. The church is God's work and not man's work. Hopefully, when remembering this, it will make us more careful when we speak about the church.

It is Jesus Christ our Saviour, who, as the great Shepherd of the sheep, gathers His church. It is He, who knows the sheep and calls each sheep individually by name. Indeed, as intimate as that! In John 10, we read that He goes before them and the sheep follow Him, for they know the voice of the Shepherd. In this figure of speech, we meet the two aspects of Christ's church gathering work. It is Christ who gathers. Yet we must come, obeying His voice and follow Him, our eyes always directed to Him, and our ears always listening to Him.

October 10

READING: JOHN 10:7-18,
HEIDELBERG CATECHISM, LORD'S DAY 21A

Christ gathers His church (1)

"I lay down my life for the sheep."
JOHN 10:15B

The church is not a voluntary institution of man but the work of God and, therefore, not an organisation we have to fight for, for it to survive. The Lord uses us as instruments in His service. Yet, the church does not depend on this. Thankfully not, since we are only weak and often unfaithful instruments. Yet despite all our unfaithfulness, God remained faithful to the promise made in the beginning, that Satan would not succeed in trying to crush the seed of the woman. Instead, this seed became the bride of Christ, for whose life He died. As the great Shepherd of the flock, Christ laid down His life for the sheep and today calls these sheep through His Word – the word of the gospel to which we may listen every Sunday. This is how Christ gathers His flock – the church chosen to everlasting life.

Chosen – this word refers to the origin of the holy catholic church. When we go back to before the fall into sin, the whole world was destined for eternal life. This was the purpose for which God had created man, that he might always glorify and praise God as the Creator. Yet we all know what happened. The first man, Adam, being the head of all mankind, turned his back upon God, choosing death instead of life.

However, this did not bring to naught God's plan made even before creation. In His sovereign pleasure, God wanted to carry on with a definite number of people already chosen by Him beforehand. That is why, after the fall into sin, God called out to Adam: "Where are you?" One could describe God's call as the beginning of Christ's church gathering work – a call full of sovereign love for us wretched sinners.

This makes it clear that there is indeed nothing we can boast of. We can only glory in God's love for us. In John 10, we read that Christ laid down His life for the sheep of the flock. By dying for us, He obtained the right to gather the church from the Father. A church, chosen to everlasting life, of which Adam and Eve were already the first members.

October 11

**READING: JOHN 10:7-18,
HEIDELBERG CATECHISM, LORD'S DAY 21A**

Christ gathers His church (2)

"And I have other sheep that are not of this fold.
I must bring them also, and they will listen to my voice.
So there will be one flock, one shepherd."

JOHN 10:16

Adam and Eve were the first members of the church chosen for everlasting life. From then on, Christ continued to gather His church throughout the entire time of the Old Testament. He did so at the time of Enosh when men began to call upon the name of the LORD. He saved His elect in the ark, when the whole human race was blotted out from the face of the earth at the time of the Flood. He was the One who called Abram from Ur of the Chaldeans, gathering His people – the church in those days – in the tents of the patriarchs. Later on, during the Old Testament history, the Son of God gathered the Israelites firstly around the tabernacle and then around the temple in Jerusalem.

Yet when the time had fully come, and the Word became flesh, a new period started. The bed through which Christ's church gathering work ran, widened. No, not straight away, since the Lord Jesus had come to redeem the lost sheep of the house of Israel first. Yet when He died, the dividing wall between Jews and Gentiles came down, which meant that now people are called from every tribe, tongue, and nation. Black and white, red and yellow – they are called and regarded as having been born on Zion's holy mount. The Moor with the Philistine and the Tyrian in many tongues confess one God, one faith (Psalm 87)!

After Pentecost, the gospel went out, first in Jerusalem and Judea, and from there to Samaria and the end of the earth, calling sinners to salvation in Jesus Christ. Through the powerful work of Christ's Spirit, they indeed came. Yes, it is only by the powerful work of the Spirit that this happened. It is the Holy Spirit who opens the closed and softens the hardened hearts, to prepare a people for Christ heartily willing and ready to live for Him.

This is how Christ gathers a church to Himself, chosen to everlasting life. He has done so from the beginning of the world, and He will do so until the last of God's elect has entered the sheepfold. He will continue to do so by His Spirit and Word.

October 12

**READING: REVELATION 12:13-17,
HEIDELBERG CATECHISM, LORD'S DAY 21A**

Christ defends and preserves His church

"...the gates of hell shall not prevail against it."
MATTHEW 16:18B

Christ not only gathers His church, but He also defends and preserves her. It was Christ's protecting hand that preserved and protected the church through the Flood and throughout the exile. Although at times only a remnant was left, He preserved His church. That is also how Christ is active today in preserving and protecting His church. Upon His ascension, Christ took a seat at the throne of God, having received all authority in heaven and on earth from the Father. With this authority, He rules the world for the sake of the church.

That is how we must look at world events. It all takes us closer to the grand finale, when Christ will bring the final harvest home. That is the comfort the church has. Christ reigns in heaven, from where He defends and preserves us in the redemption He obtained for us. We never have to doubt this.

This does not mean that, as a church, we will always lead a peaceful and quiet life. We read in Scripture that the powers of death shall not prevail against the church. They shall not succeed, but they will try! In Revelation 12, we read about the dragon raging war against those who keep God's commandments and bear the testimony of Jesus. Satan knows that since Calvary, he is on the losing end and therefore, his attacks will be all the fiercer. Satan will do his utmost to rob Christ of those the Father has given Him.

That is why the history of the church is characterised by continual war. It is a history written in blood in many ways. With respect to the New Testament church, this already started straightaway after Pentecost, when the Sanhedrin arrested Peter and John. Some time later, Stephen was stoned. James was also killed, and Peter was crucified. Fierce persecution, as it also happens today in countries where those who are in authority oppose Christ's church gathering work, perhaps even more than we are at times aware of. When the close of the age draws near, this will only become worse. In Revelation 17:6, we read about Babylon and the apostate Christianity of the last days being drunk with the blood of the saints and the blood of the martyrs of Jesus. The powers of death will gather against the church. Yet they shall not prevail, since the victory is Christ's.

October 13

READING: I PETER 1:13-2:6,
HEIDELBERG CATECHISM, LORD'S DAY 21B

Christ unites us together as a communion of saints

"…like living stones are being built up as a spiritual house…"

1 PETER 2:5

When speaking about the communion of saints, the Heidelberg Catechism first points to the vertical relationship by which together we have communion with Christ and share in all His treasures and gifts. That is what makes us one. It is only through the work of Christ that true unity became possible again. We do not come together as believers because we share the same feelings or the same experiences in faith, but we form a communion because we share in Christ. He gave Himself for us with an unconditional, self-denying total love. We were sinners who had turned their backs on God, and yet Christ died for us. Next, He also rose for us so that He could give us what He had obtained for us by His death: a new life in which sin no longer has a place, and where it becomes our joy to live according to the will of God in all good works.

If this joy is not found within us, it can quickly negatively affect our outlook on the relationships we have with one another on a horizontal level. If the joy of belonging to Christ hardly ever surfaces in our talks with others, it can be no wonder if there is a lack of fellowship within the communion of saints. In Answer 55, it reads that all believers have communion with Christ. This points to our common bond with Christ in which we are to rejoice together. Christ does not pour out His treasures and gifts on random individuals. He pours them out on His body, of which the members are united with one another.

Within that body, each member has his place in order to serve the other members. After all, that is how a body functions. To use another image, the believers all together make up a building of which Christ is the sure foundation. We are living stones built into a spiritual house. A heap of bricks is not yet a house, but these bricks cemented together become a house. Likewise, the believers are cemented together in a spiritual house, whereby every stone carries his weight through power received from above.

October 14

**READING: 1 CORINTHIANS 12:12-27,
HEIDELBERG CATECHISM, LORD'S DAY 21B**

Our task within the communion of saints

"Now you are the body of Christ and individually members of it."
1 CORINTHIANS 12:27

In 1 Corinthians 12, the apostle Paul uses a very fitting image to show how the body of Christ ought to function. In the same way as in the human body, where each organ has its specific function to complement the whole body, so it is with the members of the congregation of Christ. God in His wisdom has provided each member with their own specific task. The apostle puts a strong emphasis on God's plan, on God's choice and appointment.

In Corinth, some members considered that they alone were capable, so they wanted to do everything. However, all the different parts of a body need one another. The eye needs the hand. No one should boast, therefore, of his own gift. Moreover, whatever parts seem to be weaker, for example the eyes, these are nevertheless indispensable. The same applies to what we may call less honourable parts. Each member has received their own gifts and special function.

Within the church, there is often a great variety of gifts. This should never harm the unity of a healthy body. Instead, it is for the good of the entire body, as long as all members are willing to work together. Individualism ruins the church. Instead of individualism, our joint love for Christ should cause us to look after one another in love. After all, we need one another as members of one body.

We are to look after one another in love. In the concluding verse of chapter 12, the apostle Paul also points to the way of love. That is how that beautiful chapter 13 receives its place in the context of Paul speaking about the congregation of Christ functioning as a body. For, even the most excellent gifts are no more than hollow phrases when they are not governed by love for the other members. Whoever follows the way of love will never look down upon one of the other members. Love will never cause us to boast of ourselves. Instead, true love will give us a real desire to use our gifts readily and cheerfully for the benefit and well-being of the other members.

October 15

**READING: 2 CORINTHIANS 5:14-21,
HEIDELBERG CATECHISM, LORD'S DAY 21C**

The forgiveness of sins

"We implore you on behalf of Christ, be reconciled to God."

2 CORINTHIANS 5:20B

At first glance, it may seem that there is little connection between the two previous questions and answers from Lord's Day 21 and question and answer 56. Yet there surely is a connection, since Christ distributes the forgiveness of sins in the church. It is in the church where the gospel of our acquittal is proclaimed to us. God has entrusted the ministry of reconciliation to the church. In the church, the kingdom of heaven is open to believers and is closed to unbelievers. Therefore, it is surely not out of place whenever the church is spoken about, to also mention the forgiveness of sins. The church could be called the house of God's grace, since in the church we may listen to the gospel that declares sinners free of guilt in the blood of Jesus Christ, who was made sin for our sake so that God would look upon us in mercy. These are the glad tidings, also of which Answer 56 speaks: "I believe that God, because of Christ's satisfaction, will no more remember my sins." This is the gospel preached to us every Sunday – the gospel of our acquittal. When we accept this gospel by true faith, we may have full assurance that all our sins have been forgiven for Christ's sake.

I believe one holy catholic Christian church, the communion of saints and the forgiveness of sins. With these words, we confess that Christ gathers, defends, and preserves for Himself a congregation chosen to everlasting life – a congregation which He binds together in the unity of true faith. This congregation, though called a communion of saints, can never boast of itself. We can only glory in Christ, who has purified, renewed, and changed us by His Holy Spirit and who will grant us forgiveness of sins in His blood.

Here on earth, this will never become perfect. Even the church consists of sinful people. Yet these sinful people seek their strength in Christ, and that is what binds them together in strong unity. For this reason, we should never speak negatively about this unity. Instead, let us rejoice in it and work together more and more as a true communion of saints for the promotion of God's kingdom and the well-being of one another.

October 16

**READING: 2 CORINTHIANS 4:7-18,
HEIDELBERG CATECHISM, LORD'S DAY 22**

Christ's victory over death (1)

"So we do not lose heart…"
2 CORINTHIANS 4:16A

Lord's Day 22 first focuses on what happens to believers when they die, when here on earth we breathe our last. When speaking about death, the first thing that comes to mind is often the vulnerability and frailty of our present life. Vulnerable – for example, when all of a sudden we are confronted with a fatal accident. Frail – not only as we get older, but also when a serious illness starts ruining the human body. Human life is weak and perishable. Hence, many people avoid speaking about death, especially those who have no hope in the face of it.

Yet when opening Scripture, we cannot avoid this subject. It is there right at the beginning, in Genesis 3, where we read that death entered this world due to man's own fault, when he walked away from God and ate from the forbidden tree in the Garden of Eden. Before the fall into sin, there was no death. Initially, everything was perfect. Yet, by eating from the tree of knowledge of good and evil, man turned his back upon God. As a result, sin entered this world and also death. Man became like grass. It flourishes and is renewed in the morning, yet in the evening, it fades and withers.

The apostle Paul writes in 2 Corinthians 4 that our outer nature wastes away with all the affliction and pain often connected with it. And then finally, death, which tears body and soul apart. It tears apart what belongs together. After all, when God created man, He created him in body and soul, forming a strong unity! This unity would have lasted, if sin had not entered this world. But now, because of sin, we daily experience the wasting away of our outer nature in sickness, in diminishing strength, in pain, and then finally in death. That is life – the life of man after the fall into sin: frail, vulnerable, always living in the shadow of death.

In Scripture, however, we also read about redemption in and through Christ. He paid for our sins and conquered death. Therefore, for those who are in Christ, there is no need to lose heart, not even when death comes near. This is because, since Calvary, death no longer has the last say, but Jesus Christ instead. He is indeed our perfect redeemer.

October 17

**READING: 2 CORINTHIANS 4:16-5:10,
HEIDELBERG CATECHISM, LORD'S DAY 22**

Christ's victory over death (2)

"So we do not lose heart…"

2 CORINTHIANS 4:16A

In 2 Corinthians 4, the apostle Paul says that the outer nature wastes away, while the inner nature is renewed every day. That is why as children of God we do not need to lose heart, not even in the face of death. From a human standpoint, this may sound very strange. Yet to the one who believes, this is a very comforting message. It shows the riches of those who die in the Lord, since for them death is gain! One who does not believe will never understand this, yet for the believer it is a glorious reality.

In 2 Corinthians 5:6, Paul writes: "We know that while we are at home in the body, we are away from the Lord." In verse 8, he writes that we would rather be away from the body and at home with the Lord. Paul longs to be with Christ. This desire can indeed become so strong in a believer that he does not mind dying. After all, when we die in the Lord, we know at the very moment we close our eyes here on earth that we will open them in heaven. For this reason, Paul writes that we should not lose heart, not even when our outer nature wastes away.

What is this wasting away of the outer nature? It points to the decaying of life, for example, when a severe illness ruins our body or when people are aging. However, that is only on the outside – the things we can see with the physical eye. He, who does not believe, does not see anything more. However, the eye of faith penetrates further. It sees not only a process of deterioration, but also a process of renewal. After all, in the life of a believer, there is a twofold process. On the one hand, there can indeed be a process whereby one goes physically downhill. That is what Paul calls the wasting away of the outer nature. However, this is only one side of the coin. Concerning the upright child of God, there is also the inner nature – our spiritual life – which is renewed every day. That is why, for those who believe in Christ, there is never any reason to lose heart. Never – not even when the hour of death is near.

October 18

**READING: 2 CORINTHIANS 4:16-18,
HEIDELBERG CATECHISM, LORD'S DAY 22**

Christ's victory over death (3)

"So we do not lose heart…"
2 CORINTHIANS 4:16A

When looking at the things that are seen, we should never forget: a manger once stood in this world. Later on, a cross was erected on which the man, who was once the child that lay in this manger, was crucified and died. Briefly, we must never forget the facts of Christmas and Good Friday. Next, Easter came, which means the One who was crucified and died now lives forever. Jesus Christ conquered death. Therefore, we should not lose heart, not even when death is near. In faith, we have the firm assurance that when we die our suffering turns into glory. In that hour, our soul will be taken up to Christ, our Head, immediately.

This clearly shows that our life with Christ will never come to an end, not even when we die. In that hour, Christ as the Prince of life will bring the renewal of our life, which he the Holy Spirit already started during our life on this side of the grave. In the hour of our death, Christ will bring this renewal to initial completion. Initial completion – since in heaven the souls of those who died in the Lord wait for the reunion with their bodies. Nevertheless, this initial completion means a great gain, since death puts an end to sin. At present, every day again, we see our life stained with sin. Yet death puts an end to this. In that hour, the sinful body is destroyed, returning to dust.

This shows that there is a close connection between the life we live today and the life hereafter. When we die, there is no gap in our life with the Lord. It just continues in glory. What started on earth by the renewing power of the Holy Spirit, continues when we die. Even more decisively, in that hour there will be progress. For a believer to die is gain, since upon our death the Holy Spirit will bring His work in our lives to greater glory.

To die is gain – yet, only for those who have already let the Spirit of Christ work in their hearts today. Therefore, let us make sure that we never grieve the Holy Spirit of God, by whom we were sealed for the day of redemption. Instead, let us always rejoice in His sanctifying work, so that when the hour comes, we have nothing to fear.

October 19

**READING: JOHN 11:17-25,
HEIDELBERG CATECHISM, LORD'S DAY 22**

Christ's victory over death (4)

"Jesus said to her,"I am the resurrection and the life. Whoever believes in me, though he die, yet shall he live.""

JOHN 11:25

In the second part of Answer 57 of the Heidelberg Catechism we read: "But also this my flesh, raised by the power of Christ, shall be reunited with my soul and made like Christ's glorious body." This will happen through the power of Christ. Jesus Christ – He is the resurrection and the life. Death, therefore, has no authority over Him. Our Saviour demonstrated this very clearly when He arose from the dead on Easter morning. In Answer 57, we now read that Christ will also make our mortal bodies like His glorious body by this same power.

Mortal bodies, indeed! Dust you are, and to dust you shall return. This was the curse declared upon man. Christ, however, has redeemed us from this curse. True, one day – if Christ does not return earlier – our body will return to dust. Yet this is not the last thing that will happen to our body. For, when the trumpet sounds, in a moment – in the twinkling of an eye – this perishable nature will put on the imperishable, and this mortal nature will put on immortality. There will no longer be an initial completion of Christ's redeeming work, but both body and soul will be reunited in that hour and we will share in the full fruit of Christ's redeeming work.

Already today, we may acknowledge that we are on our way to this glorious future. This indeed gives our present life a wonderful perspective. We should not forget that the beginning of this new life starts today when, by the power from above, we live our life for the Lord. In so doing, we may experience the beginning of eternal joy about which Answer 58 speaks.

This joy is the same as what the apostle Paul writes about in 2 Corinthians 4, with the inner nature being renewed every day. Already today, Christ will sanctify us more and more through His Spirit until we are finally presented without blemish among the assembly of God's elect in life eternal. Therefore, let us never grieve the Holy Spirit of God. Remember, the Spirit who dwells in us is the Spirit of Him who raised Jesus from the dead, and who will also make your mortal body like Christ's glorious body.

October 20

**READING: JOHN 11:17-25,
HEIDELBERG CATECHISM, LORD'S DAY 22**

Christ's victory over death (5)

"Jesus said to her, "I am the resurrection and the life.
Whoever believes in me, though he die, yet shall he live.""
JOHN 11:25

In Answer 58, it reads that we may be assured of a glorious future, "Since I now already feel in my heart the beginning of eternal joy." Of course, this does not mean that this is only a matter of feelings. Instead, this is the powerful work of the Holy Spirit who wants to renew us, sanctifying us so that more and more we hate and flee from sin and, with love and delight, live according to the will of God in all good works. Therefore, this joy is not a matter of feelings, but of faith! Answer 58 also makes it quite clear that eternal life starts on this side of the grave. From this it also follows that eternal death equally starts on this side of the grave.

Spiritually, death means a broken relationship between God and man. This is why God said to Adam that he would surely die if he would eat from the tree of knowledge of good and evil. Death is the wages of sin. The opposite of death is life. Spiritual life conquers sin. It points to the renewed relationship between God and man. After all, God did not want the death of the sinner. That is why, in sovereign love, God sent His Son into this world so that whoever believes in Him should not perish but have life eternal – life in a renewed relationship with God. This is the life spoken about in Answer 58. It is our life with God through Christ that we already enjoy today. Through Christ's redeeming work, our life is no longer subjected to futility. Instead, it has been set free from its bondage to decay.

When the shadows of suffering fall deeply over our life, we may not always feel the joy of which Answer 58 speaks. Yet, even in the valley of life, God is with us to comfort us, to give us strength for today and hope for tomorrow. However, one day God will wipe every tear from our eyes. Answer 58 speaks about a blessedness so perfect that no eye has ever seen, nor ear heard, nor the heart of man conceived. It is the perfect glory to which the Holy Spirit will bring us – a glory in which God shall be all in all.

October 21

READING: LUKE 18:9-14,
HEIDELBERG CATECHISM, LORD'S DAY 23

By grace alone (1)

"God be merciful to me, a sinner!"

LUKE 18:13B

How are you righteous before God, you as a Christian? How? Am I righteous because I faithfully go to church on Sunday, because I am generous with my money, joyfully helping my neighbour when needed? Is it because I never think of myself first but like to be there for others? Are these the things which make me righteous before God?

I am afraid that although we know better, often we still measure our lives with the Lord in this light, and not only our own life, but also the lives of others. Is it not wonderful when we hear about a particular member of the congregation: "That brother is really active in the service of the Lord, a faithful member, always busy with God's Word!" Would it not be great if this were said about us? Righteous – true, we all have our shortcomings; no one is perfect. But apart from that…

Now listen to the Catechism. What testimony do we read there regarding a righteous person? Answer 60a: "My conscience accuses me that I have grievously sinned against all God's commandments." Note well, all God's commandments grievously, never having kept any of them. Yes, even worse, always inclined to all evil. So, not just occasionally a mistake here and there. As we sometimes so quickly say when someone comments on a wrong we did: "No one is perfect." No, according to the Catechism it is much worse. It gives a testimony difficult for all of us to swallow; a total deathblow for our spiritual ego.

Is there then no good in our lives whatsoever? What about our desire to serve God? Look at our church life for example: Bible Study Societies, schools where our children receive education according to God's Word. Again, it is not all perfect, but does this not count at all? Is there not any merit in all of this?

Comments like these bring us very close to the Pharisee in the parable. He was fasting twice a week and a tenth of all his income was going to the church! Did this not count? And yet, God was not pleased with this man. It was the tax collector who cried out, "Lord, be merciful to me a sinner," who went home justified. This was not because he was without sin, but he had understood that we need God's grace to be saved. We need Christ!

October 22

**READING: LUKE 18:9-14,
HEIDELBERG CATECHISM, LORD'S DAY 23**

By grace alone (2)
"God be merciful to me, a sinner!"
LUKE 18:13B

Luther, struggling as a monk in a monastery, thought that he was doing everything to please God. At the same time, he realised it would never be enough. It always fell short of what God required. Luther thought God's righteousness meant: we receive according to what we perform, and since we perform poorly, we deserve nothing other than God's wrath. The whole doctrine of being saved by works scared Luther to death until he understood that the righteousness God requires of us is given to us in Christ.

The Old Testament had already made this clear. In Genesis 15:6, we read that Abram believed the LORD, and He counted it to him as righteousness. In Habakkuk 2:4, we read that the righteous shall live by faith. That is why the apostle Paul writes in Romans 5 that we have been justified by faith. Therefore, believing in God does not mean that I can feel good about myself. Instead, it means I should feel bad about myself. The stronger I grow in faith, the smaller I should think of myself. Therefore, the testimony of the Catechism is undoubtedly not too dark. When looking into the mirror of God's Word every day again, I have to conclude: what a mess my life is in! This went wrong; there, I lacked love. Nothing in my life can stand up to the perfect law of God. It is indeed a deadly testimony.

The apostle Paul writes in Romans 7:23 that the law of sin also dwells in the hearts of the believers. It is in us, and it is only healthy to admit this. What about the bad thoughts that all of a sudden cross our minds? Where do they come from? From within – my sinful inclinations – through our eyes, which are so easily attracted to what is wrong; through our ears, which so often listen to what we should not listen to; from our tongue – also such an evil weapon when we think of the things we should not have spoken. Our hands and our feet – they too are often moved to do the wrong things. Therefore, when looking into the mirror of God's law as we bow our knees at night, we can only cry out with that tax collector: "Lord be merciful to me, a sinner."

October 23

**READING: EPHESIANS 2:1-10,
HEIDELBERG CATECHISM, LORD'S DAY 23**

By grace alone (3)

"For by grace you have been saved through faith."

EPHESIANS 2:8A

We are saved by grace alone. However, do we still marvel at it? Many know the familiar expression, "Amazing Grace!" Yet, are we still amazed? To be truly amazed, first we must learn to see see how bad things are with us. How much at times do we still mess up our lives, every day again? When seeing this, we will learn to marvel that God still wants to show mercy to us. After all, God was not bound to do so. God would have been fully within his rights if He had turned His back upon us, wretched sinners. And yet, in His love, He sent his Son, who died for us while we were yet enemies. In other words, we did not ask for a Saviour, but God in His sovereign love took the initiative, since He does not want the death of the sinner, but instead that we turn to Him and live.

God declared us not guilty, not because we believed. Faith did not precede our acquittal. From our side, there was nothing when God bestowed His love upon us. That is why it reads in Answer 61, "Not that I am acceptable to God on account of the worthiness of my faith." Thankfully not, for our faith is often very weak. It is not our faith that counts, but "only the satisfaction, righteousness, and holiness of Christ is my righteousness before God."

The word satisfaction refers to Christ's atonement for our sins. We were worthy of God's wrath, yet Christ stilled God's wrath by His suffering and death on the cross. Next, the Catechism mentions Christ's righteousness. Christ not only died for our sins, but his whole life was a substitute for our lives. In our place, He obeyed God's laws perfectly. This perfect obedience has been credited to our account. This should fill us with thankfulness, and even this is God's work. It is the Holy Spirit who works these fruits of gratitude in us. Nothing is ours. It is all by grace alone. Finally, even our sinful inclinations are covered by Christ's holiness.

In the concluding part of Answer 60, we read that all this has been imputed to us as if I had never had nor committed any sin – as if I myself had accomplished all the obedience which Christ has rendered for me. Amazing grace, indeed!

October 24

**READING: ROMANS 1:16-17,
HEIDELBERG CATECHISM, LORD'S DAY 23**

By grace through faith

"The righteous shall live by faith."

ROMANS 1:17B

God justifies sinners by grace. Yet in faith, we have to say 'amen' to this confession. The concluding part of Answer 60 reads that we must accept these riches with a believing heart. This does not mean that there still must be some contribution from our side. Faith is a gift of God worked in us by the Holy Spirit. That is why Answer 61 reads that we are not acceptable to God on account of the worthiness of our faith. God justifies sinners out of mere grace for Christ's sake. Faith is not an achievement from our side, but it is the instrument by which we embrace Christ as our righteousness – and even this instrument is given to us by God Himself.

Justification is through faith, never because of faith. Faith is not the reason for our salvation, but a means to salvation. Yet, we are to use it. We are not robots in God's service, but called upon as responsible creatures. Responsible – in this, we hear the word 'response'. Well, this is what God asks of us: a response to His love; a response in faith.

This makes it clear that justification is not a once-only affair in our life. True, already before the foundation of the world, God chose us in Christ. Having chosen us, He gave us a place within His covenant. Yet whenever the gospel is preached, it always comes to us with the command to believe and repent. The gospel is the power of God for salvation, since in it the righteousness of God is revealed 'from faith for faith', says the apostle Paul in Romans 1:17. This means that one cannot simply say, "I believe, so I am justified." This justification is realised in a living relationship with God. God preaches us the gospel of our acquittal, but this should cause the believer to render his life to God out of thankfulness for this acquittal. That is what the expression 'the righteous lives by faith' means. It points to a living relationship with the Triune God. To live by faith – this also means that the righteous cannot continue to live in sin. Having been justified by faith, we must also live by faith in a new life. That is, a life in which we have only one desire: namely to serve God.

October 25

**READING: EPHESIANS 4:17-32,
HEIDELBERG CATECHISM, LORD'S DAY 23**

A practical application of being saved by grace alone

"Do not grieve the Holy Spirit of God, by whom you were sealed for the day of redemption."

EPHESIANS 4:30

Faith is a gift of God, worked in us by the powerful work of the Holy Spirit within us. A precious gift, which we receive by grace alone. Amazing grace, yet are we still amazed? We should stand in awe of this precious gift daily– but how do we do this?

We know the gospel: Christ died for us sinners. Yet, we so easily gloss over the aspect of being sinners. After all, no one is perfect. The awareness of sin in our lives will only grow when we become more sincere in asking for forgiveness. Often we do this in general terms: Lord, graciously forgive me the sins of this day. It helps when we start mentioning sins by name – the things we actually did wrong and by which we grieved our Father in heaven. Yes, do we still feel the pain of grieving our heavenly Father with every sin we commit? Do we also realise that every single sin makes us guilty in God's eyes? Guilty – which means it makes us deserving of eternal death and of hell, if Christ had not paid for it.

When we become more sincere in our prayers, it also makes us more humble, seeing the miracle needed to save us wretched sinners. It is a miracle that makes us stand in awe of Christ's love for us. Then we will never take this for granted again. Instead, we will become more and more eager to give our whole life to Christ in active service, obeying God's commandments with joy out of thankfulness for all the blessings received in Christ. In Ephesians 4, the apostle Paul tells us what such a life looks like. It is a life of the new self, created after the likeness of God in true righteousness and holiness. It is the Holy Spirit who works all of this in us. Hence the apostle's call: "Do not grieve the Holy Spirit of God, by whom you were sealed for the day of redemption."

We are saved by grace alone. Let us always remember how precious this grace is and stand in awe of it daily. Amazing Grace, how sweet the sound!

October 26

**READING: JAMES 2:14-26,
HEIDELBERG CATECHISM, LORD'S DAY 24**

Works supply the proof that faith is living (1)

"You see that a person is justified by works and not by faith alone."

JAMES 2:24

One of the mottoes of the Great Reformation of the 16th Century was: Sola Fide – by faith alone. This was also the central message of Lord's Day 23. When we cling to Christ in genuine faith, God will count us righteous and free from guilt, even despite all our sins and shortcomings.

Yet how does this work? In 2 Corinthians 5:21, the apostle Paul writes: "For our sake He made Him to be sin who knew no sin, so that in Him we might become the righteousness of God." This is one of the crucial texts to explain what being justified in Christ means. It tells us that God regarded and treated Christ as sin, even though He Himself had never sinned.

For our sake! This means Christ became our substitute. That is how we became righteous before God. Righteous – not only because Christ bore our sins and paid for them. But God also credited Christ's righteousness to our account – an account full of debts. Yet in and through Christ, everything changed. Faith in Him gives us hope and a future again. We are saved, yet only by believing in Christ. By faith alone, and nothing of ourselves.

Yet, how is all of this to be reconciled with what James writes in his letter? James 2:24 reads: "…a person is justified by works and not by faith alone." Throughout the ages, there has been much opposition to what James writes here. Martin Luther, for example, had not much appreciation for this book of the Bible. According to Luther, the doctrine of being justified by faith alone is totally overshadowed in James' letter, especially when he emphasises that faith without works is dead. Yet, all of this is based on a misunderstanding. James wants to make it clear that faith in Jesus Christ must also be a living faith. In other words, the fact that our life is Christ-centred must also be visible – visible in the way we live.

This is also the message of Lord's Day 24. Answer 64 says: "It is impossible that those grafted into Christ by true faith should not bring forth fruits of thankfulness." In a different way, one could say, works supply the proof that faith is living.

October 27

**READING: JAMES 2:14-26,
HEIDELBERG CATECHISM, LORD'S DAY 24**

Works supply the proof that faith is living (2)

"You see that a person is justified by works and not by faith alone."

JAMES 2:24

The central theme of James' letter is that one should not only be a hearer but also a doer of the Word. Faith and actions must work together. Faith is perfected by what one does. Faith that does not show up in a god-fearing life is barren – is dead. Such faith is not genuine; it is not a living faith.

In Chapter 2, James uses an example to clarify this. He writes that saying all kinds of nice things but not showing tangible acts of love does not help a person one bit. Well, that is exactly how it is with faith. If it does not have works, it is dead. It is useless. It has no value. One may say that he loves the LORD and serves Him, but in fact, such a person has made a caricature of his faith. True genuine faith must produce fruits, expressing itself in deeds of love and thankfulness.

James makes this clear by referring to Abraham. Faith in God caused Abraham to do something of which humanly speaking, one would ask how Abraham could ever do this: sacrifice his son! As far as Abraham was concerned, there was even more at stake than just giving up his only child. This, in itself, is already quite something for a parent. Yet Abraham was not just giving up his only son. For, Isaac was also the son about whom God had promised: through him, I will make you a great nation – a nation from which one day the promised Messiah will be born. In sacrificing Isaac, Abraham was giving up the whole messianic future God had promised him. This is an element which should not be overlooked here.

Next, God did not intend to take Isaac by sudden death. Instead, God sent Abraham on a three day journey to test his faith, to see whether Abraham was indeed willing to sacrifice Isaac and this by his own hand. One indeed wonders how Abraham was able to do this.

The answer is: only by faith. James writes in verse 22: "Faith was active along with his works." These works were necessary to bring Abraham's faith to a climax and to show evidence that Abraham's faith was genuine. In this way, faith and works worked together to glorify God.

October 28

READING: EPHESIANS 2:8-12,
HEIDELBERG CATECHISM, LORD'S DAY 24

All glory to God alone

"For we are His workmanship, created in Christ Jesus for good works, which God prepared beforehand, that we should walk in them."
EPHESIAN 2:12

We are justified by grace alone. Our good works do not add anything to it. Why? Yes, why can our good works not be our righteousness before God, or at least part of it? Answer 62 says that the righteousness which God requires must be absolutely perfect, because even our best works are all imperfect and defiled with sin.

Even our best works – does this statement not put a dampener on the joys of life? The answer is no. At least, not when there is living faith! For, a living faith assures us: Christ has not only freed me from the guilt of sin by His blood, but also from the power of sin by His Spirit, that is the life-giving Spirit who renews our lives after the image of God, causing our faith to produce fruits. Nothing is of ourselves here. Because of our sinfulness, these fruits remain imperfect, and defiled with sin. Still, I may delight in it. And what is even more important, God delights in it. For in these fruits, God crowns His own work in our lives. Yes, also when it comes to our good works, God alone should receive all honour. Paul says that God prepared these good works beforehand that we should walk in them.

In Ephesians 2, Paul stresses that we are saved by grace alone. Yet, this does not undo our own responsibility. God prepared those works, yet we must walk in them, making our faith perfect and complete by our works – not to earn anything, but to honour God with it, so making God's glory perfect and complete in our lives. To say it in dogmatic terms: God wants not only our justification, but also our sanctification, and not in such a way that the justification comes from God and the sanctification from man. Instead, both justification as well as sanctification are gifts from God. The believer is justified by faith alone, yet this faith must be a living faith. Redeemed by grace alone, we must also show thankfulness for this grace by bearing fruits in the service of the Lord. It is these fruits that God will reward both in this life as well as in the next. A reward, yet at the same time a gift of grace!

October 29

**READING: REVELATION 14:1-13,
HEIDELBERG CATECHISM, LORD'S DAY 24**

A reward not earned, but a gift of grace

"…that they may rest from their works,
for their deeds follow them."

REVELATION 14:13B

In Revelation 14, the apostle John sees the Lamb in a vision standing on Mount Zion, and with Him the 144,000 having His Name and the Name of His Father written on their foreheads. This is the sealed multitude of which John had spoken about in Chapter 7, who were then still living on earth, surrounded by enemies. In Chapter 14, these same saints are enjoying the blessedness of heaven. Remaining faithful towards their Lord and Saviour had not been easy for these saints. It had called for patient endurance. But now they are blessed because they persevered to the very end. Taken by the Lord, they may now rest from their labours, with their deeds following them.

These last words clearly show that these saints are not blessed because of their works. They have already inherited eternal blessedness, and their deeds are following them. In heaven, God will reward us according to what we have done in this life. Yet after having already been justified, a reward will be given, As it reads in Answer 63: "This reward is not earned; it is a gift of grace." It is all God's work. Yet, as the Catechism says: this should not cause man to become careless.

During the Great Reformation in the 16th century, the Church of Rome said that the doctrine of justification by grace alone makes people careless and wicked. Yet Revelation 14 teaches us differently. First, it says that the redeemed find their rest in the Lamb, who by His accomplished work unlocked for them the gates of righteousness. They may rest from their labours and the hardships connected with these. The redeemed are those who, in this life, had also followed the Lamb on challenging roads. They served their Saviour, abandoning many earthly things; in some cases, they had even given their lives for Christ's sake. Yet, as Christ Himself once said, "There is no one who has left house or wife or brothers or parents or children for the sake of the kingdom of God, who will not receive many times more in this age, and in the age to come, eternal life." Thus God will reward our deeds. They will follow us. Yet this is and remains a gift of grace.

October 30

READING: HEBREWS 11:24-26,
HEIDELBERG CATECHISM, LORD'S DAY 24

Looking forward to the reward

"...for he was looking to the reward."
HEBREWS 11:26B

The reward God gives us is a gift of grace. Yet, we may look forward to this reward. Yes, we may even set our hopes on it. Like Moses did, who "considered the reproach of Christ greater wealth than the treasures of Egypt, for he was looking to the reward." This had nothing to do with human calculation. It was faith in the LORD that caused Moses to give up a bright future as a prince of Egypt, choosing God's oppressed people instead. From a human point of view, Moses could have had a much easier life, and a very wealthy life as well. However, in faith, Moses considered the reproach he would suffer with Israel to be of greater wealth than all he would receive as a prince in Egypt. Why? It was because he knew Israel was God's people – a people from whom the promised Messiah would be born. Moses considered the lasting benefit, that is the benefit of the redemption which God had promised to Abraham's seed. He considered this redemption to be of far greater value than all the wealth he would receive in Egypt. Moses knew that one day the LORD would reward him for the choice he made for Israel – a people despised by the Egyptians but precious in the eyes of the LORD. Moses lived by faith, knowing that the LORD is a rewarder of those who diligently seek Him.

The LORD extends this same reward to everyone who chooses to serve Him in faith. God will reward such a choice, both in this life and the next. This reward is the blessing with which the Lord blesses our life already today, and with which He will bless us perfectly after this life – a blessing we do not deserve. After all, when we choose to serve the LORD, it is not our work, but God's own Spirit working this within us. By His power, God causes us to remain faithful, producing fruits of faith in our lives. This is all God's work! When we remain faithful, God also promises us the crown of life as a reward. Yet this reward is and remains a gift of grace, since we from ourselves would never be able to stay faithful to the very end. Instead, God crowns His own work, in which by God's sovereign grace we receive so much.

October 31

READING: PSALM 46

Reformation Day

"The God of Jacob is our fortress."

PSALM 46:11B

Today we celebrate Reformation Day, remembering that on 31st October 1517, Martin Luther nailed his 95 theses to the church door in Wittenberg. These theses were designed to invite an academic debate on the scandalous practices of indulgences and other matters in the church. These indulgences were documents through which the sinner could purchase his salvation without any repentance before the Lord. Together with some of the other practices in those days, this practice undermined the scriptural teaching of being saved by faith through the grace of God in Christ alone. With these 95 theses, Luther called for a return to God's Word, stating amongst others – thesis 62 – "The true treasure of the Church is the Most Holy Gospel of the glory and the grace of God."

God richly blessed Luther's simple act. It became the start of the Great Reformation during the 16th century. This reformation gained momentum, especially after Luther, in January 1521, was excommunicated from the church by an official Papal decree. Having also been outlawed by the government, Luther's life was in danger. Yet he showed no fear. Instead, he found his strength in the LORD, clinging to the words of Psalm 46, where it reads that God will be our refuge and strength, a very present help in trouble. Luther expressed this trust in God by composing a hymn based on the words of this same psalm.

As far as Psalm 46 is concerned, we do not know exactly when this psalm was made. In a similar way, we do not know exactly when Luther wrote the Hymn 'A mighty fortress'. In the end, knowing these exact dates is not essential. More importantly, both Psalm 46 and Luther's hymn proclaim a message to which the church may cling at any given point in time. This message: in the heat of battle, there is no need to fear, for God is with us always. This same message is at the heart of all of Scripture. Immanuel – God with us; with us in and through His Son Jesus Christ, who according to Article 18 of the Belgic Confession, is in truth our Immanuel – God with us!

"Lord Sabaoth is His Name,
From age to age the same,
And He must win the battle."

November 1

**READING: ACTS 16:1-15,
HEIDELBERG CATECHISM, LORD'S DAY 25**

The Holy Spirit works faith by the preaching of the gospel (1)

"The Lord opened her heart to pay attention to what was said by Paul."

ACTS 16:14B

Faith is a gift of God. From ourselves, we would never believe in God. From ourselves, we are dead in sin. Scripture does not allow for a teaching, where after having heard a moving sermon, people come forward to commit their life to the Lord. Such teaching focuses more on the testimony of man than on the power of God for salvation. Faith is a mere gift of God. In Acts 16:14, we read that the Lord opened Lydia's heart to pay attention to what Paul said. It is God who graciously softens the hearts of the elect and inclines them to believe (Canons of Dort, Chapter 1, Article 6). It is indeed all God's work. Salvation is a gift, and so is the faith to embrace that salvation.

From Answer 65 of the Heidelberg Catechism, we learn that the Holy Spirit uses the Word as an instrument to work faith in our hearts. In Scripture, we read about God as the Creator and Redeemer of life. We read about God's promises of forgiveness of sins and renewal of life. When reading about all of these beautiful things, the Holy Spirit wants to kindle the fire of faith in our hearts. Only the Holy Spirit can do this. At the same time, the Spirit can only do this when we open the Word, read it, and study it.

When parents start telling their children about God and the Lord Jesus our Saviour, they use this means of hearing about Him. Yet, when our children start saying that they love the Lord and later also want to commit their life to the Lord in response to their baptism, we can only praise the Holy Spirit for His work in the lives of our children and equally in our lives too. In all of this, there is nothing from ourselves!

It is all God's work. All honour goes to God alone. At the same time, God urges us to use the means by which He wants to impart all of this to us. In Romans 10:14, the apostle Paul says: "So faith comes from hearing, and hearing through the word of Christ."

November 2

**READING: ROMANS 10:1-17,
HEIDELBERG CATECHISM, LORD'S DAY 25**

The Holy Spirit works faith by the preaching of the gospel (2)

"How are they to believe in him of whom they have never heard? And how are they to hear without someone preaching?"

ROMANS 10:14

In Romans 10, the apostle Paul stresses that man cannot contribute anything to his salvation. His heart cries out for his fellow man, that they too may come to salvation in Christ (verse 1). In verse 2, he says that they surely have a zeal for God. Yet this zeal is blinded, since they are missing the proper understanding of God's righteousness being revealed in Jesus Christ as Saviour. They are very law-abiding and as such there is nothing wrong with that. Yet they do not understand that the law finds its purpose in Christ (verse 4) who came to fulfill the law in our place.

Again, it is a gift of God, as Paul stresses in verses 6 and 7. There is no need to bring Christ down from heaven, for God had already sent Him for our sake. Neither do we have to go down to the abyss, for Christ was there for our sake, whereafter He rose and ascended into heaven, where He now is seated at God's right hand. Christ did all of this for us, so that "He could make us share in the righteousness, which he obtained for us by His death" (Lord's Day 17). That is why salvation is near for anyone who embraces the Lord Jesus Christ as Saviour.

"The word is near you", Paul says in verse 8. Through the sermons we hear on Sundays, God comes to us with His promises of salvation in Jesus Christ. This Word of God is so close to us, says Paul – it is on our lips. We can speak about it together, in church but also at home as parents with our children. It is on our lips when we respond to it. When it is a genuine response, this response comes from the heart, that is, from the place where the Holy Spirit works faith, using the Word as His instrument. Yes, says Paul, if it is indeed a matter of mouth and heart, you will be saved (verses 10 – 13). Next, Paul concludes in verse 14: "How are they to believe in him of whom they have never heard? And how are they to hear without someone preaching?"

November 3

**READING: ROMANS 10:1-17,
HEIDELBERG CATECHISM, LORD'S DAY 25**

The Holy Spirit works faith by the preaching of the gospel (3)

"How beautiful are the feet of those who preach the good news."
ROMANS 10:15B

Faith is a gift from God, who sends out preachers to proclaim the gospel of Jesus Christ. When this gospel is proclaimed in sincerity and truth, the Spirit is also at work to make people listen and believe. Faith thus comes by listening to the preaching of the gospel. It comes by a faithful listening to what God Himself has to say to us. This also means we must not look, in the first place, at the minister. Instead, we must look at God, who uses the minister as an instrument. That is why we should always speak positively about the preaching, appreciating that we may listen to it every Sunday. By listening to the preaching, we experience God's care for us, as Paul says it, quoting Isaiah 52:7, "How beautiful upon the mountains are the feet of him who brings good news."

In Isaiah 52, this refers to those who brought the exiles the good news of their imminent release from captivity. In Romans 10, it refers to the preachers of the gospel who bring the good news of release from the captivity of sin. Yes, this is also true when the gospel is preached and "It is proclaimed and publicly testified to each and every believer that God has really forgiven all their sins for the sake of Christ's merits, as often as they by true faith accept the promise of the gospel" (Answer 84 of the Heidelberg Catechism). That is why it is so important to be in church every Sunday. In the church through the preaching, the Holy Spirit will strengthen our faith. Because of the weakness of our faith, we need this strengthening every Sunday again.

This also means that we should come with eagerness and without any prejudice, as sometimes happens when a particular minister is preaching. Among the ministers, there is a variety of styles and approaches. They all have their peculiarities and weaknesses. Yet remember that God reveals His power even through the weaknesses of His servants. When coming to church, we should try to look away from the person proclaiming the Word and focus more on the Word itself, through which God Himself is extending His special care for us. Then we too will see how blessed the feet are of those who preach the good news.

November 4

**READING: GENESIS 17:1-14,
HEIDELBERG CATECHISM, LORD'S DAY 25**

The sacraments are signs and seals of God's faithfulness

"So shall my covenant be in your flesh an everlasting covenant."

GENESIS 17:13B

The Holy Spirit works and strengthens faith by the preaching of the gospel. God also gave sacraments which confirm the Word as signs and seals of God's promises – you could say these are additional. Yet, this does not mean that they are less important.

On the one hand, this means that we should not overemphasise the sacraments as more important than the Word. This easily happens when we skip one of the weekly church services, but when Holy Supper is celebrated, we make sure we are there. Alternatively, we may let disagreements linger, but before the celebration of Holy Supper they have to be resolved, lest one eats and drinks judgment upon himself. In the latter case, we forget that we can equally 'listen' this judgment upon ourselves when the preaching urges us to repent, yet we refuse to do so.

At the same time, however, we should be thankful that the Lord instituted these sacraments in addition to the Word. In Article 33 of the Belgic Confession we read that God instituted the sacraments "as pledges of His good will and grace towards us … to represent better to our external senses both what He declares to us in His Word and what He inwardly does in our hearts." This shows that the sacraments do not add anything to the Word, yet they confirm the Word as a sign and seal of God's promises.

Often we only focus on the sign portraying the promise. Yet, sacraments are also seals confirming the promise. That is why Article 33 speaks about pledges. Like a wedding ring confirms the sincerity of the "I do" spoken by bridegroom and bride, so our gracious God confirms His faithfulness to us by the sacraments as pledges of His good will and grace towards us.

When looking at the sacraments in this way, we can be thankful that God added them to the Word. Yet, we will only benefit from them when we use them in faith. This also applies to the first means of grace: the preaching of the gospel. As God's children, we are to work with both means provided by God.

November 5

**READING: CANONS OF DORT, CHAPTER V, ARTICLE 14,
HEIDELBERG CATECHISM, LORD'S DAY 25**

We are called to use the means of grace

"And they devoted themselves to the apostles' teaching and the fellowship, to the breaking of bread and the prayers."
ACTS 2:42

Through His Word, but also through the sacraments, God will point us to the promises He has given us. In faith, we must take hold of these promises and live from them. Think of the sacrament of baptism, for example. When this sacrament is administered, the Lord wants to remind all of us of our own baptism. At such a moment, we not only rejoice with the parents who present their child for baptism, but we also rejoice in the fact that we too are covenant children and may cling to these same promises. By witnessing a baptism, we feel strengthened again.

This is how the Lord wants us to use the means of grace, also concerning the preaching. You cannot lay a sermon aside by saying, that is how the minister thinks about this issue, but I have a different view. Of course, ministers have to be careful not to bring their specific opinions across. Sermons should never be issue-driven; a minister must preach the gospel. However, at the same time, the minister also has to apply the gospel in today's situation, warning against dangers that threaten the congregation. At times the minister might have to be very explicit in his warnings. Yet when doing so, he must still be able to say, "Thus says the LORD!" Then at times, a sermon may cut deeply into our sinful flesh, to the extent we are hurt by what we hear from the pulpit. Yet, this is wholesome since this is how God wants us to grow stronger in faith.

We must work with the means God has provided, that is, with the Word preached to us and the sacraments administered to us, living our faith as true covenant children, rejoicing in doing God's will. This will then never be a burden to us, but always a mere joy. When doing so, we will grow in faith. Daily we will learn to marvel at God's greatness and what a miracle it is that this great and almighty God looks upon us in mercy. Yes, then we will only have one desire – to live for the Lord in all that we do.

November 6

**READING: ROMANS 6:1-11,
HEIDELBERG CATECHISM, LORD'S DAY 26**

The comfort received in baptism (1)

" … just as Christ was raised from the dead by the glory of the Father, we too might walk in newness of life."

ROMANS 6:4B

Lord's Day 26 starts with the question: "How does holy baptism signify and seal to you that the one sacrifice of Christ on the cross benefits you?" A very personal question, which is something the Heidelberg Catechism repeatedly does. Generally, we do not like such personal questions. When office bearers visit us and ask questions about our faith and how it comforts and strengthens us, we do not always know what to answer. We find it too personal. We do not want to open up, even though we might be having certain struggles. Yet, we keep it private. The elders can feel that something is bothering us, but we do not tell them. Personal questions – we do not like them. They make us uncomfortable. At times, it gives us an unsettled feeling.

Yet on more than once occasion, the Heidelberg Catechism addresses us in a very personal way. Why is this? It wants to point us to Christ. Well, if anyone has a right to ask us very personal questions, then surely it is Christ – that is, He who stood at the very beginning of our life, when we were still laying in the cradle. At that time already, the Saviour put His saving arms around us, assuring us: 'I immerse your weak life in the communion of the Triune God, protecting it with the love of the Father, the redeeming grace of the Son, and the sanctifying work of the Holy Spirit'. That is how our life started; our life as a child of the LORD.

Having grown up with these riches, the same Saviour now asks: 'What does all of this mean to you? Do you also live from the riches of your baptism? Can people also see that these riches make you joyful?' All of this is included in this first question in Lord's Day 26.

Through the sacrament of Holy Baptism, God wants to assure us of how rich we are in being Christ's. Let us make sure that we live in the awareness of this daily, lest through a casual way of life we waste these riches. A severe warning to all who wear the mark and emblem of Christ on their forehead. A warning to heed and to enjoy life in walking with God, each day.

November 7

**READING: ROMANS 6:1-11,
HEIDELBERG CATECHISM, LORD'S DAY 26**

The comfort received in baptism (2)

"…just as Christ was raised from the dead by the glory of the Father, we too might walk in newness of life."

ROMANS 6:4B

When we were baptised we received the promise that Christ would wash away the impurity of our soul. This shows that we are impure people, right from birth – people who need help.

Because of this, there is a need for all of us to humble ourselves before God. We came into this world conceived and born in sin – an impure beginning. Therefore, even when still lying in the cradle, we needed forgiveness of sins. The Form for Baptism says that God's wrath even rests upon the baby just born. Parents rejoice in new life, and there is nothing wrong with that. However, at the same time, God's wrath already rests upon this newborn baby.

Yet, the miracle is, that Christ has taken this wrath away from us. In Romans 6, the apostle Paul writes that our baptism testifies that we were buried into death with Christ. Next, in verse 7, he writes: "One who has died has been set free from sin." Summarising this means, because of our sins, we deserved death. Yet in Christ, this death penalty has already been paid. The punishment we deserved, Christ bore for us. By His death, Christ paid the punishment for our sins. That is what our baptism tells us. I am not guilty before God. Instead, I am free from guilt, free from death and sin. Conceived and born in sin yet sanctified in Christ! As the apostle Paul writes in his first letter to the Corinthians, Chapter 6:11, "You were washed, you were sanctified."

Paul says this about people who surely did not have a blameless past. In the verses before verse 11, he writes about sexually immoral people, idolaters, adulterers, thieves, drunkards, and others. Next, he writes: "And such were some of you" – and yet, washed and sanctified in Christ. Through baptism, God had washed away the sinful past of the members of the congregation in Corinth to the extent that God would never come back on it. Christ paid for all these sins. That is how powerful the seal of baptism is. Through it, we receive a new life every day again.

November 8

**READING: HEBREWS 10:19-25,
HEIDELBERG CATECHISM, LORD'S DAY 26**

Humble thankfulness

"Let us draw near with a true heart in full assurance of faith, with our hearts sprinkled clean from an evil conscience and our bodies washed with pure water."

HEBREWS 10:22

When considering the riches of our baptism, the first thing it will teach us is humbleness. This humbleness is also referred to in Lord's Day 1, where it speaks about the need to know our sins and misery as an essential element of the comfort we may live from. I am afraid that we so quickly gloss over this at times. Often, we are very superficial in acknowledging our sins. I think of statements like, "No one is perfect; we all fall short." Yet God wants us to dig deeper and this so that we may see how much we need Christ as our Saviour. This knowledge of sin will grow when we live close to the Lord. We can then see how often we grieve Him. However, when the relationship we have with the LORD is rather casual, we also become less concerned about our wrongdoings. We start to sweet talk them: "It is not that bad, is it?"

In Hebrews 10:22, we read that we may draw near to God, assured that we are completely clean. We no longer need to have an 'evil conscience', not because of having become accustomed to sin, but because our conscience has been sprinkled clean. The addressees of the letter to the Hebrews were troubled about their sins. That is why the author reminds them of the gospel of the forgiveness of sins in Jesus Christ, assuring them: though at times your conscience accuses you, nevertheless you still may draw near to God with confidence. Cling to Christ, your Saviour, who paid for your sins. When with a contrite heart, you draw near to Him, you will find rest.

In that same faith, we too may draw near to God with confidence. These are the riches of our baptism. We are washed clean in the blood of Christ. On the day that we were baptised, Christ assured us – Lord's Day 26: as surely as this water washes away the dirt from the body, so certainly My blood washes away your sins. We may live in humble thankfulness from these riches, standing in awe of God's amazing grace each day again!

November 9

**READING: HEBREWS 10:19-25,
HEIDELBERG CATECHISM, LORD'S DAY 26**

Blessed Assurance (1)

"Let us draw near with a true heart in full assurance of faith, with our hearts sprinkled clean from an evil conscience and our bodies washed with pure water."
HEBREWS 10:22

When speaking about God's rich promises assured to us in baptism, people wonder at times how sure we can be of all this. Water is a fitting sign for the washing away of sins. But, does it indeed wash away all my sins? When I take a shower, my body becomes clean. Yet, the water of baptism cannot clean my soul, no matter how much water I use. Still, the water used at our baptism assures us that our sins have been washed away. It is certain because of God's promises, which I never have to doubt. God Himself stands guarantee that as surely as water has been sprinkled on our foreheads, so certainly are we washed from all our sins with Christ's blood and Spirit.

The Heidelberg Catechism mentions both: Christ's blood and Christ's Spirit. The blood refers to the forgiveness of sins we receive because of Christ's sacrifice on the cross. Having prayed for forgiveness, we may make a new start each time again, cleansed from all the dirt of our sins. However, since we are prone to sin, God also wants to give us a new heart, so that we become more and more willing to serve God according to His Word.

All of these are tremendous riches. Yet doubt can still creep in at times. The point is that we must accept the promise in faith, which is the evidence of things not seen. Think of the Israelites, to whom God had given the land of Canaan. It was theirs, even though they had not set one foot on it. It is true that many to whom God had said this did not enter the Promised Land. Yet this was not because God's promise could not be taken seriously, but because of their unbelief. The same applies to what God promised to us at our baptism. God will never break that promise. The only thing He asks of us is to accept this promise in faith. When we do so, we have the blessed assurance that we have never to despair of God's mercy. Never, when in true humbleness, we confess our sins, cling to God's promises, and also have the desire to break with sin.

November 10

**READING: PSALM 32,
HEIDELBERG CATECHISM, LORD'S DAY 26**

Blessed Assurance (2)

"I said, I will confess my transgressions to the LORD, and you forgave the iniquity of my sin."

PSALM 32:5B

We never have to despair of God's mercy. We may always count on forgiveness. Because of this, some people view the Reformed doctrine as being too easy. Just pray for forgiveness, and God will once again look upon you in mercy. It is that easy. Yet, it is not. True repentance will cause us to go down on our knees. It calls us to confess our unworthiness before God. Think of David, when he confessed his sins after committing adultery with Bathsheba and having killed Uriah. Read Psalms 32 and 51. These psalms are surely not a cheap confession of sins. These psalms speak of a sinner who humbles himself before God. Yet – and that is the comfort – when doing so, we may have the assurance that God will hear us; and not only hear us but also answer us. In Christ, He grants us forgiveness. We may be assured of this because of our baptism. We never have to despair of God's mercy.

When struggling with certain sins in our life, we should go down on our knees and pour our heart out before the Father. Say to Him, "Father, from myself, I will never get rid of these sins, but wilt Thou help me to fight by power from above? And whenever I stumble, graciously forgive me my sins, not because of me, but because of what Thou hast promised me at my baptism." When living close to the LORD in this way, God will indeed help and answer our prayers.

In summary, we must use our baptism daily, in a living relationship with the LORD. Then the joy of faith will prevail even in the darkest moments of our lives, because even then, God is still my Father, and He will not forsake the work of His hands. Living from our baptism simply means to trust God and walk with Him. Lay your weak life in God's almighty hands, even as He leads you through valleys. Trust Me – says the LORD – walk with Me, then you will be safe, always. You can be one hundred percent sure of this. The point is, do we truly believe this? Also, do we want to live from these riches each day in humble thankfulness, enjoying God's blessed assurance for what He gave us at our baptism?

November 11

**READING: DEUTERONOMY 4:7-9,
HEIDELBERG CATECHISM, LORD'S DAY 28**

Lest we forget

"Only take care, and keep your soul diligently, lest you forget the things that your eyes have seen, and lest they depart from your heart all the days of your life."
DEUTERONOMY 4:9

"Lest we forget!" – a well-known expression. Today at 11 o'clock, we kept a minute's silence to reflect on the lives of those killed in action throughout various wars, paying the ultimate price for our freedom. Perhaps less well-known is the fact that we also find this expression in Scripture. Even stronger, it is a very Biblical concept.

Lest we forget – we are all very prone to this. We may love songs like 'amazing grace' but do we also live daily in the awareness that all that we have received is by grace alone: not only our redemption in Christ but also the food on our tables, the wages to pay for this food and so much more? Every breath, every heartbeat is a gift of God's grace. How often do we think of this, and thank God for it?

In the Old Testament, this was why the Israelites had to celebrate Passover, lest they forgot not only what God had done for them in the past by redeeming them from Egypt, yet equally not to forget what God had done for them by bringing them to a land flowing with milk and honey. Indeed, there are always two aspects to the words 'lest we forget', also at our war memorial services. We reflect on the lives lost, but we do this in thankfulness for the freedom we may have at present.

Lest we forget – this is also the reason why we regularly celebrate Holy Supper. When celebrating this supper, we reflect on the ultimate price paid for the freedom most dear to us: our freedom from slavery and sin. At the Lord's Supper table, we remember Christ and His bitter death on the cross, where He suffered not only severe physical pain but the hellish agony of God's wrath.

When eating from the bread and drinking from the wine, we remember Christ's death. Yet not as a funeral meal. Instead, at the table we eat and drink in thankfulness that Christ died for our freedom – a freedom that far exceeds the freedom we remember on Remembrance Day. Therefore, the Scriptural call 'Lest we forget' is much more important than any other.

November 12

**READING: GENESIS 17:1-14,
HEIDELBERG CATECHISM, LORD'S DAY 27B**

Infant baptism

"For the promise is for you and for your children and for all who are far off, everyone whom the Lord our God calls to himself."

ACTS 2:39

Baptism is a sure pledge of God's grace towards us – a pledge we have to accept in faith, worked by the Holy Spirit in our hearts. Faith is what counts. Yet, what about the children of the covenant, who have not come to maturity in faith? Should they not mature in faith first, before giving them that same security as that of the adults? Even though this reasoning sounds very plausible, it is not what Scripture teaches.

Infant baptism is firmly anchored in the sure knowledge that God established His covenant with the believers and their seed. Both the Old and New Testament make this very clear. This covenantal perception is often lacking in today's evangelical circles, in which the vast majority all reject infant baptism. They come with arguments that nowhere in the New Testament do we find a proof text for infant baptism. Yet, the issue is not whether one can find an exact text. Instead, we have to listen to the overall teaching of Scripture.

Concerning infant baptism, everyone agrees that in the New Testament baptism has replaced circumcision. However, only the sacrament's outward sign changed, since bloodshed was no longer needed. We no longer celebrate Passover either, but Holy Supper instead. The outward sign changed, but not what was signified by this sign. This means we can never speak about Holy Baptism in isolation without also considering what the Old Testament teaches about the sacrament of circumcision.

Concerning circumcision, God clearly said that this sacrament should be administered to all male infants at eight days of age as a sign of the covenant. Infants too belong to God's covenant and therefore must also receive the sign of this covenant.

The LORD never came back on this. On the contrary, in the New Testament it is clear that the same applies today. The apostle Peter says in Acts 2:39, "For the promise is for you, and for your children." This text makes it clear that nothing had changed in the New Testament. The promises of God's covenant are also for the children. They share in the same promises as the adults. Therefore, they also have the right to receive the sign and seal of these promises. That is why infants too should be baptised, for together with their parents they belong to God's covenant and congregation.

 November 13

**READING: PSALM 8,
HEIDELBERG CATECHISM, LORD'S DAY 27B**

The comfort of infant baptism (1)

"Out of the mouth of babies and infants, you have established strength because of your foes, to still the enemy and the avenger."
PSALM 8:2

The gospel concerning infant baptism gives tremendous comfort; comfort in knowing that our children also belong to God's covenant and congregation, no matter how little they are. God also takes an interest in their lives. They share the same riches as we share, right from birth. Even earlier already, when they are still in the mother's womb. Yes, even then, God was numbering their days according to His plan with their lives. How amazing this is. Too wonderful to comprehend, but at the same time such a great comfort.

In Psalm 8, we read that by their mouth, God ordains strength to silence the enemy and the avenger. When crying in the cradle, these babies bring forth a cry of triumph by which Satan knows that he has lost the battle. Like no other, Satan knows that even for those little ones, Christ shed His precious blood. They too belong. That is why when still on earth, the Lord Jesus rebuked His disciples when they thought their Master had more important work to do than to take an interest in little children. But then the Lord Jesus responded, "Let the children come to Me, and do not hinder them, for to such belongs the kingdom of God."

Let us never forget that our children are covenant children. When we are busy with our children, let us remember this when we teach them and give them directions for their lives.

What a great comfort this is also for our children themselves, that they may know God is their Father. He will care for them. He will care for them when during puberty, for example, they sometimes struggle, or at times, as a teenager, find life difficult. God is there for them, also when they mess up their lives. To Him, they may return, assured of the forgiveness of all their sins, with this same God also helping them to fight these sins. When they grow older, let us tell our children to hang on to these riches, and to draw strength and comfort from them daily. Let us teach the next generation that our God is also their God.

November 14

**READING: PSALM 100,
HEIDELBERG CATECHISM, LORD'S DAY 27B**

The comfort of infant baptism (2)

"For the LORD is good; his steadfast love endures forever, and his faithfulness to all generations."

PSALM 100:5

Children too belong. Yet, what happens when these children grow older and at times become stubborn or rebel, when their elders and parents would love to see them making profession of their faith? It can turn out that they do not profess their faith or in other cases, they break the vow they made. What happens then?

Even in cases like these, we may go to God and bring the names of our children before His throne, asking the Lord – when we at times cannot reach them anymore – to reach out to these children of His. We may pray, "Lord, for Thy Name's sake, wilt Thou by the power of Thy Spirit work repentance in their hearts. Lord, keep them in Thy care". When praying this way as parents, remember the words of Psalm 100 that God is faithful. His love endures forever throughout the generations.

God has established his covenant with us and our children. We may draw great comfort from this. At the same time, it also brings with it great responsibility, since as parents we must instruct our children in these things, teaching them how rich they are in being covenant children. This requires much energy, but also a lot of wisdom and patience. At times, one can even grow tired of continually pointing our children towards the ways of the Lord, while, meanwhile, the world we live in today seems to have a much greater impact on them than the teaching of parents. Yet, we may also express this to God in prayer, asking Him to give us what is needed in this ongoing battle. Above all, in the way we live our lives, we should show our children the love of Christ which is more important than preaching to them. Children see everything. Therefore, the most crucial thing within family life is that Mum and Dad live their faith as an example to the children. If we indeed live in this way, doing what God requires of us with all the weaknesses involved, we may lay the outcome in God's hands, knowing that He will also preserve His Church throughout the generations. We may entrust our personal life and the lives of our children in the hands of our faithful covenant God, knowing that He will not forsake the work of His hands. This gives peace and rest, also when we have concerns about our children.

November 15

**READING: MATTHEW 26:26-29,
HEIDELBERG CATECHISM, LORD'S DAY 28**

Holy Supper – a festive meal

"I tell you I will not drink again of this fruit of the vine until that day when I drink it new with you in my Father's kingdom."
MATTHEW 26:29

When thinking of the Holy Supper as a meal, it is good to remember that hosting a meal was quite a festive event in the Ancient Eastern world. At the Lord's Table, this festive character is emphasised by the elements used, namely the bread and wine. These two elements were also used during the Old Testament celebration of Passover. Because of this link, it is clear that the Lord Jesus did not institute anything completely new.

Christ took bread and wine. Why? First of all, it was a sign to show that He, as our Saviour, sustains our spiritual life in the same way as bread satisfies one's hunger and wine quenches one's thirst. Yet, bread and wine also signify the festive character of the Holy Supper. In Ecclesiastes 9:7 we hear the Preacher say, "Go, eat your bread with joy, and drink your wine with a merry heart." Thus, bread and wine highlight the festive character of the Holy Supper. Festive – like the Passover meal, when the Israelites remembered the freedom God had given them by redeeming them from Egypt.

It was during this festive Passover meal that Christ instituted the Holy Supper by taking from the bread and afterward also by passing on the cup with wine. When passing the cup, Christ also spoke, amongst other things, the following words: "I tell you I will not drink again of this fruit of this vine until that day when I drink it new with you in My Father's kingdom." From this verse, we learn that one day Christ will gather all of His chosen ones, all at one table – the table of eternal joy. Holy Supper thus draws our attention to an even greater feast, which is still to come.

When Christ presented the bread and the wine to His disciples, He broke the bread, pointing them to His death. Likewise, Christ's body was broken. Not literally. Instead, the breaking of the bread points to all that Christ suffered on the cross for us so that we may live joyfully. The same applies to the wine, which points to the blood of Christ which was shed for our sins. That is why we celebrate Holy Supper as a festive meal, in thankfulness to God for all that He gave to us in Christ.

November 16

READING: JOHN 6:25-35,
HEIDELBERG CATECHISM, LORD'S DAY 28

The comfort received in celebrating Holy Supper

"Jesus said to them,'I am the bread of life;whoever comes to me shall not hunger, and whoever believes in me shall never thirst."

JOHN 6:35

By eating from the bread and drinking from the cup, we rejoice in the communion we have with Christ. Amid the brokenness of this life, we celebrate Holy Supper to be strengthened in our faith in order that we keep our eyes focused on Christ, our Saviour, who will always be there for us. Yes, throughout the ever-changing day and night, He is there to surround us with His love and His might.

When sitting at the table, one may feel lifted up, rejoicing in being Christ's. These are the blessings of celebrating Holy Supper regularly. Of course, we also enjoy these blessings through the weekly preaching of the gospel every Sunday. Yet, as it reads in Article 33 of the Belgic Confession: Our gracious God, mindful of our insensitivity and weakness, ordained sacraments, being added to the word of the gospel to represent better to our external senses both what He declares to us in His Word and what He does inwardly in our hearts. When considering all of these riches, there is no need to go to the table with a somber face, bowed down, or depressed. On the contrary, we may go joyfully, since Holy Supper reassures us that Christ is on our side in this broken life. If He is for us, who can be against us?

One may still have questions about all kinds of sorrows and worries that continue to bow us down. There may even be days when we may find it difficult to cope, even wondering whether we can make it to Holy Supper. You feel more like crying than rejoicing. This can happen. Let us never underestimate the struggles that fellow believers at times go through.

It is also especially for these struggling members that the Lord Jesus Christ instituted the Holy Supper to nourish and refresh our souls. At His table, the Lord reminds us of His sure promises which speak of mercy, peace, the forgiveness of sins, and redemption – redemption from the power of Satan. At His table, the Lord will comfort and strengthen us in the brokenness of this life. Come to me, the Lord Jesus says – eat and drink, and I will give you rest.

November 17

**READING: 1 CORINTHIANS 11:17-29,
HEIDELBERG CATECHISM, LORD'S DAY 28**

Do this in remembrance of Me

"Do this in remembrance of Me."
I CORINTHIANS 11:24B

Remembering – generally, it means you call to mind something from the past. Concerning Holy Supper, however, there is more to the word 'remember'. We indeed need to call to mind things that happened in the past. Yet, we do so because this event in the past is of paramount importance also for today. That is how Scripture uses the word 'remember'. The book of Deuteronomy often uses the word 'remember', stressing that Israel should not forget God's redemptive deeds from the past. In fact, throughout the entire Old Testament, the LORD repeatedly urges the Israelites not to forget how He led them out of the house of bondage and gave them freedom again. Israel is urged to remember these redemptive events of the past thankfully, and so to live accordingly.

This is the Scriptural meaning of the word 'remember'. It functions as a call to meditate on God's mighty deeds and also to help us stay focused on God's love and faithfulness towards us today. This is why the Israelites had to celebrate Passover annually. At the Passover, they called to mind the redemption from Egypt, remembering God's unchanging faithfulness and loving care in that critical hour of Israel's history. Yet when remembering all of this, it also reassured the Israelites of God's loving care in that moment. When celebrating Passover, the Israelites knew God's love towards them would always continue as long as they continued to live in thankfulness towards God.

From Scripture, we know that the redemption from Egypt foreshadowed the great redemption of God's people from the slavery of sin – a redemption which came true in Christ's sacrifice on the cross. Once again, a mighty deed of God worked at a particular moment in history. By instituting the Holy Supper, Christ now calls the church of all ages never to forget this momentous act of redemption, granted to us by mere grace. That is what the call "Do this in remembrance of Me" means. Never forget what I did for you. Always remember it in joyful thankfulness. That is why we celebrate Holy Supper regularly, lest we forget! At the Lord's Table, we glory in God's sovereign love towards us wretched sinners. Yes, then we marvel and ask: Lord is this really all for me? Amazing grace.

November 18

READING: REVELATION 19:6-9,
HEIDELBERG CATECHISM, LORD'S DAY 28

Holy Supper – a foretaste of the marriage feast of the Lamb

"Let us rejoice and exult and give him the glory, for the marriage of the Lamb has come, and his Bride has made herself ready."

REVELATION 19:7

At the Holy Supper table, we remember the bitter death of our Saviour. We do so, looking back in thankfulness at what we have received. Yet at His table, the Lord also directs our thoughts to the future. At the institution of the Holy Supper, Christ said that one day He would drink the wine new with us in the kingdom of His Father. These words direct our attention to the marriage feast of the Lamb. At the Lord's Table, we receive a foretaste of this feast; a foretaste that should cause all of us to await the return of our Saviour with eager expectation.

At present, we are still dealing with the brokenness of this life, which at times can hit us hard in the trials we face. Because of this, we can become disillusioned or even cynical, with not much reason to rejoice. Yet, at moments like these, we should not stay away from the table. Instead, remember that the Holy Supper was instituted to strengthen us in faith – a strengthening we all need so that we stop looking at what we are facing at present, focusing instead on God's grace in Jesus Christ. When eating from the bread and drinking from the cup, remember it was this grace that brought us safe thus far and by this same grace, God will lead us home. It is God's grace which carried us during the times when we wondered how we could possibly go on. This grace will continue in times to come, whatever the future holds, until we are finally home – home with the Father and with Christ our Saviour. It is on this day that Christ will drink the wine new with us in the kingdom of His Father. The word 'new' points to a blessedness that no eye has ever seen, nor ear heard, nor the heart of man imagined.

Every celebration of the Lord's Supper points us to this tremendous rich future. When we consider the hope by which we may live, it will help us to cope with the brokenness of this present life. Then, despite all of this brokenness, we may still rejoice, knowing the marriage feast of the Lamb is coming!

November 19

READING: EXODUS 24:1-8, HEBREWS 9:11-28,
HEIDELBERG CATECHISM, LORD'S DAY 29

Holy Supper assures us of the complete forgiveness of all our sins

"This cup that is poured out for you is
the new covenant in my blood."
LUKE 22:20B

For a good understanding of the words the Lord Jesus Christ spoke concerning the cup as a sign of the new covenant in His blood, we must read Exodus 24. This chapter informs us of the confirmation of the Old Testament covenant, which was also inaugurated with blood. First, Moses reads the Book of the Covenant within hearing distance of the people, who solemnly declare to obey these words. Next, Moses takes the blood, which had been put in basins and sprinkles it on the people, as a sign of the covenant the LORD had made with the Israelites. For the Israelites this was a sign and seal that they were reconciled with God – signified and sealed first by the sacrificial blood sprinkled on the altar and later on by the blood sprinkled on themselves.

Many centuries later, the author of the letter to the Hebrews calls this Old Testament ceremony to mind, giving further explanation of this practice of sealing a covenant through the sprinkling of blood, concluding that without the shedding of blood, there is no forgiveness of sins. This also means that without the shedding of blood, there is no possibility for a covenant, nor for any communion with God.

Of course, all the bloodshed during the time of the Old Testament could never reconcile the sinner with God. It called for the blood of the true sacrifice, which was to be brought by Jesus Christ. Only His blood was able to take away sins and to bring about true reconciliation with God. Only the blood of Jesus Christ could give the covenant of grace a legal ground. The cup with wine at the Lord's table bears testimony to this secure foundation. That is why Christ, when instituting the sacrament of Holy Supper, said: this cup is the new covenant in My blood. This new covenant received its confirmation in the blood of Christ, assuring us that because of Christ's bloodshed, we have complete forgiveness of all our sins. By drinking from the cup and equally by eating from the bread, we can be completely sure of this, without any doubt.

November 20

**READING: HEBREWS 9:11-28,
HEIDELBERG CATECHISM, LORD'S DAY 30A**

The papal mass

"But as it is, he has appeared once for all at the end of the ages to put away sin by the sacrifice of himself."

HEBREWS 9:26B

For a good understanding of what the papal mass is all about, it might be useful to note that the heresy concerning the mass did not just come into being overnight. Instead, via a process of deformation throughout the ages, this heresy became stronger and stronger until finally, in 1215 AD, the doctrine of transubstantiation became the official doctrine of the Church of Rome. So how did all of this happen?

In the early Christian church, the celebration of the Holy Supper was closely linked with the so-called love feasts – meals shared with the needy within the congregation. It was a practical example of the functioning of the communion of saints in those days. At the end of these love feasts, some of the gifts (some bread and some wine) were used to celebrate Holy Supper. During this celebration, the bread and the wine were blessed. In this blessing, the congregation rendered its thanks to God for all He had given.

It is here that the deformation started, as the thought slowly crept in: we are sacrificing something to God. As a result, bread and wine were no longer seen as signs of God's love towards man, but as a sacrifice of man to God. At the same time, due to the increasing power of the clergy, the priest was seen as one who had sole stewardship of the mysteries of the gospel. This resulted in a priest standing in front of the church congregation speaking the words "this is my body" – in Latin – making the people believe that at that very moment, the bread had changed into the body of Christ. Thus, hierarchy and false doctrine worked together to bring into being the doctrine of transubstantiation.

These few outlines show how the celebration of the Holy Supper completely deteriorated during those dark Middle Ages. A heresy came into being, which denied the rich significance of Christ's perfect sacrifice on the cross. It was taught that this sacrifice had to be repeated regularly, otherwise there would be no forgiveness of sins for either the living or the dead. All of this happened despite the clear testimony of Scripture. In Hebrews 9, for example, it is clearly stated that the sacrifice Christ made was once for all.

November 21

**READING: HEBREW 10:19-25,
HEIDELBERG CATECHISM, LORD'S DAY 30A**

The confidence received in the celebration of the Lord's Supper

"...we have confidence to enter the holy places by the blood of Jesus."
HEBREWS 10:19

After Christ accomplished His mediatorial task on earth, He ascended into heaven, where He is now seated at God's right hand in order to intercede for us. The papal mass also denies these riches. In the mass, the Church of Rome tries to bridge the distance between God and man. That is why they teach that Christ is bodily present in the signs of bread and wine. In the mass, Christ comes near to the sinner. One can even touch the sacrifice of reconciliation. The suffering of Christ becomes a tangible reality.

A superficial spectator may think that this makes the papal mass far more rich than a simple celebration of the Holy Supper. However, the church is richer with Christ in heaven than with Christ being bodily present in the signs of bread and wine. Richer, since Christ made a perfect sacrifice, once for all. According to Rome, Christ must be offered daily; otherwise, there will be no forgiveness of sins. Through this teaching, they think they have the tangible reality of Christ's sacrifice in the bread and the wine which for them changes into the body and blood of Christ, but meanwhile they are missing out on the communion with the living Christ in heaven.

Christ is in heaven, and we are on earth. Yet, there is not an unbridgeable distance between Him and us. On the contrary, when pleading with Christ's perfect sacrifice, we too may enter heaven. In the name of Christ, we may draw near to God, knowing that Christ our Advocate is seated at His right hand, having brought His blood into the heavenly sanctuary.

In the same way as during the time of the Old Testament, once a year, namely on the Day of Atonement, the high priest brought the blood of the sacrifice within the inner sanctuary. Likewise Christ, as the High Priest of the New Testament, brought His blood into the inner shrine behind the curtain. He did so when He entered heaven. The fruit of this is that we too may enter this sanctuary full of confidence "by the new and living way, that He opened for us, through the curtain, that is through His flesh."

November 22

READING: 1 CORINTHIANS 11:23-26,
HEIDELBERG CATECHISM, LORD'S DAY 30B

To proclaim the Lord's death

"For as often as you eat this bread and drink the cup,
you proclaim the Lord's death until he comes."

1 CORINTHIANS 11:26

When celebrating Holy Supper, we joyfully proclaim that Christ has died. Joyfully – is this not strange? How can you rejoice in someone's death, especially when the person who has died is dear to you? And yet, we do not sit at the Lord's table mourning, but indeed we sit there joyfully, since Christ died for our sins! To strengthen us in this sure knowledge, Christ commanded all believers to eat from the broken bread and drink from the cup until He comes, and this in remembrance of Christ's love for us sinners.

Christ commanded all believers. Does this mean that every member of the congregation without exception should participate in the celebration of the Lord's Supper? It is indeed true that with this command, Christ addresses the whole congregation, every member, even our young people. That is why young people should be keen to follow the instructions of the church in preparing themselves for public profession of their faith in order to receive admission to the Lord's Table. Parents have a task here as well. Given the challenges our children face in today's society, especially in the years leading up to adolescence, parents should point them to their riches in Christ. These are also there for the youth of the church, so that they find strength in their struggle to live in holiness before the Lord.

So, there is a clear command for every member of the congregation to celebrate the Lord's Supper. Yet, at the same time, there is another command: before attending the Lord's Supper we must firstly rightly examine ourselves, lest we eat and drink judgment upon ourselves. At times, these last words about God's judgment have made people scared. Overwhelmed by feelings of unworthiness, they do not dare to participate in the Lord's Supper. However, true self-examination can never give us any excuse to stay away from the table of the Lord. Instead, it should make us come. It is true that God is holy, and therefore He does not want His table to be profaned. Yet, this should not make us frightened to partake of the heavenly food and drink. Instead, it should serve as an incentive to amend our life so that we can come.

November 23

READING: 1 CORINTHIANS 11:27-32,
HEIDELBERG CATECHISM, LORD'S DAY 30B

Self-examination (1)

"Let a person examine himself, then, and so eat of the bread and drink of the cup."

1 CORINTHIANS 11:28

Self-examination – what does this involve? At times, overwhelmed by feelings of unworthiness, people have concluded: "I cannot partake of this food, which Christ has ordained only for those who truly believe in Him." They consider themselves not holy enough for this, lest they eat and drink judgment upon themselves. Yet, concerning self-examination, the question is not whether we are good enough to attend the table of the Lord. Instead, the point in question is whether we truly believe God's sure promises that in Christ there is forgiveness of all our sins. When trusting in this sure promise of God, we may bow our knees and fold our hands every night with a contrite heart, asking God to look upon us in mercy. Therefore, true self-examination should never cause us to doubt what God has promised us. We are God's children, and therefore we may be assured of the forgiveness of sins in Christ's blood. We should never question this.

So, what questions do we have to ask when examining ourselves? Being a child of the Lord, we have to ask ourselves whether we also live as a child of the Lord. When asking ourselves this question, we should not do so in a superficial way. True self-examination goes much deeper than just a bit of self-criticism here and there. Such self-criticism will hardly ever reach the point of starting to detest ourselves.

When examining ourselves, God wants us to look into the mirror of His law. When we do so sincerely, in an honest way, none of us can come to any other conclusion than every day we make a big mess of it all over again – a big mess of living up to God's law as the rule of thankfulness. At times, we wake up in the morning with all kinds of good intentions – today I will do things better. Yet, sometimes not even an hour passes before that bad temper flares up again, or we say something we should not have said to hurt our neighbour. True self-examination, therefore, requires being honest with ourselves and admitting the sins we have committed without any cover-up. Such honesty will enrich your faith.

November 24

READING: 1 CORINTHIANS 11:27-32,
HEIDELBERG CATECHISM, LORD'S DAY 30B

Self-examination (2)

"Let a person examine himself, then, and so eat of the bread and drink of the cup."

1 CORINTHIANS 11:28

When looking into the mirror of God's law, there is no other conclusion than that we deserve God's wrath. Our sins testify against us. Yet this should not make us conclude that we are unworthy of partaking in the Lord's Supper. After all, Christ did not give His life for righteous people, but for sinners. He gave His life for our sins – even for our remaining weaknesses and shortcomings. We all have to admit that we often fall short of doing God's will, at times even wilfully transgressing His commandments. Yet when we confess these sins with a contrite heart, God will forgive them for Christ's sake, not imputing to us wretched sinners any of our transgressions, nor the evil that still clings to us. This is a sure promise. Now it is up to us to firmly believe this promise.

God is trustworthy when He says to us, "For the sake of Christ My Son, I will graciously forgive you all your sins." This means that we must seek our life outside of ourselves to find it in Christ alone, seeking our life in His death. We know this, but we must also accept this in true faith. In true faith, that is – as it says in Answer 21 of the Heidelberg Catechism – to have a firm confidence that not only to others, but also to me, God has granted forgiveness of sins, everlasting righteousness, and salvation, out of mere grace, only for the sake of Christ's merits. Therefore, we may still eat from the bread and drink from the cup despite all of our sins. Christ gave His body and shed His blood for wretched sinners. Thus when examining ourselves we may flee to Christ, finding rest in Him.

Having received forgiveness in Christ's blood, it should now also be our heartfelt desire to amend our lives and fight against sin. Examining ourselves should function as an incentive to live our lives in thankfulness to the Lord. True, there will still be many weaknesses daily, but this is exactly why Christ has given us the sacrament of Holy Supper in addition to the preaching of the gospel – to strengthen us in our struggles.

November 25

READING: 1 CORINTHIANS 11:27-32,
HEIDELBERG CATECHISM, LORD'S DAY 30B

Self-examination (3)

"For anyone who eats and drinks without discerning the body eats and drinks judgment on himself."

1 CORINTHIANS 11:29

Christ gave His life for us sinners. Does this now mean that everyone can come to the Table of the Lord regardless, to the extent that no one need be afraid of God's holiness? Surely not! For whoever fails to appreciate what Christ has done for him, and either by his confession or life shows that he is unbelieving, such a person shall not partake of this heavenly food and drink. Otherwise, his judgment and condemnation will be the heavier.

In Corinth, some people were eating from the bread and drinking from the cup in an unworthy manner. The apostle does not speak about unworthy people. Instead, he addresses a situation in which children of God use the supper of the Lord in an unworthy manner. By eating from the bread and drinking from the cup, certain members of the congregation wanted to be reassured of Christ's love towards them, yet at the same time they fell short in showing love towards one another. The rich had no real care for the poor. In acting this way, they broke the communion with their fellow brothers and sisters, while still wanting to receive communion with Christ. This kindled God's wrath.

This shows that celebrating Holy Supper is indeed a serious matter. The table confronts us with the holiness of God, with whom we may live in a covenant relationship. This is indeed a wonderful relationship. Yet, whenever one does not live accordingly, such a person should indeed be afraid of God's holiness. Therefore, before attending the Lord's Table, we must first rightly examine ourselves, about whether we love and serve the Lord from the heart.

Because we are to take the covenant relationship with God seriously, the Christian church is duty-bound to exercise discipline over those who do not want to break with sin in their life, lest the covenant of God be profaned and His wrath kindled against the whole congregation. The Lord's Supper is a holy meal and must be maintained as such. The table should not be left open to each and everyone regardless of their walk and talk. Those who live offensive lives must be denied access, and this with the aim that they repent of their sins.

November 26

**READING: 1 CORINTHIANS 11:27-32,
HEIDELBERG CATECHISM, LORD'S DAY 30B**

Church discipline

"But when we are judged by the Lord, we are disciplined so that we may not be condemned along with the world."

1 CORINTHIANS 11:32

In Answer 82 of the Heidelberg Catechism it reads that the Christian church is duty-bound to use the keys of the kingdom of heaven in exercising church discipline over those who, by their confession and life, show that they are unbelieving and ungodly, lest the covenant of God is profaned and His wrath kindled against the whole congregation.

Unbelieving and ungodly people – the Catechism does not refer here to people from outside the church, but to church members who do not want to live from the riches of God's covenant. In doing so, they are virtually breaking their side of the covenant. In Answer 82 we read that such people cannot be admitted to the Lord's Table, and one can understand this. How would it be possible to admit those who do not want to live from the riches of this covenant to the Lord's Table? Well, that is what living in sin means. It is like a sick person not wanting to admit that he is sick, and therefore not seeking medical help, even though it is available. Such a person is not fit to partake of a meal with people who rejoice in this help. Therefore, according to the command of Christ, these members must be excluded until they amend their lives.

At the Lord's Table, we celebrate the feast of our reconciliation with God through the blood of Christ. Therefore, those who despise this blood of reconciliation cannot be admitted. God does not tolerate people despising His grace. God does not allow His bride to be assaulted by unbelieving and ungodly people. His bride must exclude these people in order to keep her life with the Lord pure. If she does not do so, God's wrath will be kindled. Yes, God will then humiliate His bride – think of the history of Achan – so that sin is put away from amongst His people, His bride once again living for Him alone.

That is why church discipline must be exercised. This is a task with much responsibility that is given to the office bearers of the church. Yet, we cannot just leave it to the office bearers. We are all given the task of encouraging one another, so that when Christ returns, we may all sit together at the marriage feast of the Lamb.

November 27

**READING: ISAIAH 22:15-22,
HEIDELBERG CATECHISM, LORD'S DAY 31**

The keys of the kingdom of heaven

"And to the angel of the church in Philadelphia write: 'The words of the holy one, the true one, who has the key of David, who opens and no one will shut, who shuts and no one opens'."
REVELATION 3:7

In His letter to the church at Philadelphia, the glorified Christ introduces Himself as "He who has the key of David, who opens and no one will shut, who shuts and no one opens." To understand these words, we have to turn to Isaiah 22 where we read about Shebna, who during the reign of King Hezekiah was in charge of the keys of the house of David. Yet because he was an unfaithful servant, the LORD appointed someone else.

In those days, a key-bearer was not just a gatekeeper, standing at the palace gates to open and close them. Instead, the key-bearer was the most influential person amongst all of the palace officials – a person with enormous authority. If someone wanted to speak with the king about a specific issue or ask for the king's judgment on a particular lawsuit, the key-bearer was in charge of saying 'yes' or 'no'. It was only through the key-bearer that one could receive access to the king. The importance of the position of key-bearer is highlighted even more when we consider that Israel's king was a theocratic king, who in his office foreshadowed the kingship of Christ. Being the key-bearer of such a theocratic king meant being in charge of giving access to the powers of redemption, which God would reveal to his people through the office of this theocratic king.

It is in this light that we are to read Christ's self-designation to the church in Philadelphia: "He who has the key of David, who opens and no one will shut, who shuts and no one opens." This means that one can only enter the kingdom of heaven through Christ. When Christ opens the kingdom to us, no one can shut it. Yet the opposite is also true. When Christ shuts it to us, no one can open it. No one can ever appeal against His decision.

This is a serious thing. Yet, it does not need to disquiet us, for Christ has our salvation at heart. He does not want the death of the sinner, but rather that he should turn to God and live, in order to enter the kingdom of heaven.

November 28

READING: EZEKIEL 33:1-20,
HEIDELBERG CATECHISM, LORD'S DAY 31

Watchmen over the household of God

"Whenever you hear a word from my mouth, you shall give them warning from me."

EZEKIEL 33:7B

In Ezekiel 33, the analogy of a watchman is used for the office which Ezekiel had to fulfill. In the event that an enemy was approaching, a watchman had the duty to raise the alarm and blow the trumpet. If he failed to do so, he would be held responsible for the blood shed. Yet if the people did not respond to the alarm, it was their own fault if they were struck by calamity.

This is a beautiful analogy to also highlight the responsibility of the office bearers today. They too are watchmen, who are to warn members of the congregation of the dangers that threaten them. This shows that serving as an office bearer is a very responsible task, even more so when remembering that the office bearer is acting on Christ's behalf. When he warns members of the congregation, he warns them on behalf of his heavenly Sender who has our salvation at heart, also when He warns and admonishes us through the ministry of the office bearers.

The office bearers are watchmen over the household of God. When these watchmen neglect their responsible task, when the sound of the trumpet to warn God's people is no longer heard, Christ's congregation is in great danger. We see this in many churches around us that have deviated from the truth of God's Word. When the office bearers no longer warn against dangers, people are led astray, and in the end this ruins the church.

That is why office bearers have to speak the word of God faithfully, even when it does not please the ears of the hearers. They must pass on the message of their heavenly Sender. Later on, no one should be able to say: "In the preaching, I was never warned against this, or the office bearers never spoke about the dangers that threatened my life."

Office bearers have the task of warning the congregation about the temptations of today's secular climate by which Satan tries to lure God's children away from the LORD. The minister has the responsibility of addressing these things in the sermons on Sundays, but the elders should also speak about them when visiting the members of the congregation at home.

November 29

READING: PSALM 84,
HEIDELBERG CATECHISM, LORD'S DAY 31

The first key: the preaching of the gospel

"My soul longs, yes, faints for the courts of the Lord."
PSALM 84:2A

Lord's Day 31 deals with the keys of the kingdom of heaven. It mentions two keys: the preaching of the gospel and church discipline. These two keys are closely connected, as church discipline is also exercised through the Word of God. Whenever the office bearers come to visit us – be it to comfort, to encourage, or to admonish – they always come with the Word of God. This is their only tool. On Sundays, the minister ministers this Word of God from the pulpit to provide the congregation with its spiritual food, but throughout the week the elders visiting the homes come armed with this same Word.

Office bearers have only one tool. It is a very powerful tool. In Hebrews 4:12 it reads: "The Word of God is living and active, sharper than any two-edged sword, piercing to the division of soul and of spirit, of joints and of marrow, and discerning the thoughts and intentions of the heart." It is by this powerful tool that Christ, through the ministry of the office bearers, exercises the authority of the keys of the kingdom of heaven.

Christ does so first of all through the preaching, by which the kingdom of heaven is opened and closed. These words highlight the tremendous importance of the preaching. Christ opens the kingdom each Sunday again when the minister proclaims to the congregation that our salvation lies in Jesus Christ alone, in whom we have forgiveness of sins through faith in Him. Every Sunday, we may listen to the gospel of our acquittal. For this reason, the apostle Paul calls the preaching of the gospel 'the ministry of reconciliation'.

Salvation is ministered to us, but only – as it reads in Answer 84 – when I accept the promise of the gospel with a believing heart. In other words, God does not allow us to take a non-committal attitude towards the gospel preached to us. According to Answer 84, if we do this, God's wrath and eternal condemnation rests on us. This means that we should not just be hearers of the Word but also doers. This shows that listening to the preaching is not only a joyful but also a serious matter. The choice between accepting and rejecting God's Word is ultimately a choice between life and death. Let us always be well aware of this.

November 30

**READING: MATTHEW 18:15-20,
HEIDELBERG CATECHISM, LORD'S DAY 31**

The second key: church discipline

"If your brother sins against you, go and tell him his fault."

MATTHEW 18:15A

Christian discipline starts within the congregation. In Matthew 18 it reads: "If your brother sins against you, go and tell him his fault." This comes first, before the office bearers become involved. We are all responsible for one another. Out of love for the brother or sister concerned, we should speak with them when we see a sinful lifestyle. We should not say, "I hope that the office bearers will do something about it." We also have to own some of the responsibility.

All church discipline starts within the congregation. Yet, the congregation remains involved also when the office bearers are dealing with the brother or sister concerned. Before it comes to the final act of excommunication, several public announcements are made by which the congregation is urged to pray for the sinner and – when the censure continues – to visit the brother or sister personally. Indeed, Christ mobilises all of us so that it does not have to come to that final act of excommunication.

Often, excommunication is considered to be too harsh. Yet, excommunication is not in conflict with God's mercy. For even in this final act of discipline, Christ has the salvation of the sinner at heart. True, Lord's Day 31 speaks about the wrath of God and eternal condemnation which rests upon the sinner who hardens himself. However, we should not forget that these words are spoken on this side of the grave, and therefore it is only the beginning of God's final judgment. As long as we are living in today's grace, there is always a way back. Yes, even for the excommunicated sinner, the way to God's kingdom remains open when there is true repentance and also amendment of life. There is joy in heaven and on earth when the lost son comes home again. Looking upon church discipline from this perspective, it is clear that it remains an act of love even in its final stage.

Lord's Day 31 speaks about the proclamation of the forgiveness of sins. However, when members of the congregation are no longer overwhelmed with thankfulness for the grace offered to them, there is no place in God's kingdom for them, not because God lacks mercy, but because they have closed their eyes to the mercy of God.

December 1

**READING: EPHESIANS 2:1-10,
HEIDELBERG CATECHISM, LORD'S DAY 32**

Why must we yet do good works? (1)

"For by grace you have been saved through faith."
EPHESIANS 2:8A

If we are saved by grace alone without any merit of our own, why must we yet do good works? Does this not mean that ultimately God's grace is still not sufficient? We have to consider this as a sincere question from someone wanting nothing other than to live by grace alone. If it is indeed all by grace alone, why must we still do good works? Yes, it even says 'must'. Does this not discredit the gospel of grace?

This question is crucial for a good understanding of the gospel of grace. Grace alone – yet we still carry responsibility for what we do, also concerning doing good works. Church members often struggle with how to gel these two together. For example, when during the preaching the minister emphasises the obligation of God's covenant, people get the feeling that this is all they have to do: obey God's commandments – whereby in that moment the whole element completely disappears that it is all about God's grace. At times it even leads to despair when we see how much we fall short of obeying God's commandments. Yet there is no need for this. We may also cling to God's grace concerning obeying God's commandments. The point in all of this is what we actually mean when we speak about grace.

Often, we limit the word grace to the fact that in Christ we have complete forgiveness of all our sins. Yet the point is that having been cleansed by Christ's blood, the call is: sin no more – yet there is sin, each day again. So more has to happen than just being forgiven. Otherwise, our life will remain the same. We must break with sin and do good works instead. Yet the point now is how to couple this with the gospel of being saved by grace alone. The simple answer is: doing good works is the fruit of being saved by grace alone. Grace does not require any additional work from our side. Indeed it is all God's work given to us in Christ, including the good works we do. God prepared them beforehand, says Paul, that we should walk in them. In thankfulness for God's grace, we must also show this in a life full of good works.

December 2

**READING: ROMANS 6:1-14,
HEIDELBERG CATECHISM, LORD'S DAY 32**

Why must we yet do good works? (2)

"...present yourselves to God as those who have been brought from death to life, and your members to God as instruments for righteousness."

ROMANS 6:13B

In thankfulness for being saved by grace alone, we must also show this in a life full of good works. Luther called this the other side of God's grace. The other side – this means there are two sides to God's grace granted to us in Christ as our Saviour. The one side is that Christ bought us with His precious blood and redeemed us. We belonged to sin, which had us completely in its grip. Yet Christ redeemed us from that bondage, setting us free. Therefore, sin no longer rules over us, but Christ instead. Out of mere grace, God declares us not guilty. That is what we doctrinally call 'our justification', that is, the forgiveness of sins in Christ's blood.

Yet, Christ did not leave it there. His grace encompasses much more. After all, Christ not only wants to forgive us of our past but He also wants to remove the sin from our life at present. He wants to renew us entirely by the powerful work of the Holy Spirit. This too is part of God's grace towards us in Jesus Christ, and no less than the first part. They belong together: forgiveness of sins and renewal of life. Our baptism testifies to this as well, since we were baptised not only in Christ's blood (pointing to the forgiveness of sins) but also in Christ's Spirit (pointing to the renewal of life).

This is also what we read in Answer 86: "Why must we yet do good works?" Is it because we still have to add something from our side? No, says the answer. It is "because Christ having redeemed us by His blood also renews us by His Holy Spirit." Both belong to God's grace, given to us in Jesus Christ as our Saviour. You cannot have the one without the other, because then we would be tearing Christ's work for us apart. That is why we must do good works. The difference is – as the apostle Paul writes in Romans 6 – that we no longer do these good works because the law requires it of us: do this, and you will live. Instead, we do this because we are living under grace.

December 3

READING: ROMANS 6:1-14,
HEIDELBERG CATECHISM, LORD'S DAY 32

Why must we yet do good works? (3)

"You are not under law but under grace."
ROMANS 6:14B

We are no longer under law but under grace. When reading this, it almost seems as if these two oppose each other: grace versus the law. By way of example, when a minister preaches a series of sermons on the Ten Commandments, he may hear comments that more attention should be paid to the fact that we are saved by grace, instead of emphasising strict obedience to God's commandments. However, comments like these create a false dilemma.

So what does Paul mean when he says that we are no longer under law but under grace? He points to God's progress in redemptive history. In the Old Testament, God gave His law and said to His people, "Do this, and you will live." Since we cannot live in perfect obedience to God's commandments, the law condemns us. That is living under the law. Yet we are no longer under law but under grace. However, this fact does not abandon the law. The law also applies to us. As God's children, today, we too are to love God with all our heart, soul, mind, and strength and our neighbour as ourselves. This command applies to us no less than it did to God's people living in the time of the Old Testament, even though we are now living under grace. In this respect, there is no difference between law and grace. The difference lies somewhere else – a twofold difference.

First, the law tells us who are living in the New Testament era: you are guilty of transgressing God's commandments, and therefore payment must be made. Christ did so with His blood, and therefore living under grace, we are no longer guilty. That is the first difference.

Yet there is more. The law requires obedience but does not offer obedience. Grace does offer this by the powerful working of the Holy Spirit within us. Hence, grace not only says we must do good works, but it also enables us to do the good works. It gives us what it requires of us. That is precisely what makes it grace! When standing in awe of what God has done for us in Christ by mere grace alone, we should have no other desire than "to show ourselves thankful to God with our whole life." It is God Himself who works this within us, making our will alive. Hence, it remains all grace and grace alone.

December 4

READING: ROMANS 12,
HEIDELBERG CATECHISM, LORD'S DAY 32

A living sacrifice

"I appeal to you therefore, brothers, by the mercies of God, to present your bodies as a living sacrifice, holy and acceptable to God, which is your spiritual worship."

ROMANS 12:1

When we have understood what grace truly means, it will change every aspect of our lives. It will change us as husband and wife within marriage. In self-denying love, we will no longer seek our own interests first. Instead, in thankfulness for what Christ has given us in marriage, forgiving us and renewing us, we will also desire to show this to one another, forgiving each other as Christ forgave us. Then, instead of finding an easy way out by no longer having the willingness to fight for our marriage, we will want to hold on to the vows we made to one another, also in difficult times. When we sincerely live as husband and wife this way, in thankfulness to God, it will also impact our children when they see mum and dad not just saying all the right things, but living them as well out of thankfulness for God's grace. Next, this thankfulness will also change how we deal with the children God has given us to raise on His behalf.

Family life – this is only one example. Yet, when truly living by grace, it will permeate our whole life: how we spend our money, how we spend our leisure time at the beach when having holidays, the way we dress. Then we will indeed want to live for and with the LORD in all that we do. That is what Answer 86 means when it says: "so that with our whole life, we may show ourselves thankful to God for His benefits." Thankfulness does not mean giving God something. Instead, it means giving our entire life to the LORD. That is what Christ wants to work in us by His grace and by the power from above. This once more shows how amazing God's grace in Jesus Christ is.

Let us never say that all of this is too difficult. Whenever this thought crosses your mind, think of Calvary and what Christ did for us there. It will give us a renewed incentive to offer ourselves to God with our whole life – a life of worship that God will work in us by His power.

December 5

**READING: MATTHEW 7:15-20,
HEIDELBERG CATECHISM, LORD'S DAY 32**

Assurance of faith by its fruits

"Thus you will recognize them by their fruits."
MATTHEW 7:20

In Matthew 7:20 we read that we will know a tree by its fruit. That is also how we may know our faith by its fruits. Look at your own life and think of that difficult day you had to face some time ago. You wondered how you would ever get through that day. Yet your faith gave you strength. Or think of that hour of temptation when you were very close to doing the wrong thing, yet your faith gave you the strength to say 'No!'. Or think of those evenings that you rejoiced in reading the Bible. All of these things are evidence of the fruits of faith, which assure us that it is not just a hoax. It is real. God is there to hold on to us, keeping us in His care. What a great thing this is when we feel reassured of our faith in this way.

Some people have criticised this, saying that in this way we are seeking assurance through personal feelings or the things we do, instead of fully trusting the promises God has given us in the gospel. Yet, this criticism is unfounded. The Catechism does not say that our faith stands or falls through what we experience. This would be rather fickle. What if we do not have these feelings or cannot testify to some of these experiences? Thankfully, we do not have to look for certainty in ourselves. This would be a dead-end road. The only foundation for our faith is God's sure and trustworthy promise that we are His always, even when we do not feel it.

Yet, like grace, assurance of faith also has more than one side. We firmly believe that God is near, even in the deepest valley, and that His grace is always sufficient to carry us. We know this, but at times we inwardly do not feel it. In other words, we do not doubt God's sure promise. Instead, we question our faith. It is in cases like these that looking at certain fruits can give reassurance. Again, the reason for this is not that we want to seek certainty in ourselves, but rather the assurance of the things God does in our life. The more we rejoice in living our life in thankfulness to God, the more we will rejoice in this additional assurance God gives.

December 6

**READING: MATTHEW 5:14-16,
HEIDELBERG CATECHISM, LORD'S DAY 32**

Winning our neighbour for Christ by a godly walk of life

"Let your light shine before others, so that they may see your good works and give glory to your Father who is in heaven."

MATTHEW 5:16

Concerning winning our neighbour for Christ, our thoughts often go straight away to evangelism, the way we live our lives amid today's secular society and being a light in the world. Of course, this too is part of it. Yet meanwhile, we often overlook the fact that it is in the church that we first meet our neighbour. You may think that this neighbour has already been won for Christ and to a certain extent, this is indeed true. Yet at the same time, especially within the church, we should have each other's spiritual well-being at heart, also in the way we live.

Do we live by example as parents at home, so that not only by the things we say but also by a godly walk of life we may excite our children into knowing how great it is to serve the Lord? Do we radiate joy in faith to other members when we do things for the Lord, so that perhaps others become enthusiastic as well? It is crucial that we seek the spiritual well-being of one another first of all within the church. Let us get excited together about how great it is to serve the Lord – excited about being children of a heavenly Father.

When we redirect the focus of our lives in this way, it will also affect the way we live our lives outside the walls of the church. If, throughout the week, our lives hardly differ from the people that cross our path, how will we ever win them for Christ? Occasionally, we may speak about the church, but when such a conversation is not seasoned with a godly walk of life, it will not get people excited about going to church.

I once watched a session of parliament during which the speaker of the house introduced the new members of parliament to the rules of the house, saying: "You are now a VIP. Do not say it, but show it." In other words: "Live who you are." We too are VIPs – ambassadors of Christ. Let us show this in the way we live so that people can see that we are genuine about our faith. This too has everything to do with being thankful to God for all that we have received in Christ.

December 7

**READING: EPHESIANS 4:17-32,
HEIDELBERG CATECHISM, LORD'S DAY 33**

The true repentance or conversion of man (1)

"To put off your old self, which belongs to your former manner of life…, and to put on the new self, created after the likeness of God"
EPHESIANS 4:22A + 24A

Repentance or conversion – what is this? How can we describe these two terms from the Heidelberg Catechism more practically? From Lord's Day 32 we learnt that in Christ, we have become new creatures. We were on the way to destruction. Yet by the regenerating work of the Holy Spirit, we are now heading towards life – putting off our old nature and putting on the new. A 180 degree conversion! Indeed, living a completely different way of life. This is what God has done in our lives. Not many of us would have difficulty accepting this as doctrinal truth. Yet, how does all of this now work in practice?

In most cases – especially with those who grew up in the church – conversion/repentance happened gradually. Remember when you were eleven or twelve years old: you loved the Lord. Catechism classes, Bible Study Club: it was all new and exciting. Yet a few years later, when you were fifteen or sixteen years old, it wore off and you became more critical, at times perhaps even rebellious. You struggled with your faith: Is it all true? Why this and why that? Slowly, however, you became more positive again. At nineteen years old, you were perhaps keen to publicly profess your faith in the church you grew up in.

As parents, you wish your child could skip those middle years. At the same time, we almost accept it as being normal and a part of growing up. Puberty, adolescence – that is how our children grow towards maturity, also in faith – a gradual process; not drastic conversions like we sometimes hear from others, and we read about in Scripture as well.

Think of the apostle Paul. On the road to Damascus, he had that wonderful experience which changed him from a persecutor of the church into a preacher of the gospel: powerful and miraculous!

Yet, even when these things happen more gradually, it is surely no less powerful and miraculous. We may think that there is nothing miraculous about it but we are forgetting the mighty deeds God has also done in our lives. Perhaps these are not so spectacular in our own eyes, but they are nevertheless still miraculous and powerful.

December 8

READING: ROMANS 6:1-11, CANONS OF DORT III/IV, 11-12, HEIDELBERG CATECHISM, LORD'S DAY 33

The true repentance or conversion of man (2)

"So you also must consider yourselves dead to sin and alive to God in Christ Jesus."

ROMANS 6:11

Chapter III/IV of the Canons of Dort describe man's conversion as follows: God penetrates man's innermost recesses, opening the closed and softening the hard heart, and installing new qualities into the will, making what was evil good and what was stubborn obedient. It describes the power by which God does this as supernatural, most powerful, and at the same time most delightful, marvelous, mysterious, and inexpressible, not inferior in power to creation or the raising from the dead. That is also how God works repentance in our hearts.

How does all of this work practically? Say there is a specific sin in your life which you find difficult to break with. How does God bring you to repentance? It is not merely by warning you in a sermon, or by a special visit from your elder or minister urging you to change, leaving it up to you what you do with it. Thankfully, it is not like that. True, the Lord also uses that sermon and that special visit as part of the process to come to repentance, yet the Lord does exceedingly more. When it comes to repentance, it is the Lord Himself who makes your stubborn will obedient, moving it so that miraculously there will be a complete turnaround in your life. It is this dramatic turnaround which is necessary in the lives of all of us. We all have to come to the stage when we say: "Lord, it is still such a mess in my life – please help me to repent." Divine power is necessary in order to change the direction of our lives.

In Romans 6, the apostle Paul writes that we were united with Christ in His death and resurrection. That is why we must consider ourselves dead to sin and alive to God in Christ Jesus. We must consider who we are in Christ, which includes a call for repentance each and every new day, not only for that person living on the fringes of the church, but for all of us. This clearly shows that even though repentance is God's work, it does not undo our personal responsibility.

December 9

READING: ROMANS 13:8-14, CANONS OF DORT III/IV, 11-12, HEIDELBERG CATECHISM, LORD'S DAY 33

The dying of the old nature (1)

"Let us cast off the works of darkness…
and make no provisions for the flesh."
ROMANS 13:12 + 14

Repentance is a continuous process. It is like a tree. A tree does not lose all its leaves at once, nor does it get new leaves all at once. It is a gradual process. So it is with repentance: the old nature has to die more and more, and the new nature has to come to life more and more. Often this goes hand in hand with the many ups and downs in our lives. We so quickly fall back into sinful habits. It is a constant battle. Yet, by grace from above, we may also make progress in this battle.

Look at it from a practical point of view, starting with the old nature. What constitutes the dying of the old nature? The Catechism describes it in terms of grieving, hating, and fleeing. The sins we have committed will bother us. It will fill our hearts with sorrow that we grieved our great Father in heaven. We grieved Him by saying those harsh words we should not have spoken, by gossiping again about that brother or sister, by bullying that fellow student at school, by being disobedient to our parents, by being dishonest towards our boss, by forgetting about the Lord during that wild night out. Having been redeemed by Christ, all of these things should indeed worry us, especially that we will so easily fall into sin again.

This entails more than just feeling sorry for the consequences of our sins. Think of a child grounded for a week because of certain wrongdoings. He says to his parents that he is sorry. Yet deep down, he is not bothered by the grief he has seen on the face of his parents. This can also happen in our prayers to God when we ask for forgiveness if we are not really bothered that we have grieved our great Father in heaven. All of this has nothing to do with true repentance. When there is true repentance, we will no longer try to cover up or smooth-talk certain sins away, saying they were not that bad and it could have been a lot worse. Instead, we will hate ourselves for having committed that sin again and make a conscious effort to flee from it.

December 10

**READING: PHILIPPIANS 4:8-9,
HEIDELBERG CATECHISM, LORD'S DAY 33**

The dying of the old nature (2)

"...practice these things, and the God of peace will be with you."

PHILIPPIANS 4:9B

In a book about Christian counselling, the author mentioned the example of a husband being frustrated with his wife. He felt depressed, since the relationship was no longer what it had been in the past, and he had no idea why this was or what to do about it. During the counselling session, the counsellor asked him: "What is on your mind? Do you at times think about other women, perhaps about one woman in particular?" The man said: "Yes. However, not that I would ever have a relationship with her. I long to have a good marriage with my wife. I love her."

This is just a little snippet of a counselling session which shows how much our mind affects our way of living. We quickly fill it with the wrong things by watching video clips or listening to music. However, we should train our minds to think about other things. When we do this, it will help us hate sin more and more and flee from it.

Sometimes, people think living as a Christian is burdensome, since you are not allowed to do this and have to live exactly like that – all kinds of rules, with no fun in life whatsoever. However, the only way that life can genuinely be enjoyed is in and through Christ. Today's society gives us a clear picture of what happens when people live their life without God. They think they are free, but meanwhile they have become enslaved to sin; a life without hope, without a future; fun one night, but a hangover the next morning. When there are difficulties to face, only things like drugs or alcohol can help to make light of the situation for a short while, but in the end it only ruins you.

In contrast to such a life, we have the riches in Christ which are truly worth living for, and this all for nothing – undeserved! I am afraid that we often forget how rich we are and then having given in to our sinful desires, God's commandments become burdensome. We grumble in discontentment, like the prodigal son who also wanted to enjoy life. Yet where did it leave him in the end? Scripture calls us to repent, filling us with joy again in doing God's will.

December 11

**READING: PSALM 84,
HEIDELBERG CATECHISM, LORD'S DAY 33**

The coming to life of the new nature
"They go from strength to strength."
PSALM 84:7A

Daily we may rejoice in the fact that God loves us, even so much so that He gave His only Son to die for us. This means that in Christ there is always a way back to God. When we go down on our knees before God in true repentance, the Lord will not hold the past against us, no matter what may have happened in our life. This is an ongoing process. The battle against sin will remain part of this life. Yet, when we fight this battle in sincere faith, that is, with a genuine desire to die to sin more and more and live in newness of life, God will also give us victories. Victories, when we receive the strength to say 'No' to certain wrongdoings and not give in to sinful desires. Victories, when we delight in doing God's will. Then we will go forward from strength to strength by grace from above.

This shows that the dying of the old nature and the coming to life of the new nature are not two different life stages where you finish the one and carry on with the other. Instead, they always go hand in hand. Think of the parable of the prodigal son. In that faraway country, this son remembered how good it was to be with his father at home. Joy returned when he remembered this. At the same time, he was overcome with grief, knowing how much pain he had caused his father. Well, the same applies to us when we kneel down at night, rejoicing in the fact that God still loves us. At the same time, there is shame that despite the unfailing love of God, we so often still grieve Him. Once I read, "The more we rejoice in God's love towards us, the more we will feel ashamed of the sins we still commit." To use an image for this: the branch most full of fruit (abundance of joy) also bends the most (is the most humble).

It is by way of genuine repentance that our life will start to bear fruit for the Lord. You will want to live for the Lord and this from the heart, rejoicing in God's love for us sinners. You will then also want to live according to God's will in all good works.

December 12

**READING: 1 CORINTHIANS 10:23-33,
HEIDELBERG CATECHISM, LORD'S DAY 33**

What are good works?

"...whatever you do, do all to the glory of God."

1 CORINTHIANS 10:31B

What are good works? These are not certain specific achievements in the service of the Lord. Instead, they refer to a Christian way of life, whereby faith determines all our thoughts, words, and actions. Deeds, of which we may say "well done," will not necessarily receive a similar qualification from God. They will not, if they were done merely out of selfish ambition and not out of a sincere love for God. If I give my neighbour a hand with a job he would like to get done and I do this only because I want to be praised or receive something in return, it is not a good work in the sight of God, since it was not done first and foremost out of love for the neighbour. Therefore, good works are only those that are kingdom-focused, out of genuine love for the Lord. This means not just church work, but also all the things of everyday life when we are busy at the worksite, in the office, at school or home, faithfully working with the talents God has given us, and this not to show off how good we are, but to bring glory to God instead.

If we indeed live in this way, our life will take on a different perspective. We would no longer be living for the material things, but living for the Lord. In all that we do, our first question should always be: "Lord, what is Thy will? Take my life and so mould it that in all that I do and wherever I am, Thy Name may always receive all glory and honour." Then in whatever we do, we will want to do it to the glory of God.

That is what true repentance is all about. It is living by faith. It is a tremendous task to live in this way, you may think. Who would ever be able to do this? However, it is God Himself who will bring this about in our lives when we entrust our whole life to Him in childlike faith and pray: "Lord, I cannot do this. Wilt Thou help me?" Therefore, let us go down on our knees daily and fold our hands, praying:

"Teach me, in your way direct me;
In Your truth, O LORD, instruct me.
Let it be my heart's one aim
To revere Your holy Name."

December 13

READING: ISAIAH 7:1-17

The gospel of the Immanuel prophecy (1)

Behold, the virgin shall conceive and bear a son, and shall call his name Immanuel."

ISAIAH 7:14B

The Immanuel prophecy was given to King Ahaz, who reigned over Judah and Jerusalem in Isaiah's day. Because of Ahaz's pro-Assyrian feelings, Pekah the king of Israel, and Rezin the king of Damascus, joined as allies to besiege Jerusalem, trying to force support from Judah in their revolt against Assyria. From Isaiah 7:6, we learn that Pekah and Rezin's real intention was the complete annexation of Judah, ending the royal reign of David's house by putting the son of Tabel on the throne. When news reached Jerusalem that Syria was in league with Ephraim and that their armies were on their way to Jerusalem, it caused panic in the palace and likewise among the population of Jerusalem. Hearts were shaking like trees in a storm.

One may think, was this not understandable? After all, the situation was critical. If these two kings with their armies succeeded, it could mean the end of the house of David. Therefore, was it not understandable that many hearts were filled with fear? From a human point of view, it indeed was. However, what about God's promises given to the house of David? Did they no longer count? I am thinking here particularly of the promise recorded in II Samuel 7 that David's house and kingdom would be established forever. If Ahaz and the people of Jerusalem had clung to these promises, there would have been no reason to fear. They would have realised the unique position of God's people in a world full of turmoil.

Yet, faith in God's sure promises was completely lacking in King Ahaz and the royal household. They had no eye for the battle behind the battle – no eye that in Pekah and Rezin, Satan was making his attack on the church. From a New Testament perspective, in Pekah and Rezin we see the dragon of Revelation 12 standing before the woman who was with child. And therefore, if Ahaz had only clung to God's sure promises made from the beginning to the patriarchs – promises later on given more specifically to David and his house – Ahaz would not have shaken like trees of the forest shake before the wind. Instead, he would have put his trust in God's promises, which are reliable – always!

December 14

READING: ISAIAH 7:1-17

The gospel of the Immanuel prophecy (2)

Behold, the virgin shall conceive and bear a son, and shall call his name Immanuel."

ISAIAH 7:14B

Instead of putting his trust in the LORD – the only One who can help in times of need – king Ahaz sought help from Tiglath-Pileser, the king of Assyria. Since this grieved the LORD, He sent his prophet to the royal palace with the following message: "Do not fear the power of Pekah and Rezin, for in the eyes of the LORD they are no more than just two smoldering stubs of firewood. It shall not stand, and it shall not come to pass." With these words, God promised deliverance. Yet this promise had to be accepted in faith.

The Lord was even willing to give Ahaz a sign to confirm the trustworthiness of the word Isaiah had spoken on God's behalf. Ahaz, however, refused to accept the sign. Piously he said: "I will not ask, nor will I test the LORD." This indeed sounded very pious, but the real reason was that Ahaz neither wanted nor dared to take the road of faith commended to him. Ahaz knew very well that if he were to ask for a sign, it would have been granted to him. But then he would also have been compelled to believe the LORD and to place his trust in God alone. Instead, Ahaz thus hardened his heart.

Despite all of this, the LORD still gave a sign: the Immanuel prophecy. Even though many a commentary sees this sign as a direct reference to the birth of Jesus Christ, the sign given here is meant firstly for king Ahaz. Therefore, the fulfillment of verse 14 cannot be related exclusively to the virgin birth of the Lord Jesus.

Who then was this virgin? Scripture does not tell us. What matters is the name of this child. The sign was in the name. At this critical time, a young woman – as the word 'virgin' can also be translated – would conceive and bear a son calling him Immanuel, that is, God with us. Through this youthful mother, who was weak in herself yet strong in faith, the LORD wanted to give a sign to Ahaz. She undoubtedly must have been known to him and the people of Judah. Yes, the fact that a young woman would call her son Immanuel would surely attract the attention of both king and people at this critical time. Immanuel – God with us. Therefore, do not fear!

December 15

READING: ISAIAH 7:1-17

The gospel of the Immanuel prophecy (3)

Behold, the virgin shall conceive and bear a son, and shall call his name Immanuel."

ISAIAH 7:14B

Immanuel – God with us! This is one of the most significant promises which God has given to His people throughout the ages. In the past, He revealed Himself in this way to the patriarchs, Abraham, Isaac, and Jacob. I am with you – that is what the LORD promised to Moses, Joshua, and the judges; and later to David, Solomon, and many a king after them. It was the constant message the LORD gave to His people, especially in times of hostility and war: "Fear not and be not dismayed, for I am with you." In calling her son Immanuel, this young woman in Isaiah 7 thus calls to mind God's revelations from the past. She knew the promises God had given to His people, and she also wanted to live from these promises, expecting redemption from the LORD alone.

The verses 15 and 16 speak about this redemption. Being born in Ahaz's time, this child would have eaten curds and honey. This indicates an abundance. The faith of this young woman would not have been put to shame. God would have been with her and her child. No matter how fearful the time in which the child to be born would grow up in, he would have lacked nothing. Even more powerful, before he would know how to refuse evil and choose the good, the land whose kings the people of Jerusalem now feared would be deserted and no longer pose any threat to Judah. This confirms the message Isaiah had given, namely that it would not stand nor come to pass that Pekah and Rezin destroyed the house of David. Syria and Ephraim would fail. Instead, their power would be broken before this child was two or three years old.

God works redemption. Yet only those who put their trust in Him will enjoy the fruit of this redemption. Ahaz would have been able to see it with his own eyes, but he himself would not experience the blessing of this redemption. The Assyrians, whom Ahaz trusted in preference to the LORD, would oppress the land instead of saving it. Ahaz himself would become a vassal of Tiglath-Pileser and be made to pay heavy tributes. Yet amid all of this turmoil, this mother and her child kept trusting God. Immanuel – God with us!

December 16

READING: MATTHEW 1:18-25

Immanuel – God with us (1)

"All this took place to fulfill what the Lord had spoken by the prophet, "Behold, the virgin shall conceive and bear a son, and they shall call his name Immanuel.""

MATTHEW 1:22-23

Immanuel – God with us! God is near to His people. This promise stands from age to age unbroken, not because of us, but because of God's faithfulness. Despite the many sins of His people, God's steadfast love endures forever. This is clear from the fulfillment of the Immanuel promise in the Old Testament. Yet, it becomes even more clear when we look at the fulfillment of this promise in the New Testament, especially when looking at the gospel according to Matthew. In a dream, an angel tells Joseph to call the child to be born Jesus, "for he will save his people from their sin." This name was also a fulfillment of repeated promises given by the Old Testament prophets. This child to be born would bring about redemption, not just from the occasional enemy, but He would take away the cause of all war and oppression, which is sin.

Next, the angel adds that all of these things would fulfill what the prophet Isaiah had already spoken about in the Immanuel sign. How are we to view this because this prophecy was already fulfilled in Isaiah's day? To answer this question, we have to look at the word 'fulfill'. In Scripture, this word means to bring about the completion of a promise which leaves room for an earlier initial fulfillment. When applying this to Isaiah 7:14, this means that the promise came to its initial fulfillment during the time of King Ahaz. This is because it was firstly meant as a sign for him. Yet the fact is that God being with His people would ultimately only come true in and through the birth of Jesus Christ. For how could God be with His people, with sinners lost in guilt? The answer is only through Jesus Christ, and only through His birth and redemptive work! In summary, the gospel of Christmas guarantees the fulfillment of the Immanuel promise: God with us! In the hour that God became man, the riches of this promise became known as never before. When celebrating Christmas, we rejoice that the fulfillment of the promise 'God with us' is founded on the birth of Jesus Christ, who became man to reconcile sinners with God.

December 17

READING: MATTHEW 28:16-20

Immanuel – God with us (2)

"And behold, I am with you always to the end of the age."
MATTHEW 28:20B

Immanuel – God with us! A rich promise! Yet, only for those who also want to live from it. At first glance this seems to be very simple. However, it requires faith. Think of the time when the Lord Jesus was born. This was again a time during which people could easily have thought that God was no longer with them. The Jews lived under the oppression of the Roman yoke. Only a few were still looking for the true redemption of Jerusalem in those days. Yet, for many others, faith in God's sure promises had faded away. However, this was the wrong way to think. For no matter how severe and challenging circumstances are, we must continue to put our trust in God alone, that is, in Him who says: "Fear not, for I am with you." This is how we too must accept the Immanuel promise. Only then will we also receive comfort from it.

In Matthew 1 we read that "all this took place to fulfill...", thereby referencing not only the miracle of Jesus' birth but also the saving nature of His work. By His accomplished work, Christ made it possible that the promise 'God with us' could fully come true also for the New Testament church on its way to the heavenly Canaan. That is how we may share in the riches of this promise today. Think of the words our Saviour spoke just before He ascended into heaven: "And behold, I am with you always to the end of the age." To this promise we may cling while on our earthly pilgrimage to the celestial city. Homeward bound, sustained by grace, and all of this because of Christ!

God with us! To this promise we may cling in days of difficulties and concern, in days of ecclesiastical struggle, wars and rumours of wars. This promise is there for us, even during times when doubt may arise in our hearts, or when we have to fight against the weakness of our faith. All of this does not undo God's faithfulness towards us. How rich a promise this is! No matter what kind of problems we may struggle with, no matter what burden we have to bear: God is with us always – with us, in and through Christ!

December 18

READING: REVELATION 21:1-7

Immanuel – God with us (3)

"And I heard a loud voice from the throne saying, "Behold, the dwelling place of God is with man. He will dwell with them, and they will be his people, and God himself will be with them as their God.""

REVELATION 21:3

God is with us, always. In and through Jesus Christ, He will surround us with His grace and power by day and by night. That is how we may draw strength and comfort from the riches of the Immanuel promise today, on our way to the complete and perfect fulfillment of this promise about which we read in Revelation 21:3 (see above). Yes, it is on the new earth that we will enjoy the complete fulfillment of the promise of 'God with us'.

When looking at this Old Testament prophecy, we see the initial fulfillment in Isaiah 7. A further fulfillment is seen in the birth of Jesus Christ, who is the male child of Revelation 12. From a redemptive-historical perspective, we may draw a line from Isaiah 7 (Ahaz) to Matthew 1 (Christmas). From Christmas to Ascension (Matthew 28) and further, we may draw a line through to Christ's return (Revelation 21, God with men forever!) That is how God will fulfill this specific promise, in coming to the perfect Immanuel communion.

At the same time, Scripture also shows that we will reach this perfect Immanuel communion via blood, fire, and vapour of smoke (Acts 2). The history of the church is written in blood. The battle has not yet finished. Yet, we have the promise which Christ gave to His church upon His ascension into heaven: "Behold, I am with you always, even to the end of the age." This means that Christ is not only present in the battle, but He is with us, at our side. Thus we are safe, no matter how severe the battle might become. Yet in addition to this, we must also accept this rich promise in faith. The same word that the prophet Isaiah spoke to King Ahaz also applies to us: "If you do not believe, it will not stand." God also requires of us that we trust in Him alone. If we do so, no matter what dark clouds may gather above the church, we have the assurance that God will be with us, always.

December 19

READING: ISAIAH 9:1-7

The true meaning of Christmas

"For to us a child is born…"

ISAIAH 9:6B

When celebrating Christmas, what do we focus on? In the world around us, the focus is on giving presents. Lots of money is spent on this. Yet, as God's children, we focus on a gift that did not cost us anything. We focus on God's gift of grace in sending His Son as a child in the manger. A precious gift, especially when we consider why this child was born: to die for our sins. That is why he was called Jesus, the Saviour, who would save God's people from their sins, which is the cause of all hunger and misery.

"For to us a child is born …" One might wonder what all the excitement is about with this announcement of a baby being born? Of course, when a baby is born, parents and grandparents are excited, and perhaps some other relatives also share in the excitement. Yet, as far as the world of adults is concerned, those little ones lying in the cradle are not considered to be of great significance, are they? That might come later, when they grow up! So, why all this excitement? Is it because this child was very special, as we know from his life later on?

Are we determining the significance of Christmas in hindsight? The answer is a definite no! We only have to read the Old Testament prophecies, which clearly speak about this specific child and the tasks He would complete. For example, in Isaiah 9. Those who are conversant with Scripture would know that these words refer to the coming of the Messiah. However, do we also know the message these words want to convey? If you were asked, what more could you say than it is just talking about Christmas?

"For to us a child is born …" These words are more than just a simple birth announcement you may find in the newspaper, for example. Neither does the prophet Isaiah speak about something that had already happened. Instead, enlightened by the Holy Spirit, Isaiah prophesies here about what God will do through this child, whose birth was still to come in the future. Yes, at a time yet to come, a child would be born – a very particular child, as we may conclude from the wonderful names this child receives: "Wonderful Counsellor, Mighty God, Everlasting Father, Prince of Peace."

December 20

READING: ISAIAH 9:1-7

Light in the darkness

"The people who walked in darkness have seen a great light."

ISAIAH 9:2

The words of Isaiah 9 lead us back to about seven hundred years before Christ was born, a time during which it had started to become dark in the Land of Promise. The Assyrians had attacked Israel – an attack which the northern provinces especially suffered under. During Isaiah's prophetic ministry, the people in the North continually heard the thud of hostile soldiers' boots and were confronted daily with military officers dressed in garments they hated the sight of.

In the South, in Jerusalem, the people sat back and laughed. They did not mind at all that the North was copping it. Had they themselves not called for the Assyrians' help when Jerusalem threatened the North? That is the reasoning the people of Judah used. But then Isaiah showed them that God's hand had caused this invasion in the North, bringing gloom and darkness upon the Kingdom of the Ten Tribes.

When celebrating Christmas, people often speak about the light and God's tender mercies, with Him visiting His people to give that light to those sitting in darkness and in the shadow of death (Luke 1:79). Yet, the reason why it is dark is often not spoken about. It is as if people think there is nothing more to say and that it does not help to talk at length about the trouble and gloom people often suffer from in this dark world. Instead, let us focus on how it can become light again.

When people have this attitude to life, one important aspect is forgotten: the reason it has become dark in this world is because of sin. Isaiah shows that the darkness that fell over the North of Israel and which was rapidly making its way to the South was God's judgment upon the sins of His people. God's divine hand caused this darkness.

Against this background, the announcement of a great light is to be considered a miracle. In his sovereign grace, the LORD dispels this darkness. The prophet Isaiah shouts for joy and cries out: "For to us a Child is born, to us a Son is given; and the government shall be upon his shoulder." Isaiah prophesies that One will be born, coming from on high. He will crush the enemy. That is how God Himself is bringing all darkness to an end.

December 21

READING: ISAIAH 9:1-7, LUKE 1:46-56

A kingdom established on justice and righteousness (1)

"He has brought down the mighty from their thrones and exalted those from humble estate."

LUKE 1:52

In Isaiah 9 we read – what one could call – an Old Testament description of Christmas, in words similar to what we read in the New Testament, for example, in the songs of Mary and Zacharias. When thinking of Mary, she did not just sing a romantic song upon the birth of her son, but she also cries out prophetically: "He has brought down the mighty from their thrones and exalted those from humble estate." Zacharias rejoices that the Son of David is coming to save us from our enemies and from the hand of all who hate us. These words do perhaps sound somewhat different to how we generally consider Christmas, or at least different to how the world celebrates Christmas. Christmas – true, Scripture also speaks about peace on earth, but not in the way the world speaks about peace.

Unto us a Child is born – not to redeem people from their earthly troubles and enemies, but from sin. The fire which burnt the boots and garments of the Assyrian soldiers was a sign of grace by which Israel was redeemed, not first of all from the thudding boots and garments covered in blood, but from God's divine judgment of their sins. It heralded a new beginning – a new beginning in God's grace. This was something totally new, for He who would establish all of this – the Child to be born, the Prince of Peace – would work in a way which was different to what people might have expected, namely by establishing a kingdom unlike that of the rulers of this world. Instead, it would be a kingdom established by justice and righteousness.

In His day, the Lord Jesus did not come to fight the Romans in order to crush them. He did not light a fire, fueling it with Roman boots and garments from the debris of a battle He had won. Instead, when hanging on the cross, His sandals were given to Roman soldiers who cast lots, dividing His garments.

This is how our Saviour established His kingdom. He, who today governs this world from the throne of God, is directing the history of this world towards that final fire – a fire much worse than the fire of which we read in Isaiah 9. That is how He will triumph.

December 22

READING: ISAIAH 9:1-7

A kingdom established on justice and righteousness (2)

"And his name shall be called Wonderful Counsellor, Mighty God, Everlasting Father, Prince of Peace"

ISAIAH 9:6B

The Child to be born will work in a way different from what people might have expected Him to do. Unlike the rulers of this world, He will establish His kingdom upon justice and righteousness. This also becomes clear from the names this Child receives.

Wonderful Counsellor. Wonderful – this word indicates that this Child will by far exceed the limits of human understanding. He will be a counsellor of wonders, just as God is wonderful in counsel and excellent in wisdom. With the birth of this Child, God's wonders of redemption will reach their climax. According to the counsel of God, this Child will obtain a perfect redemption for God's people, not only in that He defends and preserves us against all enemies, but especially in the fact that He frees us from sin.

Mighty God. This is the name that belongs to God Himself. In His Son, this mighty God came into the world, causing His power to shine over our life. Through this Child, God breaks the yoke that burdened us as well as the rod of our oppressors – the rod by which our archenemies, namely the devil, the world, and our own sinful flesh, keep oppressing us. Through the Child, God breaks this rod as in the day of Midian. This is a reference to the wonderful deliverance God gave His people in the day of Gideon. Likewise, the Child in the manger reveals to us God's power of salvation. Through this Child, God brings the forces of darkness to their knees in order to grant His people a perfect redemption.

Everlasting Father. Having become King on David's throne, this Child will be a father for His people, caring for them as a father cares for His children, taking them in His mighty arms.

Prince of Peace. The word 'peace' does not refer to an absence of war or absence of strife, but it summarises the salvation, blessing, and happiness we will receive in and through this Child. It is the peace of which the angels sang when this Child was born. A peace not of this world, but established on justice and on righteousness. We receive this peace when we acknowledge Jesus Christ as King.

December 23

READING: ISAIAH 9:1-7

A kingdom established on justice and righteousness (3)

"Of the increase of His government and of peace there will be no end."

ISAIAH 7A

The government which the Child from verse 6 will establish will have no equivalent. No one will be able to oppose His reign. Instead, all and everything will be subject to Him. There will indeed be no end to the increase of His government and of peace. "And of peace" – this is a striking notion, as most governments find increase through war. Yet, contrary to all earthly kingdoms, Christ's kingdom will grow through the means of peace; think of the gracious workings of the Holy Spirit and the preaching of the gospel by which God works peace in our hearts. Many a tyrant and dictator in this world establishes His power by oppression and tyranny. Yet, this King will establish His kingdom through righteousness. The fruit of this reign will be that the citizens of this kingdom, that is, those who acknowledge Christ as King, will joyfully obey such a righteous rule.

The words 'judgment' and 'justice' in verse 7b refer to God's covenant law, which God has given for our good and of which God Himself says in His word: in obeying this law you will be happy and it will be well with you. Thankfully, by obeying God's wholesome commandments for life, one will receive peace, real peace – peace with God through Jesus Christ! It is this peace, and only this peace, that will cause our lives to flourish.

When Isaiah spoke these words, David's house had come near to its end. Not much was left of its former glory. Yet God would restore these ruins through a child to be born in the future – a mighty King, who would be seated upon David's throne forever. Isaiah says to His contemporaries: 'Do not doubt this great future, for the zeal of the LORD of hosts will accomplish this. Judah is in a desperate condition – the Assyrian oppressor is looming on the horizon'. Therefore, how will this glorious future be brought about? Isaiah says that it will be through nothing other than the zeal which the LORD of hosts has for His own honour. God will vindicate Himself in order to secure redemption for His people. Because of His zeal, God has an intense desire to accomplish what He has promised – an intense desire to bring His work of salvation in Jesus Christ to completion as well as His plan for our lives.

December 24

READING: LUKE 2:1-14

Angels sing a song of praise of God's redemptive work (1)

"Glory to God in the highest ..."

LUKE 2:14

Angels proclaim God's glory, displayed in the sending of His Son. In the Old Testament, the glory of God is often mentioned as a sign of His majesty, splendour and power – a sign of God's divine presence – for example, when the LORD revealed Himself to Israel at Mount Sinai, full of glory and majesty. Later, the glory of God also filled the tabernacle on the day of its inauguration. Later the same happened at the inauguration of the temple.

During the time of the Old Testament, God's glory was never fully revealed. God appeared to Israel in a thunderstorm, a cloud of fire, or a cloud of darkness. Yet, the manifestation of God's glory had never been so impressive as on the very night that Christ was born.

In Luke 2:9, we read that the glory of the Lord shone around the shepherds. All of a sudden, the shepherds were bathed in heavenly light. For a moment, they could experience what it means when God embraces sinners with His glory – a foretaste of what we, as God's children, will experience permanently on the new earth when the light of God's glory will shine around us day and night. In the last book of the Bible, we read about the New Jerusalem: "The city has no need of sun or moon to shine on it, for the glory of God gives it light, and its lamp is the Lamb." The shepherds enjoyed a foretaste of this glorious future. They were confronted with a manifestation of God's glory such as no eye had ever seen before. Responding to the joyous message that the Saviour had been born in the city of David, angels sing glory to God!

Whilst the glory of God shone around the shepherds, this glory did not shine around the Child in the manger. This element shows us the significance of the Christmas gospel. This newborn King did not come into this world to seek His own honour, but he came to give light to those who sit in darkness and the shadow of death. He emptied Himself to bring glorious light to us. In the birth of this Saviour, God glorified Himself unto salvation for us sinners. Therefore, "Glory to God in the highest."

December 25

READING: LUKE 2:1-14

Angels sing a song of praise of God's redemptive work (2)

"...and on earth peace..."
LUKE 2:14

Christmas is celebrated not only as a feast of light but also as a feast of peace. The first two chapters of the gospel according to Luke clearly show this. Zacharias, for example, speaking about the Dayspring coming from on high, not only says that He came "to give light to those who sit in darkness," but also that He came "to guide our feet into the way of peace." Likewise, the angels in the fields of Ephrathah also sing about peace on earth.

Christmas – peace on earth! A wonderful message indeed! Yet what do we experience of this peace? We live in a broken world, full of turmoil. At times, there is also turmoil in our personal lives. Even within the congregation of Christ, we see brothers and sisters at loggerheads with each other: no peace at all! Maybe around this time of the year, people are willing to close their eyes for a moment to sing about peace. However, when Christmas is over, life turns back to its bitter reality. Nothing has changed. Peace on earth – it is nice to speak about it during Christmas, but the truth is different.

Angels sent by God proclaim peace in the fields of Ephrathah. Angels – they are often portrayed softly clapping their wings, so are nothing to be afraid of. Yet, in Scripture, angels are referred to as the heavenly host, the soldiers of God's army. That is how we should also consider them in Luke 2, in line with the task which they had to fulfill at that very moment; angels clothed in soldiers' attire. True, they speak about peace, but they are ready for war: the war between the seed of the woman and the seed of the serpent, which came to a climax at the birth of Jesus Christ. Because of this, one could almost speak of a military parade in the fields of Ephrathah, during the very night in which God made everything ready to start the final attack by bringing the Redeemer into this world to establish a kingdom of perfect peace. Therefore, all glory to God, who through the Child in the manger will establish peace on earth. For to men to whom He favour shows, peace nevermore shall cease!

December 26

READING: LUKE 2:1-14

Angels sing a song of praise of God's redemptive work (3)

"...and on earth peace..."

LUKE 2:14

When speaking about peace, we often associate it with the absence of war – no turmoil, no violence. Yet Scripture, when speaking about peace, places this word in a much broader context. In 1 Corinthians 14:33 we read: "For God is not a God of confusion but of peace." The apostle Paul uses the word 'peace' here in contrast to the disorder which was prevalent in the congregation in Corinth, especially concerning spiritual gifts. Over against this disorder, Paul says: God is a God of peace. God wants good order, whereby all elements of the worship service are harmonious. Of course, this does not just apply to the worship services. Being a God of peace, God wants all things to be in a healthy state, corresponding to His will – a situation in which life can develop harmoniously.

This fundamental thought must be kept in mind whenever Scripture speaks about peace. The ultimate aim of God's redemptive work is to take all disharmony and disorder away from this world and create a state in which everything corresponds to His will. That is why He sent His Son into this world. In Colossians 1:19 and 20 Paul writes: "For in him all the fullness of God was pleased to dwell, and through him to reconcile to himself all things, whether on earth or in heaven, making peace by the blood of His cross." We meet the word 'peace' here once again.

Disharmony and disorder are prevalent on earth because of sin. All our relationships are affected by it: our relationship with God, our mutual relations, as well as other relationships. Nothing is left of the perfect peace which was in Paradise before the fall into sin. Yet in the fields of Ephrathah, angels sing of the peace which God will establish through His Son, our Lord Jesus Christ who embodies this peace, that is, the peace which comes from God. Through His work, Christ establishes peace with God, taking away the disorder of sin and restoring a climate in which life can once again develop harmoniously. Therefore, true peace can only be enjoyed in communion with Christ. True peace springs from Christ and is guaranteed in Christ. Apart from Christ, there is no peace.

December 27

READING: LUKE 2:1-14, PSALM 2

Angels sing a song of praise of God's redemptive work (4)

"...and on earth peace..."

LUKE 2:14

Angels sang of peace in the fields of Ephrathah. Yet, the scene with which the shepherds were confronted was not peaceful at all, which should also cause us not to think of this proclamation of peace simply in a pietistic or romantic way. In the very night that Christ was born, the gospel of peace was proclaimed with the clashing of swords. The multitude of the heavenly host appeared to the shepherds in military tunic. Their swords were not yet beaten into ploughshares, nor their spears into pruning hooks (Isaiah 2:4), for the enemy was still active. The gospel of peace of which these angels spoke would unleash counter forces. All devils and godless people would revolt against it. Anti-christian powers would raise themselves up trying to break the peace worked by God. Yet, in Christ there is victory.

In Psalm 2 we read that He who sits in heaven is in control, no matter how proudly all of these powers raise their battle cry. In the end, all of their fierce opposition will be in vain, for the LORD laughs at them and holds them in derision. All anti-christian world powers, no matter how strong they might be, will not be able to break God's peace process.

If we live our life with the Lord in faith, we may rejoice already today in this beautiful peace as God's children, that is, in the peace we have with God through Jesus Christ. In addition, we will be on our way to the perfect peace on the new earth. On that day, there will no longer be any wars, no violence or crime any more. All enmity will be gone. Then "the wolf shall dwell with the lamb, and the leopard shall lie down with the young goat ... The lion shall eat straw like the ox. The nursing child shall play over the hole of the cobra, and the weaned child shall put his hand on the adder's den" (Isaiah 11:6-8). This peace will surpass all human understanding: no more sickness or tears, but perfect joy, always! Indeed therefore, glory to God in the highest!

December 28

READING: LUKE 2:8-20

Angels sing a song of praise of God's redemptive work (5)

"…and on earth peace among those with whom he is pleased."

LUKE 2:14

"Glory to God in the highest, and on earth peace." People may ask: what do we see of this peace today? We will only be able to see it when we open our eye of faith to the true message of Christmas, namely that through the Child in the manger God wanted to restore peace between Himself and fallen man. We will never see anything of this beautiful peace when, by a wrong or sinful attitude, we block the channel through which this peace comes to us, that is, the channel of the holy gospel. We ought to open our hearts to this gospel, and then in genuine humbleness thank God for His amazing grace in Jesus Christ.

Christmas – yes, then we sing about joy to the world but we do so in humbleness, amazed, saying to ourselves: "LORD, is this all for me? Thank Thee, O LORD, for Thy undeserving love towards me a sinner. LORD, how great are Thy mercies and never-ending faithfulness."

The gospel of Christmas confronts us with a choice – a choice between following the attitude of Mary and the shepherds or following the attitude of the other citizens of Bethlehem.

Today, when confronted with the gospel of Christmas, many do not get any further than marvelling at the things that were told to them. The gospel of Christmas does not bring about a change of heart. After a couple of days, when Christmas is over, life returns back to the same routine as before. Yet, there is also the possibility of the other attitude, like Mary, of whom we read in verse 19: "She treasured up all these things, pondering them in her heart." Mary believed. The peace of which the angels spoke reached her heart.

"And the shepherds returned, glorifying and praising God for all that they had heard and seen, as it had been told them." This time it is the angels who listen when people sing! These people are walking along the path of peace and therefore sing for joy: Gloria in Excelsis Deo! Yes:

> "All glory to our God on high
> And on the earth His peace
> For men to whom He favour shows
> Which nevermore shall cease."

December 29

READING: LUKE 2:25-32

Waiting fervently

"…waiting for the consolation of Israel."
LUKE 2:25

Simeon received a special revelation from the Holy Spirit that he would not see death before he had seen Christ the Lord. After this revelation, Simeon must have wondered continually about where he would see him, how and in what way. His whole life was determined by waiting for the consolation of Israel, but now it had become even more direct. With his own eyes, he would see the fullness of time. Because he was living in the evening hours of the Old Dispensation, he would also see the beginning of the New Dispensation. Yet, Simeon still had to wait for God's time.

Via a special revelation, Simeon knew that the coming of the Messiah was at hand. We, on the other hand, have not yet received a special revelation of Christ's second coming such as that which Simeon received regarding Christ's first coming. Nevertheless, just as Simeon's life was determined by waiting for the consolation of Israel, so our lives should be determined by waiting for Christ's second coming.

Today we live in a time in which people want their desires to be satisfied straight away. Words like self-denial and self-control are not very popular in today's society. When there is no immediate satisfaction, people become impatient. Maybe that is one of the reasons why many people have turned their back on God, asking: "Where is God? Why does He not take action in this often chaotic world, full of turmoil and tension? He promised peace, but we see so little of it." Christ promised to come back soon, but we have already been waiting for His second coming for almost two thousand years. People have given up hope in God. They have grown impatient.

This can also so quickly affect us in the same way as it affected many in Simeon's day. The church was in decline. There was only a small circle of faithful believers left. They kept putting their trust in God. This therefore should teach us not to grow impatient. The history of our lives is also closely linked with the history of God's redemption. God will take us with Him towards the day of Christ. Like Simeon, let us make sure that our lives are determined by this each day.

December 30

READING: PSALM 90

Numbering our days

"So teach us to number our days that we may gain a heart of wisdom."

PSALM 90:12

Numbering our days – how are we supposed to do this? For a moment, compare life with a book that has a new page each and every day. At night, we turn over the page – another day! However, no matter how many pages the book you are reading has, eventually you will come to the final page. The same applies to the book of our life. There will come a day when we will reach the last page, that is, the page where it no longer reads "to be continued", but instead it will read "The End!" That is the day when we die. Unless Christ returns earlier, we all will come to that final page of the book of our life.

Another year is almost over. Returning to the image of the pages of our book, soon it will read with respect the year gone by that it is the end of another chapter. How quickly it has gone by. Time flies, as we often say. Time is like water. If you try to hold on to it, it slips through your fingers and disappears. This also happened to the current year. It slipped through our fingers, just like that. One more day and it will have disappeared. The question for all of us is: as time flies by, how do we number our days?

In Psalm 90, Moses prays for the Israelites that they may receive a heart of wisdom in numbering their days. What kind of wisdom? The answer is very simple: wisdom in seeing God's hand in their lives. The same goes for us when reflecting upon another year gone by. Have we seen God's hand throughout this year, and did this bring us closer to Him? When numbering our days, do we also realise that each year brings us closer to Christ's return, and closer to our life's final destination? Throughout the past year, God has been busy working out His plan for this world, the church, and also His plan in all the things that have happened in our personal lives: joyful days and sad days, in health and sickness, in festive days, but also throughout our grief. God has used all of this so that as pilgrims on this earth we stay focused on life's final destination: the city which has foundations, whose builder and maker is God.

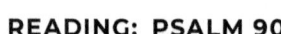 December 31

READING: PSALM 90

How to gain a heart of wisdom

"So teach us to number our days that we
may gain a heart of wisdom."
PSALM 90:12

In itself, numbering our days can become a very depressing activity. Many people see their life slipping through their fingers like water. They try to hold on to it, but they cannot. Another year has gone by. What will the new year bring? That is how the vast majority of people in this world number their days.

However, those who live by faith may number their days differently. They may do so knowing that no matter how depressing life can at times be, even in the darkness the light of God's grace still shines. That is how we have been able to cope during the year that has passed and likewise in the coming year, no matter what it may have in store for us. No doubt, the new year will have days that may be challenging for a number of us. However, as God's children, even on these difficult days we may cling to God's grace in Jesus Christ – the Son of God who came into this world, assuming our flesh, a true human nature, in which He numbered thirty three years with us. In these thirty three years our Lord and Saviour bore the wrath of God in body and soul for the sins of the whole human race. He did so for us and in our place, so that today we may number our days in the light of God's grace, no matter how dark it may seem at times from a physical point of view. In faith, we may look beyond this, and in doing so we may also number our days differently.

When reflecting upon the year gone by in this way, we can only stand in awe of God's wonderful grace during each day of the past year. Think of all that we received, not only materially but also spiritually, despite the many sins and shortcomings from our side daily. Yet, instead of being consumed by God's wrath, God's mercies were new every morning. Amazing Grace! Yes, then we will stand in awe of the goodness of the LORD: "LORD, how great is Thy faithfulness towards me a sinner."

www.ingramcontent.com/pod-product-compliance
Lightning Source LLC
Chambersburg PA
CBHW072142100526
44589CB00015B/2055